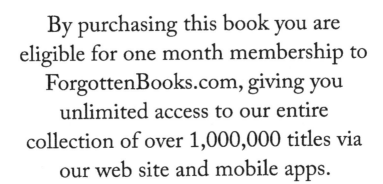

ISBN 978-0-260-44857-6
PIBN 10948842

This book is a reproduction of an important historical work. Forgotten Books uses
state-of-the-art technology to digitally reconstruct the work, preserving the original format
whilst repairing imperfections present in the aged copy. In rare cases, an imperfection in
the original, such as a blemish or missing page, may be replicated in our edition. We do,
however, repair the vast majority of imperfections successfully; any imperfections that
remain are intentionally left to preserve the state of such historical works.

The
BRYN MAWR
ALUMNAE
BULLETIN

INTERVIEW BY MISS THOMAS

THE ANNUAL MEETING

JANUARY
1924

Vol. IV   No. 1

BRYN MAWR ALUMNAE BULLETIN

OFFICIAL PUBLICATION OF
THE BRYN MAWR ALUMNAE ASSOCIATION

Evelyn Page, '23, *Editor*

Gertrude J. Hearne, '19, *Business Manager*

EDITORIAL BOARD

Lucy M. Donnelly, '93
Eleanor Fleisher Riesman, '03
Caroline Morrow Chadwick-Collins, '05

Adelaide W. Neall, '06
May Egan Stokes, '11
Leila Houghteling, '11, *ex-officio*

Subscription Price, $1.50 a Year   *Single Copies, 25 Cents*

Checks should be drawn to the order of Bryn Mawr Alumnae Bulletin
Published monthly, except August and September, at 1006 Arch St., Philadelphia, Pa.

Vol. IV   JANUARY, 1924   No. 1

THE FEBRUARY MEETING

"Nothing appears more surprising to those who consider human affairs with a philosophical eye than the easiness with which the many are governed by the few"—this observation of David Hume's applies not only to political states, but to many a minor aggregation of persons as well. Shall it apply to the Bryn Mawr Alumnae Association? That is for all of us, collectively and individually, to say. This much is certain: If the policies of our Association are determined by a small group, it will not be because some of us have an inherent tendency to be despotic—it will be because a great many of us have an inherent tendency to be lazy. In form our organization is as dem-ocratic as any organization can be, and there is every reason why it should be as democratic in reality as it is on paper. Not only do we elect our officers—elect them annually, or for a brief term of years—but none of these officers, nor all of them combined, can take final action on any important matter without our explicit consent. Such consent must be given by the Association in its regular February meeting. The more there are of us at that meeting, and the greater the interest taken by those who are there, the more truly democratic the Association will be—and, presumably, the more wisdom will reside in its acts.

True, the "business before the

meeting" is pre-determined in a general way by the Association's Council. The Council met this year in St. Louis in November, and an account of its proceedings appeared in the December BULLETIN. Its chief recommendations have to do with the raising of money for a Students' Building, the raising of money for the music department, and the reorganization of the Academic Committee. These are all matters of general interest and of immediate importance. Their passage is by no means a foregone conclusion; the last thing that "the few" in this case want is that "the many" shall follow them like sheep. Such criticism as that voiced by Jean Flexner in her able letter in the December BULLETIN is as the breath of life to an Association like ours; and those who agree or disagree with her, that the scholastic needs of the college are being neglected in the effort to secure conveniences or luxuries, should not fail to come in full force to the Alumnae meeting in February and should not fail to make themselves heard. The Bryn Mawr temper at its best is nothing if not critical, and we shall not be acting in character if we are blindly obedient to the suggestion of even the wisest of councils.

PROFESSOR CESTRE, OF THE SORBONNE, THANKS THE ALUMNAE ASSOCIATION

"Les livres sont arrivés en parfait état. C'est de nouveau un supreme envoi que nous recevons de Bryn Mawr et pour lequel la Sorbonne vous doit infiniment de reconnaissance. C'est grâce à vous que nos étudiants peuvent, en si grand nombre, prendre des sujets américains pour leurs sujets de mémoires (theses), et, quelques uns, des sujets de thèses (dissertations).

L'année dernière, j'ai eu, parmi les mémoires, les travaux suivants:

Longfellow, as epic poet.

Nature in Walt Whitman.

Hamlin Garland.

Booth Tarkington.

Thomas Nelson Page.

Comme thèse de doctorat, nous avons en préparation:

Emerson,

Walt Whitman.

Amérique et France de 1750 à 1800, (influence réciproque).

Fennimore Cooper.

L'appui que nous donnent les Alumnae de Bryn Mawr est un grand encouragement dans mon travail. Sans elles, toute recherche et toute étude d' ensemble seraient impossible, car la Sorbonne ne pourrait n'acheter que l'essentiel, c'est à dire, assez peu."

ANNOUNCEMENT

All contributions to the February BULLETIN must be in by January 10th. They should be sent to Evelyn Page, Alumnae Office, Taylor Hall, Bryn Mawr College, Bryn Mawr, Pa.

My Travels in Europe and Asia

By PRESIDENT EMERITUS M. CAREY THOMAS

(The following statement was issued to the Philadelphia newspapers shortly after Miss Thomas' return to Bryn Mawr, and many papers from every state reprinted parts of it. Due to the requests from a number of alumnae, that they be given the opportunity of reading the whole statement, we reprint it below.)

Travelling in Europe and Asia for sixteen continuous months gives one a totally different impression of the world. It is not only what one sees of different countries; it is the imaginative conception that one gets of their peoples; it is the understanding of their special problems that comes from reading their newspapers from day to day; it is, in short, a kind of first-hand knowledge that makes us look at things in a new light.

For my own part, I have come to be absolutely sure that it is the duty of the United States to delay no longer, but to use her great moral and financial power to the utmost to help to solve the many pressing problems that must be solved if the world as we know it is to go on. We should at once enter the League of Nations to which fifty-four nations of the world already belong, including the Free State of Ireland and the tiny black kingdom of Abyssinia, both of which joined this summer. There is every reason to believe that Germany and Russia also will be admitted to the League as soon as they can be persuaded to apply. In the Council and on all the League Committees a place is still kept vacant for the United States in the hope that it will soon be filled by us. Our childish isolation policy is sheer madness in the present state of the collapse of the world.

In Paris I saw a number of people who were on their way back from the annual meeting of the League of Nations held last September and October at Geneva. They one and all told me that the Italian-Greek difficulty which seemed to outsiders such a blow to the League of Nations was really a magnificent tribute to its strength and to the power of public opinion organized within the League to which even Mussolini found that he must bow.

I was in Constantinople in the summer of 1922 and I was living in the villa I had rented on the Bosphorus when the British battleships steamed past my windows as a demonstration to the victorious Anatolian Turks that they could not come back into Europe. If we had been there to stand by the side of Great Britain not a shot need have been fired, but one of the greatest and most beautiful cities of the world could have been saved for civilization. All our American schools and missions to which the lives of American teachers and the dollars of American philanthropists have been given for half a century could then have continued to carry on their beneficent educational work. Now it will, in my opinion, soon all come to an end.

I have spent four of my sixteen months in Paris and in motoring through the lovely French country during which time I read the French papers and the speeches made by leading French politicians and literary men. I also saw a great many French plays and talked to a great many people living in France. I am convinced that if we had joined Great Britain in guaranteeing France from attack what has happened since the Armistice which we all so deeply regret need not have happened. France is terribly frightened and as a consequence is now arming to the teeth. She needs us badly and our friendship for her is great but still we stand aloof.

I spent six of my sixteen months in Asia sailing back and forth across the equator visiting Ceylon, Java, French Indo-China with the splendid ruins of Angkor and India where I was for three months. In other years I have been twice in Egypt, twice in Japan, once in China, twice in North Africa (Algiers, Tunisia, Morocco and the Sahara Desert) and once in Palestine and Syria and, of course, I know the old Europe and the sad, new Europe very well indeed. We are as badly needed in the Near and Far East as in Europe. Great Britain, France and Italy cannot carry their great responsibilities alone. We must be there to help. All future civilization depends upon whether these millions upon millions of helpless people can be saved. We cannot leave them to become the prey of predatory commercial exploitation. If we do they will surely turn and rend us.

I have come back more anxious than ever before to try in every way that I can to get the United States to take the position that belongs to her at the head of the peaceful economic and industrial reconstruction of the world. For her own sake she can no longer stand aside. It is all right for us to feed the starving children of the world, but it would be still more right for us to grapple with the causes of war and of physi-

cal and moral collapse and to pour out our millions to build up an enduring economic prosperity and lasting peace. The world needs the United States, but even more the United States needs the world.

I expect to spend at least half of every year at my house, the Deanery, on the Bryn Mawr College grounds, and during the remaining six months I hope to be able to travel and see more of the world and understand it better. I am planning to write the history of Bryn Mawr College which I have known from its first beginnings as I was appointed Dean of the Faculty and Professor of English in 1884 before there was any Faculty and before there were any students. I hope also to write my autobiography. No woman who was not born before the Civil War knows out of what Egyptian darkness women came into the promised land of political equality and educational opportunity. I shall also write a little on educational subjects and I shall read some of the many books I have never had time to read in my busy life and see some of the friends I have never had time to see as often as I wished.

I hope never to serve on another new committee, never to eat another public dinner and never to make another public speech. My life for thirty-eight years has been spent on these things. Moreover, I believe in the present generation's planning the changes that it has to put through. "Elder statesmen" are a great mistake. I believe that if the men in control of affairs in this country and abroad were under forty instead of well over sixty the world would not be in its present desperate condition, and as far as I am concerned I am going to try to confine my activities to applauding and backing up the younger generation. It is possible that I may fail. All around me I see my contemporaries doing their worst, but I shall at least make an attempt to sit like a contemplative Buddha in my library.

I am a life trustee of Bryn Mawr College, and in my capacity of trustee and director I hope to be able to be of some assistance to President Marion Edwards Park by supporting her educational policies as a loyal trustee should. It is an immense satisfaction to feel, as I do, that Bryn Mawr College is safe in the hands of our new President and will grow and develop under her in a way that will rejoice every one that loves Bryn Mawr.

Annual Meeting

The Annual Meeting of the Alumnae Association will be held at 10 A. M. and 2.30 P. M. in the Chapel, Taylor Hall, Saturday, February 2, 1924.

Business

Reading of the Minutes.
Ratification of Committee Appointments.
Report of President.
　Résumé of Reports of Committees having no business to bring up.
Report of Treasurer.
　Budget.
　Alumnae Fund.
Report of Joint Committee of Trustees and Alumnae by the Chairman of Finance.
Report of Academic Committee.
　With reference to recommendations of the Council, i. e.
　· That in regard to the Academic Committee an experiment be tried of having the membership made up approximately as follows, two Alumnae Directors, two members of the Bryn Mawr Faculty, who are Bryn Mawr Alumnae, and of· the remaining members two at least to be actively engaged in teaching, one of them in a secondary school; and that the committee thus constituted should, to insure its usefulness be an active working committee, and should continue to serve the alumnae and the College as a channel of information and constructive suggestion in regard to educational matters.
Report of Alumnae Directors.
Report of Vice-President.
The Council.

New Business

Recommendations of the Council.
　That the Executive Board appoint a committee of Alumnae to discuss with the Committee on Buildings and Grounds the site, plans, and means of raising money for the immediate erection of a Students' Building, and to report to the Association at the February meeting.
　That the Music Committee be permitted to raise the funds to endow the Music Department, with the co-operation of the Alumnae.
　That the Alumnae Association make a proposal to the College with regard to sharing the cost of a yearly publication of the Alumnae Register to be published by the Alumnae.

There will be a short play given by the New York Alumnae, under the direction of F. Maude Dessau, 1913, on Friday evening, February 1st, 1924.

The Alumnae Book Club

The Alumnae Book Club will be delighted to welcome to its ranks any members of the Alumnae Association who care to join. As soon as the Secretary receives their names she will send them copies of the Constitution.

The Club acknowledges with gratitude and the Faculty with fervor the following presents of books:

The End of the House of Alard, by S. Kaye-Smith.

Inductive Sociology, by F. H. Geddings.

Principles of Relief, by E. T. Devine.

Problems of the Present South, by E. G. Murphy.

The Practice of Charity, by E. T. Devine.

Friendly Visiting Among the Poor, by M. E. Richmond.

The Good Neighbor, by M. E. Richmond.

Second Empire, by Philip Gudalla.

Italian Gardens, by Edith Wharton.

The Manhood of Humanity, by Korzybski.

French Cathedrals, by Elizabeth Pennell.

G. B. Shaw, by G. K. Chesterton.

Modern and Contemporary European History, by Shapiro.

Master-Mistress Poems, by Rose O'Neill.

French Revolution, by Johnston.

Mechanism of Exchange, by J. A. Todd.

Acquisitive Society, by Tawney.

Philosophy of Humanism, by Haldane.

Garibaldi and the Thousand, by Trevelyan (two copies).

Modern Drama, by Lewisohn.

Where the Blue Begins, by Morley.

Architecture and Democracy, by Bragdon.

Shakespearean Punctuation, by Simpson.

American Poetry Since 1900, edited by Untermeyer.

The Dark Flower, by Galsworthy.

Sartor Resartus, by Thomas Carlyle.

Humanizing of Knowledge, by Robinson.

Three Soldiers, by John Dos Passos.

These books were contributed by Peggy Ayer Barnes, Mary Bookstaver Knoblauch, Dorothy Burr, Gertrude Ely, Ruth Furness Porter, Cornelia Halsey Kellogg, Helen D. Hill, Abby Kirk, Grace Lamb Borst, Gertrude Hearne, Georgiana Goddard King, Lucy Evans Chew, M. H. Swindler, Susan Fowler, Sue A. Blake, Mrs. J. Montgomery, Mrs. Horace E. Smith, and Helen Titus Emerson.

The following people have contributed money: Marion Rawson, Mrs. Edward Rawson, Ethel Cantlin Buckley, Anna E. West, Grace Albert, Marjorie Childs, Mary K. Converse, Elizabeth Hosford Jackson, Alice G. Howland, Florence C. Irish, Bertha Rembaugh, Myra Vauclain, Mary Peirce, Jean Stirling Gregory,

Sara Archbald, Martha Tucker, Elizabeth Pharo, Esther Gist, Anna E. West, and Mary C. Smith.

One hundred and seven dollars has been sent in in all. With a part of this money Miss Reed has bought these books:

History of the United States, by Channing (two copies).

Frontier in American History, by Turner.

John Marshall and the Constitution, by Corwin.

Men of the Old Stone Age, by Osborn.

Pierre Curie, by Curie.

Valence, by Lewis.

Economic History of the United States, by Bogart.

Revolution in Ireland, by Phillips.

Manin and the Venetian Revolution, by Trevelyan.

Abigail Camp Dimon writes that she has secured a list of the books Doctor Tennant needs. Of these the last named is in five volumes: "As he did not give the price of that book I had it looked up for me and am told it is $48.50. Of course, no one person would be likely to be able to give the whole thing, and yet it is probably the one the department is most eager to have. If you know of people who would be willing to join as Doctor Tennant suggests, I would be glad to give one volume. Moreover, it has occurred to me before, and does again now, that in buying rather expensive books the Library would be able to get a large discount if they were purchased through it, and that it seems rather inefficient to have them bought by us individually, when we could afford to give more book value if the discount could be used in getting our books.

"I am eager to give my books, but will wait to hear from you, and if you have nothing to suggest about the Endocrinology, will go ahead and get one of the others."

Doctor Tennant's list follows:

The Vasomotor System, by Wm. M. Bayliss. Longmans Green & Co.

Social Life Among the Insects, by W. M. Wheeler. Harcourt, Brace & Co.

Pathologic Histology, by Frank B. Mallory. W. B. Saunders Co. $8.00.

Mind and Heredity, by Vernon L. Kellogg. Princeton University Press.

New Growths and Cancer, by Simeon Burt Welbach. Harvard University Press.

Textbook of Agricultural Bacteriology, by Löhnis and Fred. McGraw-Hill Book Co. $3.00.

Endocrinology and Metabolism, edited by Barker, Hoskins and Mosenthal. D. Appleton & Co. $48.50.

Of course, the Biology Department greatly hopes that readers of this article will be fired with enthusiasm akin to Miss Dimon's and will offer to get the other four volumes of *Endocrinology* for a New Year's Greeting to Doctor Tennant's classes.

BEATRICE MCGEORGE, *Secretary.*

With the Y. W. C. A. in the Near East

By DOROTHEA CHAMBERS, 1919

(The BULLETIN is very glad to have the opportunity of publishing the following letter from Dorothea Chambers, 1919, who went to the Near East to work shortly after her graduation. She expects to return to her post very soon.)

"I am absolutely sure that nobody has had a more interesting or thrilling three years than I have had. I started out as shopkeeper, in charge of a little gift shop on the Grande Rue de Pera, the Fifth Avenue of Constantinople. I was with the Near East Relief, and this was where the beautiful laces and embroideries and weavings of their various industrial departments were sold. With three armies of occupation, plenty of American Navy, American business and philanthropy well represented, and Russian emigrés pouring into the city, Constantinople was very cosmopolitan, and the people that came into my shop represented every group. The American Navy officer asked for "tweety tweets for twotie twos," and I guessed correctly, lace for lingerie. The British officer wanted me to make up a Christmas package of five nice gifts for ladies, his mother and three sisters, "no, four gifts for *young* ladies." A French lady who came frequently, always brought her husband with her, and his horizon blue decorated the background. The poor Russians came to sell things, and a wonderful old general used to bring carved wood boxes. His courtly greeting made me realize how difficult it is to be graceful about having your hand kissed.

Play was quite as interesting as work. At the British Officers' Club dances I seemed to be floating in a maze of Ian Hays, and when I discovered several of my partners knew him personally, all of '19 will understand my feelings. There were wonderful picnics all up and down the Bosphorus, and always another interesting site, or beautiful monument to visit. After ten weeks of this the war situation in Cilicia permitted me to join my parents in Adana. The French had occupied Cilicia after the armistice but had a lot of fighting, and for six weeks the city of Adana was in a state of siege with the railway cut and the only means of communication an "underfire" motor dash to the sea. After the French had driven the Turks back to the hills outside the city, and made the level stretch to the sea fairly safe, the trains began running and I came up from the seaport town Mersine on one of the first.

I had a very interesting year at Adana under the French régime. I was with the Y. W. C. A., and though it was only a little over a year and a half since two Y. W. C. A. secretaries had arrived in Adana, a splendid growing Service Centre had already been established. The members were mostly Greek and Armenian, and our four-room establishment was crowded with the girls who came for all sorts of classes, language and dressmaking were the most popular, and also for club and recreational activity. By the end of the year 1921 Miss Owens, the General Secretary, had secured a splendid building and our membership had reached five hundred. But politics, always the unexpected element in Turkey, reduced our membership to five and we had to begin all over again. Owing to M. Franklin Bouillon's treaty with the Turks at Angora, the French forces were to evacuate Cilicia and hand it over to the Turks. So the whole Christian population of the city decided to leave, and about fifty thousand Greeks and Armenians descended en masse to the seaport town of Mersine, and waited for opportunity to get away. The situation there became dreadful, and smallpox broke out among this uncared for mass of refugees. This resulted in practically every Mediterranean port being closed to them, and the passport red tape that officialdom imposed on these wretched people was astonishing. Miss Owens realized right away the emergency need at Mersine and she secured the use of part of a hotel (from the fleeing proprietor). We collected the Service Centre girls who were sleeping on the hard ground in church yards and gave them beds and food till they managed to get away, and we were able to make the passport business a little easier for them. Finally the French brought transports, opened the Syrian ports and took off all the refugees, and we turned back to a deserted Adana fast filling with Turks, and a winter under a Turkish régime.

An able governor kept the province in good order, and encouraged our work, so that in four months we had a new Service Centre member-ship of about a hundred. There were still about five or six hundred Christians in the city, families who preferred to chance Turkish rule than the sure fate of being refugees. The Turkish women were also much interested in what we had to offer, especially the Constantinople ones who were living a much more secluded life than in Constantinople. Just at this juncture, however, budget cuts forced the closing of the Adana Service Centre, and we had to draw out completely. It was very difficult to explain to our new members that anything American could lack money, and in their hearts they believed it was politics.

So my last year in the Near East I was in the Stamboul Service Centre at Constantinople. The Y. W. work there has prospered wonderfully, and a large Service Centre of eight hundred members in Pera, and a small one of about two hundred in Stamboul comprise the Service Centre branch of the work there. Politics again made life very interesting and one's work rather precarious. We had Turkish, Greek, Armenian and Jewish girls all busy and happy together in the Stamboul Service Centre, and very loyal to it through trying times. Smyrna was taken and a few days later was burned, the Moudania Conference gave us some rather agitated days. Then the Turks took more and more control of the city, and finally the Lausanne Treaty has brought about the withdrawal of the Allies.

The *events* in my life in Constantinople were the successive *advents* of Bryn Mawr. First, Miss Thomas and Miss King came to spend a month on the Bosphorus, and I used to have such a thrill when Miss

Thomas rolled by me on the Grande Rue in her motor, not driving, however. Then one summer night I came home from a dance to find a note on my door signed K. T. and Con Hall, and I had a most wonderful day the next day showing a most appreciative party my beloved Constantinople. In March Frannie Riker visited me. She had a musical evening in a Turkish home, and I had a ball on the Homeric looking my fill at American flappers and American clothes. Alice Hawkins, K. Gardner and V. Grace were the next group of Bryn Mawrtyrs that turned up, but theirs was one of the last of the series of tourist ships that emp-

tied their hundreds of American tourists into old Stamboul.

Mrs. J. Wylie Brown (Nanna Welles) was living in Constantinople and was president of the Y. W. C. A. committee. Frances Johnson, '17, was at Constantinople College during the winter but was called home in the spring by the death of her mother. Carlotta Welles was there a short time but left for Relief Work in Athens, and was later married.

In May I left Constantinople for leave of absence, and had a wonderful month in Beirut and a month in England. I am planning to return in December.

CAMPUS NOTES

'Varsity has had a very succcessful season. The team has lost only one game, that played against All-Philadelphia, and succeeded in defeating the Alumnae Team with a score of 11-3. The winter schedule of athletics came into effect immediately after the Thanksgiving vacation.

There have been various entertainments given lately. On Saturday, November 24, the Seniors gave a reception for the Freshmen, which included a very successful skit. On Saturday, December 8, the Freshmen gave their regular skit, in which they presented the Court of Oz. The dancing was intricate and gave evidence of the versatility of college students, and many individual stunts delighted the audience.

The Glee Club gave a concert on Friday evening, December 14, which was a great success. It was given according to a new plan. In former years the Glee Club has given an operetta, and in years in which May Day was celebrated, it gave no entertainment at all. This year, however, with great enterprise, its members invited the Rosemont Choir of male voices to sing with the Club, and also procured a group

of players of stringed instruments from the Philadelphia Orchestra. The program consisted of many Christmas carols, both French and English, several Bach Chorales, and the entire 148th Psalm, set to music by Holst. The audience received it enthusiastically.

The Music Department has planned a series of three concerts for this winter. One of these has already been given, and included Beethoven's Scotch Songs and Boulanger's Piu Jesu. The concert was so successful and was so enthusiastically received by the audience that all the tickets for the January concert have already been sold.

A campaign for scholarships to the Summer School was carried on during the week of December 10th. Two hundred dollars pays the expenses of one student during the summer. It is hoped that each hall will give a scholarship.

A conference was held at Goucher College on December 6th and 7th to discuss Students' Relations to International Affairs. Twenty eastern colleges sent delegates, two attending from Bryn Mawr.

ALUMNAE ACTIVITIES

The BULLETIN *hopes to devote a few pages in each issue to those alumnae who have become prominent in their respective fields. The Editor will welcome any articles about them that may be sent in, and will receive any suggestions as to future articles with great pleasure.*

MISS MARTHA THOMAS, FARMER

(Reprinted from the *Pennsylvania Farmer*, September 8, 1923.)

In the northern part of Chester County, Pennsylvania, in the historic Chester Valley, is Whitford Farm. If you drive through it on the Lincoln Highway you will see in a pasture along the road a magnificent herd of Guernsey cattle. Nearby you will find an old-fashioned barn that has been remodelled and brought up to date. Looking out across the valley you will see rich fields of clover, acres and acres of thriving corn, a stream winding through a pasture, a bridge, some drooping elms.

The history of Whitford Farm starts nearly 250 years ago.

In 1682 when William Penn came to America and founded a city in the southeastern corner of "Penn's woods," there came with him a certain Richard P. Thomas, a Welshman, who had purchased the rights to 5000 acres of land from the owner of the new province along the Delaware. The family of Richard P. Thomas had been for many years landholders in Wales, but he, tiring of a life of ease in his native country, embraced the beliefs of the Quakers and joined Penn's first migration to Pennsylvania. He brought with him his young son, Richard.

The elder Thomas died shortly after arriving in America. Servants dissipated his private property and left the boy Richard with nothing but his rights to a tract of land. During the interval between the death of his father and the time he became of age all the desirable land in the vicinity of Philadelphia had been taken up and it was necessary for him to locate his tract in what was then considered wilderness—the wilderness, now being northern Chester County.

Descendants of Richard Thomas living today own about 2000 acres of the tract thus laid out by him nearly 100 years before the War of the American Revolution. Whitford is one of the farms that lies on the original tract. It is in West Whiteland township, twenty-odd miles west of Philadelphia. Both farm and township derived their names from Whiteford, the seat of the original Thomas Family in Wales. Whitford Farm is owned and managed by Miss Martha G. Thomas, a member of the Pennsylvania Legislature from the Second Chester County District, and her sister, Mrs. Lardner Howell. There are five other direct descendants of Richard Thomas living on adjacent farms. They are George Thomas, Jr., Charles T. Thomas, George Thomas, III, Richard Thomas, and John Thomas.

The management of Whitford Farm devolved upon Miss Martha G. Thomas and Mrs. Lardner Howell following the death of their father, J. Preston Thomas, in 1905. Humphrey Happersett was farm manager at that time and the system of co-operation between land owner and farm manager which had been introduced by Mr. Thomas was continued.

Whitford is a farm where big things are done in a quiet, practical way. The purebred accredited herd was not acquired over night by purchase. It is the result of seventeen years of careful breeding and thoughtful planning.

The milk is sold to one of the large Philadelphia dairy companies as "Double A" quality. To be eligible to the "Double A" class, milk must come from disease-free herds, it must have a butterfat test of at least 4.5 per cent., and its bacterial count must be under 100,000 per cubic centimeter. Whitford milk averages 4.85 per cent. butterfat and the bacterial count averages about 7000.

Whitford milk won two cups at the 1923 Chester County Farm Products Show in January. Although there were 170 entries, Whitford won first place in the raw market milk class with a score of 98.8. The cup offered by the Eastern Guernsey Breeders' Association for the best milk from a purebred herd was also won.

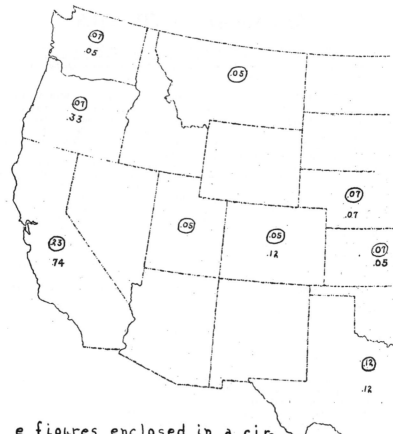

e figures enclosed in a circle indicate the percentages prepared
by public schools, those unenclosed indicate percentages prepared by
private schools.

Distribution of Alumnae, Former Students, and Presen

e Editorial Board of the BULLETIN, feeling that this information would be of interest to Br
and Registrar, Edith T. Orlady, 1902. We hope shortly to publish a map showing the

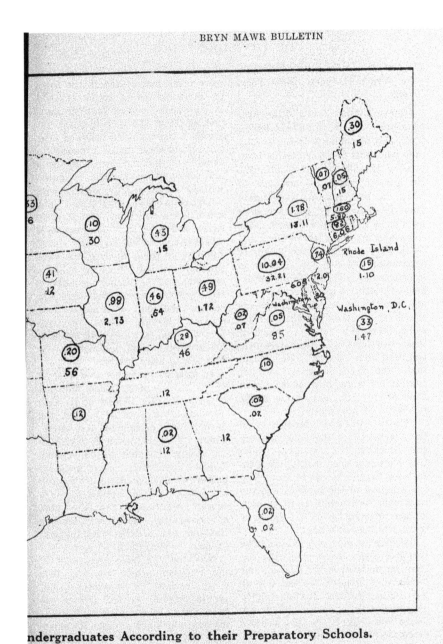

ndergraduates According to their Preparatory Schools.

wr Alumnae, has asked permission to print this map, which was prepared by the Secretary raphical distribution of alumnae and students according to their present domiciles.

The Invisible Gods

The Invisible Gods. By Edith Franklin Wyatt. Harpers. New York, 1923.

Joseph Marshfield, one of the three principal characters in *The Invisible Gods,* is a physician working in Chicago who fails to carry out his projects for the alleviation of suffering. He himself states the problem of which he is a part in a quotation from Pasteur, "Two contrary laws seem to be wrestling with each other nowadays, the one a law of blood and death, ever imagining new means of destruction and ever forcing nations to be constantly ready for the battlefield—the other a law of peace, work, and health, ever evolving new means of delivering man from the scourges which beset him. . . . which of these two laws will ultimately prevail, God alone knows." He realizes that "the invisible gods," if not against his work, have at least seen fit to destroy him, and he dies in the full sense of his failure.

"The invisible gods" brood over all the characters of the book, making and breaking the creatures whom they have fashioned, not ill, not well, each for the life he has to lead. The one conquest of the greatest and the least over destruction is to be won by the propagation of the spirit of truth, which is unfailing.

But this is only one side of *The Invisible Gods,* which is usually far from pessimistic, is not morbid, and dwells very little on the sad side of the stories it relates. It is sometimes very humorous, and one is often surprised and delighted by the writer's perspicacity. In a short outline of the late developments in poetry she says, "Verse appeared in assorted lengths and almost no rhymes. . . . The short lengths . . . were much shorter. The longer productions were much longer, and in the form of short stories in which the old ladies who soliloquized on their pasts took skeletons out of their closets instead of lavender and yellowed lace. . . . Multitudes found themselves capable of making clear statements and of writing without rhyming, without verbal melody, without connotation, without suggestion. The art of verse, which had been to some extent a limited craft now became a whelming home industry, and verses fulfilling all these requirements were produced not only by all the obliging and many of the disobliging authors, but by their wives, their sons—in college and out of college—their cousins, sisters, aunts, younger brothers, and even—as with artificial flower-making and nut-picking—by numbers of little children."

In spite of its humor and in spite of the nobility of its theme, the book occasionally fails to keep up its high standards. It does so because the author has attempted too much. There are too many stories to be told, too many thoughts to be related. The incidents often do not hang together; the conversations are too full of detail. Three characters have equal prominence, and the task of recording their simultaneous thoughts and actions, with fairness to each, is Herculean.

Now that we have given vent to the criticism which we feel that every review, of whatever book, should contain, we feel free to express our relief and pleasure in reading one which has a reason for existing. Miss Wyatt is a thoughtful writer, tolerant in mooted questions, one whose opinion is worthy of respect. *The Invisible Gods* is an oasis in a desert of trash.

ALUMNAE NOTES

The New Jersey Branch of the Alumnae Association had a luncheon on Saturday, December 8th. Jessie Buchanan, 1913, presided. Elizabeth Sedgwick Shaw, 1897, Chairman of the Regional Scholarship Committee, spoke on the organization of Bryn Mawr alumnae, and on Regional Scholarships. Edith T. Orlady, Secretary and Registrar, also spoke on Regional Scholarships. Emma Guffey Miller, 1899, gave her impressions of the Council Meeting, and Dean Bontecou brought to the meeting news of the recent developments in the College.

The meeting was attended by many New Jersey alumnae, some of whom came a long distance in order to be present. The speakers were greeted with enthusiasm, and we feel that the success of the meeting must be an incentive to other state organizations to do likewise. A great deal of praise is due to Mrs. Shaw, who was largely responsible for the interest in the Regional Scholarships in New Jersey.

After the meeting was over, Grace Lattimer Jones McClure, 1900, invited everyone to a delightful tea.

A concert will be given under the auspices of the Music Department of Bryn Mawr College by the Schola Cantorum of New York, on Wednesday, January 30, 1924, at the Academy of Music, Philadelphia. Cora Baird Jeanes, 1896, is the Chairman of the committee for the concert, which includes a number of Bryn Mawr alumnae as well as prominent Philadelphians.

The alumnae of Eastern Pennsylvania and Delaware are giving a luncheon in Philadelphia at the Bellevue-Stratford on January 19th, in honor of President Emeritus Thomas. President Park has consented to be one of the hostesses.

The Alumnae Association of New York gave a dinner in honor of President Emeritus Thomas on Friday, December 14th, at the Bryn Mawr Club on Lexington Avenue. Elizabeth Taylor Russell, 1911, the recently elected president of the club, presided. The tables were beautifully decorated with chrysanthemums sent by Julia Langdon Loomis, 1895. After dinner Miss Thomas made a most interesting address, describing her travels, and giving her audience an outline of the interesting ideas with which she has returned to Bryn Mawr.

CLASS NOTES

Master of Arts

Mary Agnes Gleim writes she is much interested in the Mount Wilson Observatory. "One October day a friend and I visited Mount Wilson. The ride by auto-stage through the blue hills back of Pasadena was well worth taking for itself alone. The road is a model highway, cut out of the side of the mountain by the government at the cost of a million dollars to carry the great telescope up to the house built for it. . . . We who had lived in the valley below for a season opened our eyes wide when we saw its extent, the number of its buildings, and its astonishing equipment. Besides the 100-inch telescope, the largest reflecting telescope ever made, there are five other telescopes each in its own house. . . . In the afternoon we visited the museum, where we found many series of photographs and lantern slides. . . . The solar eclipse, which occurred on September 10, was the occasion of a gathering of scientists in and near Los Angeles from all parts of our country and Europe."

1894

We have heard with great sorrow of the death of Mr. Randall Nelson Durfee, husband of Abby Slade Brayton, on November 24th. Mr. Durfee became ill at the Yale-Harvard football game, and died after an illness of a few hours. Mrs. Durfee has the sincere sympathy of her class and of the entire Alumnae Association.

Mary Breed spent two months of the summer in Italy and France. She took with her her eighteen-year-old niece, whose mother is Betty Martin, ex-'03, and they touched a good many high spots. In fact, they took a flying trip to England, and nearly touched the sky in a Handley-Page aeroplane from London to Paris. They flew at an altitude of 8000 feet over France, and had a glorious sunset above a floor of clouds. The descent at Le Bourget was the only unpleasant part of the flight.

1896

Class Editor, Mary W. Jewett, Moravia, N. Y.

Elsa Bowman and Margaret Hall, '99, spent six weeks last summer on the high ranges of the Rockies in Colorado, camping with a pack train.

Mary Jewett is spending December in and around Boston, and will spend January in White Plains, N. Y. She returns to Moravia in time for her busy season with her seedlings and plants.

Mary Hill Swope settled during last summer in her new home, "The Croft," in a wild piece of country on the hills above Ossining, N. Y. She and her husband have been busy cutting trails through the woods. Mary takes charge of the farm. Her daughter Henrietta is a Junior at Barnard. Isaac is a Sophomore at Harvard, and David is at the Loomis School. Mary's husband, Gerard Swope, is President of the General Electric Company. They are starting on a six weeks' European trip in January.

Elizabeth Hopkins Johnson has been in New York. Her son George, after graduating from Harvard, is doing graduate work in physics and chemistry at the University of Wisconsin. Her younger son, Stanley, has entered there as a Freshman this fall.

Anna Scattergood Hoag tells that her second son, Garrett, is engaged to Margaret Ewing of West Grove, Pa., president of the present Junior Class at Connecticut College. Garrett is manager of the Pocono Inn and Anna proposes taking a party of the Class of '96 there for winter sports. Her daughter Mary, the class baby, was married to Carl Lawrence of Groton on December 15th, at the Haverford Friends' Meeting.

Elizabeth Cadbury Jones and her husband, Rufus Jones, went abroad last February and spent two months traveling around the Mediterranean. Then they spent six weeks in Oxford working in the Bodleian for Professor Jones' new book. Mary Jones is a Sophomore at Mt. Holyoke.

Elizabeth Kirkbride moved into her new house, 1021 Clinton Street, last spring. This winter she has rented it and is with her sister in Albany.

1898

Class Editor, Mrs. Wilfred Bancroft, Harrisville, R. I.

President Park and K. Lord, '01, spent the summer in Norway.

Grace Clarke Wright has just returned from a year's sojourn in Italy. She stayed in Boston en route for Minneapolis, and her '98 friends gave her a warm welcome. Two sons are in Harvard. Lucy is studying in Florence. Anne was with her.

Etta Herr has been enjoying the desert of Sahara.

Ullericka H. Oberge is a member of the local Republican Committee.

Anne Strong is at the Hotel Hemenway, Westland Avenue, Boston, for the winter.

Lucile Merriman Farmer and family spent the summer abroad.

Frances Brooks Ackerman, her husband, and two daughters spent the summer in England and France.

1900

MY DEAR 1900:

I have nine letters on my desk in reply to pathetic appeals I sent to some of you recently, and I have thoroughly enjoyed those letters. The most intriguing thing about them is that they all say somewhere in the letter, "This is just for you and not for the BULLETIN." I don't see why I can't tell about people being presented at court or things like that,—or how awfully popular some of our children are,—but we have always been naturally modest, and besides I have assumed, apparently, a sort of Mother-Confessor rôle, which prevents my divulging these confidences.

Anyhow, I can tell you about some of our children,—for our class baby has certainly not followed our traditions, inasmuch as the child is engaged! She is, as you know, a sophomore at B. M. and her fiancé is Mr. Max Ilfeld, of Las Vegas, New Mexico, now a senior in the Engineering School at the Massachusetts Institute of Technology. My dear "Myra Frank," we offer you for your daughter our most hearty felicitations.

Lotta's daughter Cecile and her mother have been in Paris at the American University Women's Club for six months, but they are at home again now. Lotta writes that she came upon Louise Norcross and Constance Rulison having tea with Marion Reilly at the club one day. And then there was some more I can't tell.

Margaretta Morris Scott's daughter Eleanor was at the same camp on Buzzard's Bay last summer that Aletta's Barbara was. And that reminds me to say that Aletta was abroad with her husband last summer when he went to deliver some lectures. He is now teaching Eastern European history to graduate students at Columbia.

As for Margaretta, she has solved the question of team work and co-operation. She writes me that she and her husband together are going to give some lectures at the Woman's Club in Germantown on Practical Politics. She says she does not know exactly how it will work out, but says, "We have been having great fun going around acting as coach and critic for one another's speeches, but it is a new venture to appear on the same platform and take turns."

Another of our children that we have a bit of news about is Eleanor Anderson's daughter, who is a sophomore at Wellesley and who is to "come out" this winter.

Perhaps most of you know that Nina's daughter Darcy entered B. M. this fall. If you see her on the campus you will know her because she looks so very much like Nina! But with the difference that she would not be sent onto the skating pond first to try out the ice, as Nina was. Bless you, Darcy, here's the best of luck for you. Nina's eldest son, Eric, is at Groton.

We are proud to announce that our Constance Rulison is continuing her work in composition under Vincent d'Indy. She is to be in Paris this winter, having spent last summer with Louise Norcross at Château d'Oisilly, Côte d'Or.

I have a fine letter from "Billy" Crane, in which she describes a beautiful motor trip up Mt. Mitchell. I wish they would give me space to print it all, for it is full of wide visions and deep forests and "sunshiny valleys." She writes also that she had a lovely call from Jessie McBride Walsh, who was on her way from Asheville to New Orleans. Her husband retired from the Navy and is manager of the port in New Orleans. And I suppose they won't let me tell all about how charming Jessie looked either.

It is a marvel to me how Maud Lowrey Jenks could write me a four-page letter without even inadvertently leaking out a little information about herself. But she did it, she did. Anyhow, her telephone number in New York is Vanderbilt 4186.

It is always a pleasure to get a letter from Helena Emerson, and this one is no exception. She is still doing her work with the troop of colored Girl Scouts, and in the summers she works for the Negro Fresh Air Committee. I wish she, too, would tell us a little more about her work, for she always deprecates having done anything "very much" in the world and yet we all know that she's one who makes us proud.

Swalley, I believe, entertained the Northern New Jersey alumnae at her charming house in Princeton. I just know that house must be lovely. If I ever have the good luck to see it, nobody will keep me from telling you all about it.

Mary Kil is still president of the College Club, of Baltimore. That is every bit about herself I could get out of her.

And Helen Mac, me myself, can't think of anything except that I was elected president of the Council of Women of the State Department of Education. It looks imposing, so I put it in. I'd hate you to know that all we do is eat.

Yours affectionately,

HELEN.

Mrs. Charles F. W. McClure, Headmistress of the Columbus School for Girls, as president of the Headmistresses' Association of the Middle West, presided at the annual meeting on Friday and Saturday, October 26th and 27th, at the Winchester School in Pittsburgh.

1902

Jane Brown is now manager of the New York Bryn Mawr Club.

1904

Class Editor, Emma O. Thompson, 320 South Forty-second Street, Philadelphia, Pa.

Dr. Alice Boring has arrived safely in China, and started her work at Yenching College, Peking.

Miriam Chesney is suffering from a nervous breakdown. She is still in the hospital, where she has been for the past few months.

Margaret Ross Garner is very much interested in the work of the Norristown School Board, of which she is a member.

Dr. Mary James has returned from Wuchang, China, on leave of absence. She arrived the last week in November. Until the spring her address will be 4114 Pine Street, Philadelphia.

Martha Rockwell Moorhouse and Marjorie Sellers, who are members of the School Board, are busy completely furnishing the housekeeping apartment in the new Junior High School in Merion Township.

Gertrude Klein has organized a storytelling team among the girls of the South Philadelphia High School.

Kathrina Van Wagenen Bugge and her husband are stationed at the Norwegian Mission at Yiyang, Hunau, China. Kathrina has twó daughters Theodora, aged three and one-half years, and Margrethe, aged seven months.

She writes that conditions in China are still very confused. "Life is somewhat uncertain in China these days, and we wonder if there is any hope of securing a stable government."

Mrs. Scott, mother of Katherine Scott, who went out to China to spend the winter with her daughter, has remained despite her grievous loss, and is staying at St. Hilda's School, where she is planning to do some teaching.

1906

Class Editor, Mrs. Harold .Beecher, 1511 Mahantongo Street, Pottsville, Pa.

Esther White Riggs writes from Cawthron Research Institute, Nelson, New Zealand: "I am charmed with my gift from the Class of 1906 and I can not begin to tell you what joy the inscription gives me. I think I like it as much as I do the bowl and that's saying a good deal. Please ask 1906 to accept my sincerest thanks. I used to think I was busy in this servantless land, but I was living a life of ease and luxury compared to my lot now with a baby added. However, she's just about a year old now and things are not quite as strenuous as they used to be. I even find time to garden a bit now and then, write a letter or two and do a stitch of sewing. But many things go undone and my husband's socks are often neglected. However, we manage to survive, and we don't worry overmuch about socks, although we do wish sometimes that we could throw the dishes out of the window. I have become by force of necessity a thoroughly domesticated housewife. I can even bake bread and cakes and knit."

Mary Richardson Walcott was the guest of Erma Kingsbacker Stix at the Alumnae Council meeting at St. Louis in November. Mary has been elected president of the Bryn Mawr Club in Boston.

Susan Delano. McKelvey has an apartment this year at 160 Riverway, Brookline.

Adelaide Neall went to Bermuda in June and *The Saturday Evening Post* printed a poem of hers, entitled "The Charge of the Blight Brigade."

Laura Boyer's book, entitled "The World My Neighbor," is used as a text-book in the group meetings of the Nation-Wide Campaign of the Episcopalian Church.

1908

Class Editor, Mrs. William H. Best, 1198 Bushwick Avenue, Brooklyn, N. Y,

Sarah Goldsmith Aronson (Mrs. Joseph) has a second child, a daughter, Jean, born October 20, 1923.

Anna Carrere is still in Peking, visiting Mrs. Calhoun, the wife of one of our former ministers to China, and is leading a very gay life.

Margaret Vilas is assistant librarian in the Pullman Public Library, Chicago, Ill.

Josephine Proudfit Montgomery (Mrs. Dudley), her husband, and their three children went up into the northern woods of Wisconsin last August, where the temperature was down in the early thirties—"which is very chill for August."

Josephine also writes: "I visited Louise Congdon Balmer in her cunning house in La Jolla when I was in California last spring, and had a fine visit with her and her four children. Our class baby is bigger than her mother and is busy preparing for college at the Bishop School in La Jolla."

1910

Class Editor, Marion Kirk, 4504 Chester Avenue, Philadelphia.

Helen Bley Papanastasiou is connected with the Children's Bureau in Washington doing research work, particularly among German sources, along medical lines.

Constance Deming Lewis has another son, Guy Spalding Lewis, born July 1, 1923.

Evelyn Seely Jackson announces that her only work now is being a little sunshine in her home, but that they are building a new home, which they hope to have completed by next summer,—by which time the shining business will probably come easier for Evelyn.

Emily Storer, after her marvelous eight months of travel around the world, has settled down to work again, this time as Red Cross worker at Mount Alto Hospital in Washington. She and her father are living in Washington this winter.

Frances Storer Ryan has just returned from visiting Albione Van Schaack at Albione's camp in Wisconsin and also her home in Evanston. Josephine Healy was also a visitor at camp this summer. Recently Frances visited Bryn Mawr with her husband, and spent some time with Josephine Healy and Bessie Cox Wolstenholme.

Izette Taber de Forest reports that her children are hard at work at the Parents' Co-operative School in Bridgeport. Mr. de Forest has invented a magnetic testing machine for testing the treatment and durability of any ferrous product. Izette is working for the Connecticut Society for Mental Hygiene, and hopes to help establish a mental hygiene clinic for children in Bridgeport.

Elizabeth Tappan is instructor in Greek and Latin at Vassar College.

1912

Class Editor, Mrs. John MacDonald, 3227 North Pennsylvania Street, Indianapolis.

Anna Hartshorne Brown's husband has been granted leave of absence from the Westtown School, where he is now teaching, and they are going abroad shortly after Christmas. They are leaving their children at home.

Catherine Thompson is assistant advertising manager to the J. B. Lippincott Company. She is enjoying her job enormously, and is doing book reviews on the side.

Fanny Crenshaw was at the Intercity Hockey Tournament at Chestnut Hill in Thanksgiving week, on account of her position as one of the officers of the United States Field Hockey Association.

Dorothea Wolf Douglas has a daughter, Dorothea Carol Douglas, born December 11th.

Carmelita Chase Hinton is teaching at the Winnetka Country Day School. She is taking her two older children to school with her.

Julia Haynes MacDonald and Mary Peirce went to the Council meeting in St. Louis.

The class wishes to extend its sincere sympathy to Beatrice House, whose mother died recently.

1914

Class Editor, Dr. Ida Pritchett, The Rockefeller Institute, Sixty-sixth Street and Avenue A, New York City.

Madelaine Fleisher Wolf (Mrs. James Wolf) has a son, James Standish, Jr., born in July.

Montgomery Arthurs Supplee (Mrs. Frank Supplee) has a daughter, born July 5th.

Dorothy Cox, ex-1914, has just returned to New York from Constantinople, and is said to be looking for a job in a museum. Anyone having a museum in need of a job, please come forward!

Ethel Thomas is living at 4042 Chestnut Street, Philadelphia, and holds the position of field representative for the Bureau of Mental Health under the Department of Welfare of the State of Pennsylvania.

Christine Hammer has been forced to give up her position as English reader at Bryn Mawr College on account of her health,

Harriet Sheldon, dean of the Columbus School for Girls, represented the School at the annual meeting of the Headmistresses' Association of the Middle West, at the Winchester School in Pittsburgh, on Friday and Saturday, October 26th and 27th.

1916

Class Editor, Mrs. Webb Vorys, 63 Parkwood Avenue, Columbus, Ohio.

Louise Dillingham is back at Bryn Mawr as warden of Rockefeller Hall and is studying for her M.A., which she hopes to receive in June in Psychology and French.

Caroline Crowell is in her third year of the University of Pennsylvania School of Medicine.

Ruth Lautz and Elizabeth Brakeley spent their vacation together last summer at Eaton Ranch, Wyoming. Ruth is still doing the service work for the Babson Statistical Organization in New York. Brakeley is living at the Bryn Mawr Club and is in her second year of the Cornell Medical School.

Elizabeth Porter is the executive secretary of the Social Service Exchange in Wilkes-Barre.

1918

Class Editor, Mrs. Julian B. Cohn, 5154 Westminster Place, St. Louis, Mo.

Helen Whitcomb announced her engagement on December 22nd to John Sedgwick Barss, of Windsor, Conn. Mr. Barss graduated from Hotchkiss and Harvard, taking his M.A. last year. He is now teaching at Phillips Academy, Andover. Helen is still academic head and assistant to the principal at Bradford Academy. They expect to be married in June.

Charlotte Dodge says she is having a very good time at home doing nothing of particular interest.

Mary Stair is doing various sorts of volunteer work, chiefly mental testing for the Red Cross. She spent the summer playing golf from White Sulphur to Rye, ending up with the Women's National at the Westchester-Biltmore Club.

Henrietta Huff is reference librarian at the James Brown Library at Williamsport.

Penelope Turle is running a travel bureau. She took a canoe trip this summer in Canada.

Lucy Evans Chew writes that she is reading proof on her husband's book on Byron and is saving money and making plans for Europe in the summer of 1924.

Frances Buffum, who now has "R.N." after her name, spent last year in South America. She is now doing district nursing.

Dorothy Stevenson Clark, whose son is now three years old, visited Olive B. Kittle and her children, and saw Marie C. Foyler and Kate Dufourcq Kelley.

Anna Lubar studied vocal in Maine this summer and is now doing social work.

Louise Hodges Crenshaw is secretary at the Model School.

Dorothy Kuhn Minster was in Europe three months and is again doing work in the Bureau for Industrial Hygiene.

Ruth Cheney Streeter and her three sons spent the summer at Nantucket Island.

Helen Schwarz is sailling January 5th for Naples and Switzerland.

Katharine Dufourcq Kelley is keeping house and enjoying it immensely. She spent the summer motoring week-ends and visiting in Virginia.

Frances Richmond Hawes is in Loralii, Boluchistan. She has one child.

Alice Kerr has been in China since February visiting her brother, who is a medical missionary.

Elsbeth Merck Henry has a daughter and writes that she spends her time raising her.

Marjorie Smith Van Dorn's second son, Nicholas Hugh, was born in October, 1922. They have built a cottage at the Rod and Gun Club, Wisconsin, and spend their summers there.

Mary Allen is still nursing, and hopes to get into child welfare work eventually.

Ruth Garrigues is teaching at the Friends' School, Wilmington. She spent the summer in Nova Scotia and Maine.

Ella Lindley Burton is living at 15 East Padre Street, Santa Barbara, now. She holds our class record with four children.

Margaret Bacon Carey writes that she is taking care of her son, making curtains, and being exceedingly domestic.

Margaret Timpson spent two months this summer in England and France, and expects to take a trip around the world with her family in January.

"Teddy" Howell Hulburt has a son and a daughter. They send the summer in Maine, sailing.

Molly Cordingley Stevens is living in Peace Dale, and is interested in the hospital, Visiting Nurses, Red Cross and Scout Committees.

Helen Butterfield Williams writes that she is on a twenty-four hour job doing nothing that she intended to. "Polly," our 1918 baby, is fine.

Hester Quimby is engineering assistant to the Pacific Telephone and Telegraph Company. She had a month's camping in the Yosemite this summer.

Ella Rosenberg has recovered from a long illness.

Annette Gest is teaching Spanish, Italian, History and Latin at the Agnes Irwin School, going to Bryn Mawr for one hour a day to give the course in Elementary Spanish. She spent the summer in Spain and Italy and Switzerland.

We all sympathize deeply with Helen Walker in the death of her mother.

Helen Hammer Link writes that she is taking care of three children, a cunning new house, and being cook. She and Mr. Link are co-directors in a camp in New Hampshire for girls from 8 to 16 years.

Virginia Anderton Lee is back in Milwaukee and has a baby daughter.

1918's REUNION

This notice is appearing in time for 1918 to make a New Year's resolution to come back for reunion next spring. We shall then be six years old and "Now is the time for all good men to come to the help of the party." Early in November your president and vice-president met and picked out Saturday, May 31st, as the date for our class meeting and banquet. This date may not be very convenient for the married members, unless they have indulgent husbands, but it seemed much the best time for people with jobs or people at a distance, and we hope that by beginning to take thought now everyone can make plans to come. Our headquarters and banquet will be in Merion. Louise Hodges Crenshaw has already promised to be toastmistress and there will shortly be appointed a reunion manager who will send out notices keeping you fully informed of our plans.

You will also receive soon a financial statement from the treasurer, and a call for dues to cover the expenses of the class book. She and Ruth Hart Williams, class collector, will also work together to raise a reunion gift, which is just an unusually large class collection. As we gave almost nothing last year, we hope that everyone will search their hearts and their pocketbooks and produce a respectable amount this year. Do send your money in quickly, so that painful moment will be over, and then come to the reunion and have a good time.

1920

Class Editor, Helene Zinsser, 6 West Ninth Street, New York City.

Children to

"Jerry" Hess Peters (Mrs. Douglas Edward Peters)—a boy, John Milton Peters (named after both grandfathers), born April 5th.

Edith Stevens Stevens (Mrs. John Stevens, Jr.)—a second daughter, Phebe Ten Broeck Stevens, born September 10th.

Married

Dorothy Rogers to Alexander Victor Lyman; on June 5th, in Doctor Mutch's church, Bryn Mawr. Agnes Clement '23, "Peg" Connelly, Emily Kimbrough '21, and Helene Zinsser '20, were among the bridesmaids.

Elizabeth Luetkemeyer to Paul Bernard Howard, on Friday, July 6th, in Cleveland.

"Birdie" Kingsbury to Mr. Conway Macon Zirkle, on Thursday, October 4th, in Christ Church, Woburn Square, London.

Mary Hoag to Carl Lawrence, of Groton, Mass., on Saturday, December 15th, at Haverford.

Anne Eberbach to Paul Deresco Augsburg, on Saturday, December 15th, in Chicago.

Degrees Received

Dorothy Allen: M.A. in English, Columbia University, February '23.

Helene Zinsser: M.A. in political science, Columbia University, June '23

Doris Pitkin: M.A. in making clay pigeons, Columbia University.

Vocations

Dotty Allen: taught English, French, and Latin at Kimberley School, Montclair, N. J.

Elizabeth Luetkemeyer Howard: teaching at Oaksmere, Mamaroneck, N. Y.

Doris Pitkin: teaching at Brearley School, New York City.

Anna Sandford: teaching at Jacobi School, New York City.

Julia Conklin: Information Bureau of Bogue, 19 W. 44th Street, New York City.

Millicent Carey: studying Anglo-Saxon and such, Johns Hopkins, Baltimore.

Betty Weaver: teaching Latin at Thorne School, Bryn Mawr.

Helene Zinsser: working with Foreign Policy Association, 8 E. 45th Street, New York City.

Avocations

Nancy Offutt: president, B. M. Club, Baltimore.

Helene Zinsser: secretary, B. M. Club, New York City.

Social Notes

Marguerite Eilers gave a linen shower for Mary Hoag on December 8th, attended by Marjorie Scattergood '17, D. Pitkin, A. Sandford, L. Hales, C. Colman, Marjorie Canby Taylor, H. Zinsser, from '20, and H. Farrell '21.

Athletic Notes

M. Carey, together with R. Marshall '21, '24, and F. Bliss '22, and H. Zinsser, with the following Bryn Mawrtyrs reading from left to right: Eugenia Baker Jessup '14, Edna Rapallo '13, G. Rhoades '22, M. Adams '23, and H. Rice '23, went to Philadelphia from Baltimore and New York respectively to attend the Intercity Hockey Matches at St. Martins.

Both "little light blue flowers' had the ecstatic honor of meeting Miss Peg Thompson, of the Windy City, in stick-to-stick combat.

Dilatory Domiciles

Mrs. John Stevens, Jr., 985 Hillside Avenue, Plainfield, N. J.

Natalie Gookin, 321 Linden Street, Winnetka, Ill. ·

Laura Hales, Allerton House for Women, 132 E. 57th Street, New York City.

Joe Herrick, Bryn Mawr Club, 279 Lexington Avenue, New York City.

Doris Pitkin, 550 W. 157th Street, New York City.

Dear 1920:

It seems years and years since we have seen each other or done anything together. For that reason I look forward with great joy to two events: May Day, which, as you know, comes this spring; and our Fifth Reunion, which is scheduled for June, 1925. It is never too early to make plans, and I am writing this letter in hope that everyone who possibly can will come to May Day for an informal reunion, and that *everyone*, regardless of distance, time, family, finances or careers, will plan *now* to be present at the great fifth anniversary of our graduation. You probably know that according to the new schedule, 1919, 1921, 1922, and 1923 are also re-uning in 1925. The occasion will surely be worth any sacrifice. Think of what the campus will be like!

I feel as if I should produce some collegiate enthusiasm to urge us on to do something; I find, however, that with advancing years the spirit of propaganda refuses to be forthcoming. But I imagine that in you, as in me, even advancing old age does not destroy a warm feeling around the heart when you think of 1920, or the desire to see each other again.

Happy New Year!

MILLICENT CAREY.

1922

Class Editor, Serena Hand, 48 West 9th Street, New York City.

Dear 1922:

I know you always turn to the class news in the BULLETIN before you read the editorials, everybody always does. This month we haven't very many items and I

know it is because I haven't written to you one and all. You want to know what other people are doing and in the same way they want to know what you are doing. It would be a great help if you would write to me and give me all the information about yourselves. I would rather have letters that we can quote in our class notes than send out a questionnaire, which is a dull method of obtaining news.

The next news has to go in on February 10, 1924, so if you could write to me as soon as you have read this number I should be very grateful.

Very sincerely yours,

SERENA E. HAND.

Emily Anderson is working in the business office of *Life*.

Ethel Brown is finishing her course at the New York School of Social Work, and expects to go abroad later in the winter.

Barbara Clarke is studying at the School of Design in Providence, and is also working in a book shop. She continues her hockey career and is responsible for the existence of, and is manager of, the Providence team.

Edith Finch is at Oxford this winter. Fink, while traveling in Norway last summer, had the occasion to meet, in a little Norwegian inn, a lady whom she thought might speak her native tongue. "Do you speak English?" — she inquired. The stranger answered quite fluently—the story goes—and revealed herself as the President of Bryn Mawr College.

Harriet Guthrie Evans has a daughter.

Serena Hand is substitute teacher in ancient history at the Brearley School.

Katherine Haworth Leicester has a son.

Nancy Jay has a job as secretary in the Sage Foundation.

Louise Mearns is working for her M.S. at Columbia.

Katherine Peek is in the office of *Farm and Fireside* in New York. She reads manuscript and finds her occupation very entertaining.

Vinton Liddell is working with The Carolina Play Makers. This is a dramatic club connected with the University of North Carolina. Vinton is head of the properties and does some scenery and also some acting. The students of the university produce original plays and Vinton finds the work very absorbing.

Evelyn Rogers is studying at Columbia.

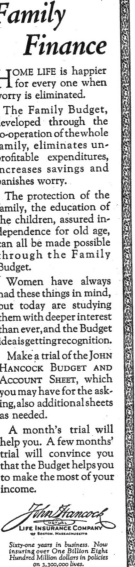

SCHOOL DIRECTORY

FERRY HALL
A Resident and Day School for Girls
LAKE FOREST, ILLINOIS
On Lake Michigan, near Chicago

College Preparatory, General and Advanced Courses. Departments of Music, Home Economics, Expression, and Art. *Supervised Athletics and Swimming Pool.*

Eloise R. Tremain, A.B., Bryn Mawr, Principal

THE
Mary C. Wheeler Town and Country School
PROVIDENCE, RHODE ISLAND
Preparation for Bryn Mawr and College Board Examinations
Out door sports   Junior Country Residence

"HILLSIDE"   NORWALK, CONNECTICUT

On a hill in six acres of ground. Three residence houses. Separate School House and Gymnasium. Preparation for Comprehensive and College Board Examinations. General and Special Courses.

MARGARET R. BRENDLINGER, A. B. (Vassar)
VIDA HUNT FRANCIS, A: B., (Smith), Principals

The Harcum School
BRYN MAWR, PA.
Prepares for Bryn Mawr and all leading colleges
Musical Course prepares for the Department of Music of Bryn Mawr College
EDITH H. HARCUM, Head of School
L. MAY WILLIS, Principal

MISS RANSOM *and* MISS BRIDGES' SCHOOL
HAZEL LANE, PIEDMONT (Suburb of San Francisco)

College Preparatory

MARION RANSOM } Headmistresses
EDITH BRIDGES }

MISS MADEIRA'S SCHOOL
1330 19th St., N. W.   Washington, D. C.

A Resident and Day School for Girls

LUCY MADEIRA WING, A.B.

MRS. DAVID LAFOREST WING
Head Mistress

The Shipley School
Bryn Mawr, Pennsylvania
Preparatory to Bryn Mawr College
Alice G. Howland, Eleanor O. Brownell, Principals

The Ethel Walker School
SIMSBURY, CONNECTICUT
Head of School
ETHEL WALKER SMITH, A.M. Bryn Mawr College
Head Mistress
JESSIE GERMAIN HEWITT, A.B. Bryn Mawr College

THE MISSES KIRK'S
College Preparatory School
Bryn Mawr Ave. and Old Lancaster Road, Bryn Mawr, Pa.

Number of boarders limited. Combines advantages of school life with private instruction. Individual schedule arranged for each pupil.

MISS WRIGHT'S SCHOOL
Bryn Mawr, Pa.

Prepares for Bryn Mawr and College Board Examinations

Miss Beard's School for Girls
ORANGE, NEW JERSEY

A country school near New York. College preparatory, special courses. Art, Domestic Arts and Science. Supervised physical work. Agnes Miles Music School affiliated with Miss Beard's School.

MISS LUCIE C. BEARD, Head Mistress

ROSEMARY HALL
No elective courses
Prepares for college
Preferably Bryn Mawr
Caroline Ruutz-Rees, Ph.D. } Head Mistresses
Mary E. Lowndes, Litt.D. . }
GREENWICH   CONNECTICUT

The Katharine Branson School
ROSS, CALIFORNIA   Across the Bay from San Francisco
A Country School   College Preparatory
Heads:
Katharine Fleming Branson, A. B., Bryn Mawr
Laura Elizabeth Branson, A. B., Bryn Mawr

THE AGNES IRWIN SCHOOL
2009-2011 Delancey Place, Philadelphia
A College Preparatory
SCHOOL FOR GIRLS
JOSEPHINE A. NATT, A.B., Headmistress
BERTHA M. LAWS, A.B., Secretary-Treasurer

SCHOOL DIRECTORY

The Episcopal Academy

(Founded 1785)

CITY LINE, OVERBROOK, PA.

A country day school for boys from second grade to college. Separate lower school beginning September 1923. Enjoys the patronage of Bryn Mawr Alumnae.

Cathedral School of St. Mary

GARDEN CITY, LONG ISLAND, N. Y.

A school for Girls 19 miles from New York. College preparatory and general courses. Music. Art and Domestic Science. Catalogue on request. Box B.

Miriam A. Bytel, A. B., Radcliffe, Principal
Bertha Gordon Wood, A. B., Bryn Mawr, Ass't Principal

WYKEHAM RISE

WASHINGTON, CONNECTICUT

A COUNTRY SCHOOL FOR GIRLS

Prepares for Bryn Mawr and Other Colleges

St. Timothy's School for Girls

CATONSVILLE, MARYLAND

Founded 1882

The Baldwin School

A Country School for Girls

BRYN MAWR   PENNSYLVANIA

Preparation for Bryn Mawr, Mount Holyoke, Smith, Vassar and Wellesley colleges. Abundant outdoor life. Hockey, basketball, tennis.

ELIZABETH FORREST JOHNSON, A.B.
Head

COLLEGE PREPARATORY

Miss J. R. HEATH
Miss L. McE. FOWLER } Heads of the School

Garrison Forest School for Girls

Less than an hour from Baltimore. A country school with all city advantages, in the beautiful Green Spring Valley. Intermediate, College Preparatory, Special Music and Art Courses. Boarding Dept. limited. Horseback riding and all sports. Catalog and Views.

MISS MARY MONCRIEFFE LIVINGSTONE, Princ'pa
Box C, Garrison, Maryland

WOMAN'S MEDICAL COLLEGE

OF PENNSYLVANIA

Seventy-fourth year beginning Sept. 26, 1923. Entrance requirements: two years of college work including certain credits in science and languages. Excellent laboratories. Full-time teachers. Clinical advantages. Well-equipped hospital. Special eight months' course of training for laboratory technicians. The Hospital of the Woman's Medical College conducts a training school for nurses which includes the advantages of class teaching by the Faculty of the College

For information address: The Dean
2101 North College Avenue, Philadelphia, Pa.

HIGHLAND HALL

A School for Girls High in the Mountains

In old residential Hollidaysburg, in the most beautiful and healthful section of the Alleghenies, six miles from Altoona on the Pennsylvania Railroad.
Spacious buildings, unusual equipment, modern educational standards.

College Preparatory, General Courses, Two years Advanced Work, Special facilities in Music, Domestic Science, Vocational Training.

Abundant outdoor life, supervised athletics including swimming, week-end camping trips.

ELLEN C. KEATES, A.B., Principal
Hollidaysburg, Pennsylvania

DWIGHT SCHOOL FOR GIRLS

Recommended by the leading colleges for

COLLEGE PREPARATION

SPECIAL FINISHING COURSES
Adequate Departments for French, Spanish, German, English, Art, Physical Education, Domestic Science, Music and Expression.

Athletics, Gymnasium, Tennis, Riding
Spacious grounds for Games
Alumnae cordially recommend Dwight because of the spirit which it inculcates;
Frankness, Self Control, Service.
Write for the illustrated catalogue telling of the life of the school. References on request.
MISS E. S. CREIGHTON, Principal
Englewood, New Jersey

He took the world to her

Twenty-five years ago a boy left a little country town to find his fortune. He found it.

Two years ago, when radio was still a novelty, he took a receiving set back to the old home and set it up in his mother's room. That evening the world spoke to her.

She could not follow her boy away from home. But the best that the world has to give —in music, in lectures, in sermons—he took back to her.

GENERAL ELECTRIC

The BRYN MAWR ALUMNAE BULLETIN

REPORT OF ALUMNAE FUND, 1923

SIMANCAS

FEBRUARY

1924

IV   No. 2

BRYN MAWR ALUMNAE BULLETIN

OFFICIAL PUBLICATION OF
THE BRYN MAWR ALUMNAE ASSOCIATION

EVELYN PAGE, '23, *Editor*

GERTRUDE J. HEARNE, '19, *Business Manager*

EDITORIAL BOARD

LUCY M. DONNELLY, '93
ELEANOR FLEISHER REISMAN, '03
CAROLINE MORROW CHADWICK-COLLINS, '05

ADELAIDE W. NEALL, '06
MAY EGAN STOKES, '11
LEILA HOUGHTELING, '11, *ex-officio*

Subscription Price, $1.50 a Year   *Single Copies, 25 Cents*

Checks should be drawn to the order of Bryn Mawr Alumnae Bulletin
Published monthly, except August and September, at 1006 Arch St., Philadelphia, Pa.

VOL. IV	FEBRUARY, 1924	No. 2

EDITORIAL

Since the new have already taken the places of the old officers, this is a fitting time for us to say what we should like to have said before. No member of the Alumnae Association is willing to allow her gratitude to the officers of the Association to remain unexpressed. We have to thank them for their toil on our behalf, their patience, skill, and energy, which has enabled them not only to carry on the work of their predecessors, but to enlarge the scope of the Alumnae Association and to perfect its organization. We cannot in any sense repay them for what they have given us, but we can acknowledge our indebtedness and strive to counterbalance it with our gratitude.

With the growth of the Association the duties of its officers have multiplied. We have called upon them for exhaustive labor not only in the larger considerations of policy, but in detail that is every day increasing in extent. We are demanding too much. If we are to have in the future, as in the present and in the past, the best to represent us, we cannot ask them to put aside their other pursuits in order to give us their full time. We have bestowed honor upon those whom we have chosen to represent us, but we have tempered the honor with the excess of our demands. In consequence we must confine our choice by narrow geographical limits, and to those within the limits who have abundant leisure or who are willing to neglect their other pursuits for our benefit. We feel strongly that the organization of the Association should make it possible to call upon those living away from Bryn Mawr, and upon the busy as well as the unoccupied.

The Nominating Committee also deserves our thanks, for in the past few years it has worked hard to secure acceptances nominations,

and in many cases has had to persuade people who felt that they were too busy to run for office. While the Nominating Committee has succeeded in the past, the time will come when the task will be impossible. At the present moment we are subjecting its members to a greater strain than we have any right to impose upon them, and we must find some solution which will at once relieve them and our officers.

The officers are yours and the problem is yours. We look to you for the solution.

ANNOUNCEMENTS

The Publicity Office has on sale some very attractive etchings of the campus, by Mr. G. A. Bradshaw, who is well known for his beautiful etchings of Princeton. He has taken for his subjects the Library, the Gymnasium, the Cloister, and the Owl Gate. His work has been very favorably reviewed by Mr. Henry R. MacGinnis, painter and instructor in painting and portraiture in the School of Industrial Arts of Trenton, New Jersey. *The Cloister* was reproduced in a recent number of *The Art News*. It was also hung at the Brooklyn Etchers' Exhibit. *The Owl Gate, The Cloister,* and *The Library* were exhibited at the Art Alliance in Philadelphia in January.

Any and all of the etchings may be ordered from the Publicity Office. Each costs eight dollars. Mr. Bradshaw intends to do

three others, one of Pembroke Hall, one of Radnor, and one of Pembroke Arch. THE BULLETIN will carry an announcement about them as soon as they are finished. It is proposed to use six of the etchings for a Bryn Mawr calendar to be sold at May Day.

The Editor is very sorry that a mistake was made in the January issue of the BULLETIN. The dinner held on December 14th, in honor of President Emeritus Thomas, was given not by the Alumnae Association of New York, but by the Bryn Mawr Club of New York.

All material for the March BULLETIN should be sent to Evelyn Page, The Alumnae Office, Bryn Mawr College, on or before February 10th.

Simancas

By VERA LEE BROWN, Ph.D.

IN the midst of the great Castilian plain, seven miles southwest of Valladolid and four hours' journey north of Madrid lies the old *villa* of Simancas. It is famous throughout the historical world as the home of the oldest of the three great archives of Spain that house the documents of that nation's history as an international power. Although picturesquely situated on one of the small hills that border the Rio Pisuerga, at the point where an ancient bridge connected the kingdoms of Leon and Castile in olden times the *villa* itself can today lay no claims to beauty. The builders seem to have been determined that views of the surrounding country, with its lovely winding river, its great pine woods and great hills, should not distract the inhabitants from the more serious business of life with the result that the houses all turn their backs to the beauty around them. Within the walls fully half the town is now in ruins and the remainder seems well on the way to dissolution. The small buildings, of adobe bricks, roofed in crumbling tiles, lean crazily against each other, straggling along narrow crooked lanes that serve as streets. Here and there about the town there are reminders of former grandeur in the stone escutcheons that adorn the faces of some of the oldest buildings, but the chances are that the visitor will be too much engrossed in choosing his way along the filthy street to give much attention to these memorials of other days. Except close to the great church, whose size seems wholly out of proportion to the resources of the village there is scarcely a blade of grass or a tree in Simancas. Everything is the color of mother earth. Indeed so perfect is the protective coloring that at a little distance the presence of a town on the hill can hardly be distinguished.

The people of Simancas, small in stature and weather-worn in appearance, resemble their houses. Of the one thousand or more inhabitants practically all are agriculturists who till the land of the nearby river valley. The passing of the centuries has left them very few of the comforts that in more fortunate places have robbed life of some of its primitive hardness. The farm implements are such as were old fashioned in Bible times, an open fire in the kitchen still serves as the only means of cooking and heating, bread must be baked in one of the half-dozen public ovens in the town, the family washing has still to be done at the river edge, and drinking water must still be brought from a central fountain. On the highway beyond the village modern automobiles and omnibuses pass to and fro on their journeys to the great centers, but in the *pueblo* the ox, the mule, and the donkey still reign supreme. So multitudinous are the services of the donkey, so intimate a part does it play in the life of a Simancas family, whose house he shares, that one finds oneself wondering how the American world gets on without him. In Simancas it is the *burro* who brings the water, the milk, and the vegetables to the door, who fetches the firewood from the pinewoods, who serves as royal mail carrier, who provides the means of transport to the nearest town, who performs much of the heavy work of the farm, and who, in short, is the ever useful friend of man from youth to old age.

The *castillo*, which alone gives Simancas its importance, rises at the edge of the town close to the highway that connects Valladolid and Zamora. The present fortress is the second on the site. It was built in the fifteenth century by the *Almirante Mayor de Castilla*, but was largely remodelled in the next century on plans drawn by Juan de Herrera, the architect of the Escorial, to whom are due the satisfying lines of the present building. In 1480 it became the property of the crown, being ceded, along with the pueblo of Simancas, to the Catholic kings, in return for other favors, by Don Alfonso Enriquez. For some years it was used solely for military purposes, but in 1508 King Ferdinand sent to it its first political prisoner in the person of an emissary from the Emperor Maximilian, whom His Catholic Majesty had discovered tampering with the loyalty of his Castilian nobles. Henceforth through the next century, Simancas was seldom without one or more famous prisoners within its walls. While state offenders were still being sent thither, Charles the Fifth created the fortress a national depository for state papers, about the year 1542, and shortly afterwards appointed the first keeper of records. His son, Philip the Second, by ordering all councils, tribunals, ministers, and other persons, in whose hands were documents of state to deliver them to Simancas, by drawing up a detailed set of instructions for the organization of the archive, and by placing his secretary, Don Diego de Ayala, in sole charge of the papers, insured the permanency and importance of the new foundation. Ayala put thirty-four years of most enthusiastic and devoted service into the enlargement and arrangement of the archive and left it firmly established. The year of his death, 1594, saw the last prisoner leave the fortress, which henceforth became merely the peaceful guardian of the nation's historical papers.

The archive of Simancas thus had its origin in the imperial epoch of Spanish history. When America meant the Spanish Indes, when the Catholic king was the consort of the English queen, when Horne and Montmorency paid their famous visits to Philip the Second to urge upon him the wisdom of a different political system for his dominions on the North Sea, when the great Armada set sail, these were the days when papers, witnessing to the world power of Spain, flowed in a great stream into Simancas. A creation of the house of Austria, the archive shared the confusion that fell upon that house in the late seventeenth century and did not thrive under the more vigorous, but alien, rule of the house of Bourbon. Indeed, the greatest of the eighteenth century kings, Charles the Third, was responsible for the idea that the papers of the Indes should be collected in a depository at Seville, devoted exclusively to documents illustrative of the history of Spain's colonial empire, and, in consequence, great wagon loads of papers left Simancas for the southern city. Under the son and grandson of Charles the Third Simancas suffered a still greater loss in the depredations of the Emperor Napoleon, who considered Paris a more suitable location for the Spanish state papers than the fortress near Vallodolid, and in his best manner ordered the choicest of them to be fetched north across the Pyrenees. While the last century has seen the return of the greatest portion of these, some still remain in the neighbor's capital, while many of those he returned bear the marks of their travels. The bustling spirit of the nineteenth century, that found fault with the inconvenience of the great distance of the archive from the national capital and the lack of modern facilities near the depository, brought the final blow in 1858 when the king ordered that state papers should henceforth be sent to the *Archivo General Central de Alcala de Henares*. When this location proved also to be inconvenient the *Archivo Historico Nacional* was created in Madrid itself.

Thus today the *Archivo General de Simancas* does not enjoy the unrivalled position among things archival in Spain that the Public Record Office holds in the English world. Nevertheless the old fortress is the mother of Spanish archives and contains within her walls the records of a longer period of the nation's history, not purely local in interest, than any other depository. Some day the remaining papers may be removed to more accessible quarters, but until that time Simancas will remain a center of interest to the historical world as a whole and an object of pilgrimage to those who make the study of the history of Spain their avocation or profession.

———

Only a few students each year reach Simancas for a sojourn of any duration. It may interest Bryn Mawr readers to learn that the two students of the present time are both Bryn Mawr graduates. The discovery of our common campus ties came about quite accidentally. One cold late afternoon of early November I was reading in my room in the depths of the village of Simancas when my landlady arrived to say that an "otra Americana" wished to see me. The visitor proved to be Miss Alice Gould, who explained that she had no reason for seeking me out other than the fact that all Simancas with one voice insisted that she must talk to the "Americana." As she later climbed the hill of one of the dark, narrow streets of the village, Miss Gould asked me the name of my American college. My reply of "Bryn Mawr" halted all progress for several minutes while my companion seized me and cried "Bryn Mawr? Why that is my college! Suppose I hadn't hunted you out!" The Spanish archivist with us, who understood not a word of English and to whom, at all events, college loyalties would mean little, looked on at this scene with extraordinary interest. Another proof of the queerness of foreigners.

Miss Gould, as many Bryn Mawr ieaders will know, is a proud member of the first graduating class of the college. Recently she has spent several years in various Spanish archives investigating the records bearing on the life of Columbus. For length of residence and study in Simancas she must easily hold the record, having been here at intervals through four years. That the history of this archive is as well known as it is, is due partly to her efforts in locating original documents relating to its history, a service which is most gratefully acknowledged in the official guide of the archive.

Bryn Mawr seems to have a large representation in Spain this year. Early in October, in the Biblioteca Nacional in Madrid, I met Miss Mary-Lapsley Caughey, whom I understood to say that she was in Spain in search of the Holy Grail, an undertaking that made the piece of ordinary historical research work that has brought me thither seem very easy of accomplishment!

Report of the Alumnae Fund, 1923

The Alumnae Fund plan, the successor to the Class Collections system of former years, has been in operation for one year. During 1923 there has been no extraordinary appeal, yet $16,801.25 has been received, against a total in 1922 of $9609.55. The Alumnae have given on an average $5.26 more than last year, an increase of 54 per cent. The Fund is proving a convenient channel through which money may pass for a great variety of College needs. $11,424.30 has actually been given to the College or is being held for later transfer, an increase of $7027.68 or 160 per cent over the amount given to the College from the 1922 Class Collections.

What are the reasons for this great increase? Probably there are many. Chief among them, certainly, is the fact that simultaneous appeal accompanied by authoritative information has been made for things of which the College was in urgent need. The Alumnae have been able to give intelligently, consequently they have given generously. Whether the sending of contributions directly to the Alumnae Office instead of to the Class Collectors is an advantage or not is an open question. While a few more Alumnae have given this year than in 1922, the increase has been far too small. It is impossible to tell after only a year's trial whether this insufficient increase in the number of contributors is due to the change in the system. What has been proved beyond a doubt is that the direct returns to the Office allow for greater ease with less chance of error in the keeping of the accounts and prompter transfer of the money to the uses for which it is intended than was possible in the past.

In accordance with the vote of the Alumnae Association at its last annual meeting the Board has appropriated the money to the various objects named by the Joint Committee. Complying with a special recommendation of the Joint Committee made at its meeting on December 17th, a large proportion of the balance at the close of the year has been given to the Library, whose need is especially acute.

The Alumnae Fund plan is new and as yet insufficiently tested. Those of us who are responsible for its administration need and invite the constructive criticisms of the Alumnae to make it a complete success. We wish to take this opportunity to thank those who have given it the success it has already had, the Alumnae who laid the splendid foundation for it in the Class Collection system, the contributors who through it have given valuable assistance to the College in 1923, and those through whom it has functioned, especially the Class Collectors who, in spite of doubts, have given the Alumnae Fund their hearty support. We hope for the continued support of all of these in 1924, and at the same time urge the co-operation of the many Alumnae who did not give to the Alumnae Fund in 1923.

Respectfully submitted,

MARY PEIRCE, *Chairman.*

RECEIPTS

Designated	$7,182.44	
Undesignated	9,582.31	
	$16,764.75	
Interest	36.50	
Total		$16,801.25

In 1922 the average Alumnae gift was	$ 9.77
In 1923 the average Alumnae gift was	15.03
Average increase	$ 5.26 or 54%

In 1922 .... $4,398.62 was given to the College— 46% of total
In 1923 .... $11,424.30 was given to the College— 68% of total
Increase .... $7,027.68 or   160%

CONTRIBUTORS

Alumnae	958
Parents	3
Bryn Mawr Clubs	3
Non Bryn Mawr Donors	6
Non Bryn Mawr Groups	1
Schools	1

DESIGNATIONS AND APPROPRIATIONS

Object	Amount Designated	Amount Appropriated	Amount Held
1. *President Park's Fund*			
From Alumnae at large	$ 140.00	$ 2,000.00	
From 1898 for Reunion Gift	1,500.00	1,500.00	
(Given to New Book Room)			
2. *Books for the Library*			
From Alumnae at large	131.50	1,626.86	
From 1914 for Reunion Gift			
New Book Room	1,000.00	1,000.00	
Books for Music Department in memory of Catherine Westling	256.00	256.00	
From Chicago Bryn Mawr Club for Dr. Scott's books	50.00		$ 50.00
3. *Students' Building*			
From Alumnae at large	107.00	107.00	
From 1919 in memory of Theodosia Haynes Taylor	651.90	651.90	
From 1921 for Reunion Gift	501.73	501.73	
From Mrs. Caldwell in memory of John Caldwell	1,000.00	1,000.00	
4. *Additional Class Room Facilities*	1.00	1.00	
5. *Academic Endowment*	10.00	10.00	
6. *Nelson's Pension Fund*	215.00	1,140.00	
7. *Special Objects* for which individual classes raised money			
From 1903 for 1921 Reunion Gift ...	324.00		324.00
From 1904 for Constance Lewis Memorial Scholarship	404.50	404.50	
From 1918 for Reunion Gift	25.00		25.00
8. *Alumnae Association Expenses*	38.50	5,376.95*	
9. *Other Objects*			
Lisa Baker Converse Memorial	356.31		356.31
Summer School	420.00	420.00	
Pictures for Art Department	50.00	50.00	
Total	$7,182.44	$16,045.95	$755.31

*Includes expenses of Alumnae Fund.

Contribution by Classes to January 1, 1924

Class	Number in Class	1922		1923		Total
		Number Contributing	Amount	Number Contributing	Amount	
Ph.D.'s and Graduate Students	..	18	$91.00	26	$154.00	$1,105.43
1889	32	18	137.00	21	671.00	10,362.55
1890	10	..	......	..	......	30,400.75
1891	16	..	100.00	..	......	15,466.90
1892	25	9	135.00	12	155.00	56,691.99
1893	37	23	103.00	16	115.44	10,010.62
1894	44	15	36.00	10	57.50	8,365.35
1895	36	15	104.00	19	191.00	12,226.86
1896	66	31	355.00	27	512.00	35,864.83
1897	80	..	250.00	4†	315.00	37,061.26
1898	59	20	163.00	47	1,505.00*	12.513.11
1899	63	32	283.00	26	336.00	40,681.50
1900	70	30	132.50	38	352.00	9,453.28
1901	88	19	300.00	26	358.00	31,174.32
1902	86	43	914.50	26	403.00	18,356.42
1903	111	21	195.50	41	931.00	33,405.42
1904	97	39	161.36	38	564.50	21,032.81
1905	119	40	221.00	33	395.50	23,781.87
1906	77	27	153.35	26	952.37	43,949.87
1907	125	65	554.00	28	262.00	110,716.39
1908	102	46	584.50	49	793.50	22,857.14
1909	108	30	195.50	38	428.00	29,216.17
1910	87	19	92.00	23	209.50	13,270.53
1911	87	7	68.63	32	379.50*	13,442.05
1912	95	40	313.00	28	322.00	23,231.34
1913	106	28	106.36	59	791.00*	16,087.85
1914	110	40	171.24	86	1,256.00*	21,168.21
1915	129	39	235.00	35	317.00	19,503.82
1916	103	25	170.20	25	406.00	12,587.90
1917	111	13	306.00	19	941.00	42,611.13
1918	97	20	95.00	2	25.00	16,107.06
1919	122	52	602.94	30	651.90	17,803.13
1920	109	48	236.50	30	264.00	722.61
1921	136	76	1,896.62	37	501.73*	2,402.12
1922	..	..	......	..	......	......
1923	100	..	......	2	20.00	20.00
Other contributors	..	..	......	..	1,268.31	......
	..	948	$9,609.55	958	$16,764.75	
Bank interest					36.50	
					$16,801.25	

* Reunion gift.   † Individual gifts to Class Chest excluded.

Total payments of collections to December 31, 1922, as per report of December 31, 1922............. $824,107.97

Total December 31, 1923............. 16,801.25

Grand total............. $840,909.22

CLASS COLLECTORS

Ph.D.'s and Graduate Students—Charlotte D'Evelyn, Mt. Holyoke College, South Hadley, Mass. Drusilla Flather Riley (Mrs. George C.), Brook Close; Dragon, Prov. of Quebec, Canada.
1889—Harriet Randolph, The College Club, 1300 Spruce Street, Philadelphia.
1890—Margaret Patterson Campbell (Mrs. Richard), 1075 Penn. Ave., Denver, Col.
1891—Anna Swift Rupert (Mrs. Charles G.), Sedgeley, Marshallton, Del.
1892—Dr. Mary Taylor Mason, School House Lane, Germantown, Philadelphia.
1893—S. Frances Van Kirk, 1333 Pine Street, Philadelphia.
1894—Abby Brayton Durfee (Mrs. Randall N.), 19 Highland Ave., Fall River, Mass.
1895—Annette Hall Phillips (Mrs. Howard M., Jr.), 1914 Pine Street, Philadelphia.
1896—Ruth Furness Porter (Mrs. James F.), 1085 Sheridan Road, Hubbard Woods, Ill.
1897—Elizabeth Higginson Jackson (Mrs. Charles), 77 Marlborough St., Boston, Mass.
1898—Elizabeth Nields Bancroft (Mrs. Wilfred), Harrisville, Rhode Island.
1899—May Schoneman Sax (Mrs. Percival M.), 6429 Drexel Road, Philadelphia.
1900—Cornelia Halsey Kellogg (Mrs. Frederic R.), 25 Colles Avenue, Morristown, N. J.
1901—Ethel Cantlin Buckley (Mrs. Monroe), 225 Kent Road, Ardmore, Pa.
1902—H. Jean Crawford, Vassar College, Poughkeepsie, N. Y.
1903—Philena C. Winslow, Cape Elizabeth, Portland P. O., Maine.
1904—Isabel M. Peters, Hawirt, Oyster Bay, Long Island.
1905—Margaret Nichols Hardenbergh (Mrs. Clarence M.), 3710 Warwick Blvd., Kansas City, Mo.
1906—Elizabeth Harrington Brooks (Mrs. Arthur), 5 Ash Street, Cambridge, Mass.
1907—Alice Martin Hawkins, 228 Madison Avenue, New York City.
1908—Marjorie Young Gifford (Mrs. Stephen W., Jr.), 5 Hilliard St., Cambridge, Mass.
1909—Margaret Bontecou Squibb (Mrs. Edward R., 2nd), Mohonk School, Lake Mohonk, N. Y.
1910—Bessie Cox Wolstenholme (Mrs. Hollis), Scotforth Road, Mt. Airy, Philadelphia.
1911—Helen Emerson Chase (Mrs. Peter P.), 104 Congdon Street, Providence, R. I.
1912—Florence Leopold Wolf (Mrs. Lester), Shoemaker Road, Elkins Park, Pa.
1913—Maud Holmes Young (Mrs. H. McClure), 5418 Cabanne Avenue, St. Louis, Mo.
1914—Mary C. Smith, Glyn-Wynne Road, Haverford, Pa.
1915—Adrienne Kenyon Franklin (Mrs. Benjamin, Jr.), 154 Lismore Avenue, Glenside, Pa.
1916—New Collector not yet appointed.
1917—Olga Tattersfield, 6807 Lincoln Drive, Philadelphia.
1918—Ruth Hart Williams (Mrs. Donald H.), 308 East 15th Street, New York City.
1919—New Collector not yet appointed.
1920—Martha F. Chase, Great Meadows, Concord, Mass.
1921—Marynia Foot, 512 Delaware Street, Southeast, Minneapolis, Minnesota.
1922—Cornelia M. Baird, 308 Park Avenue, Yonkers, New York.
1923—Agnes Clement, Wissahickon and Hortter Streets, Mt. Airy, Philadelphia.

CLASS COLLECTIONS

PH.D.'s AND GRADUATE STUDENTS

Charlotte D'Evelyn, Collector.
Drusilla Flather Riley, Collector.
Byrne, Alice Hill
Claflin, Edith Frances
Coulter, Cornelia C.
D'Evelyn, Charlotte
Dohan, Edith Hall
Dudley, Louise
Ferree, Gertrude Rand
Foster, Frances A.
Gibbons, Vernette L.
Guthrie, Mary J.
Harmon, Esther
Hussey, Mary I.
Laird, Elizabeth R.
Maddison, Isabel
Medes, Grace
Morriss, Margaret S.
Ogden, Ellen S.
Parrish, Mary Alice Hanna
Reimer, Marie
Rice, Grace Potter Reynolds
Riley, Drusilla Flather
Sweet, Margaret
Traver, Hope
White, Florence Donnell
Wood, Ida
Woodbury, Margaret
Number of Contributors 26
Amount Contributed $154.00

CLASS OF 1889

Harriet Randolph, Collector.
Anthony, Alice
Beach, Elizabeth Blanchard
Blanchard, Mary M.
Collins, Julia Cope
Cox, Catharine Bean
Dudley, Helena S.
Foulke, Frances Garrett
Franklin, Susan B.
Huddleston, Mabel Clark
Johnson, Susan Harrison
Johnson, Leah Goff
Ladd, Anna Rhoads
Lawrence, Caroline
McMurtrie, Mary
Putnam, Emily James
Randolph, Harriet
Riegel, Ella
Taylor, Gertrude Allinson

Thomas, Martha G.
Williams, Mary Rhoads Garrett
Worthington, Grace
Numbers of Contributors.......... 21
Amount Contributed $671.00

CLASS OF 1890
Margaret Patterson Campbell, Collector.
No Report

CLASS OF 1891
Anna Swift Rupert, Collector.
No Report

CLASS OF 1892
Edith Wetherill Ives, Collector.
Mary T. Mason, Temporary Collector.
Allinson, Anne C. Emery
Bartlett, Helen
Carroll, Elizabeth M.
Claghorn, Kate H.
du Pont, Alice Belin
Hall, Edith R.
Hunt, Frances E.
Ives, Edith Wetherill
Kirk, Helen Clements
Montgomery, Eliza Stephens
Pearson, Elizabeth Winsor
Putnam, Lucy Chase
Number of Contributors 12
Amount Contributed $155.00

CLASS OF 1893
S. Frances Van Kirk, Collector.
Andrews, Evangeline Walker
Brownell, Jane L.
Donnelly, Lucy M.
Emerson, Annie Laurie Logan
Flexner, Helen Thomas
Gucker, Louise Fulton
Johnson, Margaret Hilles
Kackley, Sarah Frances Atkins
Lewis, Eliza Adams
Lewis, Lucy
Oliver, Rachel L.
Seal, Harriet F.
Thom, Helen Hopkins
Van Kirk, S. Frances
Walker, Margaret Dudley
Watson, Mary Janney Atkinson
Number of Contributors 16
Amount Contributed $115.44

CLASS OF 1894
Abby Brayton Durfee, Collector.
Fay MacCracken Stockwell, Temporary Collector.
Boyd, Elizabeth Mifflin
Breed, Mary B.
Durfee, Abby Brayton
Hamilton, Sarah Darlington
Harris, Mary
Hench, Elizabeth C.
Langenbeck, Mildred Roelker
Martin, Emilie N.
Rupli, Theodosia
Speer, Emma Bailey
Number of Contributors 10
Amount Contributed $57.50

CLASS OF 1895
Annette Hall Phillips, Collector.
Borie, Edith Pettit
Brown, Madeline Harris
Clark, Elizabeth Bent
Collins, Rosalie Allan Furman
Ellis, Mary F.
Evans, Ella Malott
Flexner, Mary
Fowler, Susan
Hogue, Jane Horner
Janney, Marianna
Levin, Bertha Szold
Loomis, Julia Langdon
Louderback, Jessie L.
Phillips, Annette Hall
Shreve, Harriet R.
Steele, Esther C. M.
Stevens, Edith Ames
Tatnall, Frances Swift
Wing, Elizabeth Nicholson
Number of Contributors 19
Amount Contributed $191.00

CLASS OF 1896
Ruth Furness Porter, Collector.
Boring, Lydia T.
Bowman, Elsa
Brownell, Harriet M.
Cook, Katharine I.
Dimon, Abigail C.
Dudley, Mary Crawford
Farr, Clara
Goldmark, Pauline
Hoag, Anna Scattergood
Huizinga, Faith Mathewson
Johnson, Elizabeth Hopkins
Jones, Elizabeth Cadbury
Justice, Hilda
King, Florence
Kirkbride, Elizabeth B.
Lattimore, Eleanor L.
Nichols, Tirzah L.
Porter, Ruth Furness
Pyle, Hannah Cadbury
Ragsdale, Virginia
Slade, Caroline McCormick
Spear, Mary Northrop
Tilt, Stella Bass
Woolman, Mary Boude
Worthington, Clara B. Colton
Wyatt, Edith F.
Yandell, Elizabeth Hosford
Number of Contributors 27
Amount Contributed $512.00

CLASS OF 1897
Elizabeth Higginson Jackson, Collector.
Gift from the Class Chest, $250.00
Brooks, Clara Vail
Grafton, Anna Whitehead
Hand, Frances Fincke
Lawther, Anna B.
Number of Individual Contributors. 4
Amount Contributed $315.00

CLASS OF 1898

Elizabeth Nields Bancroft, Collector.
Ackermann, Frances Brooks
Andrews, Isabel J.
Archer, Caroline
Bancroft, Elizabeth Nields
Bertelsen, Sophie Olsen
Boericke, Edith Schoff
Bright, Mary de Haven
Browne, Jennie N.
Bruce, Sarah Ridgway
Buckingham, Elizabeth Holstein
Calvert, Mary Githens
Carpenter, Hannah
Cregar, Rebecca Foulke
Fry, Anna D.
Gannett, Alice P.
Goldmark, Josephine C.
Gray, Elizabeth D.
Haas, Anna M.
Hammond, Alice B.
Herr, Etta
Holloway, Alice Vail
Hood, Alice W.
Jeans, Charly Mitchell
Knoblauch, Mary Bookstaver
Locke, Grace P.
Meade, Addis M.
Mitchell, Catherine Bunnell
Moody, Mary Grace
Oberge, Ullericka H.
Park, Marion E.
Parker, Annie Beals
Perkins, Agnes
Pulsford, Clara Yardley
Sharpless, Helen
Sheppard, Mary
Stein, Blanche Harnish
Stoughton, Leila
Strong, Anne
Thomas, Esther Willits
Tracy, Martha
Wardwell, Florence
Warren, Louise
Wilbur, Anna Dean
Willard, M. Ella Stoner
Wood, Bertha G.
Woodall, Helen Williams
Wright, Grace Clarke
Mr. Ellis D. Williams
Number of Contributors, Alumnae.   47
One Father
Amount Contributed $1,505.00

CLASS OF 1899

May Schoneman Sax, Collector.
Allen, Helen H.
Bakewell, Madeline Palmer
Blackwell, Katherine Middendorf
Bowditch, Sylvia Scudder
Bradley, Dorothy Sipe
Darlington, Sibyl Hubbard
Dennison, Mary Thurber
Dickerman, Alice Carter
Edwards, Ethel Hooper
Ely, Gertrude
Erismann, Camille
Fordyce, Lillian Powell
Hoyt, Mary F.

Kilpatrick, Ellen P.
McLean, Charlotte F.
Miller, Emma Guffey
Motley, Ethel Levering
Riggs, Alice McBurney
Ross, May Blakey
Sax, May Schoneman
Schock, Evetta Jeffers
Sheddan, Martha Irwin
Sutliffe, May Lautz
Tyler, Eleanor J.
Vonsiatsky, Marion Ream
Walker, Evelyn
Yoakam, Aurie Thayer
Number of Contributors   26
Amount Contributed $336.00

CLASS OF 1900

Cornelia Halsey Kellogg, Collector.
Alden, Edna Warkentin
Babson, Grace Campbell
Bamberger, Edna Floersheim
Brown, Margaretta Levering
Browne, Margaret W.
Childs, Katharine Barton
Crawford, Frances Rush
Cross, Dorothea Farquhar
Davenport, Evelyn Hills
Dudley, Sara Lotta Emery
Emerson, Helena T.
Fell, Edith N.
Francis, Louise Congdon
Fultz, Ellen Baltz
Gellhorn, Edna Fischel
Gregson, Edith Goodell
Kellogg, Cornelia Halsey
Kilpatrick, Mary Grace
Korff, Alletta Van Reypen
Lanham, Edith Crane
Limberg, Marie Sichel
Loines, Hilda
MacCoy, M. Helen
McClure, Grace Latimer Jones
Miller, M. Elizabeth White
Mosenthal, Johanna Kroeber
Palmer, Emily Waterman
Perkins, Delia Avery
Righter, Renée Mitchell
Rockwood, E. Ruth
Rosenau, Myra Frank
St. John, Clara Seymour
Scott, Margaretta Morris
Tatlock, Jessie M.
Walsh, Jessie McBride
Williams, Kate
Wright, Edith B.
Number of Contributors   38
Amount Contributed $352.00

CLASS OF 1901

Caroline Daniels Moore, Collector (Re-
signed April, 1923)
Ethel Cantlin Buckley, Temporary Collector.
Buckley, Ethel Cantlin
Buell, Gertrude Smyth
Cross, Emily R.
Dillingham, Alice
Ellis, Ellen Deborah
Gould, Evelyn Louise Fisk

Hooker, Edith Houghton
Howard, Jeannie C.
Jones, Eleanor H.
Kemmerer, Frances Ream
Laws, Bertha M.
Macbeth, Lucia Holliday
Marvell, Mary Brayton
McCarthy, Edith
Miller, Jessie I.
Moore, Caroline Daniels
Newell, Ella Sealy
Righter, Jane
Rogers, Grace Phillips
Rousmaniere, Mary Ayer
Slade, Annie Malcom
Smith, Marion Parris
Thacher, Henrietta F.
Thomas, Louise Miner
Warren, Constance Williams
White, Amelia Elizabeth
Number of Contributors 26
Amount Contributed $358.00

CLASS OF 1902
H. Jean Crawford, Collector.
Allen, Marguerite S.
Amram, Beulah Brylawski
Balch, Marion C.
Barron, Elizabeth Congdon
Bouck, Harriet Walcott Vaille
Cochran, Fanny Travis
Crane, Claris I.
Crawford, H. Jean
Dodge, Elinor
Estabrook, Helen Nichols
Forman, Elizabeth Chandlee
Hackett, Frances Dean Allen
Hoppin, Eleanor Wood
Howe, Anne Rotan
Howson, May Yeatts
Ingham, Mary H.
James, Eleanor
Lafore, Anne Shearer
Paddock, Elizabeth Plunkett
Pitts, Kate Du Val
Steinhart, Amy Sussman
Todd, Anne Hampton
Witherspoon, Ruth Miles
Wright, Corinne Blose
Number of Contributors 26
Amount Contributed $403.00

CLASS OF 1903
Philena C. Winslow, Collector.
Austin, Agnes Bell
Bechtel, Emma Crawford
Bolling, Anna Phillips
Boucher, Sophie
Boyer, Martha G.
Brown, Fannie I.
Brusstar, Margaret E.
Cheney, Marjory
Cope, Evelyn Flower Morris
Crowder, Grace Meigs
Deming, Eleanor
Dietrich, Margretta Stewart
d'Incisa, Amanda Hendrickson
Fish, Margaret A.
Guild, Mary Montague

Hale, Eunice Follansbee
Johnston, Charlotte Moffitt
Lanagan, Charlotte Morton
Langdon, Ida
Lange, Linda B.
Laughlin, Agatha
Lyman, Ruth Whitney
McGinley, Elsie Thomas
Norton, M. Harriet
Parker, Elizabeth Bryan
Price, Alice M.
Riesman, Eleanor Fleisher
Sergeant, Elizabeth Shepley
Sherwin, Anne T.
Sinclair, Agnes M.
Smith, Lilian Mooers
Smith, Gertrude Dietrich
Stoddard, Virginia
Strong, Ruth
Sykes, Edith
Taylor, Marianna
Wagner, Caroline F.
Wallower, Helen Calder
White, Martha R.
Williamson, Mary Peabody
Winslow, Philena C.

Number of Contributors 41
Amount collected by Ethel Hulburd
Johnson in 1921 and turned over
this year $480.00
Amount Contributed 1923... 451.00
———$931.00

CLASS OF 1904
Isabel M. Peters, Collector.
Abbott, Mary Vauclain
Allen, Jane
Anderson, Phyllis Green
Barber, Lucy Lombardi
Bolte, Jeannette Hemphill
Boring, Alice M.
Bowen, Bertha Norris
Bugge, Kathrina Van Wagenen
Carson, Agnes Gillinder
Clark, Leslie
Clark, Alice Schiedt
James, Mary L.
Klein, Gertrude
Kreutzberg, Marguerite Gribi
Lambert, Bertha Brown
Lamberton, Mary
Logan, Sara Marie Briggs
Marcus, Bertha
Moorhead, Helen Howell
Moorhouse, Martha Rockwell
Neuendorffer, Esther Sinn
Nute, Mary Christie
Patterson, Evelyn Holliday
Peters, Isabel M.
Pierce, Katharine Curtis
Rauh, Elsie Kohn
Rossiter, Irene
Scott, Margaret
Selleck, Anne
Shearer, Edna A.
Tremain, Eloise
Uhl, Maria Albee
Ullmann, Margaret
Vauclain, Hilda Canan
Wade, Clara

Waldo, Alice Goddard
White, Louise Peck
White, Leda F.
Number of Contributors .... · 38
Amounted Contributed $564.50

Stix, Erma Kingsbacher
Torbert, Elizabeth Townsend
Withington, Mary
Number of Contributors 26
Amount Contributed $952.37

CLASS OF 1905
Margaret Nichols Hardenbergh, Collector.
Aldrich, Eleanor Little
Ashley, Edith
Ballinger, Alice Matless
Bates, Theodora
Bellamy, Frederica Fevre
Bready, Marcia
Carpenter, Olive Gates Eddy
Chadwick-Collins, Caroline Morrow
Dammann, Isabel Lynde
Danielson, Rosamond
Dunlop, Bertha Warner Seely
Flaherty, Frances Hubbard
Gardner, Julia
Griffith, Helen
Hardenbergh, Margaret Nichols
Hill, Leslie Farwell
Hill, Catherine Utley
Howell, Kathrine L.
Howland, Alice G.
Johnson, Emily Cooper
Kempton, Helen P.
Knight, Emma
Loines, Elma
Lowenthal, Esther
McLaren, Alice Day
Mallery, Louise Marshall
Paxson, Helen Jackson
Remington, Mabry Parks
Sharpless, Edith
Smith, Helen Garrett
Sulloway, Margaret Thayer
Swan, Carla Denison
Wood, Edith Longstreth
Number of Contributors 33
Amount Contributed $395.50

CLASS OF 1906
Elizabeth Harrington Brooks, Collector.
Allnutt, Phoebe Crosby
Anderson, Catherine
Barber, Elsie Biglow
Beecher, Ethel Stratton Bullock
Blaisdell, Margaret
Boomsliter, Alice Ella Colgan
Brooks, Elizabeth Harrington
Flint, Alice Lauterbach
Grant, Kittie Stone
Grenfell, Anna MacClanahan
Hewitt, Jessie
Little, Ruth Archbald
McKelvey, Susan Delano
Maclay, Louise Fleischmann
Neall, Adelaide
Norris, Mary R.
Peirce, Helen Elizabeth Wyeth
Pew, Ethel
Pratt, Anne S.
Rawson, Marjorie
Rutter, Lucia Ford
Sandison, Helen
Stevens, Anna McAnulty

CLASS OF 1907
Alice M. Hawkins, Collector.
Esther Williams Apthorp, Temporary Collector.
Alexander, Virginia Hill
Apthorp, Esther Williams
Ashbrook, Elsa-Norton
Augur, Margaret
Ballin, Marie
Barnes, Margaret Ayer
Behr, Elizabeth Pope
Cary, Margaret Reeve
Eldridge, Irene S.
Fabian, Mary H.
Ferguson, Mary
Gerhard, Alice
Gray, Mary Tudor
Hawkins, Alice M.
Houghteling, Harriot
Howson, Julie Benjamin
Lamberton, Helen.
Meigs, Cornelia L.
Miller, Dorothy Forster
Morison, Margaret B.
Richardson, Comfort Dorsey
Russell, Janet
Steel, Marion Warren
Stokes, Lelia Woodruff
Watt, Adelina Stuart
Wilson, Elizabeth D.
Windle, Letitia B.
*Wing, Marie R.
Number of Contributors 28
Amount Contributed $262.00

CLASS OF 1908
Marjorie Young Gifford, Collector.
Best, Mary Kinsley
Blatchford, Margaret Copeland
Brown, Anna Welles
Carner, Lucy
Case, Adelaide
Case, Mary C.
Castle, Ethelinda Schaefer
Cheston, Emily Fox
Claiborne, Virginia McKenney
Dalzell, Dorothy
Eldredge, Adda
Evans, Jacqueline Morris
Frehafer, Mabel K.
Gifford, Marjorie Young
Goldman, Agnes
Goodwillie, Elsie Bryant
Hall, Ethel Beggs
Helburn, Theresa
Herron, Louise Milligan
Hunt, Margaret Washburn
Johnston, Margaret Preston
Jones, Dorothy M.
Kent, Margaret Y.
King, Anna
Leatherbee, Frances Crane
Lewis, Mayone

Maynard, Margaret R.
Miller, Margaret Duncan
Montgomery, Josephine Proudfit
Mort, Dorothy
Nearing, Nellie Seeds
Pennell, Anne Walton
Perry, Lydia Sharpless
Phillips, Violet Besly
Plant, Alice Sachs
Pollak, Louise Hyman
Pyfer, Isabella
Pyle, Dorothy Merle-Smith
Rhoads, Edith C.
Roth, Helen Bernheim
Saxton, Martha Plaisted
Sherbert, Helen
Stewart, Ethel Brooks
Turnbull, Margaret Sparhawk Jones
Vauclain, Myra Elliot
Wallace, Ethel Vick
Warren, Rachel Moore
Weaver, Sarah Sanborne
Woodelton, Grace

Contributors 49
Amount Contributed $793.50

CLASS OF 1909

Margaret Bontecou Squibb, Collector.
Abbot, Edith Brown
Ballin, Florence
Berry, Fannie Barber
Biddle, M. Georgina
Browne, Frances
Cameron, Alta Stevens
Chamberlain, Dorothy Smith
Child, Dorothy
Crane, Helen B.
Dewes, Grace Woolridge
Ecob, Katharine
Ehlers, Bertha S.
Farrar, Antoinette Hearne
Ferris, Frances C.
Gilroy, Helen T.
Hall, Jessie Gilroy
Hays, Edith Adair
Henze, Paula
Herr, Mary E.
Howson, Emily
Jacobs, Sarah
Labold, Leona
Lowry, Evelyn Holt
Mitchell, Mary Holliday
Moore, Marianne
Morgan, Barbara Spofford
Nearing, Mary
Parsons, Pleasaunce Baker
Putnam, Mary
Putnam, Shirley
Shero, Julia Doe
Shippen, Ellen
Sprenger, Judith Boyer
Starzenski, Hilda Sprague-Smith
Vickery, Margaret
Warren, Catharine Goodale
Wetmore, Mildred Satterlee
Wright, Margaret Ames

Number of Contributors 38
Amount Contributed $428.00

CLASS OF 1910

Bessie Cox Wolstenholme, Collector.
Ashley, Mabel
Drinker, Katherine Rotan
Fleischmann, Jeanne Kerr
Irwin, Agnes M.
Keiller, Violet
McLaughlin, Marion Wildman
Mills, Mary Shipley
Papanastasiou, Helen Bley
Pond, Millicent
Poste, Irma Bixler
Root, Mary L.
Rosborough, Annie Jones
Ryan, Frances Storer
Scoon, Elizabeth Hibben
Selinger, Ethel Chase
Smith, Hilda W.
Stern, Juliet Lit
Storer, Emily L.
Szold, Zip Falk
*Taylor, Katherine Kelley
Turner, Julia Thompson
Voorhees, Elsa Denison
Wolstenholme, Bessie Cox

Number of Contributors 23
Amount Contributed $209.50

CLASS OF 1911

Helen Emerson Chase, Collector.
Adler, Frances Porter
Ashbrook, Mildred Janney
Browne, Norvelle
Caskey, Emily
Chase, Helen Emerson
Claflin, Charlotte I.
Cole, Blanche
Edwards, Margaret Dulles
Forster, Emma
Funkhouser, Elsie L.
Graham, Helen Tredway
Grant, Catherine Delano
Greeley, Dorothy Coffin
Holmes, Ruth Vickery
Jones, Virginia
Kruesi, Isobel Rogers
Le Vino, Margaret Prussing
Low, Margaret Friend
Magoffin, Henrietta
McKnight, Phyllis Rice
Richardson, Ethel
Russell, Elizabeth Taylor
Russell, Louise
Seelye, Kate Chambers
Sherman, Mary Williams
Shohl, Alice Eichberg
Sinberg, Hermine Schamberg
Stearns, Anna
Stokes, May Egan
Taylor, Mary Minor Watson
Thompson, Hannah Dodd

Number of Contributors 32
Amount Contributed $379.50

CLASS OF 1912

Florence Leopold Wolf, Collector
Beliekowsky, Sadie
Brown, Anna Hartshorne
Byrne, Laura L.
Chase, Dorothy
Clarke, Pauline
Crenshaw, Fanny
De Lany, Lou Sharman
Douglas, Dorothy Wolff
Gordon, Grace Rix
Gregory, Jean Stirling
Groton, Anna Heffern
Howson, Beatrice
Lamb, Emerson
Lee, Mary Morgan
MacEwen, Margaret Peck
Mannheimer, Irma Shloss
Markle, Gladys Jones
Matteson, Helen Barber
Mitchell, Pearl B.
Peirce, Mary
Railey, Julia Houston
Shaw, Katharine
Stecher, Lorle
Stevens, Cynthia
Stone, Gertrude Llewellyn
Thompson, Catherine R.
Watson, Louise
Wolf, Florence Leopold
Number of Contributors 28
Amount Contributed $322.00

CLASS OF 1913

Maud Holmes Young, Collector.
Baechle, Cecelia
Bensinger, Alice Patterson
Blaine, Margaret
Bontecou, Eleanor
Bridgman, Sarah Atherton
Brown, Josephine
Buchanan, Jessie C.
Carruth, Margaret Scruggs
Carter, Joy Tomlinson
Churchward, Beatrice Nathans
Clayton, Grace Bartholomew
Cresson, Helen Wilson
Crothers, Alice Ames
Daddow, Virginia
Davey, Keinath Stohr
Davis, Dorothy
Deming, Agathe
Dessau, F. Maude
Dewey, Marguerite Mellon
Eberstadt, Mary Tongue
Eisenhart, Katharine Schmidt
Elser, Helen Richter
Evans, Sylvia Hathaway
Faulkner, Ellen
Fox, Lillie Walton
Fraser, Mary Shenstone
Hack, Apphia Thwing
Hackett, Louisa Haydock
Halpen, Sara
Hamer, Marguerite Bartlett
Hamilton, Gordon
Harris, Alice Selig
Hayes, Yvonne Stoddard
Henderson, Louisa L.

Hodgdon, Katharine Williams
Irish, Florence
Kelly, Olga
King, Gertrude Hinrichs
Lewis, Helen Evans
Livingston, Frances
Loring, Katherine Page
Maguire, Elizabeth
Marks, Edna Potter
McCarroll, Emma Robertson
Miller, R. Beatrice
Munroe, Margaret
Murray, Marjorie
Nash, Carolyn
Quinn, Joyce Light
Rambo, Lucinda Menendez
Rawson, Gwendolyn
Shipley, Elizabeth T.
Simpson, Adelaide
Simsohn, Cecile Goldsmith
Speers, Helen Barrett
Stout, Gertrude Ziesing
Watkin, Josephine Cockrell
Young, Maud Holmes
Yow, Lucile Shadburn
Number of Contributors 59
Amount Contributed $751.00

CLASS OF 1914

Mary C. Smith, Collector.
Ida Pritchett, Special Collector for 1923.
Number of Contributors 86
Amount Contributed $1,256.00

CLASS OF 1915

Adrienne Kenyon Franklin, Collector.
Arnett, Katharine McCollin
Ash, Rachel
Bradford, Harriet
Brandeis, Susan
Branson, Laura E.
Brown, Anna
Coward, Mildred Jacobs
Erbsloh, Olga
Everett, Helen
Fitzgibbons, Angeleine Spence
Foster, Isabel
Franklin, Adrienne Kenyon
Greenfield, Edna Kraus
Hopkinson, Ruth
Hyde, Ethel Robinson
*Justice, Mildred
Kelton, Florence Hatton
Knight, Emily Gifford Noyes
MacMaster, Amy K.
Moore, Dorothea May
Morse, Ruth Tinker
Murphy, Mary Gertrude Brownell
Newman, Ruth
Nichols, Susan
Roberts, Anna
Saville, Lydia Mark
Shelby, Miriam Rohrer
Smith, Elizabeth
Smith, Isabel
Stone, Margaret Free
Sutch, Cleora
Thompson, Lillian Mudge

Thomson, Mary Majory
Wolf, Elizabeth Pauline
Zeckwer, Isolde

Number of Contributors 35
Amount Contributed $317.00

CLASS OF 1916

Anna C. Lee, Collector (resigned).
Brakeley, Elizabeth
Burt, Alene
Chickering, Frances Bradley
Davis, Anna Sears
Dillingham, Louise B.
Dowd, Constance
Garfield, Lucretia
Gayton, Rebecca Fordyce
Gordon, Jeannette Greenewald
Harding, Charlotte
Haskell, Margaret
Hitz, Elizabeth Holliday
Jordan, Mildred McCay
Kellen, Margaret Russell
Kirk, E. Buckner
Kopper, Anne Jaggard
Lautz, Ruth
Lee, Anna
MacMurray, Lois Goodnow
Robertson, Helen
Strauss, Emilie
Suckley, Margaret L.
Tyson, Helen E.
Washburn, Elizabeth
Wolfe, Nannie Gail

Number of Contributors 25
Amount Contributed $406.00

CLASS OF 1917

Olga Tattersfield, Collector.
Allport, Harriet
Beardwood, Alice
Blanton, Natalie McFaden
Hall, Constance S.
Harris, Helen
Jopling, Catharine
McPhedran, Janet Grace
Rogers, Caroline Stevens
Scattergood, Margaret
Shipley, A. Dorothy
Stragnell, Sylvia Jelliffe
*Strauss, Marion Halle
Strickland, Mary Worley
Tattersfield, Olga
Teller, Fannie
Tuttle, Marion
Willett, Martha W.
Zimmerman, Helen B.

Number of Contributors 19
Amount Contributed $941.00

CLASS OF 1918

Ruth Hart Williams, Collector.
*Newell, Marie Louise Willard
Streeter, Ruth Cheney

Number of Contributors 2
Amount Contributed $25.00

CLASS OF 1919

Mary Morris Ramsay, Collector (resigned).
Binger, Beatrice Sorchan
Cooper, Eleanor S.
Delaplaine, Meribah
Dunn, Gordon Woodbury
Hainsworth, Hazel Collins
Hall, Dorothy
Hearne, Gertrude J.
Hering, Dorothea
Hollis, Clara Jane
Hunter, Jane Hall
Hurlock, Elizabeth
Johnson, Helene
Lafferty, Mabel
Landon, Adelaide
Lukens, Frances Day
Marquand, Eleanor
Mercer, Ernestine
Moseley, Marion R.
Oppenheimer, Celia
Place, Angela Moore
Raven, Winifred Perkins
Rhoads, Margaret
Rock, Ruth Driver
Taussig, Catherine
Thorndike, Anna
Twitchell, Marjorie Remington
Tyler, Mary
Vernon, Sarah Taylor
Whittier, Isabel
Winters, Enid Macdonald

Number of Contributors 30
Amount raised in 1922 and turned
over in 1923 ....$414.90
Amount Contributed in 1923. 237.00
————$651.90

CLASS OF 1920

Martha F. Chase, Collector.
Arnold, Isabel
Bishop, Margaret Hutchins
Brown, Madelaine
Brown, Miriam
Buck, Jule Cochran
Carey, M. Millicent
Chase, Martha F.
Clark, Darthela
Colman, Charlotte
Eilers, Marguerite
Frost, Marian
Gookin, Nathalie
Hales, Laura
Hardy, Mary
*Herrick, Josephine
Hoag, Mary
Holmes, Harriet
Humphreys, Helen
Jenkins, Dorothy
Kinard, Margaret
Lindsey, Martha Jane
Lynch, Caroline
McAllister, Dorothy Smith
O'Brien, Miriam
Philip, Lilian Davis
Pitkin, Doris
Sanford, Anna Munson

Seldon, Zella Boynton
Weaver, Betty
Zinsser, Helene

Number of Contributors 30
Amount Contributed $264.00

CLASS OF 1921

Marynia Foot, Collector.
Julia C. Peyton (resigned).
Baldwin, Mary
Barton, Catherine
Baruch, Dorothy Walter
Beckwith, Lydia
Boswell, Eleanore
Bradford, Katharine Walker
Brown, Jane
Collins, Eleanor
Darrow, Ida Lauer
Donaldson, Sidney
Donnelley, Eleanor
Dowling, Louise Wilson
Eadie, Marian
Groves, Frances Hollingshead
Johns, Anne Page
Knollenberg, Mary McClennen
Ladd, Margaret R.
Maginniss, Irene
Matteson, Elizabeth
Morrison, Miriam
Morton, Margaret
Peyton, Julia C.
Platt, Marie-Louise Fearey

Reis, Elizabeth
Riker, Frances
Rubel, Helen
Shoemaker, Eleanor H.
Smith, Mabel
Stewart, Catherine Dimeling
Stokes, Beatrice
Stone, Helen H. McCalmont
Taylor, Ann
Taylor, Elizabeth
Taylor, Margaret
Walton, Marion
Warburg, Bettina
Weston, Aileen

Numbers of Contributors 37
Amount Contributed $501.73

CLASS OF 1922

Cornelia M. Baird, Collector.
No Report

CLASS OF 1923

Agnes Clement, Collector.
Goddard, Celestine
Rice, Helen

Number of Contributors 2
Amount Contributed $20.00

*Gave through Cleveland Bryn Mawr Club only. As no individual amounts were specified, the Club total only being given, the amounts could not be included in the class total.

CAMPUS NOTES

A Bryn Mawr delegation was sent to the Ninth Quadrennial International Convention of the Student Volunteer Movement, which was held at Indianapolis, December 28th to January 1st. One of the subjects most discussed was the problem of war and the education of the world for peace. The publication of the winning plan of Mr. Bok's Peace Award has brought the subject to the fore in the college as elsewhere. The students are to vote on the plan, together with the rest of the world.

The Music Department held its second concert on Monday evening, January 7th. The Letz Quartette, with Mr. Horace Alwynne, of the Music Department, at the piano, gave a delightful program. The concert was as great a success as the former one, and practically all the tickets for the final concert on February 18th have already been sold. Mr. Alwynne will give most of the program, and the College looks forward to it eagerly.

The Christmas vacation being over, together with the hurried three weeks before mid-years, the College has been very much occupied with examinations. The last thing to interfere with purely academic pursuits was the swimming competition between the classes. Two swimming meets were held, the first on January 11th, the second on January 18th, and the championship was won by the Class of 1926.

COMMITTEE ON HEALTH

The Committee on Health and Physical Education met at Bryn Mawr, February 3, 1923.

Those present were: Ella Oppenheimer and Ethel Dunham.

Mrs. Vorhees was elected Secretary but in her absence Doctor Oppenheimer acted as Secretary pro tem and submitted the following report:

Doctor Dunham reported on the history of the Committee and its activities, and presented Doctor Lange's report on the expense of the present medical service; Miss Wesson's report of Miss Applebee's work; and Mrs. Vorhees' report on the activities of the Undergraduate and Athletic Associations of the College.

It was decided that the next step for the Committee to take was to investigate the amount and character of exercise required by other colleges and universities, and that such an investigation should cover the following points:

1. Who has charge of exercise.
   Relation between Physical Education Department and Health Department of College.
   Who is directly responsible.
2. Is exercise required.
   If so, types required and number of hours weekly.
3. Is present plan satisfactory.
   If not, suggestions regarding necessary improvement.
4. Corrective work or special types of exercise.
   Amount done under supervision of Physical Education or Medical Department.
5. Relation of Athletic Association to the two departments.

The Committee then met with President Park, Dean Bontecou, the wardens, and Miss Applebee, for an informal discussion of a plan for a Department of Health and Hygiene in the College.

New members of the Committee are Dr. Ella Oppenheimer, of the Children's Bureau, Washington; Eleanor Bliss, of Baltimore, who is a student in the School of Hygiene.

The Committee regrets the resignation of Mrs. Vorhees.

Respectfully submitted,
ETHEL C. DUNHAM, *Chairman.*

ATHLETIC COMMITTEE

The Alumnae played their usual games against Varsity during the past year. During Commencement week the Water Polo, Basketball and Tennis matches were held. From an Alumnae point of view the Water Polo proved the most successful, as the score was only 7-4 against us.

The Executive Board very generously allowed the Committee $60 to pay for the Bryn Mawr Band for Alumnae Day. I am sure everyone will agree that this music adds very much to the pleasure of the day. The first prize for costumes was awarded to President Park's Class, 1898, who were cleverly gotten up as "King Tuts."

This fall the Alumnae hockey game was held on December 8th. Varsity had a splendid team this year, losing its only game to All-Philadelphia, so we did not feel too badly when they allowed us only three goals to their eleven.

We regret very much that it was not possible to have the game at Thanksgiving time, when so many Alumnae were in Philadelphia at the Inter-City Tournament. At that time there were at least eleven Alumnae here playing on the various city teams. It is interesting to know that two Alumnae are abroad with the All-American Team, Mary Morgan, 1915, and Mary Adams, 1923.

Respectfully submitted,
GERTRUDE J. HEARNE,
Chairman.

Alumnae Activities

MRS. WILLIAM C. POWELL,

Manager of Store Training

(CLARA BELLE THOMPSON, ex-1913)

[*Mrs. Powell has very kindly consented to write for the* BULLETIN *the following description of her work in that department of the John Wanamaker Stores which she organized for the training of employees. Her success in the execution of her own plans has made her an authority on employment problems. The Editor hopes to devote a few pages in each issue to those alumnae who, like Mrs. Powell, have become prominent in their respective fields.* THE BULLETIN *will welcome any articles about them that may be sent in, and will receive any suggestions as to future articles with great pleasure.*]

Have you ever been behind the scenes in a merchandizing establishment? Just at present that is my precise location as manager of training in a large department store.

"Training," you echo. "Training? What is there to train?"

Permit me to answer.

You make a purchase. The sales person who serves you has to make out a sales slip. How did she know which sales book to use and what method to employ in filling the blank spaces? Observation? No, that is too slow and too unsatisfactory. Before she had her first customer, she was given special instruction and practice in the clerical work that would fall to her lot, as well as in the handling of customers.

But, perhaps, you wish your merchandise sent to you very quickly. It is a dress which you will require tonight. The sales person cannot finish that transaction: she must consult her floor person.

And what does he do? It is to be hoped that he will do exactly as he has been taught in the training department: for then you will surely receive your merchandise on time.

But even when he arranges for a special messenger, the sale is not completed. The frock does not come to you draped on the arm of the messenger; it must be wrapped carefully, with due regard to the amount of tissue paper and the proper box. The inspector who then entered the transaction was not born with a knowledge of wrapping. She, too, had to be taught.

However, you have further business with us. You had purchased tan slippers, and you have decided to select brown instead. It is the exchange clerk who will arrange to take the first pair back and to see that you are credited with the amount of purchase. She gives you quick and complete satisfaction, if she follows the training she has received.

Of course, it is true that there are new persons to be trained all the time. But another thought: those who have been trained, they are carefully obeying instructions and are giving in every way the highest possible service, are they not? Correct: they are not!

And that brings me to the second division of our work, the more important: the effort to raise the standard of store efficiency. Dealing with errors is a very small part of the problem. Studying the various divisions of the store, talking with persons in groups or individually, checking up results, making suggestions: all of this sounds very intangible, but it is quite workable and exceedingly interesting.

In such a small compass, it is impossible to give the details which would make the work alive to anyone not engaged in it. It is never tedious: for it is all concerned with persons, differing from one another in every way and giving myriads of reactions. My experience as a "working woman" has given me a new and quite favorable impression of the people engaged in merchandizing.

It has made me very obedient, too. Headquarters said: "Write for us what you are doing." And you see—

ALUMNAE NOTES

The Bryn Mawr College Club of Kentucky was organized December 28th in Louisville, at the home of Mrs. Samuel C. Henning (Julia Duke Henning, '96). Mrs. Henning had invited the Bryn Mawr women of Kentucky to luncheon, and afterwards the Kentucky Club was formed with the following officers for the coming year: President, Frances Howard, '21; Secretary and Treasurer, Adele Brandeis, '08, Scholarship Chairman, Maria Bedinger, '91.

Miss Howard and Miss Julia Henning, '23, were delegated to speak for Bryn Mawr at the intercollegiate meetings held under the auspices of the Louisville College Club for the high school girls of the city on January 2nd and 3rd.

The Kentucky Bryn Mawr women present at the meeting were Julia Duke Henning, '96; Julia Henning, '23; Frances Howard, '21; Adele Brandeis, '08; Maria Bedinger, '91; Jennie Staadeker, '94; Augusta French Wallace, '07; Nell Roberts, '27, and Julia Haines MacDonald, '12, District Councillor. Mrs. William Speed of Louisville was an honor guest at the meeting.

The Alumnae Association of Eastern Pennsylvania and Delaware and President Marion Edwards Park entertained in honor of President Emeritus Thomas at a luncheon on January 19th in the Clover Room of the Bellevue-Stratford, Philadelphia. The room was crowded, and Miss Thomas's speech, "The Broken Globe and How to Mend It," was received with interest even greater than that which Miss Thomas's speeches usually inspire.

(The editor has just received this letter from Dr. Alice Boring, whose new address is Yenching College, Teng Shih Kou, Peking, China. We wish that many others would follow her example and send in to their class editors or to the editor direct news of the Bryn Mawr people whom they meet.)

Dear Miss Page:

Perhaps you would like a little news from Bryn Mawr in Peking. There are several of us here now and others passing through. I enclose a clipping from the *Peking Leader* in regard to the recent success of Fannie Sinclair Woods, in a play. ("Well-known Peking people are starred in the play, Mrs. A. H. Woods, whose performance as Alice in *Alice Sit by the Fire* two years ago is still remembered by those who saw her, taking one of the leading roles. In this present play, she runs the gamut of feeling from tender, yearning love to playful, spontaneous banter and she plays it all with the sure touch of an artist.")

Fannie Woods' husband is head of the Neurology Department of the Peking Union Medical College. Anna Carrere, '08, is visiting an aunt who finds Peking as interesting as Washington as a place to live in. Annie Whitney, '09, is spending the winter here with Dr. and Mrs. Emmett Holt. Doctor Holt is one of the Visiting Professors at the Peking Union Medical College. Miss Whitney has been very good about lecturing at the Peking University on her own specialty, Child Welfare. Alice Boring, '04, is here as Visiting Professor in charge of the Biology Department of Peking University during a three-year leave of absence from Wellesley College.

Recently, when a Miss Cooke, '22, was travelling through, Fannie Woods invited this group to her house for a Bryn Mawr luncheon. We were also very fortunate in having with us Mrs. Jacob G. Schurman, wife of the American Minister to China, who is mother of two Bryn Mawrtyrs.

Jane Ward, '05, of Shanghai, was in Peking for a few weeks this fall to help with the financial campaign of the Y. W. C. A.

REUNION NOTICE

In 1924 the following classes hold their reunions: 1896, 1897, 1899, 1915, 1916, 1917, 1918, and 1922. By adjustment four other classes will also hold reunions this spring, these being 1892, 1893, 1894, and 1923.

In the spring of 1925, 1900, 1901, 1902, 1903, 1919, 1920, 1921, 1922, and 1923 will have their reunions, and with them 1895 and 1924, by adjustment.

CLASS NOTES

1889

Class Editor, Harriet Randolph, 1300 Spruce Street, Philadelphia, Pa.

'89 will feel especial interest in two books in a recent list of the Yale University Press:

The Physical Basis of Life, by E. B. Wilson
Origin and Evolution of Religion, by E. Washburn Hopkins

and will readily appreciate that in these cases at least (to quote from the book notices):

"The Yale shield on a book means that it is a book of more than ordinary importance, unique in its field and of lasting value."

(These books should not only interest the members of the Class of 1889, but all Bryn Mawr alumnae, since their authors were two of the five full professors who were at Bryn Mawr when the College opened in 1885.)

Mabel Clark Huddleston, New York City.

For years I worked with all sorts of boards and committees; but having left them all for emergency war work, which came in time to a natural end, I have never been willing to return and relinquish my freedom. That is partly because my individual responsibilities have been very heavy for the last five years, and partly because in many kinds of social work so much of the available energy is wasted through friction that one's personal life is jarred and distracted with no equivalent gain to anyone. I don't think that applies to everyone, only to certain unambitious and contemplative temperaments in the years of diminishing power and vigor; but it is my one excuse for giving up "social service" in which so many Bryn Mawrtyrs are doing so much, for such individual service as may come my way.

Just now I am being absolutely domestic, dividing my time between my son, who is in the hospital with a broken leg, and my older daughter and her more than fascinating babies. To the older one, about two and a half, I am beginning to impart such classic literature as Lear's Nonsense Book, which she already tries to learn by heart.

Next summer I am planning for many months of amateur forestry and berry-raising on my neglected New Hampshire farm.

Last summer I took my school-girl daughter abroad, mostly to Italy and France. We especially enjoyed exploring for the finest stained-glass, and Gothic and Romanesque in Central France: Troyes, Gens, Amiens, Auxerre, and above all Bourges; Rouen, Nevers, Senlis and what is left of Soissons, Avallon, Vezelay, Le Puy, Clermont-Ferrand, Arles, Uzés, Vaison, etc., etc. Much of the time we were far away from the track of any tourists but the French themselves, and in the midst of the beautiful hill and river scenery of "le Massif Central."

Then we took motors from Nice for the "Route des Alpes," which was decidedly thrilling, but so fine that we would gladly do it over again—the gorges and passes and peaks making most of Switzerland seem tame by comparison. Finally, we went down to Florence and Venice, Pisa, Lucca, and Bologna, and sailed homeward from Marseilles with stops at Naples, Palermo and Almeria, and two weeks of almost perfect sea weather.

On the whole, I am simply trying to hand on to the younger generation what I myself have found most satisfying, whether it be the Nonsense Book or the marvellous apse of Bourges, trusting that the result will be education, or perhaps I should say a wide base for education.

For my personal avocation I read philosophy and that very modern science which is all but philosophy and wish I could begin all over again and really work at that and nothing else; the choice of an outlook—and the direction we move in—comes to seem of so much more importance than the rate we proceed at, or the so-called practical things we do by the way. I wonder what the rest of '89 thinks.

Perhaps it is something to be so movable, not to say nomadic, at so advanced an age—to have four homes and not to be settled down in any of them.

1893

Class Editor, S. Frances Van Kirk, 1333 Pine Street, Philadelphia, Pa.

'93 and '94 are planning to hold a joint reunion in June, 1924.

Lucy Lewis is helping to enlarge the work of The League of Women Voters in Philadelphia.

Mr. Moses S. Slaughter died suddenly on December 29, in Italy. Gertrude Taylor Slaughter and Mr. Slaughter left the United States in June to spend eighteen months in Europe.

Mr. Charles M. Moores, husband of Elizabeth Nichols Moores, died on December 7, after an illness of two months. He was a distinguished attorney of Indianapolis, and a writer.

1899

Class Editor, Mrs. Percival Sax, 6429 Drexel Road, Overbrook, Pa.

Four members of the Reunion Committee met in Overbrook in December to plan for our celebration in June. Emma Guffey Miller came from a New Jersey Alumnae meeting, where she had reported on the doings of the Council; May Blakey Ross tore herself from the League of Women Voters' duties, Elsie Andrews forgot her tutoring for the time being, and May Schoneman Sax neglected her new daughter in order to concentrate on providing inimitable entertainments which no member of the class can possibly afford to miss. During a few minutes' intermission for tea, Emma announced that as Callie could no longer give any of her valuable time to the Class Editorship, that pleasant office had fallen on May Sax's care-free shoulders. We (editorially) shall be delighted to receive and broadcast news, but we must have coöperation to be a columnist in the BULLETIN.

Laura Peckham Waring and Molly Peckham Tubby, '97, motored to Bryn Mawr in November and stopped at Overbrook to inspect '99's newest child. Modesty does not permit us to repeat what they said of her.

Molly Thurber Dennison, "Harry," and young Mary are travelling in Europe.

Aurie Thayer Yoakam, who stopped to see us en route from North Carolina, where she, Mr. Yoakam, Letitia, and her niece Dorothy Thayer spent the holidays, says that the Dennison house in Framingham burned down last spring.

Mary Churchill is living at 667 High Street, Newark, N. J., and is doing Physiotherapeutic work at two hospitals in Newark. She is anxious to see '99ers in her neighborhood.

Martha Irwin Sheddan has moved to 5223 Archer Street, Germantown.

Elsie Andrews has been helping her aunt, Ida Wood, organize the Women's City Club of Philadelphia.

Camille Erismann is spending the winter in Bound Brook, N. J.

1907

Class Editor, Eunice Morgan Schenck, Low Buildings, Bryn Mawr, Pa.

Grace Hutchins has returned from the "International Fellowship of Reconciliation" conferences in Denmark and the "Youth Movement" conferences in Germany.

Brita Horner writes further of her Mexican interests:

"During the past five years I have been greatly interested in Spanish and in the Spanish-American countries. In 1921 I spent the summer travelling in Venezuela, Costa Rica, Panama, and Cuba; in 1922, I attended the National University of Mexico, in the City of Mexico, and I visited numerous places of interest in that country. During the winter that followed I had opportunities to give a number of lectures on Mexico and was glad to do so in order to help dispel the great ignorance which exists in our own country relative to our neighbor across the Rio Grande.

"In order to be able to speak with more authority on the subject, I returned to Mexico City last summer and was even more strongly impressed by the progress and efforts for social betterment which the Mexicans are making. Along educational lines they are trying out some experiments which may well attract the attention of the world at large."

Jeannette Klauder Spencer writes from her new home, 138 Winchester Street, Brookline, Mass.:

"They told me at a tea yesterday, where I met some Radcliffe "girls," that when an alumna returns to a Bryn Mawr reunion, she is asked by her friends, not what her husband is doing, but what she herself has done and is planning to do. If I had not heard this (and, of course, believed it) I might begin now to boast of the degree of M.S. that my illustrious husband received at Yale in June and of his work in connection with radio and the thermionic vacuum tubes. But I dare not say more about him. I always avoid, if possible, alluding to my four healthy children lest I sound like a fatuously fond parent, so as I have done nothing but read a bit, write a short story during the summer and move all household effects plus our family from New Haven, Conn., to our new home in Brookline, I don't really believe that the BULLETIN will have lost news by not hearing from me. I'd adore to have any of 1907 stop to see me or call me up on the phone (Brookline 1449M) at any time, preparatory to coming to see me. I am very keen about Boston (having tried living in Washington, D. C., Philadelphia, New York, Chicago and San Francisco) and expect to thoroughly enjoy our three years' stay here."

Blanche Hecht, who had been working on a publicity campaign for the National Jewish Hospital for Consumptives, attended the convention at the hospital in Denver, with which the campaign closed and then travelled for two months in the American and Canadian Rockies and along the Pacific Coast.

The Class Editor, who had ceased to believe in miracles, had her faith revived by receiving the following letter. She offers it as a model to 1907 and promises to comply promptly with any similar requests that come her way.

"Would you be so good as to tell me what French book you want for the Library? If you were really an angel, you would buy it and charge it to me. (Here the Class Editor fainted.) I am a plagued nuisance, but if you expect to get $3—$10 out of Miss Jig, you must pay interest." Oh! wise 1907! We knew a woman when we chose our Freshman chairman.

1909

Class Editor, Mrs. Rollin T. Chamberlin, 5492 South Shore Drive, Chicago, Ill.

Esther Maddux Tennent is at home again after spending a year in China and Japan. She and Doctor Tennent lost all their possessions in the Yokohama earthquake. Esther did a great deal of singing in Japan.

Dorothy North has returned from Russia, and is supposedly living at 60 Scott Street, Chicago, Ill. Just at present, however, she is visiting in St. Louis, Mo.

May Putnam is in New York this winter, at 105 East Fifty-fifth Street.

Judith Sprenger has at last returned (January, 1923,) from Germany, and is living at 40 St. James' Place, Buffalo, N. Y. She went abroad in 1919, with her three-year-old daughter, Caroll, to join her husband at Coblenz. He was Chief Secretary of the Y. M. C. A. with the American Forces in Germany. At first, "Carol was the only American child in the area, but later there were 125 American children in the school that the Y. began, and each Sunday the Chief Chaplain of the Army of Occupation had a graded Sunday School of 130 children in the Kaiser's palace chapel. There were about 20,000 Americans there at that time, among them "Hono" and her husband, Lieutenant-Colonel Warren." Judith visited Helen King Gethman in Prague, in the "tremendously interesting, reborn land of Czecho-Slovakia," and Miriam Hedges Smith (1910) near Inverness, in 1920. "Since then, Miriam has been to the United States, to India, and back to England again." Judith has two new babies, Judith and David Francis, both born in Coblenz, in 1920 and 1921. In 1921 she came home, because of her mother's illness. Her mother died four days after she arrived. In April her father returned to Coblenz with her and her two little girls. In July, he died very suddenly. In August, David Francis was born.

Judith says, "I would like to tell you what we saw in Germany. People here do not care to hear facts. They want their comfortable diet of newspaper half-truths without disturbance, or else, they are indifferent to the fact that, with the world as with our country, 'united we stand, divided we fall.'"

Mr. Sprenger is assistant to the President of the Rand Company, makers of visible index systems for offices.

Mary Goodwin Storrs writes from China (Shaome, Fukien): "Life has been varied by inroads of soldiers, northern and southern. We have had two 'battles' of Shaown, sort of pre-arranged affairs with very little fighting. But the soldiers are sick and have thronged the doctor's clinic. The semi-brigands (northern) who were here in the winter, besides being provided with food by the Board of Trade, did a lot of looting. Then we had southeners again, and were happy; then a few blissful days with nobody, and now more northerners. We do not care for these militarists, but if it means a united China, we look forward to it, as a stepping stone. . . . For myself, Peggie and Henry and Julia keep me fully occupied." In April her husband was captured by bandits, who bound and beat him, and took all his things except the clothes he was wearing. Finally they decided to give him his life and freedom and even returned his glasses, hat, umbrella and typewriter.

Cynthia Wesson is again at the University of Wisconsin (address, 621 N. Henry Street, Madison, Wis.) coaching hockey to 300 students and playing on the Madison Hockey Club team. "The only trouble is that the season is too short. Snow on October 29th has already given me a scare."

Anne Whitney left in August for a trip to China and India with Dr. and Mrs. Holt.

1911

Class Editor, Louise S. Russell, 140 East Fifty-second Street, New York City.

Helen Tredway Graham writes that she is occupied with bringing up her two boys, now aged three and six. She is also the President of the St. Louis College Club and is serving as councillor of the Seventh District for the Alumnae Association. Her address is 4711 Westminster Place, St. Louis.

Florence Wood Winship reports herself as busy managing a lively household—two girls, Mary and Beth, six and four years, and a boy, Herring, five years—and an equally lively Girl Scout Organization, in which she is commissioner of a council and captain of a troop. As a side line she is on various committees—Parent-Teacher Association, Better Films Committee, Community Chest Federation, Bryn Mawr Summer School Committee, Church Guild and Chairman of one of the Centennial Pageant Committees. She spent September in Princeton. Her address is 203 Cherokee Avenue, Macon, Ga.

Amy Walker Field claims that she is doing nothing unusual, aside from acting on various committees. She spent the summer with her two children (and one dog) at Edgartown, Mass. Her address is 5642 Kenwood Avenue, Chicago.

Gertrude Gimbel Dannenbaum, with her husband and three daughters, aged thirteen, eleven and nine, spent last summer in France, and hopes to return again next summer. This winter she is doing dramatic coaching in social service organizations. Her address is Greenways, Valley Road, Oak Lane, Philadelphia.

Ruth Wells is district agent in the New Bedford District of the Massachusetts Society for the Prevention of Cruelty to Children. She is also Chairman of the New Bedford Chapter of the American Association of Social Workers. Her address is 122 Hawthorn Street, New Bedford, Mass.

Margaret Friend Lowe is living at 2229 Francis Lane, Cincinnati, and finds her hands full bringing up her three children. Margaret says that Alice Eichberg

Shohl spent Thanksgiving in Cincinnati "with the oldest of her little redheads." Alice's husband is in the Department of Pediatrics in the new college of medicine at Yale.

1913

Class Editor, Nathalie Swift, 130 East Sixty-seventh Street, New York City.

Marjorie Murray will finish her twenty-months' internship at the Presbyterian Hospital in New York on March 1st. Her plans for the immediate future are still somewhat indefinite.

Apphia Thwing Hack has moved to Cincinnati. Mr. Hack is teaching at the University there. Address—3338 Gano Avenue, Clifton, Cincinnati, Ohio.

Gordon Hamilton is teaching at the New York School for Social Work and is also working with the Charity Organization Society.

Alice Hearne Rockwell's third son, Francis Williams, was born on January 11th.

1915

Class Editor, Mrs. James Austin Stone, 2831 Twenty-eighth Street, N. W., Washington, D. C.

During the week Ruth Newman lives in Riverhead, N. Y., where she is still the Director of the Board of Child Welfare of Suffolk County. She has an apartment in a rambling old house which has old-fashioned mahogany furniture, a nice high boy and a fireplace. It sounds very attractive indeed. Then she goes home to New York over Sundays. Her office in Riverhead is in the County Treasurer's Building and overlooks the jail and court house, so she "gets all the excitement there is." She says they have four attractive ladies on their staff and two Ford cars. "We seem to be continually busy answering calls about children who have been beaten or women who have been thoughtlessly deserted by husbands, and left with eight or ten children. As soon as we get one vicinity nicely settled we get calls from somewhere else and a new tale of trouble, so we fill up the cars and start out again." If any classmates happen to be motoring on Long Island Ruth would be glad to have them look her up.

Frances Boyer spent the Christmas holidays with her married sister in Buffalo. Her brother and her two other sisters were also there for Christmas day. Fran will visit New York, Philadelphia and Pottsville before returning to Texas.

Anna Brown and Marjorie Tyson Forman sailed on January 5 for a trip to the Mediterranean. After completing the cruise they will travel in Italy and France, being gone from two to three months.

Helen Everett is living in Washington this winter and is working in the U. S. Department of Labor.

Mildred Justice spent Christmas with her family in Philadelphia. She had lunch one day during the holidays with Adrienne Kenyon Franklin, Cleora Sutch, Anna Brown and Mildred Jacobs Coward.

Helen Taft Manning and her husband and small daughter were in Washington over the holidays with Helen's parents. Helen was doing history research at the Library of Congress most of the time. Several Bryn Mawr people, among them Peggy Free Stone, had tea with Helen one afternoon and were completely captivated by Helen Junior.

Hadley Richardson is married and is living in Toronto. Her husband is an author and they spent the first months of their married life abroad, where he collected material for a book, which has since been published. (This news was gleaned by the Class Editor at the Council Meeting in St. Louis, but she (the C. E.) was unable to find out Hadley's married name or her address. Will anyone having this information please share it with the editor?)

Mildred Jacobs Coward has a daughter, Mildred Joan, born on October 23rd. In sending the news, the arrival was announced of "Miss Mildred Joan Coward, Bryn Mawr 1945!"

Olga Erbsloh purchased a little farm this summer near West Nyack in Rockland County, N. Y. She writes, "I bought it for the beautiful view and the bit of real woodland, but I found a cow and chickens thrown in so I had to go in for farming. willing or no . . . Quantities of fruit ripened on my hands and knocked at my conscience until either it or they simply had to turn to jelly. One hundred and twenty-six jars and glasses so far!" This was written in October, and Olga and her little girl are back in New York now, where the former expects to work on another drama.

Gordon Stevenson, to whom Candace

Hewitt was married this summer, is an artist and portrait painter. He studied and then taught at the Chicago Art Institute, winning the John Quincy Adams foreign travel scholarship. During the war she was in the camouflage service in the navy. One of his portraits is of Serge Rachmaninoff and one of his most recent ones is of Candace.

Ruth Hubbard has been living abroad for over a year now. She went there with her family in May, 1922, and they have been spending their time in Belgium, Germany and France. When Ruth wrote in September she was just finishing a three-months' course at the University of Strasbourg, where there were more than fourteen different nationalities in the class. In September, 1922, Ruth met Heleñe Evans at Oberammergau, where Helene had gone in her vacation from the American Embassy at Rome. They had not seen each other for seven years.

Hezzie Irvin is in Oxford with her mother this winter. Her address is 1 St. John's Road, care of Miss McGinnis.

Jean Sattler Marmillot is living in Bonn, Germany, and her husband is on duty in the Ruhr, getting back only for short leaves. Jean writes, "My chief interest and occupation, past, present and future, are my small daughter, born in March, and counting over millions of marks wherewith to buy a half pound of butter or a questionable egg! It's quite an education living in a country of highly depreciated currency— you learn easily to deal with millions and millions and feel quite like a financier, until you gaze upon the paltry result of your shopping trip."

Ruth McKelvey Moore and her husband are living in Covington, Ky. They have a small daughter, aged fifteen months.

Katharine Streett Robb is back in Cumberland, living at "Grey Gables" on Braddock Road. Hazel Barnett Blackburn took her baby boy over to see Streettie one day last summer.

Isabel Smith covered over 700 miles on horseback this summer, traveling in Wyoming with the Valley Ranch party. This winter she is instructor in the Department of Geology at Smith College.

Carlotta Taber for two summers has been a partner in the Wayside Tea Room, Glendon, Maine. She has a little old-fashioned house on the main road between Portland and Rockland. This winter she is in New York, at 308 West Twenty-eighth Street.

Eleanor Freer Willson spent last summer in the Catskills with her three offsprings, Ned, four; Barbara, nearly three and Archie, six months.

Will anyone who knows Lucile Davidson Middleton's address please send it to the Class Editor?

1917

Class Editor, Isabella S. Diamond, 1527 Eye Street, N. W., Washington, D. C.

Dor Shipley was married on January 12th to Thomas Raeburn White of Philadelphia. Does everyone in 1917 remember that Mr. White spoke at our commencement and that he is the College lawyer?

Eleanora Wilson, ex. '17, was married in November to Dr. Howell Peacock. She is going to live in Philadelphia.

1917's REUNION.

1917, do you realize that we have never yet had a really big reunion? Now, after seven years, the time has come for everyone to appear with or without their children. Our headquarters will be in Pembroke East.

Unless more of us come back than last time we cannot have our banquet in one of the halls. So please answer quickly the first notice that is sent you, so that we can make plans for enormous numbers.

1919

Class Editor, Mary Tyler, 1215 John. Street, Baltimore, Md.

We all send our deepest sympathy to Emily Moores, whose father died on December 7th.

Margaret Rhoads is having a most interesting time as General Secretary of the Mission Board of the Philadelphia Yearly Meeting of Friends. This Board supports fourteen American workers in Japan. She writes: "I began work three days after the great earthquake and have not recovered from the shock yet. I am learning the mysteries of cable code and the mimeograph— and a profound respect for the pluck and courage of the Japanese, who say, 'Shikataga Nai' (it can't be helped) and start living again in tin shacks on the ashes of their former homes. Of those connected with our mission only one schoolgirl lost her life, and our new buildings escaped the fire." She writes any or all of 1919 to come and see her at 304 Arch Street, Philadelphia.

Beany Dubach is still recuperating from a severe illness of last winter. She is now at 713 North Lea Avenue, Roswell, New Mexico.

On December 9th Mary Scott Spiller gave a delightful luncheon for as many 1919's as she could find around and about Philadelphia. Among those present besides Mary were—D. Chambers, E. Lanier Bolling and son, B. Biddle Yarnall, F. Day Lukens, E. Howes, M. Rhoads, M. Tyler, G. Hearne, K. Tyler, A. Stiles, M. Delaplaine. The table was most beautifully decorated with 1919 lanterns—green candles and candies, etc., and everyone had a wonderful time.

E. Marquand sailed on January 5th on the *Adriatic* for Egypt, with her aunt, and expects to be gone three or four months.

Becky Reinhardt was married on December 28th to Mr. M. Langhorne Craighill of Richmond, Va. Tip Thurman was one of the bridesmaids.

Marion Moseley is taking courses at the University of Chicago, which will help her in her work for the Grenfell Mission. She will not go to Labrador this summer, as she has not been well, but expects to go the next year again.

Elizabeth Fauvre has been traveling around the country and is now visiting in Boston.

K. T. and M. Rhoads both went to the Student Volunteer Conference in Indianapolis during the Christmas vacation.

Here are some new addresses:

Mary Ramsay Phelps (Mrs. William E.), care of H. J. Baker Bro., 25 De Mayo 267, Buenos Aires, Argentine, S. A.

Virginia Coombs Evans (Mrs. Kelvin), Scarsdale, N. Y.

Rebecca Reinhardt Craighill (Mrs. Langdon), 1107 Franklin Street, Wilmington, Del.

Jeannette Peabody Cannon (Mrs. Le Grand, Jr.), 150 Everit Street, New Haven, Conn.

Mary Lee Thurman, 9 Massachusetts Avenue, Boston.

1921

Class Editor, Kathleen F. Johnston, 1754 Massachusetts Avenue, Washington, D. C.

1921 has at last become ancient and honorable. We have a nominee for the office of recording secretary in the Alumnae Association, Margaret Ladd.

Won't all the geniuses who are working out their own salvation in silence please prepare us by sending some news to this distracted "colyumnist"? N. B. Luz, Marynia, Bickey, Vic Evans, Cloe, Gog, Eugenia, Stonie, and Biffie take notice.

Darn has gathered news of Chicago. Surrounded by twenty-three first cousins and in the midst of preparations for Christmas she stopped to say that:

First, Betty Kellogg, Marg. Archbald, Biffie, Silvine, Blissades, Jane Brown, and Luz were on the ranch with her last summer.

Second, Betsy Kales is the wonder of the Medical School—and of society, too, for at a tea she attempted to check a thigh bone in the dressing room.

Third, Nancy Porter is at the Medical School.

Fourth, Teddy commutes. She lives in Lake Forest and attends everything in Chicago.

Fifth, Nora Newell Burry is in Lake Forest with her son, "Bunny."

Sixth, Chick Parsons Storms is also in Lake Forest with a "most remarkable child."

Seventh, Chickie Beckwith was married to Mr. John N. Lee on November 11. Luz, Teddy, and Darn were bridesmaids.

Eighth, Emily Kimbrough is now assistant editor of *Fashions of the Hour*, a magazine run by Marshall Field Co. Darn says that she is now being rushed by the head of the soap department.

Ninth, Luz has gone to Little Rock after a year's absence.

Tenth, Darn herself is taking courses in English at the University of Lake Forest.

Mary Porter Kirkland was married to Mr. Arthur S. Vandervoot, Jr., on January 4, in Houston.

Ruth L. Karns was married to Mr. Norman Chapman, of Genesee, Pennsylvania, on September 6.

Rosalie Florence Henderson brought her husband and son to Washington for Christmas. They live at Charlottesville, where Mr. Henderson is an instructor at the University of Virginia.

Alice Whittier writes that she is in the

third year at the Yale Medical School. She took part in one of the National Board Medical Examinations last June and passed successfully.

Katherine Ward is at New Haven and, according to Helen Taft Manning, is working for her Ph. D.

Irene Maginnis was married to Mr. James S. Scott on September 15. Marian Eadie Farrow was a bridesmaid. She lives in Buffalo and has seen Betty Mills, who is working at the University of Buffalo and coaching basketball.

Jean Spurney is on the road in the leading part of *Abie's Irish Rose*. She was last heard of in Cleveland.

Helen Hill brought Miss Mackintosh of Barnett House, Oxford, to Washington last week but spent all her minutes interviewing government employes. Helen is working in the Law School of the University of Chicago, lives during the week in a flat with Leila Houghteling, takes some examination in March, and although she won't admit it, will undoubtedly have a Ph.D. as a result. She expects to go to the London School of Economics in the near future.

What's the use of being editor if you can't talk about yourself? I am living at home in Washington and wish anyone who passes through would telephone to me. I am like a chicken without a head and run from tutoring to scouts, from Old English to an embryonic hockey club, and from the Bryn Mawr Club and scholarship money-raising to teas, but I am always glad to see anyone.—This space was reserved for Betty Kellogg's tale of her travels and for Copey's excerpts from Kash's letters, both of which never arrived. Take warning and send me news for the next BULLETIN or you may have more fillers!

1923

Class Editor, Dorothy Meserve, 949 Madison Avenue, New York City.

Elizabeth Child has announced her engagement to Mr. Richard H. McKey of Boston and New Hampshire.

"Jackie"—Mrs. William James Buck.

"As you see, I am married and have moved to a quaint old town where we are truly living the quiet simple life. My latest occupation is the raising and selling of Police Dogs of fine pedigrees. It is loads of fun, and I have just named my kennels the 'Nordlande Kennels.' "

Polly von Hofsten.

"I have been in Sweden since July, and intend to be abroad until September, 1924, probably studying a little at the Sorbonne in Paris, and then going to Italy, England, and Switzerland."

Dorothy Burr, American School, Athens.

"Yes, I am actually here, travelling over the whole country studying stones, potsheads, and bee-hive tombs! We've been away almost continually for two months, and now we study in Athens; the Acropolis suggestively peeping into my window every morning.

"Bryn Mawr has been here. Alice Harrison was in town with Miss Goldman, and Alice Lee, ex '22, went with us into the Peloponnesus; together we carried (even I) 'Come cheer for our College' over Taygetus, 4000 feet up."

Helen Hagan Stagg, or "Hoggie."

"I married Frederick Louis Stagg, December 16th, 1923, and since then have been on the second largest cocoa plantation in the world, about sixty miles from Guayaguil. My husband is Estate Manager for Caamaño Seuguel Estate, Ltd. An English company owns this plantation. I am a British subject since my marriage, my husband being English. We will probably live in the States after this year. My only occupation is being *Patrona* to the few thousand *peons* of the estate."

Emeline Kellogg Adams.

"Married to Lewis Greenleaf Adams (architect) in July, 1921. We have a son, Richard Greenleaf Adams, born at Neuilly-sur-Seine on September 6th, 1923.

"We have lived abroad since September, 1922, mostly in Paris, but we have also travelled all through Italy, Sicily, and Spain for four months.

"My husband is a student at the Ecole des Beaux Arts, and I took the Cours de la Civilization Française at the Sorbonne last year. Now I am keeping house and being a mother.

"We'll probably be here for two or three more years."

Sophie Yarnall Jacobs writes that she is kept fairly busy with a husband and baby, the Philadelphia Editorship of the Junior League Bulletin, hospital and settlement boards and other "dull, conventional duties. Such," she writes, "is married life compared with our unbounded maidenly free-dom."

Elizabeth Jennings has been working for the past year in a fire insurance office, the Virginia Fire and Marine Insurance Company. She writes that the combined life of a working-girl and a debutante is a strenuous one.

Jean Martin is head of the Mathematics and Science Department in Smyrna High School, teaching algebra, plane geometry and solid geometry, also biology and physics.

Florence Martin has returned from a summer of travel in Europe and leaves New York on November 19th to go back to her home in California.

Eleanor Mathews is taking a secretarial course at a school in New York.

Frances Matteson is engaged to Mr. Lawrence Rathbun; the wedding is to be on January 1, 1924, and their address after February 1st will be 539 Harris Avenue, Woonsocket, Rhode Island.

Harriette Millar is teaching French at a small private school and doing graduate work in French at College.

Elizabeth Newbold is working in Glen-olden, Pa., as analytical chemist for the H. K. Mulford Company.

Harriet Price is doing secretarial work for a Doctor DuBois, who is writing a book.

K. Strauss and D. Meserve are starting on January 26th on a trip around the world.

Rosamund Raley is assistant Science Instructor at the Glens Falls Academy, which is a private co-educational preparatory school. She teaches Nature Study to the fifth and sixth grades, Elementary Science to the seventh grade, General Science to the first year High School, Biology to the Sophomore High School and American History throughout the grades.

Katharine Raht is a graduate student in history at Bryn Mawr.

Frances Young Rienhoff is living in Baltimore and doing Social Service work for the Junior League.

Helen Rice is studying the violin and also teaching the violin twice weekly in the Brooklyn Music School Settlement.

Ally Smith has been a horse wrangler on Darn's ranch all summer and now has a job as housekeeper for her mother—and is saving every penny to buy a ranch of her own some day.

Dorothy Stewart is studying Short Story and Daily Themes at Columbia and Barnard. She is also "raising police dogs, showing them, getting prizes, and making lots of money. Otherwise studying music and leading a grand lazy life."

Elizabeth Vincent is working on the *New Republic* until January, then she is going to Greece with her family until June.

Virginia Miller writes that she is very busy doing nothing whatsoever, besides which she is playing hockey on the Winnetka Hockey Team.

Julia Henning is temporarily living in Chicago and studying at the Chicago Art Institute.

Marion Lawrence is studying history of art at Harvard.

Ruth McAneny went abroad on September 8th, flew from Paris to London (never again, she says) and is now in Paris studying French and the drama.

Frieda Seligman is assistant to the director of the Louisville School of Social Work. She is taking several courses in the school and doing fine work with a child placing agency.

CONTENTS

A King's Daughter. By John Masefield, The Macmillan Company. New York, 1923. $1.75.

"And when Jehu was come to Jezreel, Jezebel heard of it, and she painted her face, and tired her head, and looked out at a window.

"And as Jehu entered in at the gate, she said, Had Zimri peace, who slew his master?

"And he lifted up his face to the window, and said, Who is on my side? Who? And there looked out to him two or three eunuchs.

"And he said, Throw her down. So they threw her down: and some of her blood was sprinkled on the wall, and on the horses: and he trode her under foot."

The High Place. By J. B. Cabell. Robert McBride & Company. New York, 1923. $2.50.

TRAVELS IN ARABIA DESERTA. By Charles M. Doughty. Boni and Liveright, New York, 1923. $17.50. Third edition.

"Arabia Deserta," says Mr. T. E. Lawrence, "is a bible of its kind . . . the first and indispensable work upon the Arabs of the desert. Doughty went among these people dispassionately, looked at their life, and wrote it down word for word . . . To have accomplished such a journey would have been achievement enough for the ordinary man. Mr. Doughty was not content till he had made the book justify the journey as much as the journey justified the book, and in the double power, to go and to write, he will not soon find his rival."

The Rover. By Joseph Conrad. Doubleday, Page & Company. New York, 1923. $2.00.

Peyrol, the rover, Brother of the Coast, comes back to France to spend the rest of his days in a place "remote from all thoughts of strife and death." But the rover's life finds him again, and "in the immobility of a smiling enchantment, of a Mediterranean fair day," he carries his last adventure to its end.

Pierre Curie. By Marie Curie. The Macmillan Company. New York, 1923. $2.25.

Antic Hay. By Aldous Huxley. George Doran & Co. New York, 1923. $2.00.

THE DANCE OF LIFE. By Havelock Ellis. Houghton Mifflin Company, Boston, 1923. $4.00.

Mr. Havelock Ellis, whom Mr. H. L. Menken called "the most civilized Englishman living today," is in some respects a follower of Pater, and especially so in his belief in the order, the art, of living. He differs from Pater, however, in believing that the conduct of life is according to the principles of art, and not only that it should be so. His subject in *The Dance of Life* is "Man as the active creator of life and knowledge, the artist of the world, moulding it to his own measure," and in the five essays which make up the greater part of the book, he considers the chief works of man, in all of which he finds evidence of the government of an aesthetic sense, that "in humbler forms, is mixed up with the most primitive manifestations of human life."

SCHOOL DIRECTORY

FERRY HALL
A Resident and Day School for Girls
LAKE FOREST, ILLINOIS
On Lake Michigan, near Chicago

College Preparatory, General and Advanced Courses. Departments of Music, Home Economics, Expression, and Art. *Supervised Athletics and Swimming Pool.*

Eloise R. Tremain, A.B., Bryn Mawr, Principal

THE
Mary C. Wheeler Town and Country School
PROVIDENCE, RHODE ISLAND

Preparation for Bryn Mawr and College Board Examinations

Out door sports   Junior Country Residence

"HILLSIDE" NORWALK, CONNECTICUT

On a hill in six acres of ground. Three residence houses. Separate School House and Gymnasium. Preparation for Comprehensive and College Board Examinations. General and Special Courses.

MARGARET R. BRENDLINGER, A. B. (Vassar)
VIDA HUNT FRANCIS, A. B., (Smith), Principals

The Harcum School
BRYN MAWR, PA.

Prepares for Bryn Mawr and all leading colleges

Musical Course prepares for the Department of Music of Bryn Mawr College

EDITH H. HARCUM, Head of School
L. MAY WILLIS, Principal

MISS RANSOM and MISS BRIDGES' SCHOOL
HAZEL LANE. PIEDMONT (Suburb of San Francisco)

College Preparatory

MARION RANSOM } Headmistresses
EDITH BRIDGES

MISS MADEIRA'S SCHOOL
1330 19th St., N. W.   Washington, D. C.

A Resident and Day School
for Girls

LUCY MADEIRA WING, A.B.

MRS. DAVID LAFOREST WING
Head Mistress

The Shipley School
Bryn Mawr, Pennsylvania
Preparatory to Bryn Mawr College
Alice G. Howland, Eleanor O. Brownell,
Principals

The Ethel Walker School
SIMSBURY, CONNECTICUT

Head of School
ETHEL WALKER SMITH, A.M. Bryn Mawr College
Head Mistress
JESSIE GERMAIN HEWITT, A.B. Bryn Mawr College

THE MISSES KIRK'S
College Preparatory School
Bryn Mawr Ave. and Old Lancaster Road,
Bryn Mawr, Pa.

Number of boarders limited. Combines advantages of school life with private instruction. Individual schedule arranged for each pupil.

MISS WRIGHT'S SCHOOL
Bryn Mawr, Pa.

Prepares for Bryn Mawr and
College Board Examinations

Miss Beard's School for Girls
ORANGE, NEW JERSEY

A country school near New York. College preparatory, special courses. Art. Domestic Arts and Science. Supervised physical work. Agnes Miles Music School affiliated with Miss Beard's School.

MISS LUCIE C. BEARD, Head Mistress

ROSEMARY HALL
No elective courses
Prepares for college
Preferably Bryn Mawr

Caroline Ruutz-Rees, Ph.D. } Head Mistresses
Mary E. Lowndes, Litt.D.

GREENWICH   CONNECTICUT

The Katharine Branson School
ROSS, CALIFORNIA   Across the Bay from San Francisco
A Country School   College Preparatory
Heads:
Katharine Fleming Branson, A. B., Bryn Mawr
Laura Elizabeth Branson, A. B., Bryn Mawr

THE AGNES IRWIN SCHOOL
2009-2011 Delancey Place, Philadelphia
A College Preparatory
SCHOOL FOR GIRLS
JOSEPHINE A. NATT, A.B., Headmistress
BERTHA M. LAWS, A.B., Secretary-Treasurer

SCHOOL DIRECTORY

The Episcopal Academy
(Founded 1785)

CITY LINE, OVERBROOK, PA.

A country day school for boys from second grade to college. Separate lower school beginning September 1923. Enjoys the patronage of Bryn Mawr Alumnae.

Cathedral School of St. Mary
GARDEN CITY, LONG ISLAND, N. Y.

A school for Girls 19 miles from New York. College preparatory and general courses. Music. Art and Domestic Science. Catalogue on request. Box B.

Miriam A. Bytel, A. B., Radcliffe, Principal
Bertha Gordon Wood, A. B., Bryn Mawr, Ass't Principa

WYKEHAM RISE
WASHINGTON, CONNECTICUT

A COUNTRY SCHOOL FOR GIRLS

Prepares for Bryn Mawr and Other Colleges

St. Timothy's School for Girls
CATONSVILLE, MARYLAND
Founded 1882

The Baldwin School
A Country School for Girls
BRYN MAWR   PENNSYLVANIA

Preparation for Bryn Mawr, Mount Holyoke, Smith, Vassar and Wellesley colleges. Abundant outdoor life. Hockey, basketball, tennis.

ELIZABETH FORREST JOHNSON, A.B.
Head

COLLEGE PREPARATORY

Miss J. R. HEATH
Miss L. McE. FOWLER } Heads of the School

WOMAN'S MEDICAL COLLEGE
OF PENNSYLVANIA

Seventy-fourth year beginning Sept. 26, 1923. Entrance requirements: two years of college work including certain credits in science and languages. Excellent laboratories. Full-time teachers. Clinical advantages. Well-equipped hospital. Special eight months' course of training for laboratory technicians. The Hospital of the Woman's Medical College conducts a training school for nurses which includes the advantages of class teaching by the Faculty of the College

For information address: The Dean
2101 North College Avenue, Philadelphia, Pa.

Garrison Forest School for Girls

Less than an hour from Baltimore. A country school with all city advantages, in the beautiful Green Spring Valley. Intermediate, College Preparatory, Special Music and Art Courses. Boarding Dept. limited. Horseback riding and all sports. Catalog and Views.

MISS MARY MONCRIEFFE LIVINGSTONE, Princ'pal
Box C, Garrison, Maryland

ROGERS HALL
A SCHOOL FOR GIRLS

Thorough preparation for college entrance examinations. Graduate course of two years for high school graduates. Complete equipment. 40 minutes from Boston.

MISS OLIVE SEWALL PARSONS, B.A.
Principal
Lowell, Massachusetts

Do not forget that the Alumnae Book Department is eager to secure your patronage. All orders promptly filled.

Write or telephone

THE ALUMNAE OFFICE
Taylor Hall

Eight thousand miles
saved on every trip

It used to be 13,307 miles from New York to San Francisco by sea; it is now only 5,262.

The Panama Canal, which seemed such a heavy expense when it was built, is an immense national economy.

A greater economy because of the 1,500 General Electric motors which do its work—pulling the ships through, pumping water, opening and closing the locks—all at such a little cost.

GENERAL ELECTRIC

The
BRYN MAWR
ALUMNAE
BULLETIN

THE ANNUAL MEETING

REPORTS OF COMMITTEES

MARCH

1924

Vol. IV   No. 3

BRYN MAWR ALUMNAE BULLETIN

OFFICIAL PUBLICATION OF
THE BRYN MAWR ALUMNAE ASSOCIATION

EVELYN PAGE, '23, *Editor*

GERTRUDE J. HEARNE, '19, *Business Manager*

EDITORIAL BOARD

LUCY M. DONNELLY, '93
ELEANOR FLEISHER REISMAN, '03
CAROLINE MORROW CHADWICK-COLLINS, '05

ADELAIDE W. NEALL, '06
MAY EGAN STOKES, '11
LEILA HOUGHTELING, '11, *ex-officio*

Subscription Price, $1.50 a Year   *Single Copies, 25 Cents*

Checks should be drawn to the order of Bryn Mawr Alumnae Bulletin
Published monthly, except August and September, at 1006 Arch St., Philadelphia, Pa.

VOL. IV   MARCH, 1924   No. 3

NOMINATIONS AND NOMINEES

We appealed, in the last issue of the BULLETIN, to the members of the Alumnae Association for a plan to relieve our over-burdened officers. At the same time we referred to another difficulty, the solution of which, we believe, already lies before us. We spoke of the efforts made by the Nominating Committee to secure the best candidates for various offices. That very little effort has been made to assist the Committee is not to be denied, and yet there is no adequate excuse for this failure. The By-By-Laws of the Association, Article V, Section 4 ("Any twenty-five members of the Association may make nominations for officers of the Executive Board"), Article VII, Section 4, a ("The Alumnae Directors shall be nominated as follows: The Executive Board of the Alumnae Association shall make at least three times as many nominations as there are vacancies among the Alumnae Directors. It may at its discretion include in such nominations names proposed in writing by any twenty-five members of the Alumnae Association qualified to vote for all Directors"), and Article VIII, Section 3, c ("Any ten Alumnae of a District may nominate a candidate for Councillor from that District"), not only offer an opportunity to choose candidates, but practically impose this duty. These provisions make the entire Alumnae Association a nominating committee, and if the Alumnae have permitted their privilege to lapse, the same inertia need not hamper them in the future.

Before very long the election of an Alumnae Director of the College will take place, and it is hoped that the Alumnae Association will begin now to think of nominees for that office. Following the policy of last year, when the new director was chosen from the Western States, the Board is looking this year for nominees from New England and the South. Yet other qualifications are even more to be stressed. The Alumnae Director, to quote a BULLETIN editorial, "should have initiative, sureness of judgment, and experience of affairs", since she acts as "intermediary between the Alumnae and the Board of Directors". But the Alumnae Directorship is not the only office to concern us.

In March two District Councillors are to be elected, one from District II, which includes New York, Pennsylvania, Delaware, and New Jersey, and one from District V, which includes Illinois, Iowa, Minnesota, and other States in the vicinity. This office is one of growing importance, and the successful Councillor must be the choice of her District, the organization and efficiency of which depend largely upon her. She is concerned not only with her own restricted area, but through the meetings of the Council she comes in contact with Alumnae from all over the United States. She must bring before them the opinions of her constituents, and carry home with her the information she receives from her fellow Councillors.

Several candidates for these offices will be nominated by the Executive Board, but the burden should lie not only upon it, but also upon the Alumnae in the districts concerned. To be a truly democratic institution, as our By-Laws make us, we, the voters of the Association, must nominate as well as elect.

ANNOUNCEMENTS

ACCOMMODATIONS NEEDED!

For Alumnae returning to Bryn Mawr for May Day, May 9th and 10th, 1924.

All Alumnae living in the vicinity of Philadelphia, which means the Main Line, Chestnut Hill, Media and Moorestown, please volunteer spare rooms for these dates, either for rent or to accommodate friends.

Please send in number of rooms available and rates per day to Gertrude J. Hearne, Alumnae Secretary, Alumnae Office, Taylor Hall, Bryn Mawr.

All material for the April BULLETIN should be sent to Evelyn Page, Taylor Hall, Bryn Mawr College, before March 10th.

The Editor is very sorry that, owing to lack of space, she has been forced to delay publication of any material not strictly official. She hopes next month to be able to print several articles for which there is no room in this issue.

She also deeply regrets that she has had to omit a very interesting letter from Miss Theresa Helburn to the class of 1908. Notes of certain classes, 1904, 1920, and 1922, had also to be cut. This material will be published as soon as possible.

The Annual Meeting

Alumnae began to gather for the Annual Meeting on Friday, February 1st. We who came early were rewarded by a delightful supper at the College Inn, at which Emma Guffey Miller, '99, presided. She not only amused the gathering herself, but called upon others, President Park, Elizabeth Nields Bancroft, '98, Julia Langdon Loomis, '95, and Caroline Morrow Chadwick-Collins, '05, to do likewise. After the dinner was over, the party adjourned to the President's House, where we had the pleasure of seeing for ourselves all of the improvements that have been made there, and were later entertained by a one-act play, *Creatures of Impulse*, by W. S. Gilbert, given under the direction of F. Maude Dessau, '13, who, together with the other actors, is to be congratulated upon both choice and execution.

The next morning we met for ends strictly businesslike. The Annual Meeting was held as usual at 10 o'clock in Taylor Hall. About 190 Alumnae were present.

MINUTES OF THE MEETING

(There is on file in the Alumnae Office a stenographic report of the Annual Meeting, giving in detail the discussion, amendments, lost and carried, etc. The following minutes are condensed.)

The Annual Meeting of the Bryn Mawr Alumnae Association was held in Taylor Hall on Saturday, February 2nd. The meeting was called to order by the Vice-President, Margaret Reeve Cary, at 10 A. M. One hundred and ninety were present.

Minutes of the Annual Meeting of 1923 were read and approved with slight change.

The following motions were passed:

That the report of the Executive Board be accepted.

That a vote of thanks and appreciation be sent to Anne Todd for her long, devoted and efficient services to the Alumnae Association, with the hope that we may have her help again.

That the report of the Treasurer containing the Budget be accepted, with the amendment of an increase of $100 to Local Association expenses.

That the report of the Alumnae Fund be accepted.

That the report of the Finance Committee be accepted as a whole, including the objects listed for the Alumnae Fund for 1924.

That the Executive Board of the Alumnae Association in appointing members of the Academic Committee be directed to appoint members of the Association of experience and training along academic lines so that the Committee may confer as an expert body.

That the continuance of the Academic Committee be a part of the Business of the Annual Meeting in 1925.

That it be a sense of this meeting that the Academic Committee be continued.

That the meeting adjourn for lunch.

The Alumnae Association is unanimous in thanking President Park for the delightful luncheon which we had with her in Pembroke Hall on the

day of the Annual Meeting. It was
a pleasure not only to be her guests
but also to enjoy the delicious luncheon and to know that it was served
by the College. Our enjoyment of it
took many of us back to the days
when Miss Martha G. Thomas entertained in Pembroke Hall. We congratulate Ellen Faulkner, 1913, the
new Director of Halls, and we look
forward to next year's meeting, when
we shall strive to be worthy of just
such another affair.

President Park's speech after luncheon dealt with the difference between
the student of thirty years ago and
the student of today. She found that
the distinction lay in the willingness
of older classes to study abstract subjects without demanding immediate
reference to everyday experience.
The present undergraduate is most
interested when her studies enter into
her life. To hold her attention, the
connection must be made between
the abstract and the concrete.

At two o'clock the gathering returned to Taylor and to work.

The following motions were passed
at the afternoon session:

That the report of the Alumnae
Directors be postponed until after
the report of the Council is accepted.

The report of the Council was
read and the recommendations were
submitted to the Association. In
connection with these recommendations the following motions were
passed:

That the Executive Board appoint
a Students' Building Committee to
carry out the plan proposed by the
temporary Students' Building Committee.

That the Music Committee be directed to raise funds for the permanent endowment of the Department
of Theoretical Music and that the
Alumnae Association co-operate with
the Committee to this end.

That the Alumnae Association
continue to publish the register providing that a suitable arrangement
can be made with the College.

That the report of the Alumnae Directors be accepted.

That the pensioning of employees
of the College is not within the province of the Alumnae Association.

That the report of the Summer
School Committee be accepted.

That the report of the M. Carey
Thomas Prize Fund Committee be
accepted.

That a vote of thanks be sent to
President Park for her hospitality
on Friday evening, and Saturday
noon.

That the Association thank Miss
Houghteling for her services and extend to her our sincere sympathy in
her loss.

That the Association express sympathy with the rebuilding of Miss
Tsuda's School, and endorse the
rebuilding.

That a vote of thanks be sent to
the retiring Board for their services
to the Association.

After the meeting the members of
the Alumnae Book Club gathered in
Rockefeller Hall to have tea and to
hear President Park speak on "The
General Needs of the Library," and
Georgiana Goddard King, '96, on
"Books Required for the Art Depart-
ment."

OFFICERS AND COMMITTEES OF THE BRYN MAWR ALUMNAE ASSOCIATION, 1924

Executive Board

President ....Margaret Reeve Cary, '07 (Mrs. C. R.)..1924-26
Vice-President ....Margaret Ayer Barnes, '07 (Mrs. Cecil).1924-26
Recording Secretary ....Katherine Sergeant Angell, '14 (Mrs. E.).1924-26
Corresponding Secretary ....Eleanor Marquand, '19 1924-26
Treasurer ....Ethel Cantlin Buckley, '01 (Mrs. M.)....1924-26

Alumnae Secretary

Gertrude J. Hearne, '19 1923-24

Editor of the Bulletin

Evelyn Page, '23 1923-24

Business Manager, Bulletin

Gertrude J. Hearne, '19 1923-24

Chairman of Class Collectors

Mary Peirce, '12 1924-25

District Councillors

District I ....Mary Richardson Walcott, '06 (Mrs. Robert).......1922-25
District II ....Emma Guffey Miller, '99 (Mrs. Carroll)...........1922-24
District III ....Margaret Free Stone, '15 (Mrs. James A.)........1923-26
District IV ....Julia Haines MacDonald, '12 (Mrs. J. A.).........1923-25
District V ....Caroline Daniels Moore, '01 (Mrs. P. W.)..........1923-24
District VI ....Helen Tredway Graham, '11 (Mrs. Evarts)........1923-26

Alumnae Directors

Frances Fincke Hand, '97 (Mrs. Learned) 1918-24
Pauline D. Goldmark, '96 1922-25
Martha G. Thomas, '89 1922-26
Louise Congdon Francis, '00 (Mrs. R. S.) 1921-27
Anna B. Lawther, '97 1923-28

STANDING COMMITTEES

FINANCE COMMITTEE

Elizabeth Caldwell Fountain, '97 (Mrs. Gerard) ....1921-26, Chairman
Caroline Morrow Chadwick-Collins, '05 (Mrs. J. C.) 1922-25
Elizabeth Bent Clark, '95 (Mrs. H. L.) 1923-27
Katrina Ely Tiffany, '97 (Mrs. Charles) 1923-27
Margaret Reeve Cary, '07 (Mrs. C. Reed) ....   Ex-officio
Mary Peirce, '12 (Chairman of Class Collectors) ....   "   "
Helen Sturgis, '05 (Chairman of Scholarships) ....   "   "
Ethel Cantlin Buckley, '01 (Mrs. Monroe) Treasurer ....

ACADEMIC COMMITTEE*

Frances Fincke Hand, '97 (Mrs. Learned) 1924-27
Edna Shearer, '04 1924-27
Eunice M. Schenck, '07 1924-27
Margaret Reeve Cary, '07 (Mrs. C. Reed) ....   Ex-officio

SCHOLARSHIPS COMMITTEE

Helen Sturgis, '05 ....1923-25, Chairman
Emma O. Thompson, '04 1921-26
Eunice Morgan Schenck, '07 1922-27
Millicent Carey, '20 1923-28
Agnes Clement, '23 1924-29
Margaret Reeve Cary, '07 (Mrs. C. Reed).........................   Ex-officio

*Four members to be appointed.

COMMITTEE ON HEALTH AND PHYSICAL EDUCATION
Ethel Dunham, '14 ....1922-26,. Chairman
Eleanor Bliss, '21 1923-25
Adrienne Kenyon Franklin, '15 (Mrs. Benjamin, Jr.) 1922-26
Ella Oppenheimer, '14 1923-27
Caroline Stevens Rogers, '17 (Mrs. Horatio) 1924-28
Margaret Reeve Cary, '07 (Mrs. C. Reed)........................ Ex-officio

PUBLICITY COMMITTEE
Caroline Morrow Chadwick-Collins, '05 (Mrs. J. C.) ....1921-26, Chairman
Adelaide W. Neall, '06 1920-25
Mary Shipley Allinson, '14 (Mrs. Page)........................1923-26
Constance Cameron Luddington, '22 (Mrs. T.)...................1924-27
Margaret Reeve Cary, '07 (Mrs. C. Reed)....................... Ex-officio

COMMITTEE ON ATHLETIC CONTESTS
Gertrude J. Hearne, '19 ....1921-26, Chairman
Elizabeth F. Cope, '21 1922-27
Leah F. Cadbury, '14 1920-25
Betty Weaver, '20 1922-27
Eugenia Baker Jessup, '14 (Mrs. H. B.) 1924-29
Margaret Reeve Cary, '07 (Mrs. C. Reed)....................... Ex-officio

NOMINATING COMMITTEE
Virginia McKenny Claiborne, '08 (Mrs. Robert) ....1921-25, Chairman
Nathalie Swift, '13 1921-25
Margaret Corwin, '12 1923-27
Anne Rotan Howe, '02 (Mrs. T. D.).............................1923-27
Margaret Reeve Cary, '07 (Mrs. C. Reed)....................... Ex-officio

Special Committee
ALUMNAE COMMITTEE OF THE BRYN MAWR SUMMER SCHOOL
Josephine Goldmark, '98 ....1922-24, Chairman
Emma Bailey Speer, '94 (Mrs. Robert)..........................1922-24
Mary Coolidge, '14 1922-24
Louise Brownell Saunders, '93 (Mrs. A. P.).....................1923-25
Eunice Follansbee Hale, '03 (Mrs. William B.)..................1923-25
Mary Herr, '09 1923-25
Margaret Reeve Cary, '07 (Mrs. C. Reed)....................... Ex-officio

REPORT OF THE EXECUTIVE BOARD

Since the last Annual Meeting there have been several changes in the personnel of the Executive Board and Alumnae Office. Owing to ill health, Anne Todd retired from office in April, and Myra Vauclain was appointed Acting President. In the autumn, finding that her health had not improved sufficiently, she offered her resignation as President. She had performed all the multitudinous duties of President faithfully and loyally, animated always and only by a desire to serve the College and the Association. Among her most valuable and permanent contributions may be mentioned her marked financial ability in budgeting the expenses of the Association, and her careful organization of Committees. Her resignation was accepted with sincere regret and Leila Houghteling automatically became President. Margaret Reeve Cary, '07, was appointed Vice-President. Our Alumnae Secretary, Caroline Morrow Chadwick-Collins, '05, lent to her office the distinction of rare judgment, foresight and executive ability, but because of her gifts along the lines of Publicity, we reluctantly gave her to the College. Gertrude Hearne, '19, has been appointed to the office of Alumnae Secretary. Mary Peirce has been appointed chairman of the Alumnae Fund.

In connection with Publicity, you will remember that the Endowment Drive brought to light the fact that the College had no contact with the Press and that the welfare of the College was seriously menaced on this account.

Realizing the importance of good Publicity, the Alumnae Association took over the financing of the Publicity for one year. The second year the Association shared in these expenses on a 50-50 basis with the College, and on October 1, 1923, the college took over the entire Publicity work as a definite part of its program of expenditure. This, therefore, relieves the Association entirely of any expenses in Publicity work. In addition, the Summer School took over the Publicity expenses for the summer of 1923 as a definite item of their budget. In 1921-22 these expenses had been carried partly by the Association and partly by volunteer work. This means that the only Publicity work which the Association is now doing is the volunteer work done by the local Publicity chairmen, who deal only with Publicity arising from their local activities and entertainments. These chairmen are still appointed by the Councillors in consultation with the Publicity Director of the College and the chairmen of the local Associations. It has been decided as a matter of policy that the Director of Publicity of the College

should, if an Alumnae, be the chairman of the National Alumnae Publicity Committee.

The high quality of editorial writing set for the BULLETIN by Martha Plaisted Saxton, '08, was a delight to all of us. As the year advanced, however, it became increasingly difficult both for the Editor of the BULLETIN and the Executive Board to have the BULLETIN edited in New York and published in Philadelphia, therefore Martha Plaisted Saxton's resignation as Editor of the BULLETIN was accepted with a sense of loss and deep regret. Evelyn Page, '23, was appointed to fill her place, with her office in Taylor Hall. The Editorial Board is glad to announce that Margaret Ladd Franklin, '08, and Frances Bliss, '22, have consented to write several editorials. Attracted by the interesting work done by various Alumnae in their chosen fields, there have been obtained from a number of them accounts of their work, which have been published and will continue to be published under the heading "Alumnae Activities." The Editorial Board would like to take this opportunity to thank those Alumnae who have written for the BULLETIN and to ask for your continued co-operation. The income from advertisements in the BULLETIN this year has been slightly higher than before, but it is not yet sufficient to pay the total costs of publishing the BULLETIN; $2,058.71 has been received from advertisements, $30.17 from subscriptions, etc., and $95.74 from Book commissions, making a total of $2,184.62. Adding to this sum one-quarter of the dues the total receipts are $3,175.67, as against $3,651.48, which is the cost of printing, mailing, and editing the magazine. This does not include the salary of the Business Manager, nor pay for the necessary clerical assistance.

The College was absolutely unable to appropriate any money to publish the *Register*. In the light of the fact that May Day is celebrated this year and for many other urgent reasons, the Executive Board felt that it was so necessary to have the *Register* published that they underwrote it, hoping that the total cost would not exceed $2,500, believing that all of the Alumnae would rally to its support by buying copies at $1.35, cost price, including postage. So far the response of the Alumnae has not been encouraging. The Executive Board is anxious to sell as many copies as possible immediately, not only to reimburse the treasury but also to avoid the use of precious storage space.

The Joint Committee on the Alumnae Fund, composed of Directors and Alumnae, whose formation was provided for last February, has held two meetings, at which were discussed the objects to be included in the appeal for the Alumnae Fund. The Association appreciated this opportunity for talking over with President Park and representatives of the Board of Directors the immediate needs of the College.

The Committee on Health and Physical Education has held two meetings. It has been decided to investigate the amount and character of exercise required at other colleges and at a meeting with President Park, Dean Bontecou, the wardens and Miss Applebee there was an informal discussion of a plan for a Department of Health and Hygiene in the College.

Interest in the Library has been stimulated by the Alumnae Book Club. Through several teas and the columns of the BULLETIN some of the Professors have been given an opportunity to tell the Alumnae their special needs. About fifty books have been given to the Library through the members of this Club. When we remember that all those who have contributed books this year, have promised for succeeding years, we realize what the Book Club may mean to the Library.

The Scholarship Committee reports that twenty-one students have received scholarships and grants in aid. The James E. Rhoads Memorial Junior Scholar is Allegra Woodworth, who has ninety-six honor points on forty-five hours work, and the James E. Rhoads Sophomore Scholar is Delia Nichols Smith, Alumnae Regional Scholar for New Jersey, with thirty-four honor points on fourteen hours work. There are eight regional scholars in the Freshman Class:

One from District I.

Three from District II—two from New York, one from Eastern Pennsylvania.

Two from District III—one of these holds a scholarship of $300 from Chicago, and $200 from Pittsburgh.

Two from District V—one from Cleveland, one from Ann Arbor holding a $300 scholarship from District V.

There are five Regional Scholars in the Sophomore Class—one from District I, three from District II, one from District IV.

There is one special Regional Scholar in the Junior Class from New York. Every District is offering at least one scholarship for 1924-25 and plans to keep on helping the scholars already in College. Northern California offers a scholarship of $300 every other year.

The Loan Fund has made loans to ten students amounting to $2,150.

The reports of the Alumnae Directors, the Finance Committee, the Alumnae Fund, the Joint Committee, the Meetings of the Council, the proposed reorganization of the Academic Committee and matters appertaining to the Students' Building, and the Music Department are of such importance that they will be considered by you at this meeting outside of this report, and the findings will later be published in full in the BULLETIN.

We have this year eleven new Life Members, seventy-four new Full Members and twenty new Associate Members, making the total members of the Alumnae Association about 2,400.

During the year the following Alumnae and former students have died, and I will ask the members present to signify their sympathy by a rising silent vote:

Lisa B. Converse, 1896, January 27th.

Edith Walton Smith (Mrs. Ritchie), '07, February 25th.

Marjory Wallace Nichols (Mrs. R. H.), '08, March 12th.

Gertrude H. Mason, Grad., April 14th.

Emily Louise Bull, '91, May 5th.

Theodora Ethel Wye, '03, May 6th.

Edith Child, '90, May 8th.

Florence Leftwich Ravenal (Mrs. S. P.), '95, May 11th.

Mallory Whiting Webster, '15, June 20th.

Catherine Dimeling Stewart (Mrs. H.), '21, July.

Margaret Wickliffe Brown, '99, July.

Clarissa Smith Ware (Mrs. H. M.), '15, August 27th.

Katherine Esther Scott, '04, September.

Emily Blodgett Sherwin (Mrs. T. E.), '05, October.

Respectfully submitted,
MARGARET REEVE CARY,
Vice-President.

TREASURER'S REPORT
THE ALUMNÆ ASSOCIATION OF BRYN MAWR BALANCE SHEET, 31 December, 1923

ASSETS

Loan Fund:
Loans to Students:

Class of 1918, and prior $1,790.00		
Classes since 1918 .... 9,528.50		
	$11,318.50	
Investments, United States Fourth Liberty Loan 4½s 100.00		
Accrued Interest Receivable ..., ... 8.50		
Cash 653.89		
		$12,080.89
Life Membership Fund:		
Investment at cost, as annexed $9,230.37		
Cash 190.26		
	9,420.63	
Carola Woerishoffer Fund:		
Investments at book values, as annexed $1,943.40		
Cash 120.24		
	2,063.64	

Service Corps Fund:
Cash 609.41
Alumnæ Entertainment Fund:
Cash 76.32
Alumnae Fund:
Cash $2,806.27
Collections Receivable 154.00
Advances for account of Alumnæ Register 776.90
           3,737.17
General Fund:
Cash 33.30

           $28,021.36

LIABILITIES

Loan Fund:
Balance, January 1, 1923 .... 12,658.86
Interest received during year 107.03

           12,765.89
Less, Uncollectible Loans of Deceased Students 685.00
           $12,080.89
Life Membership Fund:
Balance, January 1, 1923 .... $8,870.63
Life Memberships received during year 550.00
           9,420.63
Carola Woerishoffer Fund:
Principal January 1, 1923 .... $1,943.40
Interest:
Balance, January 1, 1923 .... $210.64
Amount received during year 109.60

           320.24
Less Summer School Scholarship 200.00
           120.24
           2,063.64
Service Corps Fund:
Balance, January 1, 1923 .... $599.06
Income during year 10.35
           609.41
Alumnæ Entertainment Fund 76.32
Alumnæ Fund Appropriated and Designated, as annexed 3,737.17
General Fund:
Accounts Payable 33.30

           $28,021.36

GENERAL INCOME AND EXPENSE ACCOUNT,
for the Year ended 31st December, 1923

INCOME

Dues $3,965.22
Alumnae Bulletin:
Advertising $2,058.71
Miscellaneous Income 125.91
           2,184.62

Appropriated by Bryn Mawr College for Publicity 1,125.00
Gift from President Thomas 500.00
Income from Life Membership Fund 425.13
Academic Committee Meetings, Refunded 12.00
Interest on Bank Account 49.72

$8,261.69

EXPENSES

Bulletin:
  Printing...$2,792.00
  Miscellaneous 859.39
                           3,651.48

Publicity:
  Salary 1,125.00
  Expenses 675.00
                           1,800.00

Salary of Alumnae Secretary 1,725.00
Salary of Assistant to Alumnae Secretary 875.02
Salary of Office Secretary 1,073.28
Typewriting 10.00
Traveling:
  Council $1,483.15
  Executives 50.18
                           1,533.33
Local Branches Expenses 225.00
District Councillors' Traveling Expenses 227.36
Postage 308.51
Alumnae Fund Expenses 519.90
Printing 201.75
Office Supplies 84.68
Telephone and Telegraph 173.69
Photographs and Post Cards 6.01
Alumnae Festivities 377.90
Finance Committee 22.94
Miscellaneous 822.79
                           13,638.64

Excess of Expenses $5,376.95
Amount transferred hereto from Alumnae Fund to cover excess of expenses $5,376.95

ALUMNÆ FUND,
for the Year ended 31st December, 1923

RECEIPTS:
Designated for Special Purposes $7,182.44
Undesignated 9,618.81
                           $16,801.25

DISBURSEMENTS:

	From Designated Receipts	On Account of Appropriations
President's Fund	$1,640.00	$860.00
Books	1,387.50	868.50
Students' Building	2,260.63	

Class Room Facilities 1.00
Academic Endowment 10.00
Nelson Pension Fund 215.00   70.00
Constance Lewis—Memorial, Class '04 ...... 404.50
Summer School 420.00
Pictures Art Department 50.00
Expenses of the Association for the year 1923 38.50   5,338.45
                                        ————   ————
                                        $6,427.13 $6,636.95 ————
                                                                13.064.08

Balance, December 31, 1923:
  Designated:
    Books $50.00
    Reunion Gift—Class '03 .... 324.00
    Reunion Gift—Class '18 .... 25.00
    L. B. Converse Memorial 356.31
                                          ————
                                                        $755.31
  Appropriated:
    President's Fund $1,000.00
    Books 1,126.86
    Nelson Pension Fund 855.00
                                          ————
                                                        2,981.86
                                                                  ———— $3,737.17

RECEIPTS AND DISBURSEMENTS, LOAN FUND,
for the Year ended 31st December, 1923

Balance, January 1, 1923 .... $1,164.61
RECEIPTS:
  Repayment of Loans by Students $1,536.50
  Interest on Loans 62.80
  Interest on Bank Balances 39.98
                                                          ————
                                                                  1,639.28

                                                                  $2,803.89
DISBURSEMENTS:
  Loans to Students 2,150.00

      Balance in Girard Trust Company, December 31, 1923 .... $653.89

RECEIPTS AND DISBURSEMENTS, LIFE MEMBERSHIP FUND,
for the Year ended 31st December, 1923

Balance, January 1, 1923 .... $120.26
RECEIPTS:
  Life Memberships 550.00
                                                                  ————
                                                                  670.26
DISBURSEMENTS:
  $500 Indianapolis Water Company, 1-5½s 1953 .... 480.00

Balance in Banks, December 31, 1923:
  Western Savings Fund Society of Philadelphia $181.70
  Pennsylvania Company for Insurances on Lives and Grant-
    ing Annuities 8.56
                                                        ————
                                                                  $190.26

ALUMNÆ ENTERTAINMENT FUND, RECEIPTS AND DISBURSEMENTS,
for the Year ended 31st December, 1923

Balance, January 1, 1923 .... $269.00
DISBURSEMENTS:
    Academic Committee 192.68

    Balance, Pennsylvania Company for Insurance on Lives and Granting Annuities, December 31, 1923 .... $76.32

LIFE MEMBERSHIP FUND, SECURITIES OWNED,
31st December, 1923, at Cost

$3,600 U. S. Fourth Liberty Loan 4¼s $3,546.69
   50 U. S. Third Liberty Loan 4¼s 50.00
2,000 U. S. Second Liberty Loan 4¼s 1,840.20
 500 Indianapolis Water Company, 1-5½s, 1923 .... 480.00
  41 Shares Lehigh Coal and Navigation Company, par $50 .... 3,313.48

    $9,230.37

CAROLA WOERISHOFFER FUND, SECURITIES OWNED,
31st December, 1923, at Book Values

$1,000 Ohio State Telephone Company, Cons. and Ref., 5s, 1944 .... $950.00
1,000 Chicago Railways Company, 1-5s, 1927 .... 800.00
 200 Second Liberty Loan, 4¼s 193.40

    $1,943.40

BUDGET FOR 1924
RECEIPTS

Dues .... $ 4,100.00
Income from Life Memberships 400.00
BULLETIN 2,000.00
Bank Interest 75.00
Miscellaneous 15.00
President Emeritus Thomas's Gift 500.00
Grant from College for Publicity ....
Grant from College for Alumnae Entertainment 300.00

    $ 7,390.00
Alumnae Register 2,500.00

    $ 9,890.00
Appropriation required from Alumnae Fund 4,213.32

    $14,103.32
DISBURSEMENTS
Salaries:
    Alumnae Secretary $1,800.00
    Half-time Office Assistant 700.00
    Half-time Bookkeeper, October to June 466.66
    Full-time Office Secretary and Bookkeeper, June to October .. 466.66
    Editor of the BULLETIN 600.00
        $ 4,033.32

Operations:
  Postage .... $ 500.00
  Printing 550.00
  Telephone and Telegraph 150.00
  Supplies 75.00
  Auditors 200.00
  Alumnae Fund, transferred to Printing and Postage, 1924 ...
                                                     ————— 1,475.00

Traveling:
  Executives .... $ 400.00
  Committees 300.00
  Council 800.00
  District Councillors 700.00
  Editor (now in Bryn Mawr) ....
                                                     ————— 2,200.00
Local Branches 300.00
Dues (I. F. U. W., A. A. U. W., A. M. A.) 145.00
BULLETIN—Printing $2,800.00
          Miscellaneous 150.00
                                                     ————— 2,950.00
Publicity—from Alumnae Association ....
           from College ....
Reserve Fund 500.00
Register 2,500.00
                                                     —————
                                                     $14,103.32

THE ALUMNAE ASSOCIATION OF BRYN MAWR COLLEGE
REPORT UPON AUDIT OF ACCOUNTS FOR THE YEAR ENDED
                31ST DECEMBER, 1923
                                                January 30, 1924.
MISS BERTHA S. EHLERS, *Treasurer,*
    The Alumnæ Association of Bryn Mawr College,
        Bryn Mawr, Pa.
DEAR MADAM:
    We report that we have audited the accounts of
        THE ALUMNÆ ASSOCIATION OF BRYN MAWR COLLEGE
for the year ended 31st December, 1923, and found them to be correct.
    We verified the income from all securities owned. For all other receipts our
verification was confined to making a substantial comparison of the receipts recorded
in the books of account with the deposits in the banks.
    Annexed we submit the following statements:
        Balance Sheet, 31st December, 1923.
        General Income and Expense Account for the year ended 31st December, 1923.
        Alumnæ Fund for the year ended 31st December, 1923.
        Loan Fund Receipts and Disbursements for the year ended 31st December,
            1923.
        Life Membership Fund Receipts and Disbursements for the year ended 31st
            December, 1923.
        Alumnæ Entertainment Fund Receipts and Disbursements for the year ended
            31st December, 1923.
        Life Membership Fund Securities owned, 31st December, 1923, at cost.
        Carola Woerishoffer Fund Securities owned, 31st December, 1923, at book
            values.
                            Very truly yours,
                                LYBRAND, ROSS BROS. & MONTGOMERY.

REPORT OF FINANCE COMMITTEE

The work of the Finance Committee during the past year has centered chiefly in the question of the erection of a Students' Building, and the allotment of the Alumnae Fund—together with questions relating to the Fund.

Two of these questions, that of pensioning the employees of the College, and the purchase of Doctor Scott's library, were brought before the Council in November with the result that the Council recommended to the Joint Committee the buying of the library. The Council also passed a motion that the Alumnae Directors report to the Annual Meeting with regard to the policy of the College on the question of pensions for employees. An accompanying sense of the meeting was expressed that the pensioning of the employees of the College was not within the province of the Alumnae Association.

The Council recommended also to the Joint Committee an increase in the Rhoads Scholarships from $250 to $500 each; said increase to be made yearly from the Alumnae Fund until the needed endowment of $10,000 is completed.

New interest was given to the work for the Alumnae Fund by listening to Mr. Thompson, Secretary of the Yale Alumni Fund, who spoke before the Finance Committee in February.

Other subjects discussed and acted upon by the Finance Committee were the addition of $500 to be added to the budget as a reserve fund; the taking over by the Alumnae of the publication of the Register; the Summer School and the Music Department. These, while of immediate interest and concern for the Alumnae, were felt to be beyond the scope of the fund, which would be used to greater advantage in the smaller needs of the College. This feeling was true also in regard to the Students' Building; a proposition that will have to be taken up by the College and Alumnae through some other channel.

The success of the fund, now amounting to $16,801.75, is remarkable, and should be a source of pride and enthusiasm not only to the Class Collectors but also to the Alumnae who have contributed so generously and freely to it.

The objects suggested for the Alumnae Fund for 1924 by the Joint Committee, and submitted to the Alumnae Association for approval are:

1. Alumnae Association expenses.
2. President Park's Fund.
3. Doctor Scott's Library.
4. $10,000 endowment for increasing the James E. Rhoads' Sophomore and Junior Scholarships from $250-500 each. (Increase to be made yearly from the Alumnae Fund until endowment is completed.)
5. Library.
   a. Endowment for increase of books.
   b. Current book expenses.
6. Building Fund.
   a. Students' Building.
   b. Alterations in Taylor for more classrooms, etc., and better administration offices.
   c. Enlargement of power house facilities for proposed Students' Building, etc.
   d. Wing of Library. (This is being covered by special funds.)
7. Permanent endowment for the College.

Respectfully submitted,
ELIZABETH CALDWELL FOUNTAIN.

REPORT OF THE ALUMNAE DIRECTORS

During the past year there has been one change in the Alumnae Directors. The term of Margaret Ayer Barnes expired in December and the Board saw her leave with much regret. Her record of continuous attendance at the meetings has been extraordinary and throughout her term on the Board she rendered the College faithful and efficient service. Anne Lawther is the newly-elected Alumnae Director, her term beginning in December, 1923. She comes to the Board of Directors with a record behind her of long service to the College as warden, secretary and registrar. The Board of Directors is very glad to welcome her to its membership.

The Directors of Bryn Mawr College, like most boards of directors, conduct their business through committees some of which meet frequently and some seldom. These committees are as follows:

The *Executive Committee*, which makes

all academic appointments and has power to act in the summer during the intervals of the Board meetings;

The *Finance Committee*, which performs the ordinary duties of a finance committee, passes upon the budget and takes care of the funds of the College;

The *Buildings and Grounds Committee*, which has charge of the College plant, recommends and supervises alterations and repairs to the buildings, cares for the grounds and mechanical departments of the College and has general charge of the men employed on the campus and in the power house.

The Executive and Buildings and Grounds Committees function throughout the year. The Library Committee of the Directors meet twice a year with a committee of the faculty and the Librarian. It hears requests from the departments for books and periodicals and grants these requests so far as the funds allow. The more money it has to spend, the more efficiently this committee can function. Nothing is so disheartening as to cut in two the reasonable requests of a department.

There are also committees on the religious life of the college, the Phebe Anna Thorne School and on the Summer School.

Among the twenty-one members of the Board there are now nine Alumnae. Besides the five Alumnae elected by the Alumnae Association there are President Park, Anna Rhoads Ladd, one of the thirteen Trustees all of whom are members of the Society of Friends, and Marion Reilly and Caroline Slade, Directors-at-large. The Alumnae serve on all committees except the Finance Committee. The Executive Committee, which is the most important of all, consists of ten members, six of whom are Alumnae,—President Park, Anna Rhoads Ladd, Marion Reilly, Caroline Slade, Frances Hand and Pauline Goldmark. There

are three Alumnae among the eight members of the Committee on Buildings and Grounds, — President Park, Martha G. Thomas and Louise Francis. On the Library Committee are President Park and Anne Lawther. On the Religious Life Committee are President Park and Marion Reilly. On the Summer School Committee, besides President Park, who is chairman of the Joint Administrative Committee, are Frances Hand and Pauline Goldmark. On the Phebe Anna Thorne School Committee are President Park and Louise Francis. The Alumnae will be interested to know that President-Emeritus Thomas is serving on the Committee on Buildings and Grounds and on the Phebe Anna Thorne School Committee.

Besides these standing committees there has been formed this year at the request of the Alumnae, a Joint Committee of directors and Alumnae to consider the needs of the College. This committee has met twice and as a result of its deliberations the Finance Committee of the Alumnae Association is prepared to make recommendations to the Association for the expenditure of the Alumnae Fund.

During the year the Alumnae have made gifts to the College amounting to $48,033.08. This includes money raised for the Bryn Mawr Summer School. The Board of Directors at its last meeting passed the following motion:

"It was voted to authorize the Alumnae Directors to convey to the Bryn Mawr Association the deep appreciation and very cordial thanks of the Directors for the generous gifts of the Alumnae during the past year."

The gifts received by the College through alumnae for the calendar year 1923 were as follows:

Received at College:

Regional Scholarships	$4,305.00
For Art Department	89.37
For Greek Literature Prize	50.00
From Helen Rubel for Fellowships	1,899.34
Through Mrs. Vauclain (for Athletic Association, salary of Assistant Director)	1,500.00
Through Doris Earle for Scholarships and Grants	550.00
Through Mrs. Cecil Barnes and Martha G. Thomas for the Patterson windows in Pembroke	1,050.00
For President's Fund	1,000.00

For 1914's Class Tree 25.00
Two months' salary, W. Nelson 190.00
For Library from Undergraduate Book Club and the
    Readers 128.00
Anonymous for wood for the Library 60.00
For books for Library from
    Madge Miller $500.00
    Alice Russell 20.00
    Marion Reilly 100.00
    Class of 1914 .... 256.00
    Alumnae Association 500.00
    Alumnae Book Club .... 78.50 ———
                                          1,454.50 ———
                                                  12,301.21

Received by the Treasurer
    To found Class of 1924 Book Fund 1,000.00
    To found Class of 1898 reunion gift for New Book Room Fund 1,500.00
    Added to M. Carey Thomas Prize Fund..................... 9,045.50
    Added to Students' Building Fund 4,978.74
                                                     28,825.45

Departments
    For Grace Dodge $1,775.00
    For Music Department 9,045.50
    Summer School 6,731.00
                                                     17,551.50

Two hundred and ninety-five dollars, which was received from District V during 1922 is to be added to the $4305 donated in 1923.

The Undergraduate Book Club and the Readers are two groups of students who donated a sum for books. Some of these students are now Alumnae.

The donors to the Departments are not all Alumnae. Twenty-five dollars of the Grace Dodge Department was donated by a Mr. Kendall, $1750 by an Alumna. The Music Department money was all raised by Alumnae but several donations are included from others, such as Mr. A. Strauss, Mr. Howard L. Goodhart, Mr. Cyrus H. K. Curtis, and the Glee Club.

A gift of $1676.13 is received today from the Alumnae Association from class collections which is not included in the list as it is not recorded on the college books until 1924.

One of the functions of the Board of Directors is to pass upon changes in the Self-Government By-Laws where they affect a fundamental change. One such change has been passed upon this year after it had passed the Students' Association of Self-Government and had the approval of the President. It is as follows:

"That the following exception to what is now resolution 14,—'that students shall not go in the evening to places of entertainment without a chaperon,' be made; namely, 'that three or more students may go unchaperoned to concerts or the opera at the Academy of Music, provided that they return immediately to the College.'"

A year ago a similar change was made allowing students to attend the movies in Bryn Mawr and Ardmore.

One matter of interest has recently been brought to the attention of the Board of Directors by the faculty. It seems that at present foreign students are being detained and quarantined and actually deported if the quotas of their respective countries are filled. The faculty and Board of Directors have sent petitions to Washington and it is hoped that with the new immigration bill bona fide students will be exempt from the quota rule.

The chief enterprise of the Board this year, over and above routine, has been the building of the President's House, not all that could be desired architecturally, but pleasant and commodius and well adapted to college entertaining.

At the Council meeting, in St. Louis, in November, the Council requested the Alumnae Directors to ascertain the policy of the College with regard to the pensioning of employees. Since that time the President, the Comptroller and the supervising housekeeper have been preparing figures. It is impossible for the College to commit itself at this time with regard to a policy and the Directors are unable at this time to state a definite policy with regard to any employee because the decision in the case of one employee commits the College to a policy.

REPORT OF THE ACADEMIC COMMITTEE

The Academic Committee of the Bryn Mawr Alumnae Association has had an honorable and useful career now extending over many years. Of late, however, the further need of the Academic Committee has come into question largely because of the admission to the Board of Directors of Bryn Mawr College of a number of Alumnae Directors. The inauguration of a new administration and the reorganization of the Alumnae Association have also affected the status of the Committee as an essential or necessary factor in the life of the College. The members of the Academic Committee were themselves perhaps the first to raise the question of the continuance of the committee.

In order that this whole matter may be more clearly understood by those who are but dimly aware of the many functions performed by the Academic Committee since its creation, it may be well to take time for a brief review of the history of the Committee and what it has accomplished since its creation.

The Academic Committee was founded to be the official channel of communication between the Alumnae and the College. A charter, which hangs, framed, in a corridor in Taylor Hall, established this official status. In its earliest days, it dealt with a great variety of problems and the old minutes of its meetings are a storehouse of questions and suggestions on every phase of college life that might interest or stir devoted Alumnae. We find in the minutes exhaustive reports on students' expenses, professors' pensions, on the sectioning of larger classes, on health and hygiene, on comprehensive examinations and honor courses and a great variety of other things. Many fundamental problems have been considered by one generation after another of Academic Committees. Notable among such ever-recurring matters are methods of teaching, the lecture system and quizzes, the curriculum, graduate school affairs, orals, entrance examinations. Not infrequently the thought and suggestions of the Alumnae expressed through the Academic Committee proved useful and occasionally the findings of the Committee became formulated in the policy of the College.

Essentially the purpose of the Academic Committee has been two-fold,—on the one hand to gather and present to the President and Faculty the views of the Alumnae at large on academic matters, and on the other hand to bring to the Alumnae Association a knowledge of academic development within the College. Lately the Academic Committee has also acted as a Conference Committee and has met regularly with committees of the graduate and undergraduate student bodies to discuss with them current academic questions. This seemed a wise and helpful extension of its activities.

The membership of the Committee has always been composed, in a large measure, of Alumnae actively engaged in teaching in schools and colleges, thus putting to the service of Bryn Mawr what might be termed the expert knowledge and advice of her own best qualified Alumnae. This fact is doubly important because Alumnae who are connected with the faculties of other institutions are not eligible to serve Bryn Mawr as Alumnae Directors.

The presence on the Academic Committee of Alumnae holding important positions in schools and other colleges has also proved invaluable when the Committee wished to gather material for comparative studies of progressive movements undertaken by other institutions. This facility of the Academic Committee to gather information from other colleges, proved of great help to the Alumnae Association when a few years ago the Alumnae body decided upon a change of organization. The present constitution of the Association—with its representative council—is founded in large part on the studies and recommendations made by the Academic Committee.

It was at the time of the reorganization that the question of superceding the committee was first raised. The suggestion was then made that perhaps the newly-created Council might take over the functions of the Academic Committee. Experience seems to have shown, however, quite conclusively that the activities of the Academic Committee and the activities of the Council are totally dissimilar, and can never very advantageously be combined.

Lately another proposal has been made: namely, that our now greatly enlarged body of Alumnae Directors might take over some, if not all, of the functions of the Academic Committee. In so far as the original charter goes, as official channel of communication between Alumnae and the college the Academic Committee has already been superceded by the Alumnae Directors whom the Association elects to be its representatives on the Board of Trustees of the College. Can the Alumnae Directors supplant the Academic Committee altogether?

In the hope that the question of the continuance of the Academic Committee might receive a definitive settlement, a joint meeting was called last spring of the Academic Committee and the Alumnae members of the Board of Directors, the President and Dean of the College, the President of the Alumnae Association and some members of the Bryn Mawr Faculty.

In preparation for this meeting the Academic Committee wrote to a number of former members of the Committee, whose present positions and attainments make their judgment on such a problem of special value. Excerpts from the letters received in answer, were read at the joint meeting and served to stimulate discussion. May I take time to quote from some of these letters now?

One of our most distinguished Alumnae, a former chairman of the Committee wrote, "I think the Alumnae Directors have quite a different function and that they could not replace the Academic Committee on the Academic side. I also believe in the free lance standing of the Academic Committee, though some delimitation of its functions should be made."

Another Alumna holding an important position in one of the large sister colleges, expressed herself as follows: "I think we have a real function, and ought to continue. The presence of a group of Alumnae specially interested in the educational work of the college, and known by faculty and Alumnae to be an *active* committee, keeping up its own lines of observation and investigation—this will give faculty or Alumnae a group to turn to for informed Alumnae opinion, a group in which they can have confidence that they would not have if we were a quiescent committee inactive except when called on for opinion. I do think a somewhat more informal and flexible arrangement as regards meetings with the faculty committee would be a great improvement (now that conditions are changed). I should like to have us continue as an active committee, free to ask for consultations with President, Dean, faculty committees whenever we wished, and ready to be consulted whenever anyone in the College desired."

One who holds a high place in the faculty of a New England women's college writes: "I think the Academic Committee a useful body, not the less so because it isn't, at every moment, occupied with burning issues. I think it useful to have the Committee on hand in case the Alumnae have an idea or a grievance, so that these may be rationally treated instead of creating diffused discontent."

An official in the same college, a former graduate student of Bryn Mawr, viewed the matter from a somewhat different angle. She says: "I should hope that it ought not to be necessary to have a committee always on the alert as in the earlier academic committee days to pound at certain things, such as sectioning of minor Latin, orals, science, entrance physiology, etc. It would also seem to me that the presence of a well-chosen Alumnae Director with educational experience and interest might keep the Alumnae Association informed of the academic matters at the college."

Another Alumna, who has made a distinguished name for herself in science, has this to say: "I'm emphatically for keeping the Academic Committee. When I was first on it it bewildered me. I saw no reason why I, knowing so little of the college affairs, should meddle with them. I thought it very long suffering of the president and Faculty to meet with us. But before I left I became extremely impressed with the Academic Committee and what it accomplished off and on. We are directly responsible during the last few years for three things: opening the M. A. degree to students of other colleges, revising the orals—to bring back German, and modifying the entrance examinations to a really remarkable extent.

"Now those three changes may net have been wise, but I think they were, and they are certainly very vital. I think we served the College really very well indeed and certainly tried to study the changes we proposed quite thoroughly before suggesting them."

Another Alumna, principal of an important secondary school, expresses her views as follows: "As I think of the situation in general, I should say that very likely with the system of faculty committees working well and faculty government in open co-operation with the executive, it might easily be that the Academic Committee work in its present character might not be necessary. I have always felt that a college Alumnae Association should have an Education Committee and be definitely committed to a policy of keeping up with educational interests and developments in its various communities, should keep up with its teachers and demand from them such data as will make it a useful and intelligent body! Such a committee might be of advisory use to the Faculty and College and would be an organ through which the Alumnae could do initiatory work if it wished, perhaps with the aid of the directors."

Finally, a former chairman of the Academic Committee and now an Alumnae Director writes:

"Whatever changes may seem advisable I do hope that the entity of the Committee will be preserved. It does seem to me to have a reason for existing, as an agency for getting information from 'outside' in educational matters and especially to interest the new educational policies of the College to the Alumnae. There seems real need for a committee for this purpose, as the Alumnae directors will always need to be on their guard not to seem in any way to interfere with academic policies. I do wish, however, that the Alumnae directors and the Academic Committee could function more as a unit. This seems to me a real need."

The discussion that followed was animated and covered, I believe, virtually every phase of the subject. President Park, by her keen analysis of the problem showed a deep understanding of its various implications. She spoke of the desirability of giving to the Alumnae Directors specific functions covering the work hitherto done by the Academic Committee. The amount of help that at present comes from the Alumnae Directors in the academic field is very small. Directors' meetings do not concern themselves with educational matters. And yet what Alumnae are chiefly interested in, is having the College in the forefront educationally.

By removing the restriction that forbids the election of Alumnae Directors from the staffs of other colleges, Bryn Mawr could avail herself of the educational point of view of such Alumnae. Yet in practice it might be very difficult for women in active teaching work to serve as Directors, as they could scarcely give the time for such service.

Perhaps the Academic Committee could be a purely professional committee to work as a sub-committee under the Faculty, Board of Directors or President, and give information about other colleges. School representatives might be added to put at the disposal of the College the same kind of information about secondary education. This committee could also be used to spread information among the Alumnae. The advantage of this is only that it might save reduplication and would add to the value of the Alumnae Directors by keeping them in connection with the educational policy of the College.

These interesting suggestions of President Park were fully discussed. A number of other proposals were made. One was that an educational secretary take the place of the committee. This did not rouse much enthusiasm. More favorably received was the suggestion that a large number of Alumnae holding academic positions in other colleges and in schools be appointed as an inactive advisory committee to be consulted in case of need. The objections to this plan are that such a large group would be a committee only in name; that it would lack the identity, the continuity of purpose and the cohesion of a real committee. Furthermore, it is always possible for Bryn Mawr to call upon these scattered Alumnae for information and reports on specific questions without designating them members of a committee.

It was suggested that the Academic Committee might serve merely as an education committee to keep the Alumnae in touch with educational movements in the world. The reply to this was that a committee of such limited powers would not be of great value to the College or to the Alumnae. Moreover, there are existing channels through which such information can be readily obtained.

All agreed upon the necessity of keeping the Alumnae informed regarding the educational policies of the College, but there was no unanimity of opinion as to how this could best be accomplished.

Perhaps the most significant proposal was that the work of the Academic Committee be taken over by the Alumnae Directors. A seemingly fundamental objection to this plan, however, is based upon the fact that the directors, having delegated to the Faculty all academic authority, do not concern themselves with those educational matters in which the faculties are paramount. The Alumnae Directors as such could therefore not very well assume the activities of the Academic Committee.

Another idea that was repeatedly stressed was the need of a closer contact between the Academic Committee and the Faculty of the College. The work of the Committee would gain greatly in directness and efficiency by having more definite Faculty affiliation.

One further point that was brought out very clearly in the conference was this: the President of the College should be aided in whatever she is undertaking and should be spared any unnecessary complication and effort.

As a result of all the varying ideas brought forward in the meeting a proposal finally took form that a joint committee be organized on which some Alumnae Directors and some members of the Bryn Mawr Faculty might be asked to serve, together with a number of Alumnae teaching in other colleges and schools, who should be selected especially with a view to their educational qualifications.

This plan was embodied in the following recommendations which were sent last spring to the Executive Board of the Alumnae Association:

The Academic Committee desires to submit to the Executive Board of the Alumnae Association the following report.

Owing to the increased number of Alumnae on the Board of Directors of Bryn Mawr College, and owing likewise to the inauguration of a new administration, the question has arisen whether the Academic Committee, from its creation until now a useful channel of communication between the Alumnae and the College, should be continued in its present form. After prolonged discussion among themselves, with the Alumnae Directors, with members of the Faculty, and with President Park, the Academic Committee has concluded that the Academic Committee should be continued, but that the functions which it has hitherto performed may perhaps be carried on with more directness and efficiency by an Academic Committee of somewhat different constitution. To this end the Committee would make the following recommendations:

1. That the experiment be tried of having the membership of the Academic Committee made up approximately as follows, two Alumnae Directors, two members of the Bryn Mawr Faculty who are Bryn Mawr Alumnae, and of the remaining members two at least to be actively engaged in teaching, one of them in a secondary school. The Academic Committee feels that the proposed change of personnel will result in eliminating duplication of work and in promoting co-ordinated effort.

2. That the Committee thus constituted should, to insure its usefulness, be an active working committee, and should continue to serve both the Alumnae and the College as a channel of information and constructive suggestion in regard to educational matters.

These recommendations were accompanied by the resignations of the Academic Committee, and by lists of names suggested for a committee reconstituted according to the new plan.

The Executive Board after receiving the communications of the Academic Committee, decided to defer action pending a discussion of the resolution in the council and in the annual meeting of the Alumnae Association. I have therefore been requested to lay the matter before you today for your consideration and decision.

Respectfully submitted,
ELEANOR FLEISHER RIESMAN.

CLASS NOTES

1904

Class Editor, Emma O. Thompson, 320 S. Forty-second Street, Philadelphia, Pa.

Eleanor Bliss Knopf and Anna Jones read papers at the meeting of the Geological Society of America held in Washington in December.

Gertrude Klein published an article in the November number of the *National Educational Journal,* telling of her work with the Freshmen in the Southern High School of Philadelphia. She has published a pamphlet called "Freshman First-Aid."

Marjorie Canan Fry's two daughters, who are spending the year in England, spent a delightful afternoon recently with Hope Allen in her home in Cheney Row, London.

Esther Sinn Neuendorffer has a son, born on February 3rd.

Edith McMurtrie has been appointed teacher of Art in the William Penn High School of Philadelphia. Her pictures have been shown this winter in Trenton and at the Plastic Club of Philadelphia, and also at the Corcoran Art Gallery in Washington.

Mary Christie Nute (Mrs. William L. Nute) has returned to Turkey with her husband, who is a physician, and her two sons, Billy and Cyril. Her eldest son, Miner Rogers, is staying in America with his grandmother. Mary's address is American Hospital, Adana, Turkey.

The following members of 1904 were back for the Alumnae Meeting and Luncheon at Bryn Mawr in February: Martha Rockwell, Gertrude Buffum, Amy Clapp, Marjorie Canan Fry, Emma Fries, Mary Lamberton, Edith McMurtrie, Emma Thompson, and Alice Waldo.

1906

Class Editor, Mrs. Harold K. Beecher, 1511 Mahantongo Street, Pottsville, Pa.

Our Class baby, Molly Walcott, is taller than her mother and much better looking than her mother ever thot of being (this according to Mary). She has put up her hair, goes to dances, is quick at her lessons, loves sports, is on good terms with her brothers (who really are pretty nice), and altogether is very normal, healthy and satisfactory. Of course, she is going to Bryn Mawr. She is properly trained in modern

ways so that she expects her parents will skate and dance and play tennis until they are seventy. But does she stand in awe of them? Oh, no.

Ethel De Koven writes of "Jack" Hudson, her elder son, aged ten, that he is doing extremely well at school. "He has had thirteen hundreds in succession in spelling, which sets a school record. His instinct for knowledge is terrier-like, for he worries and shakes at you with questions until he has extracted every bit you know from the recesses of your memory. The other day he asked about the theory and composition of the universe, and I had to call on every atom of learning I ever possessed to answer his queries. He is evidently cut out for a lawyer."

Reggie, born on his grandfather's birthday and named after him, is five years old. He is being taught a few odds and ends at his mother's knee and appears to like it much better than his mother ever did, though his mind does not seem so keen.

Charles Prichard (Marion Mudge's oldest child) was thrown while riding a motorcycle and has been in a hospital for several months and is now convalescing from a serious operation. Charles is sixteen years old. Billie, aged nine, has just had his tonsils out, so Marion is busy amusing her two invalids. Katherine, aged fourteen, is at Rogers Hall, Lowell, preparing for Bryn Mawr, to enter in 1926.

Lucia Ford is entirely too silent concerning the four little Rutters, Elizabeth, Peter, Patty and Tom, ages ten to four. They are devoted to farm life and resent any request to go near Philadelphia or even to Pottstown. They do go to school at Pottstown, which is five miles from the farm. Their mother writes she cannot say she is preparing her daughters for B. M., for she doubts the wisdom of keying a child up to such a standard as is required there now, but thinks educational ideas may change.

Beth Harrington Brooks is equally uncommunicative with four to talk about, but all four are attending an open-air school in Cambridge and it seems to agree with them physically, mentally and morally.

Helen Brown Gibbons writes glowingly of her brood (thus it is to have an authoress-mother) and suggests the editor send a round robin to the class with news of all its children. (Editor is willing. Come on, 1906.)

Christine Gibbons is as tall as her mother and slightly heavier. She is blue-eyed and has a gorgeous mane of goldy-brown curls, and wants to put it up. "Is giving her first dance, February 29th, with a mob of Princeton students to help her see that we do not have a single wallflower. She hates mathematics, but she loves to write, and has written and produced in our house twelve plays for children. Has done some short stories and this winter is devoting her spare time to planning a series of books, juveniles, of which the first volume is on the way. Although she was born in a school house where there were 350 people and a hideous massacre was raging—she is the most placid person I know. I call her my "old reliable." She has been entered at Bryn Mawr. Will probably go about 1927. Date indefinite at present because we are planning another year in France in the near future."

Lloyd, twelve years old, is the most ardent Princeton fan in the U. S. A. He is clever at drawing or modeling maps of the countries his father writes about. Sings in the Episcopal choir and is a Tenderfoot Scout. Both he and Christine are good horsemen and ride with the soldiers of the Princeton Field Artillery Unit.

Mimi, aged ten, wants to meet Pavlowa. "I want to dance for her so as to find out whether my talent is going to be a profession or is only something for domestic purposes."

And Hope, aged eight, is well into the second year of Latin.

Yes! they make a sure-enough "Gibbons Good Gang."

1908

Class Editor, Mrs. W. H. Best, 1198 Bushwick Avenue, Brooklyn, N. Y.

Helen Shurbert, of the class of 1908 was taken ill on Thanksgiving Day, and died a week later from chronic heart trouble and the complications resulting from it. She was at Bryn Mawr College a year and a half, and then had to leave because of her mother's death, and her own ill health. However, these handicaps only delayed her education. She persisted in spite of them, and received her A. B. from Goucher in 1916. Since then, she has been teaching,— first in the public schools of Baltimore, and

later in the Teachers' Training School, where she was instructor in the theory of Arithmetic and Geography at the time of her death. As a class, we pay honor to her brave spirit, undaunted by suffering, and send our deepest sympathy to her family and friends.

Margaret Duncan Miller (Mrs. Geo. F. Miller) reports that a husband and two small sons, one three years old and the other a year and a half, occupy most of her time and thoughts; but that a French study class and a Drama study class, both made up of Faculty members and their wives, are stimulating and help her keep out of too deep a rut. Margaret is connected with the University of Oklahoma.

Nellie Seeds Nearing (Mrs. Scott Nearing) writes: "I am still married, living happily with my family on a farm twenty-three miles outside of New York City, where I commute every day. I have a full-time job as Associate Educational Director of the Rand School of Social Science. I have also published two books of my husband, "The Next Step" and "Oil and the Germs of War," and one book of poems by Ralph Chaplin, "Bars and Shadows." My oldest son is almost ready for high school, but we are famous pals and far from feeling old, I feel younger each year. I don't know whether it is second childhood or arrested development. But I find life more wonderful, more stimulating, and more worth while every year."

From Helen Cadbury Bush (Mrs. Arthur Bush) comes a delightful sketch of life in Sommerfield, Bovey-Tracey, S. Devon, England. We housekeepers in free America, struggling with "helpless help" can heave an envious sigh when we read Cad's letter: "My dear, now can you beat that? Four paragraphs, to my address, four twigs to the Cadbury-Bush, and four servants to match 'em. You ask for private life. There isn't any such thing in an ancient English village. The town crier sees to that and he is ably assisted by every cottager in Bovey-Tracey. This is what 'every lady' knows, so I'll let you in on it. The three maids get up before dawn and scrub and scour and polish and dust a house that is already perfectly clean. Nurse gets the four children in line for breakfast and as for me, why, I just turn over and take another nap.

"At 9.30 I stroll down to breakfast, where

my father is reading the *Times* all properly aired in front of a coal fire. Then the governess comes for the two older youngsters, and nurse goes a-pramming with the two babies. If I can get a whack at the *Times* I take it, and if I can't I go to see if the tits need a new piece of cocoanut or if the peas are up or if any snowdrops need cutting. When the governess leaves, my hard work begins, for I have to exercise the children and get up an appetite for that roast beef of old England plugged down with boiled pudding. Off we start through the rain and mud of this bewildering Devon country. Dartmouth is just beside us, crowned with that great rock Hayther. Little streams, red Devon cows, thatched farm houses, quickset hedges, a hunt ariding by, jaunting carts, all the daily English things that we enjoy so much are ours for a few seconds' brisk walking. "Dinner is a rite, and needs another tramp to work it off. We had to abolish tea. Sheer incapacity. And we have met with many other defeats along the same line. However, this holiday in England is a tremendous lark. Best love to everybody. Cad."

The four servants for the four twigs are Edith (cook, the Queen-mother), Gertrude (housemaid, parlor, maid, the Queen), Milly (scullery maid) and "Nurse." The four twigs are Deblois, Anne Head, A. P. B. 3rd, and Martha Comfort.

1910

Class Editor, Marion Kirk, 4504 Chester Avenue, Philadelphia, Pa.

A. Maris Boggs in December became Director of the Bureau of Commercial Economics, assuming full charge of the organization. The free educational films of the Bureau are now sent in weekly shipments to all parts of the world.

Gertrude Kingsbacher Sunstein is completely occupied with the business proposition of making the Community School of Pittsburgh a financial and educational success, and this job, together with managing four small children, is all that Gertrude finds time to do.

Katharine Liddell exhibited last summer in the annual exhibition of the Provincetown Art Association, and at Miss Grace Horne's gallery in Gloucester, and in October at the Arts and Crafts Club in New Orleans, and she expects soon to show two small canvasses at the Boston Art Club.

Lucie Reichenbach Sayler announces the birth of a daughter, Ida Lou, on November 27, 1923. She also reports the completion of twenty-five illustrations for her husband's book, "Our American Theatre," which appeared recently, and the publication, in portfolio form, of her sketches made in Salzburg, Austria, last summer. The Saylers are now living in Hartsdale, New York.

Mary Boyd Shipley Mills reports from China that she is president of the Bryn Mawr Club of China, an organization now in process of voting whether to live or to die. Her two children take most of her time, but she also does a little teaching, entertains guests going through Nanking, has a Sunday School teachers' training class, and enjoys life generally. She expresses the wish that the members of the Bryn Mawr Alumnae who from the BULLETIN are traveling in China would drop in on her and give her a chance to extend a welcome to them.

Julia Thompson Turner has a daughter, Julia, born October 21, 1923. She says she and baby Julie have an hour's exercise each day during which they pace the floor and sing to the glory of Bryn Mawr and 1910. Julie is not yet ready to make a statement as to the relation of art to domestic life, but says emphatically that she feels no regret over the years spent in art and athletics rather than in studying domestic science.

Florence Wilbur Wyckoff writes from Norway that they are having a delightful winter at the head of a fiord surrounded by lofty mountains. They ski and coast and go sleigh riding for daily exercise. There are quite a few nice English-speaking people in the village where she is staying. Florence and her family expect to return to America in the spring.

1914

Class Editor, Dr. Ida W. Pritchett, The Rockefeller Institute, 66th Street and Avenue A, New York City.

Marion Camp Newberry (Mrs. Roger Newberry) has been traveling in the Orient with her husband this winter. She expected to return some time in February.

Elizabeth Atherton, ex-1914, is living in New York this winter and is doing dietetic work with undernourished children. She is living with her sister, Mrs. Donald Storrs Bridgman, 1913, at 27 Beekman Place.

1916

Class Editor, Mrs. Webb I. Vorys, 63 Parkwood Avenue, Columbus, O.

Katherine Scriven was married on January 31 at her father's house in Washington to Mr. Detlow M. Marthinson. Her address is 714 E. Garfield Street, Glendale, California.

Chloe McKeefry Usis (Mrs. Felix Max Usis) has a young son Felix, junior, born December 12th, 1923.

Rebecca Fordyce Gayton (Mrs. Oscar F.) has a young son, George Fordyce Gayton, born on August 23, 1923.

Kathryne Batchelder Smythe has a daughter born in October.

Lucretia Garfield writes: "Having summarized my activities last year as divided between scouting in the southern mountains, filling out at Pine Mountain Settlement School, Kentucky, and trying to second mother as hostess at the Institute of Politics here in August, I have little to add this year, excepting to say that the development of the Girl Scout work in the southern mountains continues to be my first interest.

"I have been back at Pine Mountain School this fall and shall return there in March for five or six weeks. During January and February I am hoping to give short training courses for Girl Scout Leaders at Berea, Lincoln Memorial University, and Eastern Kentucky State Normal School."

1916!! All hail!

This June will witness the greatest reunion of the class ever held. MAKE READY NOW. Don't disappoint any of us by not coming. We need a reunion with every member answering "present" to the roll call. Bring your sunny face and make this a *real occasion.* 1915, 1917, 1918 are coming back in throngs, and so are WE!

1918

Class Editor, Mrs. Julian B. Cohn, 5154 Westminster Place, St. Louis, Mo.

Mary Scott is studying at the Sorbonne.

Harriet Hobbs Haines has a second son, Frederick, born on the sixth of December.

Evelyn Babbitt is engaged to Mr. A. W. Hastings, an engineer. After their marriage they will live in Michigan.

Gertrude Reymershoffer was married in December to Dr. Thomas St. Clair Cuddy. They are living at 125 Audubon Road, Boston.

Jeanette Ridlon Piccard writes that she spent the summer in the Swiss mountains, protecting her child from his cousins and his cousins from him.

Mary Safford Hoogewerff is living in Long Beach, California, to be near her husband, who is stationed on the U. S. S. Oklahoma. She saw Margaret Worch in Tacoma.

Rebecca Rhoads is in New York, living at 2 Gramercy Park.

Gladys Barnett spent the summer, she writes, "studying the occult writings of Rudolph Stein at his colony in Dornack, Switzerland, and clambering over the heathery hills of Wales up among the old Druid arches."

Virginia Pomeroy McIntyre is remodeling an old farm house on Long Island.

As spring draws near, 1918's thoughts turn toward Reunion, and then we are confronted by a dilemma. Can we go both to May Day and to Reunion, and if not, which not? It is too bad that we have both the same year, but the College wouldn't change, and we can't help our age. But we hope that if anyone is in doubt, she will finally decide on Reunion, for we are very anxious to get together as many of our classmates as we possibly can.

If someone should announce a prize for the Busiest Person in the class, I think Annette Gest would have a very good chance at it; she is teaching full time at the Agnes Irwin School in Philadelphia, and giving a five-hour course at College in addition. But she has promised to be our Reunion Manager and she will keep you posted from time to time as to the development of our plans. She will appoint an Athletic Committee and a Costume Committee to help her, while Louise Hodges Crenshaw, as previously announced, will be Toast-Mistress at the Banquet and Sidney Belville Coale will make the Banquet arrangements.

Another big piece of work which is already under way is the editing of the Class Book. We know that, under the capable direction of Helen Walker, this will prove to be an interesting and varied record of 1918's "past." If each member of the class will answer Helen's inquiries fully and promptly, it will simplify her task very much, and help to make complete our record of six years' attainments.

1920
Class Editor, Helene Zinsser, 6 West Ninth Street, New York City.

Children to

Helen Hartman Russell (Mrs. Henry Allan Russell), a second son, Bruce Hardy, born last spring.

Dorothy Griggs Murray (Mrs. Francis King Murray), a second daughter, Carolyn Lee Murray, born December 17th.

Helen Humphrey Jackson (Mrs. William Ratcliffe Jackson), a son born December 13th.

Engaged

Margaret Ballou to David Hitchcock, Dartmouth, '15, now doing research work at Rockefeller Institute.

Nominee for Hall of Fame!

First 1920 to go into politics (evidence just unearthed by Detective Gookin):

"Belinda" Rood was elected a committee-woman in Evanston with a grand total of eight votes, which is a landslide in Republican Evanston, and this January was a delegate from Evanston to the Democratic Star Advisory Convention in Springfield.

Vocations

Anne Coolidge: studying at Recreation Training School in Chicago.

Social Notes

Dorothy Jenkins: sailed on Cunard liner "Samaria," January 26, for a trip round the world.

Nat Gookin: having Anne Coolidge to spend every week-end and going to the opera with Belinda Rood Saturday afternoons.

Dilatory Domiciles

Dorothy Griggs Murray (Mrs. Francis King Murray), 41 Chilton Avenue, Garden City, Long Island.

Virginia Park Shook (Mrs. John Hoover Shook), 2519 Thayer Street, Evanston, Ill.

Anne Coolidge, Chicago Commons Settlement, Chicago, Ill.

Joe Herrick, Pebble Hill Plantation, Ga., recuperating from "flu."

Esther Jenkins Willcox (Mrs. Westmore Willcox), Bronxville, N. Y.

Anne Eberbach Augsburg (Mrs. Paul D. Augsburg), 10 East Erie Street, Chicago, Ill.

1922
Class Editor, Serena Hand, 48 W. Ninth Street, New York City.

Emily Anderson sailed for England the 29th of December to be gone until the middle of March.

Ursula Batchelder is teaching at a school somewhere in Wisconsin.

Custis Bennett is a Junior bursar at the University of Pennsylvania.

Frances Bliss is sailing the end of February to join Josephine Fisher in England.

Jane Burges was married to Mr. Preston Perrinault on the 16th of January at El Paso. Mary Douglass Hay was one of the bridesmaids.

Barbara Clarke is going to California with her family for a few months. Mary Douglass Hay is going with them and is meeting them in New Orleans.

Dorothy Ferguson has gone to Florida with the little boy she is taking care of.

Olive Floyd is teaching at Westover.

Audrey Fountain is working at the Art Students' League in New York.

Story Kirkbride is living in Florence.

Marion Rawson is working in the public schools in Cincinnati, giving mental tests. Elizabeth Hall went out to stay with her during Christmas vacation.

Prue Smith has a studio in Paris and is studying art.

Jane Yeatman Savage has a son, born Sunday, January 13th.

Sylva Thurlow is at Cambridge University. Jean Gowing writes: "I had a delightful note after Christmas. It is full of enthusiasm for Wales, where she spent her Christmas holidays, and her professors under whom she is working on enzymes."

Dear 1922:

As some of you know, and as some of you do not know, at our last Reunion, which was a grand and glorious one, although we did miss those who couldn't get there most awfully, we voted to come back for an informal Reunion at May Day, instead of having the formal Reunion at Commencement. You see, next year, that is in 1925, according to the new schedule, all the classes that were in college our Freshman year will be back, to make us young again, and 1923 will be there too, so for our third anniversary, we will want to be back in great crowds. But for this year we have decided to combine the joys of seeing May Day, with the joys of seeing 1922 once again.

MARGIE TYLER.

CONTENTS

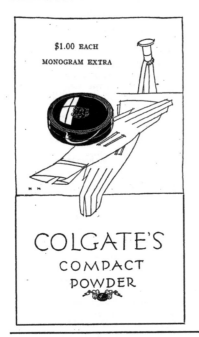
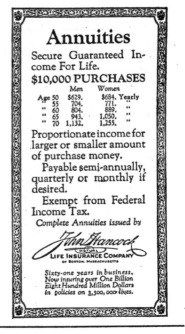

SCHOOL DIRECTORY

FERRY HALL
A Resident and Day School for Girls
LAKE FOREST, ILLINOIS
On Lake Michigan, near Chicago

College Preparatory, General and Advanced Courses, Departments of Music, Home Economics, Expression, and Art. *Supervised Athletics and Swimming Pool.*

Eloise R. Tremain, A.B., Bryn Mawr, Principal

THE

Mary C. Wheeler Town and Country School
PROVIDENCE, RHODE ISLAND

Preparation for Bryn Mawr and College Board Examinations

Out door sports   Junior Country Residence

"HILLSIDE" NORWALK, CONNECTICUT

On a hill in six acres of ground. Three residence houses. Separate School House and Gymnasium. Preparation for Comprehensive and College Board Examinations. General and Special Courses.

MARGARET R. BRENDLINGER, A. B. (Vassar)
VIDA HUNT FRANCIS, A. B., (Smith), Principals

The Harcum School
BRYN MAWR, PA.

Prepares for Bryn Mawr and all leading colleges

Musical Course prepares for the Department of Music of Bryn Mawr College

EDITH H. HARCUM, Head of School
L. MAY WILLIS, Principal

MISS RANSOM and MISS BRIDGES' SCHOOL
HAZEL LANE, PIEDMONT (Suburb of San Francisco)

College Preparatory

MARION RANSOM } Headmistresses
EDITH BRIDGES }

MISS MADEIRA'S SCHOOL
1330 19th St., N. W.   Washington, D. C.

A Resident and Day School
for Girls

LUCY MADEIRA WING, A.B.

MRS. DAVID LAFOREST WING
Head Mistress

The Shipley School
Bryn Mawr, Pennsylvania
Preparatory to Bryn Mawr College
Alice G. Howland, Eleanor O. Brownell,
Principals

The Ethel Walker School
SIMSBURY, CONNECTICUT
Head of School
ETHEL WALKER SMITH, A.M. Bryn Mawr College
Head Mistress
JESSIE GERMAIN HEWITT, A.B. Bryn Mawr College

THE MISSES KIRK'S
College Preparatory School
Bryn Mawr Ave. and Old Lancaster Road,
Bryn Mawr, Pa.

Number of boarders limited. Combines advantages of school life with private instruction. Individual schedule arranged for each pupil.

MISS WRIGHT'S SCHOOL
Bryn Mawr, Pa.

Prepares for Bryn Mawr and
College Board Examinations

Miss Beard's School for Girls
ORANGE, NEW JERSEY

A country school near New York. College preparatory, special courses. Art, Domestic Arts and Science. Supervised physical work. Agnes Miles Music School affiliated with Miss Beard's School.

MISS LUCIE C. BEARD, Head Mistress

ROSEMARY HALL
No elective courses
Prepares for college
Preferably Bryn Mawr

Caroline Ruutz-Rees, Ph.D. } Head Mistresses
Mary E. Lowndes, Litt.D. }

GREENWICH   CONNECTICUT

The Katharine Branson School
ROSS, CALIFORNIA   Across the Bay from San Francisco
A Country School   College Preparatory
Heads

Katharine Fleming Branson, A. B., Bryn Mawr
Laura Elizabeth Branson, A. B., Bryn Mawr

THE AGNES IRWIN SCHOOL
2009-2011 Delancey Place, Philadelphia
A College Preparatory
SCHOOL FOR GIRLS
JOSEPHINE A. NATT, A.B., Headmistress
BERTHA M. LAWS, A.B., Secretary-Treasurer

SCHOOL DIRECTORY

The Episcopal Academy
(Founded 1785)

CITY LINE, OVERBROOK, PA.

A country day school for boys from second grade to college. Separate lower school beginning September 1923. Enjoys the patronage of Bryn Mawr Alumnae.

WYKEHAM RISE
WASHINGTON, CONNECTICUT

*A COUNTRY SCHOOL
FOR GIRLS*

Prepares for Bryn Mawr and Other Colleges

The Baldwin School
A Country School for Girls
BRYN MAWR   PENNSYLVANIA

· Preparation for Bryn Mawr, Mount Holyoke, Smith, Vassar and Wellesley colleges. Abundant outdoor life. Hockey, basketball, tennis. ·

ELIZABETH FORREST JOHNSON, A.B.
Head

Garrison Forest School for Girls
Less than an hour from Baltimore. A country school with all city advantages, in the beautiful Green Spring Valley. Intermediate, College Preparatory, Special Music and Art Courses. Boarding Dept. limited. Horseback riding and all sports. Catalog and Views.

MISS MARY MONCRIEFFE LIVINGSTONE, Princ'pal
Box C, Garrison, Maryland

ROGERS HALL
A SCHOOL FOR GIRLS

Thorough preparation for college entrance examinations. Graduate course of two years for high school graduates. Complete equipment. 40 minutes from Boston.

MISS OLIVE SEWALL PARSONS, B.A.
Principal
Lowell, Massachusetts

Cathedral School of St. Mary
GARDEN CITY, LONG ISLAND, N. Y.

A school for Girls 19 miles from New York. College preparatory and general courses. Music. Art and Domestic Science. Catalogue on request. ·Box B.

Miriam A. Bytel, A. B., Radcliffe, Principal
Bertha Gordon Wood, A. B., Bryn Mawr, Ass't Principa

MISS GILDNER'S PRINCETON SCHOOL
FOR GIRLS

Prepares for best eastern colleges and Board examinations. Also for Advanced College-entrance Two-year Graduate Course. Music. Art. Expression. Sports. Riding. Outdoor and Indoor. Athletics. Estate of beauty. Mile from town.

Miss Laura M. Gildner, A.M., Director
Princeton, New Jersey

WOMAN'S MEDICAL COLLEGE
OF PENNSYLVANIA

Seventy-fourth year beginning Sept. 26, 1923. Entrance requirements: two years of college work including certain credits in science and languages. Excellent laboratories. Full-time teachers. Clinical advantages. Well-equipped hospital. Special eight months' course of training for laboratory technicians. The Hospital of the Woman's Medical College conducts a training school for nurses which includes the advantages of class teaching by the Faculty of the College.

For information address: The Dean
2101 North College Avenue, Philadelphia, Pa.

St. Timothy's School for Girls
CATONSVILLE, MARYLAND
Founded 1882

COLLEGE
PREPARATORY

Miss J. R. HEATH }
Miss L. McE. FOWLER } Heads of the Schoo l

Every idle stream or waterfall that is put to work, and furnishes light and power to homes and factories many miles away, means a saving in coal and, what is more important, a saving in human energies.

How far can a waterfall fall?

Improvements in electrical development do not "happen." They come from the tireless research of trained scientists. The General Electric Company invests in the work of its Research Laboratories more than a million dollars a year.

In 1891 General Electric Company equipped an electric plant at San Antonio Canyon for transmitting electric power 28 miles—a record.

Today electric power from a waterfall is carried ten times as far.

Some day remote farm homes will have electricity and streams that now yield nothing will be yielding power and light.

GENERAL ELECTRIC

The
BRYN MAWR
ALUMNAE
BULLETIN

FELLOWSHIP AWARDS

THE GRADUATE SCHOOL

THE ALUMNAE FUND

MAY DAY

APRIL

1924

Vol. IV

No. 4

Bryn Mawr Alumnae Bulletin

OFFICIAL PUBLICATION OF
THE BRYN MAWR ALUMNAE ASSOCIATION

EVELYN PAGE, '23, *Editor*

GERTRUDE J. HEARNE, '19, *Business Manager*

EDITORIAL BOARD

LUCY M. DONNELLY, '93
ELEANOR FLEISHER REISMAN, '03
CAROLINE MORROW CHADWICK-COLLINS, '05

ADELAIDE W. NEALL, '06
MAY EGAN STOKES, '11
LEILA HOUGHTELING, '11, *ex-officio*

Subscription Price, $1.50 a Year　　　　　　　　　　*Single Copies, 25 Cents*

Checks should be drawn to the order of Bryn Mawr Alumnae Bulletin
Published monthly, except August and September, at 1006 Arch St., Philadelphia, Pa.

VOL. IV　　　　　　　　　　APRIL, 1924　　　　　　　　　　No. 4

THE MUSIC DEPARTMENT

The experiment of a Department of Theoretical Music at Bryn Mawr College draws to the close of its third and final year. As the moment has approached for deciding on the permanent establishment of the department through Alumnae effort, the original committee has received satisfactory assurance that within its scope, it has proved the right to a place among the departments of a college whose scholarship is the attribute most cherished by us all. The question still to be answered before steps could be taken to secure the department to the College was whether it were desired by the Faculty and students within the walls and approved by the Alumnae without.

A fair referendum has been taken on Alumnae opinion, and the reply to the Music Committee's question is so absolute a mandate that the task of raising the necessary endowment can be undertaken with confidence. Four months general inquiry through every channel open to the committee has revealed that the experiment has been conducted, not before an especially endowed minority, but before a large and critical company, comprehending almost every Alumna, all the Faculty and all the students, the entire Bryn Mawr countryside, musicians great and small, and particularly, the fathers and mothers of the new generations on their way to the college of their choice but confronted with the possibility of sacrificing during college life a vital element of education—a company comprehending, in point of fact, that general public which we are.

This, then, is the work now before the Alumnae; we are to find the money to maintain a new department which has proved its value, offering, along with an added element of culture and enjoyment for the general college community, intellectual training of high quality in a field hitherto untouched by Bryn Mawr. This general opinion says it has done. But when all the evidence is in, the truth remains that the majority of our people believes the final warrant of any educational undertaking to lie in the measure of its ultimate service to the public. That public has in the last few years taken into its life of American drive and pressure, almost, it seems, as a measure of self-protection, the saving grace of music. The heartening tale is told by the serious study of music from the lowest to the highest class of the public or private school, the modern exacting individual training in singing and playing, the free concerts, the locally supported orchestras throughout the country, the use of music in settlements and Americanization centers, above all, by the recognition by the confessedly non-musical of music's place in every-day life. That single voice among our Western peoples whose untaught audience has always been the greatest next to Shakespeare's, is the voice of Beethoven. And through the training of the fine musical mind which shall, according to its nature, criticize or create, Bryn Mawr makes her contribution to the satisfaction of a very beautiful and appealing need of our people and our day.

JULIA LANGDON LOOMIS, 1895.

ANNOUNCEMENTS

The following Alumnae have accepted the nomination for Alumnae Director: Elizabeth Winsor Pearson, 1892, (Mrs. Henry Greenleaf Pearson), Dudley Road, Newton Centre, Mass.; Katharine Page Loring, 1913, (Mrs. Charles Loring), 8 Otis Place, Boston, Mass.; Helen Taft Manning, 1915, (Mrs. Frederick Manning), 107 Avon Street, New Haven, Conn., and Natalie McFadden Blanton, 1917, (Mrs. Wyndham Blanton), 3015 Seminary Avenue, Richmond, Va.

The Executive Board would be very glad to receive the names of further nominees. Any twenty-five Alumnae qualified to vote for Alumnae Directors may nominate a candidate, and the name of their nominee will be printed on the ballot to be sent out in a few weeks.

After April 10th copies of the *Alumnae Register* will be on sale in the Alumnae Office, Taylor Hall, and in local Bryn Mawr Clubs.

All material for the May BULLETIN should be sent to Evelyn Page, Alumnae Office, Taylor Hall, before April 10th. The Editor hopes very much that she will receive many unsolicited contributions.

The Fellowship Awards

On the morning of March 21st, President Park announced the names of the European Fellows to a crowded chapel. The Helene and Cecil Rubel Fellowship was won by Eleanor Grace Clark, of Oberlin, O.; The Mary E. Garrett Fellowship by Rose Lucile Anderson, of Jamestown, N. Y., and the M. Carey Thomas European Fellowship by Louise Bulkley Dillingham, of Millburn, N. J., A.B., Bryn Mawr College, 1916.

For the first time in the history of the college, the Bryn Mawr European Fellowship was divided between two Seniors, Virginia Fleek Miller, graduating Summa Cum Laude, with 270 points, and Katharine Van Bibber, graduating Magna Cum Laude with 259 points, both majoring in Mathematics and Chemistry, and hence easily to be com-

pared. The rest of the Honor Roll for the Class of 1924 is as follows:

Magna Cum Laude

Martha Lewis Fischer 258
Lesta Ford 220

Cum Laude

Katharine Bishop Neilson 216
Priscilla Harriet Fansler 205
Beatrice Talbot Constant 192
Elizabeth Kissam Henderson 188
Roberta Murray 184
Roberte Godefroy 178

Mary Minott 177
Pauline Gardner Sharpe 177
Elizabeth Thorn Pearson 175
Mary Katharine Woodworth 171
Esther Lowrey Rhoads 170

THE GRADUATE SCHOOL

(A speech delivered by President Park at the Graduate Fellowship Dinner on Friday, March 21st)

"My speech must begin with renewed and warmer congratulations to the three new graduate European Fellows on the year that lies ahead of them. I think with delight of their happy journeys by sea and land, of their long adventurous days, in new lecture rooms and libraries, of their experiences, their discoveries and their rewards. When my own mind dwells on a winter in Athens broken with voyages through blue Aegean islands and journeys on foot, on bicycle or on horseback through the mountains and uplands of inland Greece I feel almost sorry to know of their stern determination to stay in workaday England or France, but I realize, honestly, that their memories have every chance of being as glowing as mine.

"When at the instance of President Thomas the graduate school was established simultaneously with the undergraduate college at Bryn Mawr she made what seems to me perhaps her wisest contribution to women's education in America. Adequate undergraduate education for women was hard enough to get in 1885; graduate instruction was impossible. The mature woman student could neither work in the lecture room or laboratory where she wanted to work nor be supervised by the

professor whose instruction she wished to follow. With her own experience of graduate work in Germany and in Paris fresh in her mind, experiences which seem to us now almost romantic, Miss Thomas threw open to the college graduate an opportunity for solid graduate work, solid and at the same time stirring. She saw the need in women's education for immediate contact with scientific accuracy, with intellectual truth. And in the years that have seen increasing undergraduate opportunities open to women we have many of us felt that in the graduate seminary or the advanced laboratory that contact first came.

"Another contact Miss Thomas made from the very beginning for the graduate student, the contact with a wider culture, with a different type of education. The direct connection of the Bryn Mawr graduate school with the training given in the European university existed from the beginning of the college. Almost every member of the faculty has had his year or years of foreign study. With the graduation of the first class at Bryn Mawr its ablest student was chosen to continue her work abroad and its thirty-sixth European fellow was named today. Within five years the Mary E. Garrett Graduate European

Fellowship was founded and within eight years the President M. Carey Thomas European Fellowship. Much more recently the Rubel Foundation Fellowship has added another and freer opportunity for the advanced student. The current was set flowing too in the other direction. Since 1909 a fraction of the graduate school itself has been yearly made up of the Bryn Mawr foreign scholars. These two fundamentals of advanced education in America, solid and independent work, and first-hand connection with European intellectual standards are strengthened yearly, we trust, in the Bryn Mawr graduate school.

"So much President Thomas did for the American woman graduate student and in our gratitude for the opening of many other doors since then, none of us can forget or for an instant minimize her gift to us. The Graduate School, with its unique and honorable record, is a reminder of her acumen and wisdom, but in establishing it she did at the same time an equally great service for undergraduate education. She laid down as principles that undergraduates should be taught by a faculty keen on its own research work and able to instruct and actually instructing students maturer than the most mature senior, that the library used by undergraduates should contain the books and journals of research and advanced study, that the younger students should never be without the stimulus of

contact with older students working on subjects in which they themselves were already interested, usually working harder and using other and freer methods, set loose a little from the bondage of the beginner.

"I believe in nothing more whole-heartedly than in the value of graduate work per se for women but if I disbelieved that I should still believe in it as a necessary part of a college from the undergraduate point of view. The graduate school is like the eyes of the college through which we all look at learning or it is like the hands of the college feeling the way in our steep up-hill climb. There have always been and there always will be places for improvement in our graduate work. We must always look for better and better students. We must make their conditions of working more and more satisfactory. We must never drop the standard of the graduate degrees but we can perhaps find adaptations to the individual in the working out of their routine. We must try to establish more research fellowships and we must try to increase the stipend of our travelling fellows so that they will not need to dig so deep into their own pockets when they sail out as our ambassadors. In other words, we must work continuously for a higher standard, we must direct ourselves with a bolder aim and we must rest contented only with a more honorable accomplishment."

THE OBJECTS OF THE ALUMNAE FUND

Of the objects chosen by the Joint Committee for the Alumnae Fund several are self-explanatory or so well known that little further information about them need be given. The need for increased Academic Endowment, for instance, is obvious, so obvious that we are apt to overlook it. Yet if the College is to go on developing it must be assured of a constantly increasing income from endowment, the only sure source of income outside of the students' fees. Such a regular income will provide in large part for the needs which can be foreseen. But emergencies are constantly arising for which provision can not properly be made in the College budget. To meet these, President Park's Fund was established by the Alumnae last year. From this fund President Park has been able

to assist two brilliant graduate students, to provide more comfortable furnishings for the New Book Room so that the students may be encouraged to do more reading there, to refurnish in a simple way the Graduate Club Room, to provide proper lighting for the Faculty Room, to finance the preliminary work on the *Alumnae Register* (this was a loan), and to give the College and many of its friends the pleasure of hearing Amy Lowell speak and read some of her poetry. Finally, there are the expenses of the Alumnae Association met by the dues which are kept at the present nominal figure so that it may be possible for every Alumna and former student to belong to the Association. It must never be forgotten that a strong, well-informed Alumnae Association is a valuable asset to the College. Consequently, funds used for the maintenance of the Association are indirectly a contribution to the College. The other objects on the 1924 Alumnae Fund are more fully explained in the accompanying articles. The need of Bryn Mawr is clear. Equally clear is the responsibility of the Alumnae to relieve this need.

MARY PEIRCE, 1912, *Chairman.*

THE RHOADS SCHOLARSHIPS

When the question arose of a memorial to our first president, Dr. James E. Rhoads, the suggestion that we found two scholarships in his name met with an immediate response from the Alumnae Association, and it seemed especially fitting that he should be so remembered. At that time there existed but few scholarships which would enable an undergraduate in need of financial aid to continue her college course; so the James E. Rhoads Sophomore and Junior Scholarships were founded, to be awarded to such students who also should deserve the honor because of the excellence of their work.

The value of each scholarship then was $250.00, a sum at that time equivalent to two-thirds of the amount representing the minimum for tuition, board, and residence; today the value of each scholarship represents only one-third of this minimum charge, which is now $750.00. For this reason the raising of a $10,000 fund to increase these scholarships is now included among the objects of the Alumnae Fund. They stand for our first realization of an important need, a need which is still and always will be very great.

Those of us who were so deeply interested in their foundation should be proud to think how worthily they have been held. Among the James E. Rhoads scholars between the years 1897 and 1922 we have had seven Bryn Mawr European Fellows and a President's Fellow; three of the ten Alumnae who have graduated from Bryn Mawr *summa cum laude* were James E. Rhoads scholars. Of the other holders of the scholarships nine have returned to Bryn Mawr as Fellows or Scholars, or graduate students. Ten of our scholars are married; of the rest the majority are upholding the standards and ideals of Bryn Mawr as teachers in schools and colleges.

We do not wish to lose from Bryn Mawr a single student of the type which these scholarships have kept for us. They have always been considered the most distinguished scholarships to be awarded, but they cannot continue to be so regarded if other scholarships have a greater money value, and if students of high standing feel obliged to apply for these instead.

The friends of Dr. Rhoads, who remember him with friendship and gratitude, will wish to help in raising the fund that his name may live on associated with the best that the undergraduates have to give; later Alumnae will remember how their friends and classmates have been benefited by the scholarships, and will wish to help, in order that other undergraduates may be given a like opportunity to contribute to the name of Bryn Mawr. HELEN J. ROBINS, 1892.

THE LIBRARY

I have heard with keen interest the discussion of an increased appropriation for the library and have eagerly watched its development. For several years the library has been adding little more than the most necessary books for immediate use. There has been money for current needs but not for the "source material" so urgently needed by the Faculty and graduate students.

In every institution, regardless of size, the amount of money necessary for the library depends largely upon the character of the teaching and the nature of the work done. A college with a relatively small number of students doing first grade work requires a comparatively larger per capita for books. In a college such as Bryn Mawr, which is small, but which stresses research work, a well-equipped library is of prime importance, and a large annual appropriation for books is a necessity. The present income is not sufficient for development. The library ought to have an income of at least $12,000 a year and an immediate sum of $25,000 for the purchase of much-needed sets of serials and older books. The work of the Faculty and students—I speak from experience—is often seriously handicapped for lack of material. I am frequently obliged to tell a professor that some much-needed book cannot be purchased because the funds of the department for books have been exhausted for the year.

The present income of the library is $7,000, appropriated by the trustees from College funds and, in addition, the money that comes from late course book fines, condition fees, late registration, change in courses, and academic records. This amount varies from $1,000 to $1,200 a year. There are a few invested funds which give an annual income of about $250. Last year, the library received from individuals and classes, gifts, the largest in some time, amounting to $1,195.37. For the past three years the total library income has averaged $9,785 and this is higher than for the previous years, but the increase has not been sufficient to keep pace with the growing cost of books. During this period the average expenditure for books has been $4,860; for periodicals $3,050; for binding periodicals and books $1,390; for supplies, for library catalogue cards, printing, etc., $417; for postage and express $68. The appropriation of $7,000 is divided each year among the several departments of instruction. The additional funds are apportioned among the professors by the Library Committee where most needed.

No college or university library can hope to have all the books necessary for research, but there are certain standard and primary "source" books that must be in every library of the kind Bryn Mawr requires. These older books were issued in small editions and are rapidly vanishing from the market. The recent development in the United States of research libraries has gradually reduced the supply of the complete sets of the fundamental research publications, and in many cases the available supply is already exhausted. The longer Bryn Mawr delays the purchase of this kind of material, the harder it will be to secure and consequently the more it will cost. There should be at least $25,000 donated for the purchase of these "source" books for research. This sum is not excessive when the professors of one department alone say they need $15,000 to get the books necessary to make the work of the department what they wish. We make constant use of the library at the University of Pennsylvania and borrow extensively from other university libraries, often requesting books that should be here. It will only be through an increase in the income for the purchase of a greater number of books that the library can hope to meet the growing demands made on its resources.

LOIS A. REED, *Librarian.*

MISS SCOTT'S LIBRARY

In acquiring Miss Scott's library, the College comes into possession of some volumes that would otherwise be practically unobtainable. In the early days, when the funds for books and periodicals were even more limited than now, Miss Scott from her own resources acquired the volumes needed for purely working purposes. These form the bulk of the library. They deal mainly with Geometry, the field in which Miss Scott was most interested. But, on account of the interconnection of the subjects and the constant reference in Geometry to developments in the Theory and Functions, many standard works on the Theory of Functions and on Analysis in general were also acquired. In addition, there are complete sets of a number of periodicals, to many of which Miss Scott was an original subscriber. These include "The Proceedings of the London Mathematical Society," the first six volumes of which are practically unobtainable, "The American Journal of Mathematics," "The Palermo Rendiconti," "The Bulletin of the American Mathematical Society," and the first three volumes of "The New York Mathematical Society" which are very rare. There are thirty volumes, too, of the "Revue Semestrielle," which, issued twice a year, gives a brief account of every mathematical paper published for the preceding six months. For a number of years, it was Miss Scott's task to contribute to the "Revue" the reports on the articles appearing in all the American Mathematical Journals, and as a result of this work, she was made an honorary member of the Amsterdam Society. This "Revue" is absolutely indispensable, so that provision will have to be made for the College to subscribe to it.

In addition, there are a number of books bearing on the History of Mathematics, acquired as a hobby. As a luxury Miss Scott secured some really old books which are among the most interesting in the collection. These include a 1650 vellum edition of Cavalieri's "Geometry of Indivisibles," and a 1647 edition of the sequel to it;

Vieta's works in vellum, from the Elzevir press of 1646—a fine specimen of old English binding; Halley's edition (1710) of the "Works of Apollonius," which was once the property of Thomas Taylor, the Cambridge Platonist; a 1710 edition of MacLaurin's "Description of Linear Curves" and his "Treatise on Algebra," published after his death by his wife, Anne MacLaurin. There are, too, a number of original editions of Euler, Lagrange, Legendre, a copy of Cramer's "Analyse des Lignes Courbes," the only original work on "Curve Tracing." Then there are eleven volumes given Miss Scott at the time of her Mathematical Tripos, among them Todhunter's "Theory of Probability," very precious and almost unobtainable today. There are also various complimentary copies, including all of Cayley's works, and about thirty-five volumes of bound pamphlets.

One might think that with the acquisition of this splendid library the mathematical needs of the College would be provided for for many years. In reality, the College is no better off than before. Though the books were the property of Miss Scott, they have always been used freely by the students, as there were no others available. In some cases the College has duplicates, a few of which Miss Scott feels should be retained, others of which can be disposed of to great financial advantage. Immediate provision must be made for subscribing to the periodicals heretofore supplied by Miss Scott, so that the sets be kept complete. Funds must be secured, too, to bind the recent issues. But the collection forms a splendid foundation for future building. It is the duty and privilege of the Alumnae to see that the superstructure is equally fine.

MARGARET E. BRUSSTAR, 1903.

THE BUILDING FUND

The Building Fund has been brought to the fore this year by the drive for the Students' Building. This long-discussed project seems about to take form and to exist for the benefit of students twenty years younger than those for whom it was first planned. But even the Students' Building, since it does not define itself, is still subject to argument. Shall it be large or small? What rooms shall it contain? Shall we bind ourselves by present necessity, or look forward to the need of the future?

Such were the questions discussed at a delightful luncheon given by Marion Reilly, 1901, to which President Park, Mrs. Chadwick-Collins, the presidents of the classes and of the Associations, the editors of the News and the Lantern, the Chairman of the Students' Building, several Alumnae, and a few others interested in the subject were invited. In general, the gathering considered that the need of a Students' Building was certain; that the building should be simple, but not so small as to defeat its own end; that it should contain an auditorium, which could be enlarged by the use of folding doors to adjacent rooms; that there should be some place for costumes and scenery, and at least one room for records, and a room for meetings. The undergraduates expressed the hope that the Students' Building might soon be got under way, since only the appearance of a few workmen in overalls would make them believe that it had come at last.

But in our enthusiasm for the Students' Building we must not forget that in a few years the College will be forced into an extensive building program. The wing of the library is already provided for by a special fund, but another dormitory, which is just as urgently needed, must soon be financed. The entering Freshman class was so large this year that the College had to rent a house below the College Inn to accommodate fourteen of them. Such a situation not only is uncomfortable, but cannot be allowed to continue indefinitely. The infirmary must be enlarged, there must be more classrooms, and with every addition to the buildings, the facilities of the powerhouse must be increased.

An invested fund, established now, will earn interest and increase by contributions from year to year, so that when the time for building comes, and it will soon come, the College need not consider that it is impossible to do what it is impossible not to do.

MAY DAY

The sixth Bryn Mawr May Day will take place on Friday and Saturday, May 9th and 10th. In case of rain, says our preliminary announcement, it will be postponed until the first clear days of the following week, but the prayers of loyal Alumnae are now invoked to prevent such a contingency. It is at least one which we shall not have to face for another month.

In the meantime, the campus is possessed by meetings, rehearsals, conferences and fittings to an extent only to be imagined by one who has already been through this exciting period of preparation. To enlighten the ignorant, we need only describe the larger aspects of May Day organization.

May Day this year is governed by an Executive Committee, of which President Park is Chairman. Its members are Mrs. Otis Skinner, May Day Producer; Mr. Samuel Arthur King, Director of Plays; Miss Constance M. K. Applebee, Director of the Green; Mrs. J. C. Chadwick-Collins, May Day Manager, and Miss Pamela Coyne and Miss Eloise ReQua, Student Representatives. This committee meets frequently to discuss plans and policies. It serves to link up all diverse elements, graduates and undergraduates, the college administration, the Alumnae, and so forth.

There are seven student committees, which oversee casting, costumes, dances, music, refreshments, the green, and scenery and properties. The chairmen of these committees form a Central Students' Committee, by means of which the overlapping of functions is eliminated, and an understanding of general plans of the Executive and Central Committees is given to those who control specific parts.

Outside the College, Alumnae District Chairmen are already at work. The territory to be covered has been divided into a number of districts, each of which has its chairman. The names of these chairmen are listed in the preliminary announcement, which has just been sent out, and cannot be given in full here. Mrs. Thomas Raeburn White is to be Chairman for Philadelphia, Mrs. William Carter Dickerman for New York, Miss Kathleen Johnston for Washington, Miss Millicent Carey for Baltimore, Mrs. Bradley Dewey for Boston, and Mrs. Evarts Graham for St. Louis. Each local Chairman is responsible for the prosperity of May Day in her particular district.

The College has once again been extremely fortunate in securing Mrs. Otis Skinner as May Day Producer. Not only those who worked with her in 1920, but also everyone who saw May Day in that year can bear witness to her ability to cope with this tremendous task. She possesses a combination of charm and keen artistic sense which is unique. As to her plans, Mrs. Skinner said recently: "I am often asked how this May Day is to differ from those that preceded it. I regard May Day from a somewhat different point of view. To me the most important aspect of its production is the adherence to the tradition which has been given to us by earlier generations, a tradition which is not as important in point of time as in perfection of feeling. Bryn Mawr was one of the first places to give such a pageant, and is consequently bound up with the development of pageantry in this country. As this idea of pageantry grows, May Day changes, and, in return, the Bryn Mawr May Day gives a very definite contribution to its growth."

In answer to a question regarding proposed changes in costuming, Mrs. Skinner said: "I do not think that we should speak of costumes being more elaborate. There has never been any May Day lovelier than the second, but with the passing of time and styles we unconsciously change our ideas of the beautiful and the fitting. An amusing illustration of this occurs to me. The last May Day took place at the time when it was the fashion to wear short skirts. Now the Elizabethan costume calls for an ankle length skirt, and yet no efforts on my part could induce the actors to conform to historical accuracy. It seemed to me that at every rehearsal skirts grew shorter. The same thing is true with regard to color. At the present time we delight in bright colors, and possess a feeling for color which has been increasing for the past twenty years, and therefore the colors of May Day costumes have grown gradually brighter and brighter.

"Some costumes are time honored, and, we hope, will never be changed. Of these, I need only mention the lion and the head of the ass in Midsummer Night's Dream, and the famous and beloved dragon which was originally designed and made by a student, Emma Wines, 1894, and has been in use twenty years. For fifteen of those years he has slept in peace, but at every May Day he is awakened and expected to roar.

"One aspect of May Day," Mrs. Skinner continued, "has greatly developed with the passing of time, and that is the Green with its English country dances. Mr. Cecil Sharp has been responsible for the preservation and the practice of many dances which twenty-five years ago were about to die out entirely. This is especially true of the Morris, which Bryn Mawr has done much to revive."

Led by Queen Elizabeth (Martha Cooke, 1924, of Honolulu) and the Queen of the May (Margaret Wylie, 1926, of Washington, D. C.), the procession will follow the traditional route past Taylor and Denbigh, behind Radnor, and up Senior Row to the green, where the May Pole Dance will take place. The companies will then scatter to their plays.

Robin Hood, of course, is the most important of all. The title role will be taken by May Morrill Dunn, 1925, of Natchez, Miss., and Maid Marian is to be played by the May Queen. *The Old Wives Tale*, *Midsummer Night's Dream*, and the *Masque of Flowers*, all of which featured in the May Day of 1920, are to be given again. *Campaspe*, which was last presented in 1914, has been readopted, but this time, rather than the spectacular, the dramatic element is to be emphasized. Sir Philip Sidney's *Lady of the May*, which was produced in the first May Day in 1900, is to be revived, although as a masque rather than as a play. The Alumnae play is entitled *The foure PP*.

Mr. Samuel Arthur King has again consented to direct the production of these plays, and his rehearsals are in full swing. The leading characters rehearse eight and ten hours a week, and we are confident that their industry and Mr. King's able and vigorous tutelage will show splendid results.

The plays are to be given in the same places as before with the exception of *Campaspe*, for which a charming stage has been planned. It is to be played on the plateau beside the Deanery, against a background of fir trees. The semi-circular stage will be bounded by a white colonade.

The growing importance of the Green in May Day is wholly due to the interest and labor of Miss Applebee. This fascinating spectacle is to be still further developed this year. Mr. Charles Rabold, of the English Folk Dancing Society, Mr. Cecil Sharp's representative in America, has been asked to take charge of the Morris dances, and he is introducing several which have never before in America been danced by women. Miss Applebee plans to make the Green a more connected performance than it has ever been. She is making still greater efforts to cling to historical accuracy, both in costumes and in the "village" and its characters, and to produce a rustic and an

Elizabethan atmosphere. The Alumnae have been invited to take part in the Green, and any Alumna who would like to accept the invitation will be given a sketch from which to make her costume. Only the Alumnae who are acting in May Day are requested to appear in costume.

Thanks to the Music Department, it has been possible to give more intelligent attention to songs and accompaniments. Most of the music to be used consists of old English folk tunes. The music for the masques, however, has been selected by Mr. Horace Alwynne with a view rather to appropriateness of feeling than to historical accuracy.

A preliminary announcement concerning May Day has been sent to all Alumnae, and to a large number of others. The cover of this pamphlet was drawn some years ago by Elizabeth Shippen Green Elliott for the College Song Book. The same cover will appear on the May Day program. The posters are also drawn by her.

It is hoped that the Sixth May Day will be a worthy heir to its predecessors. It is no small task to carry on the tradition to which other May Days have contributed so much. The College takes it up with a sense almost of inadequacy, but with the determination to renew as far as possible the impression of vitality, order, and beauty for which May Day is known.

THE CHINESE LOAN EXHIBIT

Marjorie LaMonte Thompson, 1912.

Following its policy of awakening interest in China, in order to gain support for the Chinese Scholarship Fund, the committee this year gathered together a Loan Exhibit which was just put on view in two of the galleries at the Art Alliance in Philadelphia. No one who did not share the varying emotions of the committee during the weeks of collecting and arranging can realize their surprise and intense pleasure when finally out of the chaos emerged something that seemed to them miraculously to stand for the spirit of China, as they knew and loved it. It was literally the Sixth Day that their small miracle of creation took place; they suddenly saw dignity, suavity, restraint, and strangely satisfying charm rising out of intolerable confusion.

On the walls of the east gallery were the pictures loaned by Mr. Charles Ludington—the room glowed with the mellow red of the robes of high officials. In one corner burnt the clear green of the gown "of an old lady of high degree." One forgot, however, one's pleasure in pure color, and in the mellowness of the landscapes, and in the decorative value of the Korean panels, in amazement at the living quality in the faces of the portraits. In each face one felt intensely the dignity, the suavity, the restraint, the humor, the wisdom. The conviction grew that character was to those men and women an even greater art than painting. One of the pictures that comes outside the general category was a T'ang picture of a Lohan, strikingly and unmistakably Jewish. Vague memories of the Jewish emigration came into one's mind as one looked at the amazing drawing of the thing, and again one's thoughts crept back to the Chinese people who could absorb into themselves all invaders.

In the other gallery were more pictures, some of Mr. Ludington's, some lent by the University Museum, some by Florance Waterbury, '05, and some by Captain Dmitri Dubassoff. In a measure the pictures here, in spite of their beauty and interest, served as a background for the Han, T'ang, and Lung pottery loaned by the University Museum, and for the charming early Chinese and Cambodian figures sent by Mr. Ludington. No one will easily forget a slim Cambodian girl, standing on a great Korean chest with the gray-blues of a rare piece of Kosu behind her, throwing her slender lines into sharp relief.

In the other half of this room was a more heterogeneous collection of things, but even in these things one was conscious of a curious essential unity of impression. Color was never raw; design never became an end in itself. In the case where the crystals caught the light, the gleam was like that of water—the white water of springs, the clear tawny water of mountain brooks that have flowed past pine trees.

Particularly lovely were the snuff bottles loaned by Dr. Howard Gray, and the stone flowers loaned by Mrs. Ellis Thompson. Not far away stood the case of delicate, lace-like ivory fans, and two fragile baskets, very arresting in their perfection of workmanship, which bore the initials of Washington's mother, and had been brought from Virginia with some of the Washington china. This china was displayed near them. For lack of a better name the committee called the porcelain of this type, clipper-ship china. The name explains exactly what it was. The thin cups and saucers, the tall jugs, the teapots and tea-caddies, had all been brought as part of the rich cargoes of sailing ships. Most of the pieces had been for three and four generations in the possession of the families who loaned them. A few of the plates, bearing quaintly enough, English or French coats-of-arms, were sent by the Pennsylvania Museum. Beyond these were other porcelains, and red lacquer boxes and embroideries, glorious embroideries that made pools of color on the wall. Some of the loveliest of these were sent by Miss Waterbury, a red Ko'see robe, sold by the Boy Emperor last spring, that blazed above some Tibetan Buddhas; on another wall an Imperial yellow manchu coat with its warm lining of fur, flanked on either side by exquisite sleeveless jackets that in their soft blues repeated the blue of Hawthorne jars near by. Looking down the room again, one was more conscious than ever of the curious impression of unity, and still unable to analyze it.

The exhibition made one feel that perhaps it was ironic to offer our civilization to one who would come to us with such art as her cultural inheritance, and that perhaps the Chinese scholarships ought to mean that we send a scholar to China. Yet, even while playing with that idea, one knew with absolute conviction that China needs cruelly some of the things we can give; but because we in our turn need some of the things China can give, the Chinese girl who comes to study at Bryn Mawr, on the scholarship, is a greater ambassador than she or we can realize.

ALUMNAE ACTIVITIES

MRS. JOHN JOSEPH MOORHEAD
*Observer at the Opium Advisory Committee
of the League of Nations.*

Helen Howell Moorhead, 1904, served as a volunteer hospital worker from 1914 until 1916. From 1917 until 1919 she was a volunteer worker in the American Red Cross in Washington. When the war ended, The Foreign Policies Association invited her to join the work it was doing on international questions. To prepare herself she went to Harvard and Columbia and studied there under the professors of International Law. Her especial problem was the traffic in opium.

Last year Mrs. Moorhead was chosen by The Foreign Policies Association, the Young Woman's Christian Association, the Young Men's Christian Association, the International Institute of Education, and the American Association of University Women to be their sole representative at the meetings of the Opium Advisory Committee of the League of Nations. She went to Geneva as a private person, but although in an unofficial capacity, she was accorded all the courtesies and given access to all the documents provided a member of the committee, the entire session of which she attended.

The Opium Advisory Committee was created by the League of Nations in 1919 to carry out the Treaty on Opium signed at the Hague in 1912. This committee at its five meetings drew up a program to which every member agreed. The program was submitted to the Council of the League, which, in turn, requested the nations concerned to conduct an investigation of the recommendations, and to pass laws in accordance with their findings.

There are four ways in which the sale of opium may be controlled. The growth of the poppy and the manufacture of drugs from opium may be limited to medical and scientific needs. The countries concerned may bind themselves by an international treaty to forbid the drug traffic. Lastly, fines and punishments may be imposed by the individual countries to prevent their sale. In the first case, little can be done as yet, since China and Persia, where the poppy is grown, suffer from unstable governments, and India, a third producing country, has not accepted the principle of limitation. However, through the agency of the Chinese students in America, information about opium is to be spread in China. The town crier in each village, who is also the ballad singer, is to sing and to tell his audience of its evils. The manufacture of drugs from opium is largely carried on in the United States, England, Germany, and Switzerland, and a careful inquiry is being carried on among the medical authorities in these countries as to the amount of the drug actually needed in medical practice. Since these countries have stable governments it is hoped that drug manufacture may soon be controlled by legislation.

Almost all nations signed The Hague Treaty of 1912, but those who did not, such as Switzerland, do not, of course, carry out the provisions of that treaty. Since the problem must be treated from an international standpoint, it is imperative that every nation be convinced of the necessity of such an agreement.

The findings of the Opium Advisory Committee to a large extent concern the fourth method of control, by specific legislation in the individual countries. There is an investigation being carried on in the United States as to the amount of heroin needed as a medicine, and also an inquiry is being made in the courts of the different states to find out whether offenses against existing laws are best punished by fines or by imprisonment.

The committee seeks to create everywhere an enlightened public opinion on the subject, believing that the proper laws will follow almost automatically. Since Mrs. Moorhead has returned to this country from Geneva, she has been occupied in writing articles, delivering addresses, supplying information to all types of institution, and in instigating statistical research. As the result of a pamphlet which she assisted in composing, a bill has been introduced in Congress forbidding the manufacture of heroin. Above all, the committee emphasizes the necessity of a fair realization of the problems which each country has to face. Certain obstacles exist in China, or in Turkey, which exist nowhere else, and unless the public recognizes that these obstacles must be removed before the laws of China and Turkey are judged on the same basis as those of the United States, there will be a great deal of irritation and bad feeling aroused between the nations. This the Opium Advisory Committee avoids. It cannot persuade further than the facts justify.

Bryn Mawr may be very proud to have as distinguished a representative as Mrs. Moorhead in this field. It is not only true that she was the only woman present at the meetings in Geneva, and there represented many well-known associations, but it is also true that since she has returned to the United States she has done a brilliant piece of work in making public the findings of the committee.

CORRESPONDENCE

TRIPOLI, SYRIA, January 18, 1924.
Editor of the BRYN MAWR ALUMNAE BULLETIN, Bryn Mawr, Pennsylvania, U. S. A.

MY DEAR MISS PAGE:
You will find enclosed a notice which I should be glad to have inserted in the BULLETIN. I am sending copies to several colleges, in the hope that through some one of them we may find just the right person to fill the position mentioned; but it would naturally be a special pleasure to a Bryn Mawr Alumna to find some one with Bryn Mawr tradition back of her to join her in this work.

Very sincerely yours,
MARGARET DOOLITTLE, 1911.

WANTED, to teach in Tripoli Girls' School next year, one woman, a college graduate, preferably with some experience in teaching. Her work will be entirely in English, and will include such subjects as English language and literature, elementary science, history, mathematics, and Bible, her preference being consulted as far as possible. It will add greatly to her usefulness if she has had some experience in directing athletics and school societies. A knowledge of Arabic is not expected; but some acquaintance with French is desirable.

As compensation we can offer full maintenance during the school year, including the short vacations if spent at the school, $500 salary, and full traveling expenses if a three-year term is completed.

The school stands in the midst of a city of more than 30,000 people, two-thirds of whom are Muslims. The pupils number at present about 140, ranging in age from four to twenty, and in grade from kindergarten to high school. They represent six different sects, Christians and non-Christians; about thirty are boarders.

The American community consists of three families and three teachers in the schools. Though vacations may easily be be spent in Beirut, sixty miles away, it is impossible to join in the general social life there; and the woman who comes to Tripoli must be prepared to find her pleasure in her work, in reading and study, in music, and in simple social gatherings. The Syrian community is very pleasant, and ready to welcome a newcomer, even if she is without Arabic.

The position requires some one with a determination to do her best, regardless of circumstances. Life in the Near East, in a Muslim city, brings with it new experiences in food, climate, and especially in customs, some of which are not at all pleasant. The woman who depends largely on others, or on the surroundings to which she has been accustomed, ought not to attempt to come. On the other hand, one who can make up her mind to like what comes, who can accommodate herself without too much strain to new conditions and social restrictions, and whose health is good, will find the life rich in interest and even in pleasure.

More than all else, I need not say, it is a chance to interpret Jesus Christ to those who do not know Him.

(The following letter was recently received from Gordon Woodbury Dunn, 1919, by her Class Editor, who very kindly permitted the Editor to print it here, believing that it would be of interest not only to the members of Mrs. Dunn's class, but to every reader of the BULLETIN.)

—

January 8, 1924.

We sailed on September 8th with a precious month ahead of us for vacation purposes until the American and British Arbitration Tribunal should meet in London. (My husband is secretary.) We planned to put in the vacation in Italy, but, of course, we stopped in Geneva on the way. The Assembly was in session that month, and we leaned over the balcony while Betty Brace Gilchrist pointed out the celebrities. We had the good luck, too, to go to a meeting of the Disarmament Committee, and Lord Robert Cecil was in particularly good form that day. Incidentally, we concluded that for anything so "dead," the League appeared to be a pretty lively corpse.

After that we had an enchanted week in Venice, and went on to Florence and Rome, where, while contorting ourselves to look at the Sistine Chapel ceiling, we found Peggy Dent (1920) in a similar state of contortion.

The Arbitration Tribunal met in London on October 15th, and it was really wonderful to see international disputes in the process of settlement in a rational, good-tempered fashion. The cases were mostly old ones that had defied settlement by diplomatic means, but the decisions taken will be used as precedents in international law in the future.

The machinery of the thing is this : Each country has an agency which gets up and presents its cases to a court of three arbitrators, one from each side, and one from a neutral country. Colonel Olds was the American arbitrator, a former partner of Ambassador Kellogg; Mr. Mitchell-Innes was the British, and the umpire was M. Fromageot, a very well-known French jurist.

The first day every member of both agencies seized their "toppers" and were presented to Lord Curzon at Downing Street. Then they met in the courtroom and MacNiel, the under-secretary for foreign affairs, made a most impressive speech, that set the keynote for the whole session. The two agencies met less with the attitude of two opponents, than with that of trying to discover where justice really lay.

However, I'm rambling on at an appalling length. We took a little flat in Tite Street, Chelsea, and "Unt," a treasurer of a maid, contrary to our expectations, knew how to cook a few things besides Brussels sprouts.

After the session (in which, we modestly report, the U. S. won six out of the eight cases) we went to The Hague and heard the World Court handing down a decision between Poland and Czecho-Slovakia, and from there we proceeded via Paris to Cherbourg, took the *Leviathan*, got stuck in the mud, and arrived grandiloquently at the dock in New York in a Staten Island ferry.

(The extract which follows is taken from a letter from Fung Kei Liu, 1922, a former Chinese scholar, to Jean Gowing, 1922, who says it is the most optimistic that she has received since Fung Kei left this country.)

Canton, China, November, 1923.

. . . It certainly has been long since I wrote you last. It means that I have had too much in my hand. Don't you know that I have been playing the Father's part for three children besides running a home? I have to earn enough to send two children to boarding schools, one to a day school,

besides giving some spending money to two other sisters who are still studying in college. The houses here are not built for sanitary living or convenience. I had to spend much money as well as time to fix up the house for just simple living. Father is now an invalid forever and I have to do much in keeping my brothers and sisters in decent behavior. Canton has been in constant tumult. The constant moving and escaping means much money and anxiety. Besides such conditions mean that regular work is impossible. I had a great worry for fear of not getting a job at the beginning of this term. Thank heavens! I have gotten a pretty satisfactory one three days before school opened and everything was well for a while. Unfortunately, when I just sat down and wrote my Christmas list, another disturbance broke out. I was not able to do any shopping. In fact, I was a refugee for a week. . . .

What do you think? Before I joined the Y. W. C. A. they elected me to the Board of the National Y. W. The city now insists to give me a lot of work. Perhaps you already know that I am teaching English to the pre-medical students here besides doing some office work. I am here from 8 A. M. to 5 P. M. every day. You can imagine how much work I am doing. But I am glad. I am enjoying the work. Most of my students are boys and they have been really nice to me. In fact, they listen to my orders much more than to their men teachers. They said I had the most attentive classes in the school. I am really thankful for that. . . .

By the way, we got a letter from my brother a few days ago, saying that he was going to sail home in a freight boat as a sailor boy the 28th of last month. It will take him over two months to get home, but will not cost him a penny to do so. You know that we had no previous idea of his return and expected that he would not come back till next year. We are now just counting the days and wishing that he only could be back by Christmas. . . .

(The following letter from Fumi Uchida, 1920, carries with it its own plea. Anything sent to her Class Editor, Helene Zinsser, 1920, 6 West Ninth Street, New York City, will be gratefully forwarded. Packages can be addressed directly to Fumi

Uchida, 29 of 2 Nagatacho, Kojimachi, Tokyo, Japan.)

"I suppose you know about our terrible disaster and you may think that I may be killed, but I'm still alive, Helene. But it was indeed a frightful shock. On the morning of September 1st I went to the Higher Normal School, and if I had stayed there longer something might have happened to me, for the school was badly damaged and afterward completely burned down. However, I was at home when the first shock came. When the first one subsided we went out of doors. There we saw already smoke rising at a distance and the wind blowing towards us. We thought we were in danger and after a while we began to carry some of our things to our friend's house at the top of the slope in front of our house. The water supply had stopped and we committed the whole matter to the direction of the wind and kept on carrying things in the midst of hot smoke. But toward evening at the most dangerous moment the direction of the wind changed and we got out of danger. In the evening it was a frightful sight to see the whole burnt-down field with bluish, reddish, yellowish and greenish (it sounds like B. M. colors, doesn't it?) flames arising. We had fire on two other sides later on, but it did not reach us. For fear of severe after shocks and on account of horrible rumors we slept three nights out of doors, on the hill of the Mexican Embassy. We had no water, no gas, no electric light, no newspapers and scarce food for many days. At first we thought we were near the biggest fire, but we heard later that there had been many much worse places, and we saw refugees in half-burnt tatters passing in the street. They were all walking, for we had no street cars.

On the morning of the 4th I walked to my school with a cousin of mine. Large bridges had gone down and I had to crawl over a narrow remnant. The school had been completely burnt down excepting the gate-keeper's house and the outer wall. It was like a dream. I could hardly believe that the buildings in which we used to have classes and the precious books in the library and other things were no longer. The school office had been moved to the Music School at the top of the Ueno Hill farther on, and we walked on to the temporary office. We walked in the midst of a vast devastated field of ashes. Streets were crowded with refugees and their bundles. Some houses were still burning or smoking. It was simply incredible to think that it had been one of the most prosperous sections of the city.

Most of the large stores are no longer. Many schools are either burnt or hopelessly damaged. Five important government schools were burnt, including the Imperial University. My school is one of them. A great many private schools were burnt. Miss Tsuda's School, to which, as you know, B. M. C. A. sends money each year, was also completely burnt. Ordinarily the school has many friends in the city, but at this time some of them are sufferers themselves. It has to ask some of its American friends for help. The other day when I went to see Miss Tsuda she asked me to send the enclosed printed matter to any of my friends who might be interested in her school and willing to help it. I send the copy to you, not because I think you are the richest in our class but because I know you are willing. I shall be very grateful for the sake of Miss Tsuda's school if you will kindly tell some of our classmates and some of your friends who might be willing to help the school, to get interested in it. Miss Tsuda told me a library of two or three thousand books had been burnt and I am sure gifts of books will be gratefully accepted. The school is at present using part of a mission school and it is planning to build a temporary barrack on the same site, but if you are doubtful as to the place where the gifts are to be sent, my home address might do, for I shall see that they will be sent to the school at once.

The Peeresses' School, where I also teach, is very little damaged. It is said to be earthquake proof. From the second of September till the beginning of October the school kept about 300 refugees and we teachers took turns to take care of them. We also bought some stuff and made clothes for the sufferers in the city. The students brought many things. We sorted them and sent them out to some of the sufferers. But now all the schools except those that are unable to reopen are reopened and we are doing our regular work. The Higher Normal School for Women is a huge school with many departments, so it is using part of four different schools and two others for dormitories. I go to three of them.

Everybody is very grateful to the United States for her most generous and prompt help and gifts. I am glad not simply because the sufferers are helped by them but because the friendship between the two countries is deepened. Mr. Woods, the Ambassador, who has done so much for the city and sufferers, is leaving for the United States today and the city is gratefully sending him home. Please give my love to my other Bryn Mawr friends in New York when you see them.

Yours as ever,

FUMI UCHIDA.

CAMPUS NOTES

The Athletic Association has recently adopted a new constitution, which provides that the officers shall consist of a President, a Vice-President with the duties of Treasurer, and a Secretary. These officers are to be elected in the spring from the Junior, Sophomore, and Freshman classes respectively. In the following autumn, the entering Freshman class is to elect an Assistant Secretary. Each sport is to be controlled by a sports manager, nominated by the officers of the Association, and elected by the Association as a whole. The President is not eligible for such a managership, nor can any person be manager of two sports unless one of them be Water Polo or Track.

The Self-Government Association entertained the Presidents of Student Government of Vassar, Smith, Wellesley, Radcliffe, and Barnard over the week-end of March 8th. The meeting discussed the rules, concerning proctoring, cutting, and so forth, prevailing in the different colleges, and compared their usefulness. It was found that the regulations governing cuts varied. In Barnard, Radcliffe, and Wellesley cuts are limited by public opinion or by the preference of individual professors. The Curriculum Committee later took part in the discussion. The meeting decidedly approved of comprehensive examinations in Major work, or the substitution of reports for examinations when so elected by upper classmen. There will be an intercollegiate conference on these subjects next year at Vassar.

On Friday, February 22nd, Miss Amy Lowell gave a short address before an enthusiastic audience on recent developments in American poetry. She paid special attention to the school of the vers libre and to the school of poets reacting against it. Miss Lowell illustrated her remarks with readings from her poetry.

His Excellency, Prince Gelasio Caetani, Italian Ambassador to the United States, spoke in Taylor Hall on Friday evening, February 29th, before the Italian Club and the College at large. President Park introduced Prince Caetani, who afterwards discussed the Fascisti Movement. He declared that Italy has now completed a cycle, whose downward curve followed the Renaissance, and whose upward curve ended in the Fascismo, under which the individual sacrifices himself to the good of the community. After the meeting a reception was held in Rockefeller Hall in honor of Prince Caetani.

Dr. John L. Lowes delivered the second Ann Elizabeth Sheble Memorial lecture on Friday night, March 14th. His subject was "The Deep Well, a Chapter in the History of the Rime of the Ancient Mariner." Dr. Lowes discussed Coleridge's philosophy in general and its expression in this specific instance. He has written several books on English literature.

The Senior Class won Water Polo, defeating the Sophomores 8-0 in the final game. The play was scrappy and the shooting became wild towards the last.

The Seniors also succeeded in winning the two Gymnasium meets, the first of which took place on Friday, March 7th, and the second a week later. Mildred Buchanan, 1924, won the individual championship.

CLASS NOTES

1889

Class Editor, Harriet Randolph, 1300 Spruce Street, Philadelphia.

At the Annual Meeting of the Alumnae Association on February 2nd, at Taylor Hall, the following members of the Class were present: Alice Anthony, Julia Cope Collins, Anna Rhoads Ladd, Lina Lawrence, Harriet Randolph, and Martha G. Thomas.

Gertrude Allinson Taylor, Haverford, Pa.

"My husband and I are living very much as usual in our quiet home at Haverford after a pleasant summer in our little camp at Pocono Lake Preserve.

"I have .been learning recently how absorbing an occupation it is to acquire a new son-in-law. The details of our daughter's marriage belong in the class notes of 1921. During the summer her new home has been growing up in our vegetable garden and is now (November) ready for occupancy; and instead of corn have come up some little fir trees.

"Our older son, Ted, is now at the Institute of Technology in Boston and our younger boy, Larry, is at Haverford College. Ted spent his vacation working for an electric company in East Orange and was able to come to us for his week-ends.

"In June Larry and a college friend set out for the West in a very forlorn little Ford with a fine engine. They slept and ate by the roadside and accomplished their trip on time as planned. Their little car, 'The Empty Bucket,' took them to the top of Pike's Peak and through the Yellowstone Park. They spent several weeks at a pioneer ranch in Wyoming, and altogether gained fresh knowledge of their country and fellow-citizens."

Some members of the Class have been unable for various reasons to write for '89's notes. They send to the Class Editor explanatory letters as follows:

Letter No. 1.

"I dread to think of what your opinion must be of my lack of response to your letter asking for news for the BULLETIN, but the way of it was this:

"When your letter came I was very busy with many things and I put it aside undecided in my own mind as to what the nature of the reply might be. I continued to be busy until I was laid low with a carbuncle. This not only took the perfectly good time, but made my time much fuller when I returned to active life.

"The more I meditated on the desirability of sending a communication to the BULLETIN, the less I thought it would interest the readers. There is no doubt about our being back numbers from the point of view of most of the readers of the BULLETIN." (Probably an allusion to the inducement to write freely offered by the Class Editor that '89's column is the most sequestered place in the universe, as no Alumna reads notes of classes earlier than her own.— *Editor*.) "Not that I would grant it, for the older I get the less I realize the flight of time and the more I am impressed with the tolerance of the aged compared to the young.

"But the letter was never written and my enthusiastic admiration for Mussolini was never voiced for the readers of the BULLETIN.

"There is one thing I fear greatly and that is that you will think me unfriendly, on account of this silence. Nothing is further from the truth. I hope that you will realize that I really have been compelled by an untoward combination of circumstances to leave this undone."

1897

Class Editor, Mary M. Campbell, Walker Road, West Orange, N. J.

Mary Levering Robinson's daughter, Mary L., is a member of the Freshman Class at Bryn Mawr. Through a careless mistake this item was omitted from the last issue.

Elizabeth Higginson Jackson's older son, Charles, is at St. Paul's School, and will be prepared there for Harvard College.

The Shipley School, of which Eleanor Brownell is Principal, will celebrate its thirtieth anniversary in June.

Molly Peckham Tubby's daughter, Ruth, will graduate from Bryn Mawr in June. Molly and Ruth and Mr. Tubby sail for Europe on June 21st.

Beth Caldwell Fountain's daughter, Olivia, will graduate from Bryn Mawr in June. Her elder son is a student at Yale.

Clara Vail Brooks' oldest son, Harry, will enter Yale next fall. Her second boy,

Tom, is at the Buckley School in New York, and the youngest one, Gordon, six years old, is at a little school in Ardsley. When Clara is not at a committee meeting (she is on very many Westchester Boards) she is on the golf-links of the Ardsley Club. She does not like golf, but feels that she must keep pace with her husband, who is assistant vice-president of the American Telephone and Telegraph Company, and who spends his idle hours indulging in the game.

Elizabeth Higginson Jackson, Beth Fountain, Elsa Bowman, 1896, and Mary Campbell spent the week-end of Washington's Birthday at Sharon, Conn. They had wonderful coasting, sleighing, skiing, and skating.

Edith Edwards, president of the Rhode Island Society, United States Daughters of 1812, visited Little Rock, Ark., in October, and New York City in January, attending meetings of the National Executive Board of that organization.

Julia Duke Henning's daughter, Julia Duke, is studying in Chicago this year, after graduating from Bryn Mawr.

1903

Class Editor, Mrs. Herbert Knox Smith, Farmington, Conn.

Alice Lovell Kellogg had, in the fall, a wonderful two months' trip through Ecuador. She says she believes it has the greatest variety of climate and scenery in the smallest amount of area of any country in the world. "It is only a few hours from the tropical coast to the sub-arctic highlands, cocoa and banana groves to eternal snow. Within a few hours, too, we went from the ever-steaming wet jungle of the Oriente to the dryest, densely populated spot (I believe) on earth, the Indian village of Licto, where Indian huts touch shoulders. We climbed the extinct volcano of Pichinaha and looked into its crater."

Elizabeth Shepley Sergeant is in the East this winter after a long stay in New Mexico writing a book on the Pueblo Indians and taking an active part in the national "Indian Movement" hoping to help preserve the last of the Indian Culture.

1905

Class Editor, Mrs. Clarence Hardenbergh, 3710 Warwick Boulevard, Kansas City, Mo.

Jack Paxson enjoyed showing her child over Bryn Mawr last fall and Jane was properly thrilled. Jack has been working in "a whirl of non-political politics trying to persuade a reluctant city council to vote money for city playgrounds—results gratifying."

Curly and husband and son spent Christmas in Biloxi, where Teddy joined them from the Walker School.

Rumor has it that Po's husband has a new job in Indiana. Is she moving there? Some one please answer.

Kempy is taking a sabbatical year, studying at Columbia.

Freddy is still active in religious drama, lecturing and advising. She staged a big church Christmas pageant. She sang the title role in the Denver municipal opera during music week. Her eight-year-old Frederva is a keen horsewoman.

During December and January, Putty's three children had measles, chicken-pox, and mumps.

The following members of the Class of 1905 attended the Alumnae meeting and President Park's luncheon in Pembroke on February 2nd: Alberta Warner Aiken, Caroline Chadwick-Collins, Mabel Austin Converse, Julia Gardner, Alice Heulings, Katharine Howell, Miriam Johnson, Louise Lewis, Elma Loines, Helen Read, Mabry Parks Remington, Anna Workman Stinson, Helen Sturgis, and Edith Longstreth Wood.

1907

Class Editor, Eunice Morgan Schenck, Low Buildings, Bryn Mawr.

Mrs. James L. Houghteling, the mother of Harriot Houghteling and of Leila Houghteling, 1911, died suddenly at Warm Springs on January 28th. The Class extends its deepest sympathy to Harriot and to Margaret Morison, whose father, Robert E. Morison, died in New York on February 10th.

Harriot Houghteling spent part of February and March in California and expected to be at her home in Winnetka on her return.

Margaret Augur spent three weeks in February on a ranch in Arizona and stopped in Chicago on her way back to attend some conventions of Head Mistresses and Secondary School teachers.

Marie Wing, who is now the Honorable

Marie Wing of the City Council of Cleveland, honored Pennsylvania with her presence on February 23rd and spoke at a luncheon of the League of Women Voters in Erie.

1907 has two new children born in February: Sarah Elizabeth Jamison, daughter of Athalia Crawford Jamison, and Stoddard Wilder Daniels, son of Grace Brownell Daniels.

Adele Brandeis has been studying painting in New York this winter and living at the Bryn Mawr Club. She was in Bryn Mawr for the Alumnae Meeting, as were Letitia Windle, Mary Ferguson, Alice Hawkins, Mabel O'Sullivan and Eunice Schenck.

Dorothy Forster Miller spent a week-end in March in Bryn Mawr visiting her sister, who is warden of the temporary off-campus house for Freshmen. She reported that she and her family had been delighted with their country winter at Cold Spring Harbor, Long Island.

Julie Benjamin Howson has also spent this winter at her country home. She and her entire family will sail on April 14th for a summer in England and Wales.

Elma Daw, whose letterhead tells that she is specializing in "Physical and Musical Re-education," writes that she expects to be in Bryn Mawr for the May Day Fete, and to teach again this summer at the University of Chicago.

The Class Editor wishes to thank all members of the Class who have sent her items for the Class notes, and hopes they will go on and that others will follow suit.

1909

Class Editor, Mrs. Rollin T. Chamberlin, 5492 South Shore Drive, Chicago, Ill.

Katherine Branson's School, at Ross, Calif. is reported by a visiting 1909er "to be one of the most beautiful places I have seen." Whether Kate likes it or not, she lives in a palace. "She makes a most delightful and dignified principal."

Frances Browne was "seen in New York last week looking very handsome with some beautiful new clothes." She says for herself, from Bryn Mawr, "the Model School is still running, and still more fun to be in."

Helen Crane is working hard as an educational secretary of the Student Volunteer Movement, with headquarters in New York. She went to Indianapolis for the Student Volunteer convention during the Christmas vacation.

Jessie Gilroy Hall is at home again (in a suburb of St. Louis) after her year abroad. She spent last spring in England, renting an old house built by Cardinal Newman for his mother, in Iffley, just outside of Oxford. Now she is at home and says, "If we can ever decide about styles and materials, we shall build a permanent dwelling-place before long. At least we have the hill and an old barn and a tarn for a beginning."

Evelyn Holt Lowry is in New York, "much interested in her clinical work." Further details lacking.

Mary Nearing is abroad, studying gardens and landscaping.

Dorothy North was in New York recently, "spending some time with her sister in a fascinating house on Fifth Avenue just above Washington Square." A returned relief worker from Russia should have more news than this, but the Editor has called in vain.

May Putnam "has been appointed chief of Pediatrics at the Woman's Infirmary, as well as continuing on the staff at the Bellevue. She is preparing a monumental work on rickets for the Federal Children's Bureau, and will be a chief authority on that subject."

Shirley Putnam was married on Thursday, March 6th, to Elliott O'Hara, of Waltham, Mass. The wedding, which took place at the studio apartment of her sister, the sculptor, Brenda Putnam, 49 West Twelfth Street, New York, was attended only by the immediate families. The Reverend John Haynes Holmes, of the Community Church, performed the ceremony. Mr. and Mrs. O'Hara sailed on March 11th, on the *President Wilson,* for Spain, North Africa, Sicily, and points further north; returning in June by way of London. "We shall live somewhere near Boston, as Elliott is head of the O'Hara Waltham Dial Company in Waltham. Besides inventing machinery, and being a manufacturer, he paints, and we expect to bring home sketchbooks full." Shirley has resigned from being editor and manager of the *Greenwich Press,* after a four-year term there.

Mildred Pressinger Kienbusch is "training" with a prize-fighter and dancing.

Ellen Shippen, is still living in South Orange and working in New York for the *New Republic*. She says "everything is with me exactly as it has been for the past five years. We are hoping to go to Pocono in June, and then perhaps West." ("West" meaning the Rockies.)

Margaret Bontecou Squibb "has a most attractive daughter," whom she has been "showing off" in New York.

Janet Van Hise is reported in New York. Her class mates wish she would tell her address, and would "turn up at the club."

Lucy Van Wagenen did her "first travelling" last summer, going to the Pacific coast and to Alaska. She "took a look at the Grand Canyon" on the way out, and "swam on different beaches all the way to Alaska." Going to Alaska, "I stood the captain of our ship on his head on the cabin floor, and studied navigation in return." "We camped up the river in the interior opposite five glaciers, where the Alaskan brown bears and grizzlies were so dangerous that we were not allowed out of camp without a gun and a man, too. We fished our ice out of the river. There I swam, with a current you can't row against, and there's no doctor's treatment that can beat it." Lucy has an apartment in New York, "with a thirty-foot roof-garden. There my patients sleep in the sun after their lessons. The library makes a fine private gym. My work is thrilling. My patients range from two to eighty-two, and I have fat grandmothers who do back somersaults and hang upside down in the rings. I am known as the beauty doctor. They say, 'Don't lace—go to Lacy,' and 'Dollar a pound, on or off.'"

Anna Platt is living in New York "working hard at Cornell Medical, also Mah Jong."

Anne Whitney is at home again in Milton, Mass. She had a fine trip to Japan and China, "with a month in Kobe, and travelling in Japan in spite of the earthquake. In Peking she gave several lectures. Also she was very gay."

1911

Class Editor, Louise S. Russell, 140 East Fifty-second Street, New York City.

Isobel Rogers Kruesi has a third son, Oscar Rogers, born January 22nd. .

The Class will sympathize with Leila Houghteling in the sudden loss of her mother, January 28th. Leila had come east to preside at the annual meeting of the Alumnae Association, but was called back immediately after her arrival.

Margaret Doolittle, who is head of a girls' school in Tripoli, spent Christmas with Kate Chambers Seeleye in Beirut, Syria.

Marion Scott Soames landed in New York, January 29th, and after a visit to Catherine Delano Grant, went west to spend two months with her family in Chicago. She will return to Wales about April 1st.

1911 was represented at the Alumnae meeting at Bryn Mawr by Margery Hoffman Smith, Helen Ott Campbell, Hermine Schamberg Sinberg, Willa Alexander Browning, Norvelle Browne, Elizabeth Taylor Russell and Louise Russell. Saturday afternoon we had tea with hospitable Miss Applebee and Miss Taylor and talked over old and new times and customs.

Margery Hoffman Smith's trip east was described as a shopping trip, taken at a few hours' notice. After a few days in Bryn Mawr and Philadelphia, she came up to New York, where she shopped and collected artistic inspiration. Hoffy knows an awe-inspiring amount about dyeing, and those of us who watched her pack away in her suitcase various articles in bright, still unnamed colors were much impressed.

Helen Ott Campbell and her family arrived in Seattle last July to spend their furlough. Helen had not been well and they therefore came home a little early. She tells most interesting tales of her experiences in Korea, and showed very attractive pictures of the country and of her three pretty little children. Helen is giving some lectures in this country on their work in Korea. They expect to stay for about a year longer.

Virginia Canan Smith and her family have taken a house outside of Altoona. Her address is R. D. 2, Hollidaysburg, Pa.

Helen Parkhurst is now living at 27 West Ninth Street, New York, and Mary Taylor has moved to 78 Bedford Street, New York. .

Florence Wyman Tripp sailed for Europe in January.

New York has had visits this winter from many members of the Class—Margery Hoffman Smith, Marian Scott Soames, Ruth Tanner, Beulah Mitchell Hailey, Mary Case Pevear, and in the fall Ethel Richardson and Leila Houghteling on their way home from Europe.

Mary Williams Sherman recently accompanied her husband to Springfield, Mass., where he was a delegate to the Exchange Club Convention. She and her family will spend the summer on Lake Erie at their cottage at Mitiwanga, Ohio, six miles east of Huron, and she wants to hear from all members of 1911 passing through.

Ruth Roberts McMillen refuses to admit that she is doing anything of interest to the Class. She has three children, a boy and two girls, and lives at 465 W. Macon Street, Decatur, Ill.

1913

Class Editor, Nathalie Swift, 130 East Sixty-seventh Street, New York City.

Yvonne Stoddard Hayes is Chairman of the Committee on Efficiency in Government of the New York League of Women Voters.

Mary Tongue Eberstadt has a second daughter, Mary Van Arsdale, born in Baltimore on February 18th.

William Beebe's new book, *Galapagos; World's End,* contains twenty-four illustrations in color by Isabel Cooper. The New York Zoological Society's Expedition, of which Isabel is official artist, has recently gone to Haiti.

The following notes were contributed by our special correspondent in Boston:

Louisa Haydock Hackett has a daughter, Mary, born January 25th.

Alice Ames Crothers works three mornings a week at the Children's Hospital, and entertains with true Western hospitality, as the 1913 Lunch Club can testify.

Marguerite Mellen Dewey manages with surpassing skill the New England Bryn Mawr Alumnae Scholarship Committee; is on the Board of the Shady Hill School; gives large dinner parties with éclat; and successfully engineers her family of three children.

Clara Crocker is immersed in educational psychology and has chance for endless field work with her three energetic, active children.

Katharine Page Loring headed the Committee of the Junior League, which has just produced a much-lauded musical comedy, "Mlle. Modiste."

Margaret Blaine has succeeded to the honors of Chairman of the House Committee of the College Club, and, together with Miss Merryweather, runs an excellent hostel. She is also Chairman of the American Committee to collect funds for Crosby Hall.

Iki Irwin works on, with increasing fame attaching itself to her. Her researches are not such as can be understood by the uninitiated, but they find favor in the eyes of those in high scholastic circles. For the laity, she continues to be the best of companions and hostesses.

The Boston coterie has sustained a severe loss in the removal of Apphia Hack to Cincinnati.

Peanut Hodgdon tries to bring her Bryn Mawr training into play in executing the common round, the daily task, and continues her education by imbibing thoughts on the Moscow Art Theatre from her truly Bostonian cleaning lady, on English history from Dr. George Trevelyan, and viewing the latest thing in movies under the guidance of Clara Crocker.

1915

Class Editor, Mrs. James Austin Stone, 2831 Twenty-eighth Street, N. W., Washington, D. C.

The representatives of 1915 at the Alumnae meeting and President Park's luncheon were Kitty McCollin Arnett, Zena Blanc, Frances Boyer, Adrienne Kenyon Franklin, Mary Mitchell Moore and Helen McFarland Woodbridge.

Frances Boyer liked the East (or North?) so much when she came up for the Christmas holidays that she did not return to Texas as she had intended. Her brother is stationed in Philadelphia for intensive training in the Graduate School of Medicine of the University of Pennsylvania and Fran is studying French at the University. She is living at 4009 Baltimore Avenue.

Gertrude Emery visited Vashti McCreery at her home in Benton, Ill., for ten days during the mid-year vacation at Radcliffe, where Gertrude is still in the Physical Education Department. Her mother is on a cruise around the world and will arrive in New York on June 3, so Gertrude hopes to combine coming to reunion with a trip to New York to meet her mother. Vashti is also expecting to help celebrate our "tenth."

Olga Erbsloh was married in January to Robert Miller. She will keep her own name.

Ruth Hubbard and her sister have been studying at the University of Grenoble this winter. The card conveying this news gave no indication of when Ruth expects to return to her native heath.

Dora Levinson Kramer wants us to correct her address in our address books, as her college mail has been going astray. She is living at 2007 Pine Street, Philadelphia.

Ruth Tinker Morse and her husband had a short vacation at Pinehurst in March.

Elizabeth Smith Wilson says that for probably the next two years at least her address will be 2322 Grandview Avenue, Cincinnati. If nothing unexpected happens, she will spend the latter part of June and most of July at her father's summer home at Mt. Desert, Maine, where she was married in the fall. She writes: "I should love to see any one who happens to be in the neighborhood. Last summer I was fortunate to see a number of people from Bryn Mawr who were in Maine for a time and encountered Iki Irwin unexpectedly on a mountain top. Our post office address is Mount Desert, Me., but we are reached via Ellsworth or Bar Harbor or Northeast or Southwest Harbor."

Here is a message from Hat entitled Reunion:

"The Class of 1915 will meet"—by a certain flowering crab-apple tree outside the Library. . . . It's true, girls; this is reunion year, so you had better be getting out those green class-song books and humming through "We come from the East" and "As in the days of old" and "As the fragrant breath of spring." And then you had better gather together those tattered bits of sentiment for which 1915 was famous (?) and then write or telephone to your most best particular classmates, and be sure they get to reunion. Then all of us will be turning up and our "tenth" will be a real one, even if the Alumnae Association's arithmetic put us in 1924. Tradition has given place to schedule, which evidence of modern progress should delight the hearts of such as the notorious authors of "Pale lasses thin and fair."

Well, thin or fair or fat or tall or short—come on and reune, and answer all Adrienne's postals and questions and send your Reunion gift and make it a big one.

Yours as ever,

Hat.

P. S. (by the Class Editor). Adrienne begs me to say that a little help with the clerical work will be greatly appreciated, and asks anyone living in or near Philadelphia who has or can find any spare time to get in touch with her. Her address, as you all know, is 154 Lismore Avenue, Glenside, Pa.

1917

Class Editor, Isabella Stevenson Diamond, 1527 Eye Street, N. W., Washington, D. C.

Hel Harris writes from Kingsley House, Lorimer and Auburn Streets, Pittsburgh, Pa., and says she has been there since November 15th and bids fair to stay for some time to come. Hel says, "Kingsley House is a settlement house, of course, and I am its associate head resident. We have a new building almost finished—with a gym and a pool that rival Bryn Mawr's. All '17s are urged to stop off in Pittsburgh and try our spring board. Hildegarde Kendig is here as our personal service worker. Ruth Levy Falk and Heloise Carroll Hancock are in the vicinity."

Ilsa Knauth Dunbar writes:

"Dear 1917:

"I wish you'd all write to the BULLETIN. I just live from one class notes to the next. We are living at the village of Hurley, N. Y., two miles from Kingston. My husband teaches physics in the high school and we farm on the side—chief product—babies, four so far, two boys, two girls, all well and of normal intelligence according to Binet-Simon tests. Other live-stock consists of two cows, some hens, ducks and guineas—enough to keep me out of mischief. I keep up music and occasionally sing in concert here. I have no paid job, haven't published anything, haven't won any peace prizes. Try to read psychology in odd hours and do some thinking while I darn the stockings. If any Bryn Mawr people pass through Kingston, you know where to come and have lunch."

Bertha Greenough writes that she really has no news about herself, but that she visited Thalia over January 22nd and that she, Harold, and Diana are all well. Thalia acted in a play in December in Jamaica Plain—I know that seemed like old times to Thalia.

Frances Colter Stuart has a son born last September and named Archibald Stuart V for his father and grandfathers. Frances writes that Pete Iddings and Gladys McMillen also have new sons.

Will Elizabeth Hemenway send me her present address, please? The plea for news about herself sent her recently was returned unclaimed.

Con Hall wrote me that Eleanor Jencks is still studying art since she returned from Paris in October and that she received Honorable Mention the other day at the Charcoal Club Exhibit. Con added that she got the ring in Dor Shipley's wedding cake— she leaves us to draw our own conclusions about that!

Fran Curtin was a real honest-to-goodness lady and sent me word about her daughter, Ann De Armond Haynes, born last July. Fran adds that she *does* hope there is going to be a reunion this spring— is there?

Anna Coulter Parsons wrote that she had no particular views about herself this time but she enclosed excerpts from letters from Mildred Foster Elliston, who is again in China with her husband, who has a most interesting job with the Chinese Government Bureau of Economic Information. I am extremely glad Anna enclosed the excerpts, for they give a most interesting picture of Shanghai. The address "560 Avenue Joffre" impressed me particularly. Mildred's letter follows:

"Thanks muchly for your letter. They seem like manna from Heaven out here, so please keep them up.

"I am enclosing a picture of our house with H. and me sitting like landed proprietors on the porch. We were very lucky to get this place, because furnished houses for rent are rare in Shanghai and this one has *three* bathrooms. Imagine that after Peking, where I had none, or at least only a makeshift. We also have five servants, so I am not overburdened with household labor. But you are right about ease as compared to friends. I have been as homesick as the devil since landing here this time—before I felt all the time that it was just a temporary lark, but now I must stay for a time at least. Anyway, I am going to get everything out of it that I can. I have started doing some writing, but, of course, one can never tell whether one's effusions will ever reach the light of day. I feel, though, that I ought to make use of more of the experiences that I have had.

"Shanghai is a strange hybrid place. I am sure you would be surprised when you first saw it out here in what people think of as the wilds of China—it is a bona fide city—tall buildings—broad (at least some broad) paved streets, trams, big hotels, roof-gardens for dancing, restaurants, department stores—even soda fountains with real American drinks. And it is seething and buzzing with the eternal rush of city life. And yet in its standards it is very provincial, because each nationality here makes, as it were, a small town of its own with small-town gossip and small-town notions. There are no theatres—only movies with an occasional stock company—and amateur concerts play as important a part here as in a small town at home. And people discuss the three or four-year-old movies at the Carlton as they would speak of Galsworthy's latest play in New York. And then underneath all this respectability (there are more rich people here in proportion to the population I should say than in any place on earth) is the real Shanghai of poverty and licensed horrors in the shape of gambling and opium houses—restaurants that stand outside the international settlement and therefore outside the law, sweating of Chinese labor, and exploiting of the poor Russian refugees. Almost all the girls who serve as dancing-partners in semi-respectable restaurants like the Del Monte and the Creet are Russians of good family, who have been forced either to do this or starve. I have seen some of them and, as a whole, they are charming—entirely different from the type that you see at home. The gulf between the high and low is more marked here than in any place I have been—starvation elbowing with the most profligate extravagance.

"I am studying Chinese and can already carry on a rather skimpy conversation with my teacher that consists in phrases somewhat like this:

Sleep time, I take off coat.
Eat time, I eat very good foreign food.
Afternoon time, I go out play.
I sit private yellow vehicle, go.

This being a literal translation. The *private yellow vehicle* is a ricsha.

"I have also been studying Buddhism and have become quite enamoured of it (but don't tell Bob this—he will visualize me doing the three observances before a grinning Buddha and going altogether completely mad). The point is, like Christianity, Buddhism has declined until it is no longer reconcilable with the earlier tenets. And originally it was quite wonderful—a sort of cross between Couéism, Freudism, and the moral ideas of Christ. You ought to read something about it if you get a chance. I have been reading furiously since I got here, because it's the first time I haven't had a job taking up all my spare time."

1919

Class Editor, Frederica Howell, 211 Ballantine Parkway, Newark, N. J.

Frannie Day Lukens has a son, Allan Wood Lukens, born February 12.

Mrs. Louis Schwartz writes that our oldest child does not belong to Pi Driver Rock, but to her. Her son, Anthony, was born before she joined our Class, in July, 1908, and he now, at the age of fifteen, is the youngest Freshman at Cornell. Mrs. Schwartz is living in New York, at 1506 University Avenue.

Amelia Warner Wyllie has a daughter, Nancy, born November 18 last. Her present address is 159 East Fifty-fifth Street, New York.

Peggy France Caulfield has a son, Robert Lee, born last September, who, she writes, "has blue eyes, yellow hair, and is altogether most beguiling. His father being a baby specialist, we are trying to bring him up scientifically." Peggy's address is 31 Owen Street, Hartford.

Georgia Bailey Seelye has a daughter, Caroline Reily, born last August.

Helen Karns Champlin announces the birth of Carolyn King Champlin on June 11, 1923. Helen is teaching psychology in her husband's department at Southwestern State Normal School, California, Pa.

Dotty Walton Price claims as her sole great creative works Marion W. Price, born May 22, 1922, and Charles R. Price, May 28, 1923. Her address is Holt Street, Bronxville, N. Y.

Win Kaufman Whitehead has two children, John, who will be two this month, and Margaret Hope, born last November. Her address is 721 Sherman Avenue, Evanston, Ill.

So much for vital statistics for the moment.

Ann Stiles has accepted the job of Class Collector in Buster's place for the next few months.

Eleanor Marquand has been elected Corresponding Secretary of the B. M. Alumnae Association, but is a free woman for the present, having fled to Europe shortly before the election.

Buster Ramsay Phelps' new address is Wineberry 2783, Olivos F. C. C. A. Argentina. She writes of a darling house and very gay times, but pleads for letters.

A great occasion in the lives of six of our spinsters and two marrieds was the night of December 28, when B. Sorchan Binger allowed the invasion of her home by Tip and Nan, down from Boston. for Becky R's wedding, Peggy Janeway, Amelia Wyllie, Eleanor Marquand, Dot Chambers and Freddy Howell. A great deal of plain and fancy eating and talking was done between 7 and midnight, and all parted friends.

Gordon Woodbury Dunn is moving on April 1 to an old house in Georgetown, and is "looking forward to a lot of refurbishing." Her new address is 3126 O Street, Washington.

Marion Mosely is hard at it in the University of Chicago, taking work along nutrition lines. She is sailing June 11 for London with Dr. and Mrs. Grenfell to help with the Grenfell Mission booth in the British Empire Exhibit there, and plans for the rest of the summer in Brittany and Italy with Louise Wood.

Isabel Whittier is teaching English and History in the Senior High School of Hazleton, Pa.

Our deepest sympathy is with Louise Wood, who was called home from Florence in December by the death of her mother, Mrs. Ira Couch Wood. All '19 remembers Mrs. Wood with a great deal of admiration and real affection, recalling particularly her coming from Washington, when she was the head of the Woman's Committee of the Council of National Defense, to help us organize the War Council at Bryn Mawr.

1921

Class Editor, Kathleen F. Johnston, 1754 Massachusetts Avenue, Washington, D. C.

Katherine Ward has announced her engagement to Mr. Robert Seitz, a graduate student and instructor at Yale. Kath is still at Yale and on her way to her Ph. D. She had her M. A. last June.

Clarinda Garrison is working with the J. Walter Thompson Co. in New York and from all accounts is an ardent advertising fan. She makes flying trips to far-off points in search of copy and leads a pleasantly variegated existence.

There are two members of 1921 at Miss Parker's School in New York, Wiestie, who has been there for several years, and a newcomer, Margaret Weisman.

Mary McClennen Knollenberg has just set off on a most delightful journey. She and Bernhard left New York for San Francisco by rail. From there they will sail for China, Japan and Russia, making little side excursions through the Inland Sea, Honolulu, the Fiji Islands, and the South Sea Islands. They arrive home about the end of May.

Helen Irvin Murray is still librarian for the Association of the Bar. She is also doing some research work at the Rockefeller Foundation.

Florence Billstein has an apartment at 141 MacDougall Street, New York, and is working as secretary to an architect.

Lulu Cadot Catterall and her husband are moving to Richmond on April 1st. Her husband will practice there.

Mary Baldwin writes from Rome, where she had arrived after six months' travelling in England, Scotland, France and Italy. She has seen all sorts of Bryn Mawr people,—Gertrude Steele in a tea-shop on the Riviera, Betty Barber about to start for Greece, and Sydney Washburn on the Piazza di Spagna. Mary says that she is having a wonderful time travelling with three friends and doing everything from riding horseback and climbing mountains to dancing with Italian princes. She is going to Sicily, and then to England for May, June, and July, stopping en route at Florence, Venice, Milan, Lausanne, and Paris. Her address is care of The Farmers Loan and Trust Company, Rue d'Antin, Paris.

Postscript. If anyone wants to see the most adorable baby in the world go to see Ellen Jay and Clarinda Garrison, Junior, in East Seventy-eighth Street, New York

1923

Class Editor, Dorothy Meserve, Madison Avenue, New York City.

Pick is engaged! and very much so, to Mr. Sherman Loud, of New York City, who is Dena Humphrey's cousin; so it's all in the family. We are far more pleased than surprised. Pick is going on with her work at the May Day office in spite of outside interests.

Dena appeared as the nun in Morris Gest's *Miracle* on Saturday, March 22nd. She made a great hit. All of Bryn Mawr was there and claimed her with pride.

Scribie is also joining the younger married set, announcing her engagement to Mr. John Abbott of New York.

Gussie Howell is staying with Wang Holt in Chicago. It is rumored that Lucy Kate Bowers went also, but the report lacks confirmation.

1923 had a Birthday dinner in Rockefeller Hall on March 17th. Pick, Ratz, Grace, Dusty, Hellie Wilson, Sara Archbald, and Harriett Millar were present. Postcards from Ally were read and much applauded.

Frances Childs is to be May Day Vice-Chairman in New York and Anne Fraser Brewer May Day Vice-Chairman for New Haven. We are very proud that the class holds such important offices.

Everyone in the class is very busy.

CONTENTS

SCHOOL DIRECTORY

FERRY HALL
A Resident and Day School for Girls
LAKE FOREST, ILLINOIS
On Lake Michigan, near Chicago

College Preparatory, General and Advanced Courses, Departments of Music, Home Economics, Expression, and Art. *Supervised Athletics and Swimming Pool.*

Eloise R. Tremain, A.B., Bryn Mawr, Principal

THE
Mary C. Wheeler Town and Country School
PROVIDENCE, RHODE ISLAND

Preparation for Bryn Mawr and College Board Examinations

Out door sports   Junior Country Residence

HILLSIDE
A School for Girls
NORWALK   CONNECTICUT

In a beautiful New England town, one hour from New York. Girls from all parts of the country. Four residences, schoolhouse, gymnasium. Extensive grounds. Preparation for all colleges. Special courses. Outdoor life. Horseback riding. Catalog.

Margaret R. Brendlinger, A.B., Vassar
Vida Hunt Francis, A.B., Smith, *Principals*

The Harcum School
BRYN MAWR, PA.

Prepares for Bryn Mawr and all leading colleges

Musical Course prepares for the Department of Music of Bryn Mawr College

EDITH H. HARCUM, Head of School
L. MAY WILLIS, Principal

MISS RANSOM *and* MISS BRIDGES' SCHOOL
HAZEL LANE, PIEDMONT (Suburb of San Francisco)

College Preparatory

MARION RANSOM } Headmistresses
EDITH BRIEGES }

MISS MADEIRA'S SCHOOL
1330 19th St., N. W.   Washington, D. C

A Resident and Day School
for Girls

LUCY MADEIRA WING, A.B.

MRS. DAVID LAFOREST WING
Head Mistress

The Shipley School
Bryn Mawr, Pennsylvania
Preparatory to Bryn Mawr College
Alice G. Howland, Eleanor O Brownell,
Principals

The Ethel Walker School
SIMSBURY, CONNECTICUT
Head of School
ETHEL WALKER SMITH, A.M. Bryn Mawr College
Head Mistress
JESSIE GERMAIN HEWITT, A.B. Bryn Mawr College

THE MISSES KIRK'S
College Preparatory School
Bryn Mawr Ave. and Old Lancaster Road,
Bryn Mawr, Pa.

Number of boarders limited. Combines advantages of school life with private instruction. Individual schedule arranged for each pupil.

MISS WRIGHT'S SCHOOL
Bryn Mawr, Pa.

Prepares for Bryn Mawr and
College Board Examinations

Miss Beard's School for Girls
ORANGE, NEW JERSEY

A country school near New York. College preparatory, special courses. Art. Domestic Arts and Science. Supervised physical work. Agnes Miles Music School affiliated with Miss Beard's School.

MISS LUCIE C. BEARD, Head Mistress

ROSEMARY HALL
No elective courses
Prepares for college
Preferably Bryn Mawr

Caroline Ruutz-Rees, Ph.D. } Head Mistresses
Mary E. Lowndes, Litt.D. }

GREENWICH   CONNECTICUT

The Katharine Branson School
ROSS, CALIFORNIA   Across the Bay from San Francisco
A Country School   College Preparatory
Heads
Katharine Fleming Branson, A. B., Bryn Mawr
Laura Elizabeth Branson, A. B., Bryn Mawr

THE AGNES IRWIN SCHOOL
2009-2011 Delancey Place, Philadelphia
A College Preparatory
SCHOOL FOR GIRLS
JOSEPHINE A. NATT, A.B., Headmistress
BERTHA M. LAWS, A.B., Secretary-Treasurer

SCHOOL DIRECTORY

Kindly mention BRYN MAWR BULLETIN

BRYN MAWR ALUMNAE BULLETIN

OFFICIAL PUBLICATION OF
THE BRYN MAWR ALUMNAE ASSOCIATION

EVELYN PAGE, '23, *Editor*
GERTRUDE J. HEARNE, '19, *Business Manager*

EDITORIAL BOARD

LUCY M. DONNELLY, '93
ELEANOR FLEISHER REISMAN, '03
CAROLINE MORROW CHADWICK-COLLINS, '05

ADELAIDE W. NEALL, '06
MAY EGAN STOKES, '11
LEILA HOUGHTELING, '11, *ex-officio*

Subscription Price, $1.50 a Year   *Single Copies, 25 Cents*
Checks should be drawn to the order of Bryn Mawr Alumnae Bulletin
Published monthly, except August and September, at 1006 Arch St., Philadelphia, Pa.

VOL. IV   MAY, 1924   No. 5

WE REFORM OURSELVES

We intend, in this issue of the BULLETIN, to advocate a reform, not in regard to another phase of the Alumnae Association, but in regard to ourselves. We have realized in the past few months that we must adopt a new system of class notes. Again and again, to our own disappointment and that of our readers, we have been forced to cut or to hold over material, not one but two months, until the next issue scheduled to contain the notes of the class in question. Although we cannot increase the amount of space devoted to class notes, we can devise a plan by which we may use the space at our disposal to better advantage.

The inadequacy of the present plan of division by odd and even classes is obvious. This arbitrary distinction often forces us to omit news of im-mediate importance because the BULLETIN about to be published carries the notes of the even rather than the odd classes, or vice versa. A month later the psychological moment has passed. Secondly, the material for the BULLETIN is unevenly distributed throughout the year. In one month we have ten pages to devote to class notes, in another five. It is our aim to give every class its desserts in the matter of space, and this we have been unable to do. Indeed, although we publish a monthly magazine, we have imposed upon ourselves the disadvantages of one published half as often.

We therefore propose, beginning with the issue of next October, to carry in each number of the BULLETIN the notes of every class, whether odd or even, sent in to us.

Whatever space we may have we shall allot as evenly as possible among the different classes. Among the notes sent us by each class we shall give precedence to news of time importance, or to that which the Class Editor especially requests us to print. Whatever remainder there may be we shall insert in the next issue of the BULLETIN.

We have said nothing so far about the Class Editors and their work, although we are in a position to ap- preciate both. They supply the Alumnae Association with information, through the pages of the BULLETIN, and form the indispensable connection between the individual and the group. In the past it has been our ungracious duty to punish not only the hard-working Editor but also the eager Alumna. In the future it shall be our endeavor no longer to turn a deaf ear to the many who say to us, "I pray you, tell me how my good friend doth."

DISTRICT COUNCELLOR ANNOUNCEMENT

Sarah Atherton Bridgman (Mrs. Donald Storrs Bridgman), '13, of 27 Beekman Place, New York City, has been elected Councillor of District II for the years 1924-27.

Caroline Daniels Moore (Mrs. Philip Wyatt Moore), '01, of Private Road, Hubbard Woods, Ill., has been elected Councillor of District V.

THE ALUMNAE FUND AND THE CAMPAIGN

Two appeals for contributions for the College are being made, one through the Alumnae Fund and the other through the $400,000 Campaign for the Music Endowment and the Auditorium for the Students' Building. Both appeals were authorized by the Alumnae Association at the Annual Meeting in February. The first is primarily an appeal to the Alumnae, the second to the outside world through the Alumnae. That there may be as little duplication as possible very close relations have been established between the two committees in charge. Gifts for the Campaign will be received by the Alumnae Fund.

Gifts from Alumnae to the Campaign are reported immediately to the Alumnae Fund, thereby being reported to the Class Collectors and credited to the classes of the donors. Second appeals for the Alumnae Fund will not be sent to those Alumnae who have contributed to the Campaign. A supplementary report will be published with the 1924 Alumnae Fund Report of all contributions made by Alumnae to the Endowment of the Music Department and the Auditorium of the Students' Building.

MARY PEIRCE,
Chairman of the Alumnae Fund.

ANNOUNCEMENTS

Mary Rodney, Merion Hall, Bryn Mawr College, will be very glad to receive the names of any Alumnae who wish the Class Book of 1924.

The Editor was forced by lack of space to omit a part of the notes of 1892, 1904, and 1908. These notes will appear in the July BULLETIN.

If any copies of the programme remain unsold after May Day they will be available for Alumnae at a price of $1.00 each. The illustrations for the programme have been drawn by Elizabeth Shippen Green Elliott, and are extremely beautiful.

All contributions to the June BULLETIN should be sent to Evelyn Page, Taylor Hall, Bryn Mawr College, before May 10th.

The Nominees for the Alumnae Directorship

Elizabeth Winsor Pearson

ELIZABETH WINSOR PEARSON, 1892

Elizabeth Winsor Pearson of the Class of 1892 has many qualifications for Director of Bryn Mawr College; but I should put first a life-long experience, study and love of the problems and methods of education. She is a New Englander by inheritance as by marriage and both tradition and marriage have contributed to her knowledge of the teaching profession. Indeed, she comes of a family which teaches the young and builds schools for them to grow in as easily and creatively as other families swim or sing.

Her mother was a teacher and a member of a line of distinguished educators. This remarkable woman who founded a school after her marriage in a suburb of Boston where her seven children got the beginnings of their education launches four of the seven as educators in their turn. All four have taken a notable place.

Elizabeth Winsor's college years belong to the era when a Bryn Mawr education was a radical and deeply prized adventure, for which real sacrifices were made. When she began to teach Latin and Greek and English in her sister Mary P. Winsor's Boston school, after her graduation, the glory of Paul Shorey's legendary classes under the cherry tree hung about her and a whole generation of· young Bostonians started headlong for Bryn Mawr. She taught six years in the Winsor School, until her marriage in 1898 to Henry G. Pearson. Mr. Pearson was also a teacher of English— at the Massachusetts Institute of Technology, where he now directs the English Department.

Mrs. Pearson's interest in the Winsor School, like her loyalty to Bryn Mawr, never slackened. If her husband's profession led her to follow very closely the problems of teaching in technical schools, if her growing family stimulated her to study and experiment in elementary teaching, and to create a "secondary" neighborhood school on her beautiful street in Newton—as her mother had done ·in Winchester—she also found time to be assistant secretary of the then much larger Winsor School in 1910-11, and to serve two terms on the. Academic Committee. Time for civic work ·and responsibility was not lacking either, or for literary work in collaboration with Mr. Pearson.

There have been no water-tight compartments in Mrs. Pearson's life between home and school, family and community, private and professional careers: what life brings her she immediately examines, reacts on, and puts to constructive use. ·She was, for example, one of the first "academic" educators to apply the Montessori method to primary teaching in America; and her work on the progressive education of children from 2-5 years begun in her own home has been extended into one of the tenement districts of Boston where the Ruggles Street Nursery School and Training Centre—which she was instrumental in establishing—has proved a most valuable social experiment.

As a pupil of Elizabeth Winsor in her sister's school, as a friend of later years, who has watched the truly creative development of her life and work and family, I suggest that few if any Bryn Mawr graduates have a grasp as complete as Mrs. Pearson of the whole problem of education. Her success as mother, teacher and citizen has been striking and I know no woman more fitted to cast a vote in the destinies of her Alma Mater; of a college like Bryn Mawr which must increasingly meet the demands of the experimental schools, without sacrificing the gifts and standards of the academic education. Elizabeth Pearson has poise, intellectual integrity and complete disinterestedness, combined with that affectionate faith in the young of the hu-

Katharine Page Loring

man species, that joy in life and intelligence forever renewing itself, that eagerness to bring opportunity and expansion to minds and souls in need of sustenance that is the gift of all true teachers—and should be of all true directors of institutions of learning.

ELIZABETH SHÉPLEY SERGEANT, 1903.

KATHARINE PAGE LORING, 1913

Katharine Page was born in New Rochelle, New York, in 1891. Her father, Walter Hines Page, was a Southerner; her mother is of Scotch descent. Somewhere woven into the family is a French strand which may account in her for a most lovable touch of gaiety.

Katharine went first to the Buckingham School in Cambridge, then to Friends' Seminary in New York, then, her family again moving, she entered and was graduated from the Dwight School in Englewood, going immediately afterwards to spend two peaceful summers in England and a winter studying German and French on the Continent. In 1909 she entered Bryn Mawr, taking her A.B. in Latin and French. Here, as in school, she did everything easily and well without self-consciousness, with a sort of simplicity, which is part of her charm. She was three and one-half years president of her class and then permanent president, a member of every varsity team in college—except that I am not sure about water polo,—tennis champion two years, and an unforgettable Babbie in the *Little Minister.*

Immediately after leaving Bryn Mawr she joined her father, then Ambassador, in England. One catches delightful glimpses of her in her father's published letters. One cannot altogether weigh what this London experience meant, but I know that her quick perceptions, tact, good judgment and real ability in practical affairs must have been a great comfort in those trying days; and I do know also that when she returned there had been added something fine and strong to her personality.

In 1915 she had married Charles Greeley Loring at the Chapel Royal, St. James Palace, which showed, I think, how close she and her family were to the heart of the English people. Afterwards she returned with her husband to his home in Boston, where she is now living. She has now two little girls, four and six years old.

Since her marriage her interest in educational, civic and social matters has been rapidly growing and to these things she has been giving serious attention. Her interests are at the same time wide and discriminating. Besides her ordinary engagements she has found time to be director of the Boston City Club, director of the Boston Children's Aid Society, director and later president of the Board of Directors of the Beaver Elementary School; and, in more immediate college activities, she has been secretary of the Bryn Mawr Club, chairman for two years of the New England Scholarship Committee, of which she is still a member, and—a rather characteristic note—she is treasurer of the United States Field Hockey Association.

If one thinks of Katharine Page Loring as being young for the position of Alumnae Director—well, so she is, but she brings an experience and equipment unusual for her age. Cultivated in the best meaning of the word, by tradition, by association, by education; with a keen, far-reaching balanced mind, never hurried or driven, because with all her interests she has a nice sense of values; with a love of ideas; with a love of everything beautiful; with a real appreciation of the significance of people and things, and events; with humor, poise, and loyalty like that of a ship's captain, —with all this, she understands a certain graciousness and *art of living* and this understanding she could bring to Bryn Mawr.

A. GORDON HAMILTON, 1913.

HELEN TAFT MANNING, 1915

Helen Taft Manning's career speaks so definitely for itself that it seems unnecessary to make any comment on it at this time, the eve of her running for the nomination as Alumnae Director.

She was born in Cincinnati on August 1, 1891. Prepared by the National Cathedral School, Washington, and by the Baldwin School, Bryn Mawr, she entered the College in 1908 as the first Matriculation Scholar for Pennsylvania with one of the highest averages that has ever been made in the history of the College. Her college course was interrupted at the end of her Sophomore year, when she left for two years to help her mother as hostess at the White House. At the close of her father's term of office as President of the United States, she returned to college. Her part in undergraduate activities was an important one; she organized the Debating Club, was a member of the English Club and Editor of "Tipyn o' Bob" and of the "Lantern," she was a member of the Advisory Board of the Self-Government Association and was Vice-President of the Christian Association. In her chosen line of Modern History and Economics and Politics she did brilliantly and she also won the George W. Childs Essay Prize.

After graduating from Bryn Mawr, she became a graduate student at Yale, where she took her Master's Degree in 1916. In 1917 she returned to Bryn Mawr as Dean for two years, and as Acting President for

one, the year, as it happened, of the Endowment Drive. Although her marriage in 1920 to Mr. Frederick Manning, an Instructor in History at Yale, meant that she left Bryn Mawr, it did not mean that she in any way lost touch with the College; that same year she became one of the Alumnae Directors. She also continued to prepare her Doctor's thesis, both at Yale and in London, where she and Mr. Manning were in 1922-23 with their year-old daughter.

To those who knew Mrs. Manning as an undergraduate and realize the part she played in undergraduate life and remem-

Helen Taft Manning

ber the great debate with President Emeritus Thomas on the Cut Rule—"It was a famous victory,"—to those who knew her as a singularly delightful hostess at the White House, and to those who knew her as Dean, and as Acting President, one need say nothing. To the college generations before and after her, one may say that her utter lovableness, her humor, her sense of justice, her keen, fearless logical mind and her generosity of point of view, make one singularly sure of the value of the gifts of spirit and intellect that she, as a Director, would again give to the College.

MARJORIE LAM. THOMPSON, 1912.

Nathalie McFaden Blanton

NATHALIE McFADEN BLANTON, 1917

Nathalie McFaden Blanton was born in Marion, Virginia, in 1895, and graduated from Miss Ellett's School in Richmond in 1913, entering Bryn Mawr the next autumn with the Class of 1917. At school she was president of her class and throughout her whole career there showed uncommon ability both in her classes and in her power of leadership. In college her capacity manifested itself in many directions. She was on her class teams in basketball and hockey, manager of the track team, acted in certain of the class plays, was secretary of her class, and president of the Christian Association.

The winter after her graduation she married Dr. Wyndham Blanton of Richmond, then in the Army. She has now three handsome sons and a charming little daughter, all bright, all good, well-trained children, and all fairly bursting with health. But in spite of so much family, which shows her constant, personal care, she has had time for anything that pertains to or forwards the cause of Bryn Mawr. She is one of the firm supporting pillars of a rather frail College Club. She has been president and is still one of the executive board of the Virginia Randolph Ellett Alumnae. It was she who organized the Bryn Mawr Summer School Committee here, and she was the first Alumnae Councillor for this district,—a district involving much labor and heart-breaking discouragements, for, with the exception of Washington, there was no group of Alumnae as large as the one in Richmond, where we had, I believe, at that time about seven. Seldom does one have opportunity to hear so delightful or so effective a speaker as she is. She has a most uncommon gift of speech. Easy, poised, enthusiastic, convincing, inspiring, she completely controls her audience, yet is, withal, restrained, graceful, modest, and altogether charming. And I think I might say that it is mostly she and her undaunted spirit and enthusiasm that keep the Bryn Mawr spirit alive in this community of few Alumnae and little college interest.

No rehearsal of mere offices and concrete achievements could give one an idea of Nathalie Blanton's real self, nor of her brilliant mind and ready and convincing tongue, her initiative, her executive ability and power of organization, her indefatigable energy, her enthusiasm, her willingness to tackle the seemingly impossible, her entire competence for any task laid on her shoulders, and her deep abiding love for Bryn Mawr. We who know her love her, admire and honor her; Bryn Mawr should be proud of her, and if she is chosen a director the Alumnae may indeed be happy.

HENRIETTA RUNYON WINFREY, 1912.

By Evangeline Walker Andrews, 1893

(This article is taken from the preface of a book on May Day which Mrs. Andrews is now writing. It was originally intended for publication in the May Day programme, but owing to a lack of space had to be omitted.)

Almost a quarter of a century has passed since the first "Merrie May Games" were given "by Ye Scholars of Bryn Mawr on Ye Colledge Greene, Ye first day of May, Anno Domini 1900;" and at that time, I venture to think, no one dreamed that this historic revival of Elizabethan sports and revels would become as traditional a part of the life of the Bryn Mawr undergraduates as Lantern Night or the Sophomore Play. This production of 1924 is the sixth of a series begun twenty-four years ago, and produced, on an average of once every four years since that time.

One afternoon in March, 1900, a group of students, mainly seniors, came to my house on the campus to discuss the possibility of giving an out-of-door entertainment by means of which a substantial sum of money might be raised towards a Students' Building, needed almost as much then as now. For two hours or more we discussed plans without producing any that seemed to express what we liked to call the spirit of Bryn Mawr; and the meeting broke up, all of us promising that we would try to think of something concrete and entertaining to present at the mass-meeting to be held the following evening.

Then while I stood watching my guests as, talking and laughing, they crossed the athletic field, climbed the steps on the opposite side, and drifted—a charming little procession—across the campus towards Denbigh and the Pembrokes—at that very moment the inspiration came, literally out of the blue sky of Bryn Mawr. Of course! With an English setting all made for us—rolling hills and well-tilled fields; grey stone, ivy-covered buildings of Elizabethan architecture; with spring and May coming over the hills, and youth, almost 500 strong, waiting merely for the word—why not an Elizabethan May-Day? Not the gambols of the court with which everyone was familiar—but those of the common people with their planting of the may-pole on the village green, their country dances, games, and plays, and pageants; with Robin Hood and his band, Maid Marian, the hobbyhorse, the worthies nine, and all the gay, grotesque, and charming festivities and characters beloved by the rustics of Elizabethan England? It was entirely suitable

that the May-Day sports and pastimes, suppressed by Puritan Old England as well as by Puritan New England, should be revived, without its evils, by the adventurous and talented young Elizabethans of Bryn Mawr. Such was the idea that took possession of me, as I stood enjoying the color and rhythm of that little procession of students crossing the campus on a bleak afternoon in March of 1900.

The suggestion that we should revive an Elizabethan May-Day on the Bryn Mawr campus was received by cheers that made the gymnasium ring with an enthusiasm that promised success from the start; and from that moment until May 1—six short weeks, one of them a college holiday—every undergraduate, and many Alumnae, both in New York and Philadelphia, worked incessantly, giving most generously of time, interest, and labor. Having the idea was a simple enough matter, and more or less familiarity with the period made not too difficult the necessary research work and the arrangement of the programme; but had it not been for the fine spirit of co-operation on the part of groups and individuals, who subordinated personal preferences and worked for the glory of the College as a whole, the task of casting, training, and costuming almost 500 persons in so short a time, would have been impossible. The great danger that college work might suffer and the opposition of faculty and authorities thereby be justly incurred was minimized by the fact that the undergraduates, as a body, agreed not to cut classes for any cause except illness, and that the available Alumnae assumed the responsibilities of costumes, properties, rehearsals, business and financial arrangements. Thus the undergraduates were left more free to devote themselves to training for the parts they were to take in the production, although the four who served on the Executive Committee not only served as class chairmen and maintained at a high level the *esprit de corps* of the student body, but contributed largely to the general work of organization, and to the solving of the new and difficult problems that confronted the Committee from moment to moment.

A special feature of the first May-Day,

and one calculated to create atmosphere, as we say today in the Moving Picture world, was the programme, the cover of which is made of a soft, tinted paper and printed in black, yellow, red, and green from a design by Miss Violet Oakley. In the background are the towers and arch of Pembroke, and one of the old wild-cherry trees in full bloom; while in the foreground vivacious Elizabethans weave in and out the gay streamers of the may-poles. The spirit of the English Renaissance and of a Bryn Mawr spring breathes in every detail of this design, which was used for the programmes of 1900, 1906, and 1910, and again in 1914 for the cover of the May-Day Announcement.

It is a cause for great regret that the original of this design was lost, for it was to have been one of the cherished possessions of the much-wished-for Students' Building; but in 1900 the best color work was done in Boston and our programme had to be printed there. The hand-made plates from which were printed the inside sheets—Elizabethan as to form, lettering, and spelling—were returned in safety; but unfortunately for all of us, Miss Oakley's delightful design never found its way back to Bryn Mawr. Some day, perhaps, we may be able to induce her to reproduce it for all of us from one of the old programmes.

Elizabethan music proved to be difficult to assemble and arrange, and we should have fared badly in this respect had it not been for the expert knowledge and assistance of the late Dr. Hugh Clark of the University of Pennsylvania, who not only orchestrated the music for the songs and dances, but trained and directed the various musicians and directed the orchestra on May-Day. In this connection I recall with real gratitude the fact that when some of the union musicians struck because of the long hours of the Elizabethan revels —they were not Elizabethans—the musical clubs of Haverford College came to the rescue, donned cloaks and caps, marched in our pageant, and furnished much of the music with which we made this May-Day an historic, as well as a very merry, one.

Then, too, the dances of the milkmaids and chimney sweeps, as well as the sword and morris dances, had to be worked out painfully from such books as Brand's *Observations of Popular Antiquities*, published in 1813; for not until many years later did a Cecil Sharpe arise to give us invaluable books of accurate music and the detailed figures of the traditional country and morris dances of England. The many and varied dances of this sort which were given for the first time at the May-Day of 1920 added a new and very beautiful feature to the spectacle, and are to be given again, in even greater numbers, in this production of 1924.

And then the questions of costumes and publicity! Bryn Mawr was about to appear in a new and very public way, and it was for the May-Day committee to see that nothing was done that was not highly creditable to her. Newspaper reporters who appeared on the campus during the last days of rehearsals were told that they could not take photographs, but that they might use some of the official photographs, provided that every plate be returned to the committee, and that students taking part in the plays, etc., should not be identified by name in the printed accounts. Personal publicity, they were told, was to be scrupulously avoided; and what seems most extraordinary, considered from the angle of today, is that both photographers and reporters promised to regard the wishes of· the committee and kept their word.

Today, when we are accustomed to see women of all ages wearing street gowns fourteen or more inches from the ground; or dressed for sports in bloomers or breeches; or dancing rhythmic and ballroom dances in the scantiest of clothing— it is difficult to realize that as late as 1900 such things were not only "not done," but that storms of criticism were aroused because college girls even ventured to wear their sport skirts an inch above their shoe-tops. At that time Bryn Mawr students playing men's parts in men's costumes were not allowed to go out on the campus to have their photographs taken; and at Vassar, the students met the various prohibitions by wearing men's coats and vests with their own long dark skirts, or by masking the unmentionable trousers by means of small black aprons.

As I look over the photographs of the first May-Day, I find that the Bryn Mawr Elizabethans were, if anything, overburdened with clothes, even the most daring of them, such as Robin Hood and his merry men, wearing leather leggings and garments coming well to the knees. However, many were the hours spent over the troublesome questions as to whether girls should wear men's costumes at all in public—fortunately the period that offered smocks and cloaks helped greatly at this point; whether materials were too gaudy or too diaphanous; and whether the shepherds and rustics should wear their smocks one inch or four inches below the knee. And even though all the costumes had been designed with great discretion and passed upon in every instance by an efficient and wise costuming committee, it was possible for a Philadelphia critic to say that the Elizabethan crowd at Bryn Mawr was "as leggy as young colts"; and for the delightful old farmer who came all the way from Lancaster to drive his handsome belted oxen in the pageant, to exclaim, as the procession started, "Never again will I allow my oxen to see such a sight as this."

May-Day of 1900 dawned bright and clear, and almost with the sun, students, faculty, neighbors, and college workmen were assembling to help decorate the floats, and to give the finishing touches to the may-poles, especially to the rose-wreathed pole that was to have the place of honor in the middle of the green. Neighboring farmers arrived with sheep and lambs for the Senior play, *The Lady of the May;* and children from far and near were on hind with their donkeys and ponies, proud to have them ridden by the Nine Worthies, without whom no English May-Day was ever complete. By noon the campus presented the appearance of a village fair.

Thanks to the generosity of the late Mr. Theodore N. Ely, always a staunch admirer and supporter of the College, the procession was allowed to form in his beautiful grounds of "Wyndham"; and just as the bell in the tower of Taylor Hall struck three, a blare of trumpets sounded, and twelve heralds came through the arch of Pembroke, announcing the approach of the pageant. The first May-Day revels at Bryn Mawr had begun. Many of those who took part in the May-Days have said that the thrill they experienced when for the first time they found themselves transformed into Elizabethans and saw the procession about to move, made them forget everything except the fun of the experience and the real joy of living.

Such was the character and spirit of the first May-Day, and the second was much the same; but quite aware of our shortcomings in 1900, we took six months for the production, and put more thought and time on costumes and the coaching of the plays and dances. The Elizabethan banners which now decorate the towers of the various buildings date from 1906, and do much toward creating the proper atmosphere. Then owing to the fact that by May of 1906 the beautiful cloisters of the new library were finished we yielded to the temptation of using the cloister garden, and departed from our May-Day of the common people to the extent of giving three masques—distinctly entertainments of the court—the *Masque of Queens,* the *Masque of Flowers,* and the *Masque of Cupid.*

Thus, although the May-Day of 1900, both in its choice of plays and dances, and in the crudeness and simplicity of its costumes, was more accurate from an historical point of view, that of 1906, with its costly masques and more elaborate costumes, has proved to be the type to which the Bryn Mawr May-Day conforms. From time to time, a play here and there is omitted in favor of another not tried before, and special features, like dances, are added which enhance the beauty of the whole, but the essential form and spirit remain the same from May-Day to May-Day. The productions of 1910 and 1914 were most ably directed by Miss Elizabeth Daly of the Class of 1901, who not only helped with the original production, but arranged the version of the Robin Hood plays which has been used from that time to this. The fifth and sixth productions owe their direction to Mrs. Otis Skinner, who though not a Bryn Mawrtyr, academically speaking, interprets our ideals so sympathetically and is so entirely one of us in spirit and association that we claim her as one of our very own.

Many of the more conservative friends of the College who refused to lend their names for the first production, became later most enthusiastic supporters of the May-Day; but from the moment of its inception there was one who has always had faith in Bryn Mawr students and stimulated them to put forth their best efforts for the College. Anyone who has had the privilege of studying the Elizabethans with President Emeritus Thomas, and has seen the lovely campus and the beautiful buildings grow as if by magic under her hand, knows that at heart she herself is a great Elizabethan, and that in the last analysis, the inspiration for our Elizabethan May-Day sprang from the atmosphere and environment which she has created at Bryn Mawr.

The $400,000 Drive

In the combination of the drives for the Students' Building and for the Music Department, the Alumnae Association looks for the fulfillment of two desires, which, although they have arisen in different generations, are not alien to each other. From a practical point of view, the auditorium of the Students' Building is linked to the establishment of a Music Department, which to be of value to the entire student body must sponsor a number of formal and informal concerts. From a point of view which cannot be called impractical, both the Music Department and the Students' Building are phases of a new trend in college life. The student of today asks that she be not only equipped for the special occupation which she is to pursue, but also trained to appreciate the work of others and to employ her leisure moments intelligently according to her interests. In establishing a Music Department at Bryn Mawr, the college hopes to give those especially endowed an opportunity to cultivate their faculties, and to train the average person to a keen appreciation of good music. In erecting the Students' Building, the college will provide an adequate working centre for student activities.

At the request of the May Day Manager with reference to the objects of the drive, President Park recently made the following statement for publication in the May Day Programme:

Musicians and musically minded laymen have always sacrificed and toiled for the art of their love, but only lately have persons of general education in the community realized the relation of music to their own and to the common life, and spent themselves to secure and make permanent opportunities for hearing music and for learning to understand it. They are providing the musician for the audience and the audience for the musician. The great increase in local symphony orchestras, and in the development and enriching of the music settlements and music schools is a result of their efforts. In the public and private schools more music is actually taught today and the instruction is directed from a new angle. The ordinary child who a generation ago would have been regarded as thoroughly unmusical learns now to understand the structure of music so that he can not only listen with intelligence but even in a small way create music himself. The colleges in their turn must concern themselves with the problem of music as a subject of study for the undergraduates and graduates.

"Through a gift of the Alumnae and friends of the college a modest experiment in musical education has been tried at Bryn Mawr. Technically difficult courses in harmony have been given along with sound courses in the history of music and in the appreciation of music, the latter training the faculty of attention in a way which is unique in our college curriculum. And to those of us who cannot register for these courses, good measure pressed down and running over has been given by the generosity of the department,—delightful concerts, informal musicales open to all the students, choir and glee club training, talks explaining the programs of the Philadelphia Symphony, and aid in preparation for May Day. In the short, close packed Bryn Mawr year we have all found something for our odd moments which is different from and yet closely in harmony with the other intellectual work of the college.

I came to the college two years ago hesitant as to the inclusion of music in the Bryn Mawr curriculum. I saw in it all the dangers of the superficial, the sentimental, and the momentary enthusiasm. I have come to feel that the courses offered and the contribution made by the department to the life of the college are as stimulating intellectually as they are pleasing aesthetically. It is already hard for me to imagine academic Bryn Mawr proceeding on its way through the years without its Music Department.

Every Alumna knows the inconvenience of our only two places of meeting—the chapel which is not large enough even for our own student body, and the gymnasium which has no dignity or appropriateness for many of its uses. The college life could go on more usefully, more pleasantly and more interestingly with a convenient place of assembly for addresses, meetings, plays and concerts. In the old Taylor Chapel partitions could give us three more large, light classrooms and two more offices. All the small classrooms and offices are already in constant use. A few committee rooms for important student organizations, a few shelves and cases for student records would solve problems in the college life in a way out of all proportion to their actual cost.

"There is a busy, active-minded generation at Bryn Mawr which asks not for more playing space in a Students' Building, but more working space, not necessarily work set by instructors and done in libraries and laboratories, but something which will use the common fund of intelligence in one more way on late winter afternoons and Saturday mornings and make the college able to add to its proper work by the quality of its play."

The needs of the Music Department can be stated briefly. It must have $300,000, $100,000 to be expended immediately for housing and equipment, and $200,000 to serve as a permanent endowment fund, the income from which will cover the yearly operating expenses of the Department. These expenses amounted in 1921-22 to $15,597.14, in 1922-23 to $14,958.07, and are estimated for 1923-24 at $10,903.40. The cost of the auditorium of the Students' Building is estimated at $100,000. The endowment fund of the building will be covered by the $46,000 which has been earned and saved by students over a period of thirty years. It is hoped that this sum will be raised to $50,000 by the proceeds of the sixth May Day.

It is proposed to house the Music Department in a wing of the Students' Building, of which the Auditorium will form the centre. The remaining wing will be financed later by gifts from classes or groups of classes.

Mrs. William Carter Dickerman, Chairman of the Music Committee, sends the following message to the Alumnae Association: "The Music Department is about to complete its third and final year under the guarantee of the committee, which, in response to considerable pressure from parents of prospective students, critical friends, and Alumnae interested in the academic potentiality of music, undertook its organization. The question now before us is how to enable the department not only to continue but to develop usefully and brilliantly. Hard facts and many difficulties lie before us. The college has no money to spare— and not even a room—and the public is manifestly tired of campaigns and causes; but if music is to thrive on the campus and animate new generations of students, the Committee must drive on in search of endowment in spite of college poverty and public humor. Organization is essential; friends and foundations are immensely helpful; publicity incalculably useful, but the *sine qua non* is the loyal and enthusiastic support of the Alumnae body.

"I ask, therefore, every Alumna near and far, to give money and strength if she can, but above all and unreservedly her interest, and to evidence that interest by sending to headquarters any information of value. In this way only can the future be secured for Music at Bryn Mawr!"

As the object of the Music Department is to train the minds, quicken the feelings, and stimulate the imaginations of the students, so the object of the Students' Building is to give them a place where they may organize and learn to govern their community. The college can spare neither, and looks again to the Alumnae Association for the help it has never failed to receive.

DAUGHTERS OF ALUMNAE AND FORMER STUDENTS

(This list of the daughters of Alumnae and former students who have entered Bryn Mawr was compiled by Edith T. Orlady, 1902, Secretary and Registrar, who has very kindly allowed the Editor to publish it.)

NAME	DAUGHTER OF
Ethel Andrews, ex-1919	Evangeline Holcombe Walker, 1893
Blanche Butler Borden, ex-1924	Sarah Hildreth Ames, ex-1897
Alys Boross, 1925	Josephine Bowen Holman, ex-1896
Eugenia Boross, 1925	Josephine Bowen Holman, ex-1896
Lysbeth Knickerbacher Boyd, ex-1925	Elizabeth Hornli Mifflin, ex-1894
Margaret Vail Brooks, 1927	Clara Warren Vail, 1897
Margaret Millicent Carey, 1920	Margaret Cheston Thomas, 1889

Susan Shober Carey, 1925 .... Margaret Cheston Thomas, 1889
Harriot Cristina Coney, 1925 .... Harriot C. Reitze, graduate student, 1890-93
Hilda Ferris, 1921 .... Anna Peirce Shoemaker, ex-1891
Anne FitzGerald, 1924 .... Susan Grimes Walker, 1893
Rebecca FitzGerald, 1926 .... Susan Grimes Walker, 1893
Audrey Fountain, 1922 .... Elizabeth Miller Caldwell, 1897
Olivia Fountain, 1924 .... Elizabeth Miller Caldwell, 1897
Katharine Lucretia Gardner, 1922 .... Katharine Taber Willets, 1890
Mary Deshon Hand, 1927 .... Frances Amelia Fincke, 1898
Lucy Weygandt Harris, 1917 .... Sophia Weygandt, 1889
Julia Duke Henning, ex-1923 .... Julia Blackburn Duke, ex-1897
Helen Rockwell Henshaw, 1925 .... Jessie Darling, graduate student, 1895-96
Eleanor Straus Hess, 1926 .... Sara Straus, ex-1899
Mary Scattergood Hoag, 1920 .... Anna Scattergood, 1896
Elizabeth Ives, 1924 .... Edith Wetherill, 1892
Angela Johnston, 1926 .... Grace Douglas, 1902
Mary Darcy Kellogg, 1927 .... Cornelia Van Wyck Halsey, 1900
Margaret Rhoads Ladd, 1921 .... Anna Ely Rhoads, 1889
Marjorie Taylor Mackenzie, 1919 .... Mary Lewis Taylor, 1893
Ruth Meredith Miller, 1927 .... Mary Anna Meredith, graduate student
                                          1896-97
Emily Bishop Moores, 1919 .... Elizabeth Nichols, 1893
Mary Zelia Pease, 1927 .... Laurette Eustis Potts, 1896
Nancy Foster Porter, 1921 .... Ruth Wadsworth Furness, 1896
Anna Pratt, 1924 .... Agnes Woodbury Gray, graduate student,
                                          1895-96
Helen Cloyd Quinn, 1925 .... Helen McKee, ex-1901
Mary Levering Robinson, 1927 .... Mary Armstrong Levering, 1897
Bertha Pauline Rosenau, 1926 .... Myra B. Faith Frank, 1900
Anna Swift Rupert, ex-1922 .... Anna Vaughan Swift, ex-1891
Mary Swift Rupert, 1918 .... Anna Vaughan Swift, ex-1891
Olivia Saunders, 1926 .... Louise Sheffield Brownell, 1893
Silvia Saunders, ex-1924 .... Louise Sheffield Brownell, 1893
Dorothea Caroline Shipley, 1925 .... Caroline Warder Cadbury, ex-1898
Delia Nichols Smith, 1926 .... Margaret Parsons Nichols, 1897
Margaret Bailey Speer, 1922 .... Emma Doll Bailey, ex-1894
Constance Lynch Springer, graduate stu-
   dent, 1918-19. .... Gertrude Mason Lynch, ex-1891
Edith Stevens, 1920 .... Edith Ames, ex-1895
Harriet Lyman Stevens, 1922 .... Edith Ames, ex-1895
Mary Swift Tatnall, 1926 .... Frances Dorr Swift, ex-1895
Margaret Wood Taylor, 1921 .... Gertrude Allinson, ex-1889
Anna Hazard Tierney, 1926 .... Lydia Mitchell Albertson, 1897
Ruth Peckham Tubby, 1924 .... Mary Peckham, 1897
Susan Dudley Walker, 1926 .... Margaret Dudley, 1899
Sylvia Vail Walker, 1927 .... Margaret Dudley, 1899
Helen Hutchins Weist, ex-1921 .... Alice Longfellow Cilley, 1897
Elinor West, 1924 .... Anna Ervina West, ex-1895
Elizabeth Dean Wilbur, 1926 .... Anna Elliott Dean, ex-1898
Mary Dorothy Whitall Worthington, 1910
   (Died, 1912) .... Mary Grace Thomas, ex-1889

Book Reviews

(The following review was sent to the BULLETIN by Alys Smith Russell, 1890. It was written by Mrs. M. G. Fawcett and was first printed in "The Woman's Leader." Ray Strachey, the author of "Marching On," was graduate student at Bryn Mawr in 1908-1909.)

Marching On. By Ray Strachey. Harcourt, Brace & Co. New York, 1923. $2.00.

This is an intensely interesting book. If it were written by one who was a stranger to me, I should not hesitate to call it a "great" book. But I do hesitate, lest I should by my affection be beguiled: so I must ask all readers to judge for themselves. What seems to me "great" in the book is the power of the writer so to visualize in her own mind every detail of the narrative that the whole thing lives before us; one does not think of it as a story, but as a detailed account of some of the most interesting years in the history of the world, the years which immediately preceded the Civil War in America, and determined once for all whether the great Republic was to be a Slave or a Free State. I will only say here that Mrs. Strachey has, in my judgment, the same power which Defoe had of imagining all the details, both preceding and following extraordinary events, and thus makes the whole series of situations living realities.

I have called the period of the story one of the most important in the history of the world. The Northern States were for freedom: the Southern States were for slavery; every kind of compromise and dodge had been suggested with the view of reconciling these irreconcilables. . . . Into this world of intense antagonism over a vital human problem, Mrs. Strachey introduces her heroine, Susan Bright: and the interest lies in watching her part in it and her strong, simple, vigorous character; we see the extraordinarily unfavorable atmosphere by which the girl was originally surrounded, a peevish, foolish mother, a harsh, tyrannical father; no education, no church, no newspapers, the mail fetched once a month from the station forty miles away; no outlet for the really noble qualities of her mind and character. Susan is devoured by a desire for education. Her elder brother is being sent to college, with the view to his becoming a Baptist minister, but he gives her neither sympathy nor aid. Her duty was to marry and bring up children, "and pray the merciful Lord, Susan, that he curse you not with children like yourself," said her father, while her mother added, "What have I done that she should be a child of mine? God knows I am sorry for the day she was born."

Finally she runs away, penniless and forlorn, and gradually gets absorbed in the Abolitionist movement and also in the movements for Women's Education and Women's Votes. The three dove-tailed into each other; Susan is no longer lonely and forlorn: she makes friends, and they quote to each other Hosea Bigilow's

Wy it's jest ez clear ez figgers,
Clear ez one and one makes two;
Chaps that make black slaves o' niggers
Want to make white slaves o' you.

Susan marries and has children, and there is a chapter describing the pain and peril of childbirth, far surpassing Tolstoi's efforts in the same direction in *Anna Karenina.* The book is brought to a close with the John Brown escapade at Harper's Ferry. He had murdered five men in cold blood a few weeks earlier, and now he had taken up arms against the United States Government and had to pay the penalty. One of the characters in the book pronounces the verdict: "John Brown was a good man, in spite of all. What he did was wrong, but he himself was right." The last words of the story quote the marching song of the Northern armies:

John Brown's body lies a-mouldering in the grave,
But his soul goes marching on!

Alumnae Activities

BY MRS. HERBERT RADNOR-LEWIS

Publicity Director, H. B. Mallinson and Company

My dear Editor:

Your request for a short résumé of my activities coming just at this time, when '99 is preparing for the Twenty-fifth Reunion, focuses the fact that I have been treading a path diametrically contrary to that laid out for me in the class prophecy.

What even I didn't realize at the time when the life of a social diplomat was predicted for me was the force of that little "up and doing" virus so constantly stimulated by an unusual vitality and tireless energy. Executive positions on hospital boards and with sewing schools didn't satisfy, and social affairs frankly bored. There was just one thing to do—challenge that "place for a married woman is in the home" attitude, strong at that period (although right here I want to say that my husband and family have always been staunch, enthusiastic shouters) and launch out on what has proved a twenty-four-hour-a-day life work.

The beginning of this strenuous career was as a cub reporter on the *Philadelphia Public Ledger*. It was only a few weeks before I was made Editor of what was then called "The Third Page," a page devoted to society, art, musical and club affairs and all feature stories. Eighteen months and I had attained the highest position that a metropolitan newspaper has to offer a woman then or even now—that of signed feature writer.

By this time Mr. Lewis was able to arrange his business affairs so that we could live in New York. Here my first interview landed me in the editorial chair of *Dress Magazine*. As the name signifies, it was primarily a fashion magazine established by members of the advertising staff of *Vogue*. I was "it"—everything from editor to stamp-licker.

When I seated myself at my desk the first day I knew nothing about printing, engraving, art work and make-up. My newspaper work had called for just one factor—copy. I had to figure it all out for myself, and it was to obtain this very experience that I had accepted the position, for I wasn't interested in clothes and never have been, except in the impersonal way demanded by my business.

I was concluding my third year when I was asked to write a series of articles on fabrics for *Good Housekeeping Magazine*. These articles brought me the Associate Editorship of that magazine.

During my occupancy of this editorial chair Mr. Hearst bought *Harper's Bazar* and made me Managing Editor of it, continuing my connection with *Good Housekeeping*.

A few more annual turns of Father Time's pendulum and I was fronted with the fact that I was, or should be, at the turning of the ways. I naturally longed to try the "wings" I believed I had been forging in a, what shall I call it?—certainly not literary—mold. I had scarcely launched a free-lance bureau with Mr. Lewis when as bait the Rotogravure Editorship of the *New York Tribune* was dangled before my eyes with the added inducement, "You will be the first woman editor of a metropolitan Graphic." The first anything apparently has an irresistible lure for me, for all through college I was accused of starting precedents from the day I entered college without any study of Latin to the day I took my A.B. as a married woman.

When our entry into the War offered me the opportunity to make a graceful exit I took it. I had always been tremendously interested in advertising. The Advertising Manager of the *Tribune*, who had also been the Advertising Manager of *Harper's Bazar*, remarked once in conference, "Mrs. Lewis is the only editor who knows how to work with an advertising department." Easy enough when one's interests are there.

Again at the forking of the ways, I determined to follow the path of desire and "go in" for advertising. My friends argued that it was suicidal and that I was throwing away years of hard work and a splendid editorial training. I disagreed with them and experience has proved that this editorial training and viewpoint has bee invaluable to me, so much so, in fact, that I wonder how anyone can be a successful advertising manager without some experience either in the newspaper or the magazine world.

There was an Advertising Manager at H. R. Mallinson's & Co., Inc., when I joined the staff of this great silk house, so I was compelled to develop a position for myself, largely along the publicity line. Two years later when this man resigned I was given charge of the entire department, certainly one of the most absorbingly interesting positions the advertising world has to offer— the selling of the finest qualities of a fabric as replete with beauty and romance as silk to women, who are acknowledged 85 per cent. of the buying public.

The preparation of the advertising appearing in the magazines and newspapers in point of time is one of the smallest factors in the advertising office of a large national advertiser, especially one in which publicity other than space advertising is as important a feature as with us. The merchandising of the product is today as vital a factor of advertising. This means close connections with the merchants of the country, studying their policies and supplying as their requirements may demand selling aids in the way of direct-by-mail literature, window displays, counter displays, posters, etc.

These include with us the *Blue Book of Silks De Luxe*, a magazine of thirty-two pages of fashion and fabric illustrations and data; an Ad-Suggestion Book twice a year, and at least monthly booklets.

The mail that comes to my desk is enormous, for the advertising department is invariably the catch-all for mail not specifically designated, and, according to Mr. Mallinson, I am the "language factory."

About two years ago I decided that our three-reel film depicting the silk industry from the cocoon culture through the various intricate mill processes was not being used to the best advantage and instituted a drive with the women's clubs, schools of all kinds, colleges and department stores on a special showing with a talk illustrated by the silks. This met with such an enthusiastic reception that I am forced to do some very fine juggling with my work in order to "make" the time to give these talks. I believe my present record is seven talks in one day which is necessary when I can only be away from my office for a limited period and there are so many different types of audiences to which I could appeal. Much as I enjoy and benefit from thus getting directly in touch with consumers, from the clerks behind the counters who are the links between the manufacturer and the women, and the consumers themselves in their most critical club moods, these are anything but joy-rides, for there is no substitute at the office to carry on.

Then by way of variety there are always articles to be written ranging from statements on financial and business conditions to authentic fashion news; a fashion show or two (we give at least two at the store every year and are always exhibiting in innumerable others); an art or fabric exhibition, to say nothing of a varied but always long waiting line of solicitors to be interviewed. There are days which are just one solicitor after another in such a steady procession that it is almost impossible to even answer the necessary telephone calls and all dictation is out of the question.

I fear that this little résumé has grown into too long a one and I truly hope it doesn't sound egotistical, for I can assure you I realize fully that there is a long, long way still to go. I do want to add that not one inch of the way has been attained by pull of any kind; in fact, I put it all down to just hard work and lots of it.

Always cordially,

CAROLYN TROWBRIDGE (BROWN) LEWIS.

Class of '99, Bryn Mawr College.

In Memoriam
EMILY BLODGETT SHERWIN, 1905

Emily Blodgett Sherwin continues to live vividly in our thoughts and imaginations. Her appreciation of all that came to her in life was so exquisite, that many of the things we see have taken on a tinge of Emily's personality. Gardens, flowers, friendships are more lovely and valuable to us because we have had glimpses of them through her eyes. Her vision was more perceptive of detail than that given to most of us. Even when we were not with her she was showing us in her letters the gay pattern of life where we might be seeing only gray. The very look of those letters was pleasure giving. With that neatest of tiny handwritings, with the perfect margins and spacings, they were a calling away from hurried living and carelessness.

Whatever Emily did had a delicate precision and perfection. Her sewing, her writing of English, her way of speaking were without bungling or clumsiness. She was always charming and interesting looking. Her features were piquantly beautiful and her wonderful gray eyes were full of understanding.

It was because she saw so clearly, physically, mentally and spiritually, that she did not hurt and bruise. She was delightfully aware of the whimsicalities of life. The faults of her friends she had understood from the beginning, and her constancy was unswerving.

CLASS NOTES

1892
Class Editor, pro tem., Mrs. Edward C. Kirk, Villanova, Pa.

As '92 is to have a reunion on June 2nd, all the members of the Class were asked to send in a brief sketch of their lives from graduation to date. The Class Editor wants to thank the twelve who responded. Six of their letters follow, and six more will appear in the July BULLETIN.

Anne Emery Allinson.

After 1892 I took four more years to be educated, winding up with a Ph.D. in 1896, after work at Bryn Mawr and in Germany. For a year out of these four I was "Secretary to the President" at Bryn Mawr. I went, in 1897, to the University of Wisconsin as Dean of Women, until 1900. In that year I came to Brown University as Dean of the Women's College. In 1905 I gave up this position to marry the professor of Greek, Francis G. Allinson. Since then my professional work has consisted only of writing and occasional lecturing. In 1920-21, and again in 1922-23, I went back to the Women's College in Brown University as acting dean, finding the same office, a very new generation, and very old human nature. Outside of strictly professional work, I do the usual things, under my own roof and in the city where I live.

Helen Bartlett.

Since graduation my chief interests have been education and travel. Specialization in Modern Languages continued through preparation for advanced degrees, and through five years' residence abroad with study in Paris, Italy, Spain, and lectures at Berlin University. As Head of the Modern Language Department of the Portland, Oregon, Academy, and as Dean of Women and Head of the Modern Language Department of Bradley Polytechnic, Peoria, Ill., I was interested in the education of others.

Travel in Europe included every country except Russia, and in the United States, especially the South and West. Eight years were spent high in the New Mexico Rockies, where glorious scenery, flowers and birds, and even lobo-wolves and mountain lions, made life fascinating. Finally, three years in Chicago of slow recovery from illness have paradoxically proved that city beneficial as a rest-cure.

Alice Belin du Pont.

My thirty-two years from 1892 to 1924 have been filled with a great deal of happiness and but little public usefulness. They were spent at Scranton, Pa., and, after I was married to Pierre S. du Pont in 1915, at "Longwood," Pa.

I have traveled more or less, seven times to Europe, three times to California and once to Honolulu. Motor trips from Paris to Rome, and from Gibraltar to Paris were delightful incidents. Hospitals, visiting nurse associations and the American Red

Cross have been my favorite charities and my war work was done with the Red Cross. "Longwood" is my greatest interest. It is becoming widely known, because of the gardens and greenhouses that are open at almost all times for public enjoyment of flowers and music.

Frances Hunt reports that she is just through the task of moving into a new home in Scranton and is, as usual, very busy with church and welfare work, which have always been her chief interests.
Edith Wetherill Ives.

I spent the summer of 1894 and the years of 1895-96 abroad and did volunteer work in the Civic Club of Philadelphia, first as Recording, then as Corresponding Secretary till my marriage, November 15, 1900, to Dr. Frederick Ives. Since then we have lived in New York City in winter; in summer, first at Southampton, then at our farm near Brewster, N. Y.

I have been busy for twenty-three years from early morning till late at night with the following result:
Elizabeth Ives, Senior at Bryn Mawr; Gerard M. Ives, Junior at Yale; John W. Ives, Freshman at Yale; Chauncey B. Ives, VI Form at Groton.

I am spending the winter of 1923-24 with Dr. Ives in Italy. With the exception of this winter, I have been Secretary of '92 since graduation.
Elizabeth Winsor Pearson.

On the hill where we built nineteen years ago there presently grew up a neighborhood school, where I experiment in the profession on which I ignorantly embarked in 1892. A teacher as husband intensifies my congenital preoccupation, and nowadays my chief "outside" responsibility is a modest effort to reform education, in the shape of a nursery school and training center. Puzzling over such problems (for which our boys, now 11, 14, and 20 furnish illustration), occupied together with my husband's writings, and solaced by folk, by home-made music, and by our outlook toward Blue Hill, we pass "uneventful" years.

1898

Class Editor, Mrs. Wilfred Bancroft, Harrisville, R. I.

Elizabeth Delano Gray was married to Mr. Thomas Joseph Mocock in New Haven on January 27th. They are living at 29 S. High Street, New Britain, Conn.

1900

Class Editor, M. Helen MacCoy, State Education Building, Albany, N. Y.

It is with deep concern and profound sorrow that we have learned of the sudden death of Baron Serge Alexander Korff, husband of Aletta Van Reypen Korff. Baron Korff died on March 7 in the very midst of his inspiring and interesting career, and in the death of this cultured and distinguished Russian gentleman who has given so much of his intellect and power to our country, we have indeed suffered a most poignant loss.

Baron Korff had been professor of Russian law and the history of law at the Universities of Petrograd and of Helsingfors. He had been Lieutenant Governor of Finland, and since his transplanting to this country, had been a teacher and lecturer at Williamstown, at Georgetown, at Johns Hopkins, at Northwestern and at other universities. He had been of the staff of the newly founded Academy of International Law at The Hague, and last year he was called to the Faculty of Political Science of Columbia University. "Simple, modest, genial, a man of rare cultivation and of delightful spirit, with no trace of bitterness in him, this gentleman and scholar of the Old World won the respect and affection of everyone with whom he came in touch. . . . The passage of his bright and winning personality will long be gratefully and tenderly cherished."

Edna Fischel Gellhorn, '00, has just been in California in the interests of the League of Women Voters. She spoke on Tuesday, February 26th, at the San Francisco center luncheon, where ten Bryn Mawrtyrs turned out and had a table together. On Wednesday afternoon the Bryn Mawr Club gave a tea in honor of Mrs. Gellhorn at the A. A. U. W. rooms. Receiving with Mrs. Gellhorn were Amy Sussman Steinhart, '02, Helen Brayton Barendt, '03, Caroline Sloane Lombard, '00, Elizabeth Perkins Lyders, '00, and Ruth Babcock Deems, '10.

1902

It is with the deepest sorrow that we record the death of Beulah Brylawski Amram, which occurred in the latter part of March.

The Class of 1902 wishes to extend its sincere sympathy to Harriet Spencer Pierce, whose husband died very suddenly. Mr. Pierce's death was the result of heart disease and occurred while he was driving with his wife and daughter.

1904

Class Editor, Emma O. Thompson, 320 S. Forty-second Street, Philadelphia, Pa.

The following is a letter received from Phyllis Green Anderson, who is so anxious for news from the rest of us that she is willing to tell us something about her own affairs. Perhaps this will encourage others to do likewise:

"I suppose that the majority of us have nothing really important to relate, and yet we all know, down in our hearts, that our classmates would be interested in accounts of just our ordinary life. Anyway, here goes—This is written not because it has anything of importance in it; but in the hope of shaming other 1904s into writing of their lives.

"Of course, I am busy like everyone else. I'm chairman of our Girls' Club here, 300 members, all working girls, the most democratic kind of a club—self-governing, and splendid in every way. Then I'm chairman of a committee consisting of eight women, each representing a college club—our purpose to raise scholarships for the Bryn Mawr Summer School. It's a fine committee and great fun to work with. And drives! I've been on so many drives to raise money that it's a crime. Of course, the Bryn Mawr Endowment almost killed Sadie Briggs and me. Since then I've helped endow hospitals and charities, so that I can hardly refrain from begging for funds whenever I get a crowd together. I'm also much interested in politics. I belong to the Republican City Committee, and we did some fine work this winter, getting rid of a poor Mayor who has managed to stay in for four years. I go to Philadelphia every winter or spring to visit my family; the rest of the winter I'm here in Worcester, working hard and playing hard—I skate, coast, ski, and snow shoe with the kids for exercise. I generally spend my summers with my boy at Jamestown, R. I., my husband coming down week-ends. Last summer my husband, boy, and I had a fine visit at Southwest Harbor. Then after five weeks at the shore we went to a camp up in Maine, motored up there, had ten days of loafing in boats, and then motored over to the White Mountains, where we played

much tennis and golf. It was a wonderful vacation."

Jeannette Hemphill Bolton, 17 Irving Place, Pelham, N. Y.

I recently heard some one say that unusual happenings constitute news, and, as both my children are very healthy and normal, their life flows on in an even stream of school, church, and outdoor play, which is very convenient for me. I therefore fear that they can have no place in the news column.

Marjorie Canan Fry, 2131 Ritner Street, Philadelphia.

I had meant to get this note written to you last week but was generally upset by a call from St. Luke's School at Wayne, saying that my younger son, Christopher, had developed scarlet fever. Fortunately, he has only a light case and is doing very well.

My other son, Humphrey, so tall that he wears long trousers at fourteen, is home with me for a rather dull spring vacation. Not only was he without his brother, but being a "suspect" for a week he could not go about with other people. My small daughter of six has been attending a public school just across the street this winter, but this has not been satisfactory.

My other daughters, Elizabeth ("Betty") and Lucy are still in England. They have had a very delightful and unusually educative year. They have not attended any school but have kept up their work under two of the masters from St. Edmund's, a boys' college near Standen, where they are living with their aunt. Betty is planning to enter Bryn Mawr in 1926 and will take her preliminary either this spring in London or here in the autumn. They hope to spend a month or two in France before returning. Next winter, as I am planning to take a house here again, I expect to send them to Miss Irwin's school, thus having them with me for a while before they are altogether grown up. England, I am glad to say, keeps girls young in many ways, so that neither of them seems in the least anxious to become a sophisticated young lady.

Hope Woods Hunt, Locust Farm, Lincoln, Mass.

In response to the appeal to Proud Mothers, I feel I should write something about my offspring, but having three very normal children in no wise either talented or brilliant it is difficult to find anything to say. Merrill, Jr., is conspicuous only for his beauty, which is of little or no use as far as I can see to any male member of society. I believe also he is physically remarkably strong and does shine as a woodchopper. He and his daddy cut all our wood Saturdays and Sundays, and this winter small Merrill has cut nearly three cords himself (he is ten years old and weighs only seventy pounds). We have about forty acres of woodland, so if he keeps up his enthusiasm for this particular sport we shall never suffer from lack of fire wood. Sophie Lee, my next, is eight years old and is a bookworm, and is already planning to go to Bryn Mawr. Martha Jane, my baby, is two and a half, adorable and much spoiled by everyone. She walked at nine months and at fifteen months climbed alone the ladder going up our 30-foot water tank, thereby giving her father, who was watching her from the top and not daring to speak for fear she'd fall, heart failure.

In winter we all ski together (the children are great at it) and skate and slide, and in summer we garden and play tennis. We live on a farm miles from neighbors (inadvertently three or four from school), and for sheer content I recommend anyone at any time to a farm and the companionship of children.

Miriam Frederick Holtzinger, Kenwood, Helena, Mont.

How much I should like to be with you all in May! But miles are such stubborn things and pocketbooks won't stretch, not in Montana. As to my youngsters, they are darlings, of course! Phyllis, the eldest, will celebrate her eighteenth birthday next month. She is completing her freshman year at Intermountain College, doing very creditable work and somewhat of a musician. Beatrice, sixteen, nicknamed "Pete," is finishing her Junior year at Intermountain Academy, sings well and has a wonderful time wherever we sojourn for a while. Wesley Burns, aged nine, is finishing his fifth grade work, active and athletic, proud of his Y. membership and his swimming badge.

I have tooted the little tin horn; you see, they are just "kids" and mayhap this is not the kind of news you want. I might add that beyond their other "accomplishments" they are full of the "glory of Bryn

Mawr." I wish the girls might do their college work there.
Helen Arny Macan, Easton, Pa.

Linette Arny Macan, age seven years, height four feet one and one-half inch, weight fifty pounds, school, College Hill School, grade third. Has lost and regained the proper number of teeth and, in fact, seems pleasantly normal.

Patty Rockwell Moorhouse, 111 Wister Road, Ardmore.

The young Moorhouses now number four Wilson, Jr., aged nearly eleven; Martha, nearly nine; Anne, nearly six, and June Rockwell, aged one and a half. The first two go to the fifth and third grades respectively of the public school while the next child pines to go with them. The baby looks more like a butter ball than anything else. Wilson, Jr.'s, chief delights in life are swimming at the Y. M. C. A. and reading Lucy Lombardi's history. He announced at the table the other day that he hoped if we had any more babies that they would be boys, as we had too many girls. Anne then suggested that we have two more boys so we could have three boys and three girls.

From this you can see that there is not likely to be a dull moment around 111 for some years.

1906
Class Editor, Mrs. Harold K. Beecher, Pottsville, Pa.

Ida Garrett Murphy is rejoicing in the possession of a brand new son, Malcolm by name. The Class extends heartiest congratulations. Ida writes that her other two kiddies are just normally intelligent youngsters. Campbell finishing his third year at school is deeply engrossed in stamp collecting and Mercet starting school next fall has her eye firmly fixed on the Phoebe Thorne School with Bryn Mawr as the ultimate goal.

Irene Houghtaling Carse writes that Prof. Driggs says a good story requires two elements, people and trouble, and therefore there is "nothing doing" in the six acres of woods where the Carses live, Irene, husband and boy of six.

Edith Durand McColl had her youngest child ill with pneumonia at Christmas time, but writes she is as hale and hearty now as her two sisters, Ellen and Margaret, who are both in Grade 5 at school. Edith does all her own housework and sewing, and still finds time to be head of a Managing Committee of a Current Events Club of 400 members, and also Secretary of The University Women's Club.

Virginia Robinson and her home-partner, Jessie Taft, have added a little adopted girl to their family—of a boy.

Ruth MacNaughton plays the church organ, organizes the musical work, and teaches Latin, Piano, and Singing in the colored school at Thomasville, Georgia.

1908

Class Editor, Mrs. William H. Best, 1198 Bushwick Avenue, Brooklyn, N. Y.

The following letter was sent in for the March BULLETIN, but the Editor was obliged, on account of lack of space, to hold it over until May.

Dear 1908,

The next time I want to complain I'll suppress the desire. I protested about the paucity of news, I manufactured a questionnaire, I even replied to it just to show Lou Hyman how inspiring the questions were—and, of course, the inevitable happened! The whole business of the Alumnae notes was wished on to me. To the kicker belong the toils. Having only three productions under way at the moment, it it great to find something to do with my leisure time.

Frankly, I would have struck, but Molly's letter enclosing all the others ran:

"We are fairly distracted here because my middle child, John, ran a nail through his foot while playing over a week ago, and the wound is not acting properly at all. He has had lockjaw serum, with a terrific reaction, and now the puncture is getting deeper and deeper." What could I do? If Molly had sent me the preliminary data for an encyclopedia with a note like that I should undoubtedly have gone ahead and finished it for her without a word. Luckily, she didn't. And more luckily still, John is well on the road to recovery at the present writing.

Well, now, for the notes themselves. No, not quite yet. I must first remark that I have never been more convinced than at the present moment of the wisdom of keeping one's own name whether married or not. Quite apart from the fact that one's husband keeps his no matter how many wives he may have during his career—there

is the immense convenience to one's friends. I've been having a dreadful time recognizing my former classmates. There's Mrs. L. G. Phillips, for example, from New Rochelle, who writes:

"I have no news of general interest except perhaps that I have been trying 'electronic reactions of Abrams' on my persistent streptoccus infections with great success. In consequence I may be a plump person the next time you see me." She signs it "Violet," and I have my suspicions, but in our editorial capacity we take no chances.

I haven't even my suspicions about Mrs. Benj. L. Bird of Bala, Pa. Perhaps her maiden name might not be so alliterative. She writes: "I am sorry I haven't any news for the BULLETIN, as I like to hear about others. My time seems to be well filled with domestic work, raising my three sons. Ethel Vick Wallace has been visiting her brother near us and I enjoyed seeing her very much. She is wonderfully brave."

By the way, I must stop here again to protest about these homemakers who protest their own dullness. Methinks the ladies do protest too much. There's Jack Morris, for example, who begins:

"As for news, alas, I have none! My private life is very uninteresting to anyone except myself." How do you know, Jack? Try us. "But," she continues, "I really love the monotonous routine of looking after the house and kids. . . . The Evanses spent the summer with the Rhoadeses and enjoyed their society muchly. I could write much more about Fatty's life than mine. If any 1908er is looking for a summer resort come and join the throng at Beach Haven, N. J. I'll guarantee a good time. . . . I have a niece in the Freshman Class at B. M. It is great to hear her unceasing enthusiasm."

And Frances Crane Leatherbee begins: "I still firmly maintain a mother of three adolescent sons has very little to report of interest to others." Well, speaking editorially, we wonder. The more so as we have met one of the sons who hopes to go Gordon Craig and Max Reinhardt one better. Frances admits, however, "a keen interest in the struggles civilization is making to keep from disintegrating" and a real desire to "find a path to a better world of peace and brotherhood."

"Fatty" Chambers Rhoades is properly confident of her audience. Her private life she chronicles as: "Care of one house, and five children, a new baby being added last October, a future Bryn Mawrter I hope, This makes three girls for us. I've decided I can help the College best by furnishing raw material. Having decided to specialize in this fashion, my public life is practically nil."

Marjorie Young Gifford is also specializing with conviction. "Well, here's a bit of news," she writes. "I have a little daughter born on December 5th." (Only our champion shot putter would feel impelled to specify that the daughter is little. But ye ed. has inspected the child and can confirm the report.) "I know that does not look particularly exciting in print, but it is a matter of great importance to me," Marjorie goes on. "I did quite a little talking about her in the notes I wrote raising money for the class fund. You will be glad to hear we have about $800 in hand and a little trickles in from time to time."

Molly Kinsley Best besides bringing up her three children—and nursing them through disasters—is serving on the local School Board and "working overtime on the district music contest," and functioning vigorously in the Mothers' Club of her school. "My private life," she says, "only a housewife could appreciate, with three kids, a doctor's office, a house and 'helpless help.'"

"I am bursting with pride, as I have something to tell," writes "Milly," and ye ed. is also bursting with pride because she has just remembered that Milly's last name is Heron. "We are now stationed at Fort Sill, Oklahoma. We like it very much and have all been riding till Bill, aged seven, fell off his horse, and broke his arm. Since then, of course, I have done nothing but read aloud. . . . Did you know that Lou Hyman Pollack attended the meeting of the B. M. Club of Indiana in Indianapolis on November 12. She represented Cincinnati."

Margaret Carroll Jones (Mrs. Bayard Turnbull) writes: "My life has suddenly assumed a rural aspect, for after many years as a city dweller we are about to build a country house and to live under the shadow of very ancient trees. 'We' means, my architect husand and Frances Andrew and Eleanor. These four people make life for me in both its private and public aspects. I have found Baltimore a very welcoming and sympathetic spot, full of delightful people and endless opportunities." . . . She goes on to recount some adventures with President Park when that lady was visiting her brother near Annapolis. "A morning basking in the sun on the beach, and an evening around a wood fire, after sharing the intimacies of scrambling eggs and washing dishes," made Margaret "rejoice in the future of the College, guided by so sane, so intelligent and so vivid a personality."

So much for the domestic group. Dorothy Merle-Smith Pyle, frivolous as of yore, omits all mention of her offspring in her laconic statement. "Sailing February 6 for England, France, Spain, and Italy: partly business, partly fox-hunting."

Dorothy M. Jones TYPES. Thank you, Dorothy. "Have been in touch with College this past year trying to get girls to apply for the scholarships offered; this has been very interesting. I wish reunion were not so far off."

Margaret Kent writes: "I am living a very quiet life, working in a large trust company in Philadelphia and acting as notary public on the side. The most exciting thing I've done lately was to take a trip to Bermuda last June."

Ina Richter sends the following from California: "1. Private life: I'm still single and childless and like Walt (do you have him in the East?) I 'know when I'm well off.' I do manage to support myself, but I don't believe I could manage a husband; doctoring children may be difficult, but from what I can see of it bringing them up is far more so. Q. E. D. 2. Public life: (a) an interesting and growing practice; (b) clinic work; (c) member of and secretary to the staff of the Children's Hospital; (d) lecturing to the nurses and various other minor jobs of that nature." Ina also reports that the Bransons have a very flourishing and popular school near her and ends with "If I don't get to the next reunion I shall just burst—so there!"

"Mother and I are living in a co-operatively owned apartment house," writes Lucy Carner of her Private Life, "and I'm learning something of the 'co-operative movement' first hand, especially as I am now on the board of our Beekman Hill Coop. Ass'n." Lucy says her Public Life is entirely vicarious. She "belongs to an appallingly large number of organizations, having become a 'joiner' in my old age. Of course I vote, predominantly socialist." Civil liberties, internationalism, and the modernist movement are also "predominantly on her mind." She is, in addition, doing graduate work in Sociology and Economics at Columbia, although, she says, "there's not much *glow* about college from this angle." Her final paragraph we promised Lou Hyman we wouldn't cut. "One of the best things I could wish for 1908 would be a reunion in the shape of a theatre party to see 'Saint Joan.' (I meant to write Terry after I saw 'Liliom' that I was ready to dust her boots for the thing she and the Theatre Guild had done. Now I'll do it twice.) My next would be that everyone would subscribe to *The World Tomorrow*. It gives me more ideas in a month than all the other periodicals I read put together. Try it."

My humble and hearty thanks to you, Lucy. And now that you've mentioned the Theatre Guild you've relieved me of the responsibility. That's all there is to my Public Life. But there's enough of it to leave me very little time for anything else. We're at present busy on our new theatre, which ought to be ready to receive Bryn Mawrtyrs—and others—early next year. I wonder if any of you "out-of-towners" saw the repertory company which we had on tour this season.

My private life consists of one husband, who believes quite as sincerely as I do in our keeping our own names, our own jobs, and our own friends, a system which seems to me to provide the greatest amount of freedom and the least friction possible in the debatable institution of matrimony.

Out of ninety-odd (is that right?) of the original class of 1908 the questionnaire brought answers from sixteen. Most of us have, probably, received formal announcements of the fact that Fanny Passmore was married in December to Mr. Justus Lowe. But Fanny has apparently not communicated with anyone since. Which is intended as a hint not only to her but to the other seventy silent ones to drop a line before next June to Mrs. William H. Best,

1198 Bushwick Avenue, Brooklyn, N. Y., this being the first and last time matters will be left to,

Yours apologetically,
THERESA HELBURN.

1910

Class Editor, Marion Kirk, 4504 Chester Avenue, Philadelphia.

Anita Uarda Maris Boggs, 607 Northbrook Court, Washington, D. C.

"It may be of interest to the Class of 1910 that as Director of the Bureau of Commercial Economies I have been asked by the Pan Pacific Union to establish Visual Education in all of the countries bordering on the Pacific and to direct such work for a period of ten years, the same to be known as the Pan Pacific Visual Education Bureau. It will be allied to the Pan Pacific Union and be the Pacific division of the Bureau of Commercial Economies. At the conference I am calling to meet in Honolulu, August 1st-15th, there will be present official representatives from the following countries to work out the details of the organization: Japan, China, the Philippines, Siam, Dutch East India, India, Straits Settlements, Malay Peninsula, Australia, New Zealand, Chile, Peru, Ecuador, Colombia, Panama, Costa Rica, Nicaragua, San Salvador, Guatamala, Mexico, Canada, Russia, and the United States, and the various South Sea Islands.

Considering that the nations outnumber the white race by a large percentage, the possibilities ahead of such work are enormous and the problem most fascinating, as it gives one unparalleled opportunity for development of minds on such huge scale that it is almost overwhelming."

1912

Class Editor, Mrs. John A. MacDonald, 3227 N. Pennsylvania Street, Indianapolis, Ind.

Julia is very glad to publish news if you send it to her. If you don't tell her what you and other 1912 people are doing she can't pass on information to you through this column. For months you have sent her nothing, in spite of which omission on your part some of you have dared to complain because "1912 never has any notes in the BULLETIN." You've had more than you deserved because I, Mary Peirce, happen to be on the spot and am somewhat of a gossip and news collector. In November and January I passed on what I'd heard. In March I heard nothing. The only things I know now are that

1. Dorothy Wolff Douglas' husband has been appointed a full professor at Amherst.

2. Maysie Morgan Lee has recently moved into her new house (please send your address, Maysie).

3. Florence Leopold Wolf has a son, Thomas, born January 7th.

4. Agnes Morrow has been traveling around the country helping to manage the exhibition of work done by the Oberammergau Passion Players.

5. Pauline Clarke is abroad, in what capacity I do not know.

6. Christine Hammer is to teach at the Brearley School next winter.

7. Jean Stirling Gregory, Julia Haines MacDonald, Gertrude Llewellyn Stone, Gladys Spry, Catherine Terry Ross, Lorraine Mead Schwable and Louise Watson are planning to come to May Day.

8. I am going to California in May to visit my sister and Mary Alden Lane, I hope.

If you want to see your names in print hereafter send word to Julia.

1914

Class Editor, Dr. Ida W. Pritchett, The Rockefeller Institute, Sixty-sixth Street and Avenue A, New York City.

Isabel Benedict went to Bermuda for ten days in March with her mother.

Katharine Huntington Annin (Mrs. William Stuart) has a second daughter born on February 26th.

Elizabeth Baldwin Stimson and her husband are going abroad this summer.

1916

Class Editor, Mrs. Webb Vorys, 63 Parkwood Avenue, Columbus, O.

Dorothy Packard Holt (Mrs. Farrington) and her husband have just built a new home in Birmingham, Mich., a suburb of Detroit.

Margaret Dodd Sangree (Mrs. Paul) writes that she has a third daughter, Margaret, born on December 13th. "The new baby is a prize fat baby fed entirely on buttermilk." Doddie also writes that she

is Secretary of the League of Women Voters in Moorestown.

Anna Sears Davis (Mrs. Warren G.) writes "the only news I know is that we have bought a house and expect to leave this apartment and move into our own home about April 1st. My address after that will be Otsego Road, Worcester."

Ruth Alden was married to Ralph Wescott Lester in December. Mr. Lester is a cousin of Constance Dowd's and is a graduate of Williams.

Constance Dowd has spent the winter in Cincinnati as Assistant Director of the Psychology Laboratory of the Vocation Bureau of the Cincinnati Schools.

Helen Holmes Carothers (Mrs. Ralph) has a second daughter, Harriet, born March 14th.

Charlotte Harding has moved to 303 West Bradley Lane, Chevy Chase, Md. She is keeping house for her brother and attending the George Washington University.

Agnes P. Smith is head of the Science and Mathematics Department of the Shipley School. She has been living at the College Inn this winter.

Clara Heydemann is teaching Latin and Physics at the Wright School.

Louise Dillingham was just awarded the M. Carey Thomas European Fellowship. She gets her A.M. at Bryn Mawr this June and expects to go abroad immediately to continue her work in Paris at the Sorbonne.

Larie Klein Boas (Mrs. Benjamin) is coming East sometime this spring.

Helen Robertson is living at home and working on the Board of the International Institute and "doing church work with a Sunday School class of boys age twelve, whom I adore, and especially with the Women's Alliance, which is the uniting body of the Women's organizations of the Unitarian Churches, sometimes to speak, sometimes just for conference and acquaintance. . . . I have just been at college and getting thrilled at the attractiveness of the present undergrad."

Georgette Moses writes: "I am a full-fledged real estate saleswoman, selling New York City property, tenements, lots, private houses and everything from Avenue C to Riverside Drive. I enjoy the work tremendously and have had some very thrilling experiences in my travels about New York

City. I discovered Buckner Kirk in an apartment on Waverly Place and met Agnes Grabau in Greenwich Village."

Margaret Mabon Henderson (Mrs. David K.) is living in Glasgow, Scotland, and has two small daughters.

It is with deep regret that 1916 has heard of the death of Mr. Garret. To Dr. and Mrs. Branson and Polly the deep sympathy of the Class is extended in this great loss. Of *Reunion* you will all hear more anon. But make your plans to include a trip to B. M. No excuses listened to. WHERE THERE IS A WILL THERE IS A WAY.

1918

Class Editor, Mrs. Julian B. Cohn, 5154 Westminster Place, St. Louis, Mo.

When 1918's Reunion was set for Saturday, May 31st, it was done in the hope that members with jobs or from a distance would profit by the holiday on Friday to spend an extra long week-end at Bryn Mawr. We still hope that this may be the case, but we find that the College cannot give us rooms in Merion until Saturday, as the Undergraduates are still taking examinations on Friday. So, if any out-of-town members expect to come to Bryn Mawr before Saturday, May 31st, and have not already made their own arrangements for bed and board will they please notify Annette Gest, 5979 Drexel Road, Overbrook, Pa., *at once* so that she can see that they are taken care of.

Ruth Cheney Streeter has been put in charge of 1918's athletics and wishes to call your attention to the schedule of Alumnae Association games as printed in the Commencement Calendar which you will receive shortly. Any member of 1918 who is still able and willing to play water-polo, basketball, or tennis is besought to notify Ruth at Morristown, N. J.

1918's own private Reunion starts at noon Saturday, May 31st, when the Class will meet in Merion and sojourn to a picnic at the Old Mill. The Class Meeting is to be Saturday at 4 P. M., when several matters of importance will come up, such as election of Class Secretary (and Class Collector), and consideration of memorials. The Class Banquet will be at 8.30 P. M. in

Merion. Then Annette has asked the Class to her home for tea on Sunday afternoon.

1920

Class Editor, Helene Zinsser, 6 West Ninth Street, New York City.

Married: *Caroline Lynch*, ex-'20, to Mr. William Claude Byers on Tuesday, March 25th, in Harrisburg, Pa. *Katherine Thomas* to Howard Park Stallman on December 31st in Columbus, Ohio.

Engaged: *Teresa Donahue James* to Edward Karrick Morris, Williams, ex-'19.

Dilatory Domiciles: *Caroline Lynch Byers*, 257 South Sixteenth Street, Philadelphia, Pa. *Katharine Thomas Stallman*, 35 Franklin Park West, Columbus, O. *Lois Kellogg Jessup*, 141 High Street, New Haven, Conn.

A letter from Fumi Uchilda appeared in the Correspondence of the April BULLETIN.

1922

Class Editor, Serena Hand, 48 West Ninth Street, New York City.

Emily Anderson got home from Europe in March. She spent a week in Cambridge with Josie Fisher. Saw Gink in London, and Prue and Ikey Coleman in Paris. In June she is going into a new job in the J. Walter Thompson Advertising Company.

Barbara Clarke and Mary Douglass Hay are having a perfect time in California. Burge came to the train to see them as they passed through El Paso bringing a "box of cookies that she had made herself."

Mary Ecroyd spent her Easter vacation in Florida with one of her pupils from Foxcroft.

Virginia Grace is teaching English at the Wadleigh High School.

Margie Tyler and Serena Hand spent their Easter vacation in Washington, where they saw Picoll, and ran into Mary Ecroyd, who was on her way back to school.

Vinton Liddell has announced her engagement to Mr. Robert Sylvester Pickins. She is to be married April 26th and will live in Hickory, N. C., where Mr. Pickins is editor of the newspaper.

Cornelia Skinner is playing in "In the Next Room."

Likewise the Daughter

By Strickland Gillilan

DID you ever sit and weep and thrill through Dave Belasco's presentation of Lenore Ulrich in "The Son Daughter"?

That play is based on an old Chinese mistaken obsession that girl-children were always a liability and boy-children always an asset. The girl Lenore personated in that thrilling play believed this, and wanted to be so much like a son that she might amount to something. And she did amount to something — by being like a son? No! By being the best possible daughter.

We are not chinese; yet it hasn't been long since we acted very much along the lines of that hidebound superstition. Usually we decided, when Henry was born and had to be named Henrietta, that we'd keep her anyway. But we just as usually, mother and all, hid a little disappointment that it hadn't been Henry himself instead of his little sister that came to board with us.

In the language of the comic strip, "them days is gone forever." We hail the girl-child as another human being come to bless the world, bringing her meal-ticket with her just as certainly as if she had been of the other sex. For her to work for a living is no stigma. For her to know practical, self-supporting, self-pro-tecting things is no disgrace.

Therefore when we are considering insuring any youthful member of the family, why pass up the *daughter* of fifteen and a-half? She must be educated, she must undergo a period when she is an expense, she must be tided over till she becomes self-supporting, in her own home or in some other livelihood than home-making—for we have come to admit she has the right to choose or reject the maternal and home-building role.

Then: Every argument holds for her, that obtains for the insuring of the boy—to compensate the parents for the expense of the schooling, if she should die; to start the insured's insurance career on a low-priced basis easy for her to keep up when she goes "on her own"—every solitary argument FOR insurance (and there is no argument against it) goes double, for daughter as well as son.

So if you have a daughter coming sixteen, be good to her, be wise for yourself, and take out a long-term endowment policy—some day she will accept a few thousands dollars from an insurance company, and through grati-tude-blurred eyes thank the one whose effective thoughtfulness granted her that boon.

John Hancock

LIFE INSURANCE COMPANY
OF BOSTON, MASSACHUSETTS

Sixty-one years in business. Now insuring over One Billion Eight Hundred Million dollars in policies on 3,300,000 lives.

Reg. Trade Mark

McCutcheon's
New Imported Underwear

Simple or elaborate, these underthings proclaim a French origin in many subtle ways—by novel trimmings, by pressed-in tucks, by their fine fabrics and inimitable grace.

Night gowns $1.95 to $50

Night gowns are here in an infinite variety—plainly tailored models, daintily embroidered garments; or a robe de nuit that is rich with lace and handiwork.

A special collection of fine white opaline Gowns, featuring pastel tinted pipings and colored applique cunningly set in with Turkish Point. All hand made. All sizes *$3.25.*

An attractive assortment of Nainsook Gowns is also displayed. These gowns are trimmed with hand embroidery or real filet lace and all of them are hand-made. All sizes *$1.95, $2.95.*

Other Intimate Accessories

Of course, there is every fabric and every new style in Costume Slips, Step-ins, Vests and Chemises. Every garment is perfectly made and moderate in price.

Orders By Mail Promptly Filled

James McCutcheon & Co.
Department No. 62
Fifth Avenue, 33d and 34th Streets, N. Y.

SCHOOL DIRECTORY

FERRY HALL
A Resident and Day School for Girls
LAKE FOREST, ILLINOIS
On Lake Michigan, near Chicago

College Preparatory, General and Advanced Courses, Departments of Music, Home Economics, Expression, and Art. *Supervised Athletics and Swimming Pool.*

Eloise R. Tremain, A.B., Bryn Mawr, Principal

THE
Mary C. Wheeler Town and Country School
PROVIDENCE, RHODE ISLAND

Preparation for Bryn Mawr and College Board Examinations

Out door sports   Junior Country Residence

HILLSIDE
A School for Girls
NORWALK   CONNECTICUT

In a beautiful New England town, one hour from New York. Girls from all parts of the country. Four residences, schoolhouse, gymnasium. Extensive grounds. Preparation for all colleges. Special courses. Outdoor life. Horseback riding. Catalog.

Margaret R. Brendlinger, A.B., Vassar
Vida Hunt Francis, A.B., Smith, *Principals*

The Harcum School
BRYN MAWR, PA.

Prepares for Bryn Mawr and all leading colleges

Musical Course prepares for the Department of Music of Bryn Mawr College
EDITH H. HARCUM, Head of School
L. MAY WILLIS, Principal

MISS RANSOM *and* MISS BRIDGES' SCHOOL
HAZEL LANE, PIEDMONT (Suburb of San Francisco)

College Preparatory

MARION RANSOM } Headmistresses
EDITH BRIDGES }

MISS MADEIRA'S SCHOOL
1330 19th St., N. W.   Washington, D. C.

A Resident and Day School for Girls

LUCY MADEIRA WING, A.B
MRS. DAVID LAFOREST WING
Head Mistress

The Shipley School
Bryn Mawr, Pennsylvania
Preparatory to Bryn Mawr College
Alice G. Howland, Eleanor O. Brownell, Principals

The Ethel Walker School
SIMSBURY, CONNECTICUT
Head of School
ETHEL WALKER SMITH, A.M. Bryn Mawr College
Head Mistress
JESSIE GERMAIN HEWITT, A.B. Bryn Mawr College

THE MISSES KIRK'S
College Preparatory School
PREPARATORY TO BRYN MAWR COLLEGE
Individual instruction. Athletics.

Clovercroft, Montgomery Avenue, Rosemont, Pa .
Mail, telephone and telegraph address: Bryn Mawr, Pa.

MISS WRIGHT'S SCHOOL
Bryn Mawr, Pa.

Prepares for Bryn Mawr and
College Board Examinations

Miss Beard's School for Girls
ORANGE, NEW JERSEY
A country school near New York. College preparatory, special courses. Art, Domestic Arts and Science. Supervised physical work. Agnes Miles Music School affiliated with Miss Beard's School.
MISS LUCIE C. BEARD, Head Mistress

ROSEMARY HALL
No elective courses
· Prepares for college
Preferably Bryn Mawr
Caroline Ruutz-Rees, Ph.D. } Head Mistresses
Mary E. Lowndes, Litt.D. }
GREENWICH   CONNECTICUT

The Katharine Branson School
ROSS, CALIFORNIA   Across the Bay from San Francisco
A Country School   College Preparatory
Heads
Katharine Fleming Branson, A. B., Bryn Mawr
Laura Elizabeth Branson, A. B., Bryn Mawr

THE AGNES IRWIN SCHOOL
2009-2011 Delancey Place, Philadelphia
A College Preparatory
SCHOOL FOR GIRLS
JOSEPHINE A. NATT, A.B., Headmistress
BERTHA M. LAWS, A.B., Secretary-Treasurer

SCHOOL DIRECTORY

Broadway around the world

The biggest machines built by the General Electric Company are steam turbine generators of 80,000 horse power, used in great power houses.

One of these giants could generate enough current to run all the street cars in twelve cities as large as Wilmington or Spokane. Ten could light a street as bright as Broadway running around the world.

Compare these huge turbines with the tiny lamp used by surgeons to examine the inside of an ear, and you will realize the variety of G-E products. Between these extremes are lamps, motors, generators, switch-boards and other equipment—all tools by which electricity works for you.

GENERAL ELECTRIC

The
BRYN MAWR
ALUMNAE
BULLETIN

WHY IS THE SUMMER SCHOOL?

FOREIGN SCHOLARSHIPS

JUNE

1924

Vol. IV   No. 6

BRYN MAWR ALUMNAE BULLETIN

OFFICIAL PUBLICATION OF
THE BRYN MAWR ALUMNAE ASSOCIATION

EVELYN PAGE, '23, *Editor*
GERTRUDE J HEARNE '19, *Business Manager*

EDITORIAL BOARD

LUCY M. DONNELLY, '93
ELEANOR FLEISHER REISMAN, '03
CAROLINE MORROW CHADWICK-COLLINS, '0(

ADELAIDE W. NEALL, '06
MAY EGAN STOKES, '11
LEILA HOUGHTELING, '11, *ex-officio*

Subscription Price, $1.50 a Year   Single Copies, 25 Cents
Checks should be drawn to the order of Bryn Mawr Alumnae Bulletin
Published monthly, except August and September, at 1006 Arch St., Philadelphia, Pa.

VOL. IV   JUNE, 1924   No. 6

MAY DAY

The Sixth May Day took place not on May 9th and 10th, but on May 10th and 12th. We might well exclaim, to quote from the *Old Wives Tale,* "O fortune cruel, cruel and unkind," for on this occasion fortune ceased to be capricious and definitely rejected the advances of the college. Friday was rainy, Saturday cloudy, so that a trembling Executive Committee prepared for a downpour at any moment, and Monday first clear and then stormy. In spite of the weather on Monday, May Day went on. The plays were presented in the dining rooms of Pembroke, Rockefeller, Denbigh, and Merion, and in the Gymnasium. At five the rain stopped long enough to allow the pageant to take place. As the last dance began the downpour was resumed and the audience fled.

The most notable aspect of this May Day was the courage with which it faced difficulty. The work done by Mrs. Otis Skinner, the Producer, on her enchanting costumes; by Mrs. Chadwick-Collins in her sound and far-reaching business arrangements; by Mr. Samuel Arthur King in his production of the many plays, and by Miss Constance Applebee in the management of her Green, made it possible to hold May Day suitably even under the worst conditions. But it was the attitude of every actor, no matter how unimportant, that made May Day successful. The definite postponement Friday and the complete performance Saturday made few demands upon anyone. The test came on Monday when on account of the widespread announcements May Day had to be given, although the idea of an outdoor fete on such a day seemed absurd. There was not an undergraduate who grumbled at the inconvenience and discomfort of the performance. Not one who did not try above everything else to entertain the damp and patient audience before her. There were no breaks in the self-imposed discipline, no lack of good humor. The courageous players received their reward, for their audience was most generous and appreciative. We have concrete evidence that the makeshift May Day of Monday attracted people even after it was obvious that it must take place under difficulties, for many standing in the pouring rain bought tickets to enter the grounds, so that the gate receipts for Monday were almost a thousand dollars.

If there had not been an enormous advance sale of tickets, however, May Day would almost certainly have run a deficit. As it is, the Endowment of the Music Department and the Auditorium of the Students'

Building is assured of a sum of money varying in size with every rumor, but substantial in the most pessimistic.

We have often been asked if May Day is "really worth while" and after this most discouraging experience we can be trusted to give a thoughtful answer. May Day may have. overgrown its proper limits. A few of the plays, the more elaborate types of costume, and the more adventurous business arrangements may be dispensed with. May Day must go on. There is no sight more beautiful than the pageant marching to the sound of the heralds' trumpets beneath Pembroke Arch and along the road that every May Day has followed, up Senior Row and on to the Green. There is nothing more inspiring in color, sound and motion than the may pole dances—nothing more expressive of order and gaiety and beauty. When one is able to create beauty it becomes an obligation to do so, one that may be troublesome at times, but one that will always be fulfilled as long as youth possesses the campus and tradition endures in the spirit of the college.

ANNOUNCEMENTS

The Associate Alumnae of Vassar College have very generously extended to the members of the Bryn Mawr Alumnae Association the privileges of their club house at Vassar. Any Alumna who wishes to stay there this summer should obtain a card of introduction from Gertrude J. Hearne, 1919, Alumnae Secretary.

Alumnae who would like to have copies of the May Day programme

should order them at once from the Publicity Office, Taylor Hall, the price being 50 cents each. The beautiful illustrations in the programme were drawn by Elizabeth Shippen Green Elliott, who painted the cover of the Song Book.

All contributions to the July issue of the BULLETIN should be sent to Evelyn Page, Taylor Hall, Bryn Mawr College, before June 10th.

Why is the Summer School?

By HELEN D. HILL, 1921

Why is the Summer School? Will the end of the fourth year, which will have started as this BULLETIN goes to press, bring any more definite, let alone unanimous answer than has been formed as a result of the preceding three? Those who lived through many kinds (not to mention degrees) of heat of that first summer are accustomed (after the manner of veterans) to refer to it as the historic period. They did, indeed, establish the fact that a school as a joint venture of women in industry and Alumnae could work. But the following years have made it apparent that there are a number of bases on which such a school can work, and the choice among these which must inevitably be made in these present years is probably as important as the original concept of the school.

The idea that the school is part of the general movement for workers' education has been very easily accepted; the exclusive enrolment of women workers in industry, i. e., those who work with the tools of their trade, the ruling, with regard to the ineligibility of typists, comptometer operators, etc., and the cooperation of the W. E. B. have all been evidences of it. But are not the implications of this idea much deeper than these outward signs? Do they not involve whatever difference there is between workers' education and ordinary adult education? If there is no difference between these, surely the summer school is an enormously costly mistake, for the summer terms of our State universities supply at far less cost good, sometimes excellent, liberal arts courses scaled to the adult mind on the assumption that the summer enrolment, with its large proportion of teachers, is considerably above undergraduate age. If there is a difference sufficiently genuine to warrant the present $30,000 expenditure, it ought to be reflected throughout the school, in students, in curriculum, in faculty.

Should not the minimum standard in the selection of a student be that she shall have shown a genuine interest in the structure and operation of the industrial system of which she is a unit? By this I do not mean necessarily a trade union affiliation; while the best students of each year have been almost entirely from the union group, the half and half proportion of union and non-union girls has perhaps contributed more to the education of each half than any other single factor in the school, and our national representation plan included non-unionized trades and geographical sections of great importance. As a parallel to the lost sheep story, is it not perhaps more important for the girl from the remote Southern company-owned mill town to come than for the trade unionist from a section of more advantages, *provided* she be really interested in industrial matters? But there have been undeniably girls each year to whom the school has signified little more than a healthful period of recreation plus certain required mental activity. If it is not possible to get one hundred girls without these, should we not run with a smaller school until our methods of selection produce a larger number of students? It would seem as though this should certainly be true of the second-year students. If we are to content ourselves with the interested girl, even though she be without experience or much information, as our first-year student— and the general level of our national community with regard to industrial matters would appear to make this wise—we are committing ourselves for most of the first season to the teaching of very primary facts. As for the second-year or advanced students, however, is it not better to admit less than the fifteen now allowed, if it is not possible to secure the return of such girls as have a genuine capacity for training in the use of facts which they already possess?

If a connection of the student's life with industry is the basic reason which justifies the existence of the school, must not the economic training which she gets there be recognized as the backbone of the curriculum? The strong feeling of the girls for the literature and science courses is alone a sufficient indication of the necessity of having them in the school: the sense of the past and of contact with other peoples which can come through good books, or the appreciation of an infinitely transferable scientific method are among the treasures of any education. But we expect our students to continue in the labor movement—an attempt to draw off the best minds of each generation of workers would be the deadliest blow that could be aimed at the working class. Must we not then remember that for eight, nine, nine and a half hours of every day our student is part of the industrial machine, and that if the school is to be effective it must supply her not only with a means of escape but also with tools for a solution of its problems? Anyone who has ever been an observer of industrial disputes knows the mass of hazy allegations, partial facts, widely repeated sayings which by their very indefiniteness increase ill-feeling into malice and hatred. The community is continually demanding fact-finding commissions; trade boards and arbitrators cry for the concrete; the owner or manager of a business has a trained staff for this purpose. The worker too often comes out of a dispute with the bitterness of incoherence. Surely it is with this aspect of its students' lives that a school founded for the education of women in industry ought primarily to deal.

If a genuine interest in industrial

problems is to be regarded as a prerequisite for all students, should not a similar standard be applied to faculty, no matter what subject they teach or tutor? The presence of a certain number of people with previous experience in workers' education is essential; this the school has always been able to secure. While at present it seems not to be possible for the entire staff to have had such experience, the various workers' classes springing up in most large cities should make this decreasingly true. It can hardly be doubted that there is a recognizable difference between methods suitable for teaching preparatory or undergraduate college classes and classes of adult workers with definite experience to correlate with their work. But until there are more people with actual technique available, ought not the school to require at least a working knowledge of current conditions of production and the recent history of the American labor movement? Every year we have had tutors, whose innocence was almost as spotless as that of a philanthropist at a certain Liberal Club meeting who inquired if there were points of difference between the A. F. of L. and the I. W. W.; and I need look no further than my own experience in the first year to realize how dearly the ignorant tutor, even though she be doing English and history, can cost the school.

I realize that there are many people who will answer in the negative most of the questions I have raised. It seems to me less important how they are answered than that they be discussed. For I believe that in the next year or so decisions regarding policy will be taken that will determine whether the school is to have any future value to the worker. Inertia, if undisturbed, will allow it to crystalize on what has been found to be a workable basis, and considering the rate of advance of the workers' education movement at present, such a crystalization will leave the school behind in the ranks of "welfare" organizations. Yet if a vigorous policy should now require from both students and faculty a persistently high quality of constructive work it could take a strong position in a pioneer movement. Whatever result occurs, let us know our reasons for our decisions.

Summer School Statistics

The following Alumnae are members of the staff of the Summer School for 1924:

Hilda Smith, 1910
Director

Caroline Morrow Chadwick-Collins, 1905
Publicity Director

Dr. Marjorie Jefferies, 1918
Physician

Emilie Strauss, 1916
Assistant Librarian

Anna Haines, 1907\
Nurse

Lucy Carner, 1908
Tutor, Economics

Millicent Carey, 1920
Tutor, English

UNDERGRADUATE ASSISTANTS

Susan Carey
Janet Seeley

Frances Briggs
Helen Henshaw

Mary Woodworth
Assistant in Physical Education

The students for this year can best be described by the following statistics:

Native Born 82
Of native-born fathers 49

Of foreign-born fathers 33

Austria-Hungary 2	
Bohemia 1	
Canada 3	
Czecho-Slovakia 2	
England 4	
France 1	
Germany 6	
Holland 1	
Italy 3	
Ireland 1	
Latvia 1	
Lithuania 1	
Nova Scotia 1	
Poland 2	
Portugal 1	
Russia 1	
Sicily 1	
Wales 1	

Foreign Born 38

Austria-Hungary 1
England 6
Germany 2
Italy 1
Macedonia 1
Mexico 1
Norway 1
Poland 4
Roumania 1
Russia 17
Scotland 2
Sweden 1

SECOND YEAR STUDENTS—1924
GROUP I

Mrs. Ethel Halliwell	Lawrence, Mass.	Textile-mender
Helen America	New York, N. Y.	Garment-Dresses
Rose Lerner	Brooklyn, N. Y.	Milliner
Sarah Panitsky	Chicago, Illinois	Garment-Dresses
Gladys Myers	Springfield, Ill.	Elec. Motor Tester
Katherine Norman	Durham, N. C.	Hosiery-seaming
Mary Burnette	Durham, N. C.	Hosiery-inspector
Mrs. Ida Lambert	Portland, Ore.	Laundry-marker

GROUP II

Annie Hollingsworth ....Phenix, R. I. ....Textile-warper
Elizabeth Nord ....Pawtucket, R. I. ....Textile-weaver
Mildred Dahl ....Tonawanda, N. Y. ....Horse Shoe Nails (insp.)
Lucile Stortz ....Chicago, Ill. ....Shoe
Sarah Greenberg ....Philadelphia, Pa. ....Garment
Hanna Blasius ....Pittsburgh, Pa. ....Metalworker
Anna Scabora ....Pittsburgh, Pa. ....Railroadworker

THE UNION AND NON-UNION GROUPS

District	Union		Non-Union		Total Union and Non-Union		
	Total 1st & 2nd yr. Group	Total 1st yr. Group	Total st & 2nd yr. Group	Total 1st yr. Group	Total 1st & 2nd yr. Group	No. of 2nd yr. Students	Total 1st yr. Group
Boston................	6	6	15	12	21	3	18
New York..............	14	11	13	13	27	3	24
Pennsylvania..........	5	4	20	18	25	3	22
Cleveland.............	1	1	5	5	6	..	6
Chicago...............	11	9	7	6	18	3	15
South................	4	4	7	5	11	2	9
St. Louis.............	..	..	3	3	3	..	3
West.................	4	4	5	4	9	1	8
	45	39	75	66	120	15	105

TRADES REPRESENTED

	Boston	N. Y.	Pa.	South	Chicago	St. Louis	Cleveland	West	Total
Automobile........................	..	..	..	..	..	..	2	..	2
Button............................	..	..	1	..	..	..	..	..	1
Cigar.............................	..	..	2	1	1	..	..	..	4
Corset............................	1	..	..	..	..	..	..	..	1
Curtains..........................	..	..	1	..	..	..	..	..	1
Electrical........................	..	..	2	..	2	..	1	2	7
Embroidery........................	..	..	1	..	..	..	..	..	1
Foodstuffs........................	..	..	..	..	2	..	..	..	2
Garment { Dress...................	2	8	3	..	8	1	..	..	22
Men's...................	..	1	..	4	..	..	1	2	8
Underwear...............	..	1	1	..	..	..	..	..	2
Waists..................	..	1	..	..	..	..	..	..	1
Horseshoe Nails...................	..	2	..	..	..	..	..	..	2
Hosiery...........................	..	..	3	2	..	..	..	..	5
Jewelry Box Maker.................	1	..	..	..	..	..	..	..	1
Laundry...........................	1	..	..	..	..	..	..	2	3
Metal.............................	2	..	1	..	..	..	..	..	3
Millinery.........................	..	6	2	..	1	..	..	..	9
Novelty...........................	..	1	..	..	1	..	..	..	2
Paper.............................	1	..	..	..	..	..	..	..	1
Printing..........................	1	1	..	..	..	..	..	1	3
Railroad..........................	..	..	1	..	..	..	..	..	1
Rubber............................	..	..	..	..	..	..	1	..	1
Shoe..............................	2	1	..	..	1	1	..	..	5
Telegraph.........................	..	..	..	..	1	..	..	..	1
Telephone.........................	..	..	4	1	1	..	..	..	6
Textile...........................	9	2	3	2	..	..	..	1	17
Tobacco Bags......................	..	..	..	1	..	..	..	..	1
Toilet Articles...................	..	..	..	..	..	..	1	..	1
Typewriter........................	1	2	..	..	..	..	..	..	3
Waitress..........................	..	1	..	..	..	1	..	..	2
Woodworkers.......................	..	..	..	..	..	..	..	1	1
									120

Foreign Scholarships

By ISABEL MADDISON, Ph D., Recording Dean and Assistant to the President

In the fifteen years from 1909 to 1924, ninety-nine European students have held scholarships at Bryn Mawr College. It therefore seems a favorable time to take stock of the results as far as figures can give us light on the benefits due to the far-seeing generosity of the late Miss Mary Elizabeth Garrett, who founded these scholarships.

In 1909, 10 scholarships, 5 for British and 5 for German women were offered to be paid from Miss Garrett's annual gift to the College.

They covered the cost of board, residence and tuition for the academic year, which was then $405 for Graduate Students. In the year 1913-14 the first French Scholar was appointed, and in the year 1916-17 a Swiss Scholar. At present 9 scholarships covering the cost of board, residence and tuition, now amounting to $720, are open to women from all European countries. The total awards from 1909-10 to 1923-24 and the number of scholarships awarded in each year were as follows:

	BRITISH	GERMAN	FRENCH	MISCELLANEOUS
1909-10	2 British	4 German		
1910-11	4 British	1 German		
1911-12	4 British	3 German		
1912-13	4 British	6 German		
1913-14	3 + (4)* British	4 German	1 French	
1914-15		1 German	1 French	
1915-16	4 British	1 German		
1916-17	2 + (2)* British	1 German		1 Swiss
1917-18	1 + (2)* British			
1918-19	2 British		5 French	
1919-20	3 British		4 French	
1920-21	4 + (1)* British		3 + (1)* French	1 Swedish
1921-22	2 + (1)* British		3 French	1 Swedish, 1 Spanish
1922-23	4 (1 of these Australian)		2 French	1 Norwegian, 2 Spanish
			2 French	1 Norwegian, 1 Dutch, 1 Italian
1923-24	2 British		2 French	2 Czech, 1 Danish, 1 Italian
Total	41	21	23	Miscellaneous 14

*The numbers in parentheses indicate scholarships awarded for a second time.

The College by means of the questionnaire sent out annually to all its former students has kept in touch with the greater number of these women, and from the questionnaire the following figures have been compiled.

The present occupations of holders of these scholarships are:

College Lecturers: 11 British (1 a Warden); 1 German (Science Assistant), 1 Dutch, 1 Spanish.

School Teachers: 12 British; 4 German; 5 French; 2 Norwegian; 1 Swiss.

Students: 3 British; 1 German; 3 French; 2 Czech; 1 Italian; 1 Danish.

Not Stated: 3 British; 7 German; 5 French; 2 Spanish; 1 Swedish.

Married, No Occupation: 3 British; 2 German; 4 French; 1 Italian.

Married, Occupation: 3 British (1 Physician, 1 Statistician, 1 Research Worker); 3 German (1 Business, 2 School Teachers); 1 French (School Teacher).

Artist: 1 French.

Statistician: 1 French.

Research Worker: 1 British; 1 Swedish.

Business: 1 German (Drug Store).

Y. W. C. A.: 1 British.

No occupation: 1 British; 1 French.

Barrister: 1 British.

Factory Supervisor: 1 British.

Work in Embassy: 1 British.

Dead: 2 German; 1 French.

The academic work of the holders of these scholarships has been done in almost all the departments of the college. A great many of the candidates have worked in the English Department and in the Department of Education.

The following items are of interest in regard to the Scholars of different nationalities:

British Scholars:

2 have done Mathematical Research work in regard to aeroplanes.

2 are Lecturers in Education.

1 is a Lecturer in English.

1 is an Assistant Professor of Latin at Smith College, Northampton, Mass.

1 held an important post as Manager of a Munitions Factory in Scotland.

1 has become a Barrister in England.

1 is doing statistical work for the U. S. Coal Commission in Washington.

1 is Principal of a Missionary College for Women in India.

1 is Lecturer in Biology in the University of Birmingham.

1 is a sub-warden of Ashbourne Hall, University of Manchester.

1 is Instructor in English, Newcomb College, New Orleans, La.

German Scholars:

6 are teaching in schools.

1 is Science Assistant in a University.

7 have not replied to the questionnaires sent out.

French Scholars:

5 are teaching in schools in France.

3 are still studying.

1 is teaching in Tangiers.

1 is teaching in Algeria.

Spanish Scholars:

1 has distinguished herself by p a s s i n g the examinations which entitle her to be a Professor of Latin in a Spanish University, being the first women to obtain this honor.

The extent of the interest in Education in the United States which has developed in European countries since the War and since the foundation in other colleges of scholarships for European students has been shown in the increased number of applicants. The task of the Committee in choosing the best candidates is becoming increasingly difficult. In the present year the Committee has received applications from 27 students: 7 British, 1 Belgian, 2 Norwegian, 2 Swedish, 4 Dutch, 9 German, 1 Hungarian, 1 Greek, and from an unknown number of French and Polish students whose applications have not yet reached the college. In the interests of international friendship and mutual understanding these scholarships for European women undoubtedly play their part.

May Day Awards

" Sunny Jim ".

On Thursday, May 1st, President Park announced in chapel the names of the winners of prizes and scholarships for this year.

Elizabeth Howe, 1924, has been awarded the Mary Helen Ritchie Memorial Prize, which carries with it the title of "Sunny Jim." This award, which consists of a set of books, is given each year to the Senior who in the opinion of a committee of her classmates and the faculty possesses "the qualities of courage, cheerfulness, fair-mindedness, good sportsmanship, whose influence is widely felt, who has the courage to live up to her own convictions and who is respected by all."

Miss Howe has been on the Board of the Athletic Association since her Freshman year and was President in 1923-1924. She was class songmistress in 1922-23 and took the part of The Town Crier in May Day.

(The following lists of undergraduate and graduate awards was announced on May 1st. A number of other awards were also made, but are not published here, since they were not won by Alumnae or former students of Bryn Mawr College.)

PRIZES

Maria L. Eastman Brooke Hall Memorial Scholarship. Value $100. Emily Pepper Watts, of Quincy, Mass.

Charles S. Hinchman Memorial Scholarship. Value $500. Anne McDowell Shiras, of Pittsburgh, Pa.

Elizabeth S. Shippen Scholarship in Foreign Languages. Value $100. Barbara Hyde Ling, of London, England.

Elizabeth S. Shippen Scholarship in Science. Value $100. (Also the Anna M. Powers Memorial Scholarship). Janetta Wright Schoonover, of Trenton, N. J.

The Sheelah Kilroy Memorial Scholarship in English. Value $125. Emily Pepper Watts, of Washington, D. C.

The Sheelah Kilroy Memorial Scholarship in English. Value $125. Anna Clinton Adams, of Philadelphia.

Horace White Prize for Greek Literature. Value $50. Kathryn Mae Elston, 1924, of Woodland, California.

Mary Helen Ritchie Memorial Prize. A set of books. Martha Elizabeth Howe, of Fulton, New York.

SCHOLARSHIPS

To Be Held in Senior Year—

Anna M. Powers Memorial Scholarship (Also Elizabeth S. Shippen Scholarship in Science). Janetta Wright Schoonover, of Trenton, N. J.

Amelia Richards Memorial Scholarship. Allegra Woodworth, of Philadelphia.

Thomas H. Powers Memorial Scholarship and *Special New York Alumnae Regional Scholarship.* Catherine Kirke Gatchell, of New York.

Foundation Scholarship. Margaret Edwards Gardiner, of Haddonfield, N. J.

Frances Marion Simpson Senior Scholarship. Mayo Castleman, of Lexington, Ky.

To Be Held in Junior Year—

James E. Rhoads Junior Scholarship and *New Jersey Alumnae Regional Scholarship,* and *Elizabeth Duane Gillespie Scholarship in American History.* Delia Nichols Smith, of East Orange, N. J.

Elizabeth Wilson White Memorial Scholarship and *A Special Scholarship* and *The Alice Ferree Hayt Memorial Award.* Elizabeth DuBois Burroughs, of West Park, New York.

Mary E. Stevens Junior Scholarship. Dorothy Couvenhoven Lefferts, of Lawrence, Long Island, New York.

Anna Hallowell Memorial Scholarship and *Cincinnati Alumnae Regional Scholarship* and *A Special Scholarship.* Grove Alma Thomas, of Cincinnati, Ohio.

A Special Scholarship. Anna Clinton Adams, of Philadelphia.

Constance Lewis Memorial Scholarship. Deirdre O'Shea, of New York.

Alumnae Regional Scholarship for New England. Edith Greenleaf Nichols, of Boston, Mass.

New York Alumnae Regional Scholarship and *A Special Scholarship.* Barbara Joan Sindall, of New Brighton, Staten Island, N. Y.

Eastern Pennsylvania and Delaware Alumnae Regional Scholarship and *A Special Scholarship.* Mary Swift Tatnall, of Wilmington, Del.

Frances Marion Simpson Junior Scholarship. Ellen Sudders Young, of Rosemont, Pa.

To Be Held in the Sophomore Year—

One-Half James E. Rhoads Sophomore Scholarship. Lucy Taxis Shoe, of Philadelphia.

One-Half James E. Rhoads Sophomore Scholarship and *First Maria Hopper Scholarship.* Eleanor Faxon Woolley, of Detroit, Mich.

Mary Anna Longstreth Memorial Scholarship. Mary Wyckoff, of Penfield, Delaware County, Pa.

Second Maria Hopper Sophomore Scholarship. Constance Cromwell Jones, of Washington, D. C.

Alumnae Regional Scholarship for New England and *Anna Powers Memorial Scholarship.* Agnes Ellen Newhall, of Boston, Mass.

Washington Alumnae Regional Scholarship. Euzelia Ernestine Jennett, of Takoma Park, Md.

Special Scholarship. Beatrice Louise Pitney, of Washington, D. C.

Frances Marion Simpson Sophomore Scholarship. Florence Elizabeth Day, of Philadelphia.

GRADUATE SCHOLARSHIPS OF THE VALUE OF $350 AWARDED FOR THE YEAR 1924-25

Department of English:
Beatrice N. Spinelli, of Philadelphia. A.B., Bryn Mawr College, 1921.
Priscilla Fansler, of Frazer, Pa. A. B., Bryn Mawr College, 1924.

History:
Elizabeth Kissam Henderson, of Stamford, Conn. A.B., Bryn Mawr College, 1924.

Economics and Politics:
Henrietta Cooper Jennings, of Danville, Pa. A.B., Bryn Mawr College, 1922, and M.A., 1923. Fellow in Economics and Politics, Bryn Mawr College, 1923-24.

History of Art:
Roberta Murray, of Chappaqua, N. Y. A.B., Bryn Mawr College, 1924.
Delphine Fitz, of Philadelphia. A.B., Bryn Mawr College, 1923.

Mathematics:
Rose Lucile Anderson, of Jamestown, N. Y. A.B., Mount Holyoke College, 1922. Graduate Scholar in Mathematics, Bryn Mawr College, 1922-23, Fellow in Mathematics, 1923-24, and Mary E. Garrett European Fellow-elect for 1924-25.

Chemistry:
Sara Thompson Archbald, of Pottsville, Pa. A.B., Bryn Mawr College, 1923. Graduate Scholar in Chemistry, Bryn Mawr College, 1923-24.

Horace White Greek Literature Prize,
Value $50:
Ruth Lea Lustbader, of New York City.
A.B., Barnard College, 1923. Graduate Scholar in Archaeology, Bryn Mawr College, 1923-24; and Fellow-elect.

Danish Scholarship Renewed:
Johanne Magdalene Stockholm, of Copenhagen, Denmark. Candidate for the degree of Doctor of Philosophy at Bryn Mawr College.

NEW NOMINATIONS FOR FELLOWSHIPS AND SCHOLARSHIPS FOR 1924-25
RESIDENT FELLOWSHIPS OF THE VALUE OF $810 AWARDED FOR THE YEAR 1924-25

Department of Greek:
Dorothy Burr, of Philadelphia. A.B., Bryn Mawr College, 1923. Holder of the Bryn Mawr European Fellowship and Shippen Foreign Scholarship, American School of Classical Studies in Athens, 1923-24. Miss Burr has just been awarded one of the two fellowships in Archaeology given by the American School of Classical Studies in Athens of the value of $1000, and resigns the Greek Fellowship to accept this fellowship and study in Athens for one more year.

Department of Romance Languages:
Anne Cutting Jones, of Des Moines, Iowa. A.B., Grinnell College, 1918. Graduate Scholar in Romance Languages, Bryn Mawr College, 1921-22. Fellow in Romance Languages, Bryn Mawr College, 1922-23. Holder of the Mary E. Garrett European Fellowship and student in Paris, 1923-24.

Department of History:
Mary Albertson, of Magnolia, N. J. A.B., Bryn Mawr College, 1915. Teacher in the Baldwin School, Bryn Mawr, 1918-24. Candidate for the degree of Master of Arts, Bryn Mawr College, 1924.

Department of Economics and Politics:
Cora Luella Gettys, of University Place, Nebraska. A.B., University of Nebraska, 1920, and M.A., 1921. Instructor in Political Science, University of Nebraska, 1921-22. Susan B. Anthony Scholar in Politics, Bryn Mawr College, 1922-23. Holder of a Carnegie Fellowship in International Law and graduate student, University of Illinois, 1923-24.

Department of Social Economy and Social Research:
Wilmer Shields, of New Orleans, La. A.B., H. Sophie Newcomb Memorial College, Tulane University, 1923. Grace H. Dodge Scholar, Bryn Mawr College, 1923-24.

Department of Psychology:
Dorothy Doris Durling, of Cambridge, Mass. A.B., Mount Holyoke College, 1920. Assistant in Philosophy and Psychology, Mount Holyoke College, 1920-21. M.A., Cornell University, 1923. Graduate Scholar in Psychology, Bryn Mawr College, 1923-24.

Department of Education:
Hazel Austin Wentworth, of Wayne, Pa. A.B., Smith College, 1921. Assistant Demonstrator, Department of Experimental Psychology, Bryn Mawr College, 1922-24.

Department of Classical Archaeology:
Ruth Lea Lustbader, of New York City. A.B., Barnard College, 1923. Graduate Scholar in Archaeology, Bryn Mawr College, 1923-24.

Department of Mathematics:
Laura Guggenbühl, of New York City. A.B., Hunter College, 1922. Instructor in Mathematics, Hunter College, 1922-23. Graduate Scholar in Mathematics, Bryn Mawr College, 1923-24.

Summary of Receipts and Expenditures of Bryn Mawr College for the Year 1922-23

(It has been found impossible, on account of lack of space, to publish in the BUL-
LETIN *the entire. financial statement of the college. We are glad to have the opportunity, however, of bringing before the Alumnae Association the following summary
of that report, a complete copy of which may be obtained from the Alumnae Office.)*

RECEIPTS:

From Investments	$209,753.27
From College Halls and Productive Real Estate	105,735.74
From Special Funds	6,452.03
From Students' Fees	131,700.39
From Donations	19,766.93
From other sources	6,792.66
	$480,201.02

DISBURSEMENTS:

Teaching Salaries	219,424.77
Administrative Salaries	35,204.73
Teaching and Administrative Pension Contribution	12,357.73
Fellowships and Scholarships	49,670.80
Laboratory Expenses and Class-Room Supplies	10,049.16
Maintenance of Academic Buildings including Books for Library, and Salaries of Librarians and Athletic Instructors	68,611.09
Other Academic Expenses	38,183.15
Non-Academic Expenses	36,439.17
Permanent Improvements and Restoring Buildings and Grounds to pre-war standard of repair	19,118.12
Total	$489,058.72

Appropriation unexpended at close of year 1922-23 . $5,031.80
Less unexpended appropriation carried from
1921-22 . 3,832.59

Increase of unexpended appropriations chargeable to current year . 1,199.21

	490,257.93
Deficit on Operating for Year 1922-23	$10,056.91

Paid by Treasurer for Alterations to Penygroes—now President's House . $14,662.53
Accumulated Charges to Grace H. Dodge Current Account . 6,245.97

Charges Added to Deficit on Operating for 1922-23	20,908.50
Debt of College as of September 30, 1923	$30,965.41

Alumnae Activities

MRS CARROLL MILLER

Councillor for District II, 1921-24

If the Alumnae Council is a success, its success is due to the untiring energy and efficiency of the District Councillors. To all of those Alumnae who have been the organizers of the several districts the gratitude of the Alumnae is due. But by none of them is so much praise merited as by Emma Guffey Miller, the first Councillor of District II. This is the largest district and it contains a large majority of all the Alumnae of the college.

At a memorable meeting held in Merion Students' Sitting Room in the fall of 1920, the country was divided into districts and District II was made to comprise New York, New Jersey, Pennsylvania and Delaware. Abba Dimon, 1896, made the prophetic remark at that meeting, "Do you realize that this means that New York may be run from Pittsburgh?" And New York has been run from Pittsburgh most efficiently for three years and the rankest New Yorker has had to acknowledge that no one could have done a better job. New York City would undoubtedly have been organized in any case, but Mrs. Miller has organized the whole of her district as well. New York State has the beginnings of an organization, and New Jersey has a flourishing state organization. Eastern Pennsylvania and Delaware are organized fully and so is Pittsburgh. Harrisburg has a nucleus for future work.

This district has six regional scholars now in college, one from New Jersey, three from New York and two from Eastern Pennsylvania and Delaware. The fact that there are four from New York and none from Pittsburgh is due to the magnanimous attitude of the Pittsburgh Bryn Mawr Club. Having raised their money, and having no suitable candidate, they generously offered the money to New York, where there were more candidates than money. Such magnanimity reflects the able work of the Councillor. It shows that she felt that the district was a unit and that she was able to convey this sense of unity to the loyal Alumnae of Pittsburgh, who had labored so hard to raise their scholarship and who would so have liked to see a girl from Pennsylvania at college on their scholarship.

Next year will see at least three more regional scholars at Bryn Mawr from District II, and we hope that as the district is more and more organized under Mrs. Bridgman, new parts of New York and New Jersey will send scholars.

Mrs. Miller as a pioneer Councillor has set a standard for us to live up to. It will be hard indeed to equal her record of devotion and efficiency. She has held meetings all over the district, has spoken innumerable times and has written countless letters to her constituents. We regret exceedingly that her term of office has expired, but we feel sure that she has only transferred her activities and that wherever she is she will work whole-heartedly for Bryn Mawr and the Alumnae Association.

LOUISE CONGDON FRANCIS, 1900.

CLASS NOTES

1889

Class Editor, Harriet Randolph, 1300 Spruce Street, Philadelphia.

On a beautiful afternoon late in April Emily Greene Balch spent an hour at Bryn Mawr showing the college to thirty or forty of her friends, representing about twenty-three different countries, who were delegates to the meetings of the Women's International League for Peace and Freedom.

From the close of the war to the autumn of 1922 she was the secretary of this organization at Geneva, Switzerland. Being for various reasons a little tired she spent the winter before last in Egypt and last winter in California. This summer she is expecting to be in Maine with her sister.

Elizabeth Blanchard Beach, Bellefonte, Pa.

"I cannot think of Bryn Mawr without Miss Scott. She will always be in my picture of the college. I am delighted that our old friends and helpers, her books, are to be part of the library.

"The future of Bryn Mawr looks very bright to me. I like so much President Park's view of education. The Summer School, too, opens new views of life and life's opportunities. The reports that appear in the BULLETIN speak of the education which these girls are bringing from the busy walks of life to their teachers. I wish that the BULLETIN might find a way to let us hear more about the mental reactions of these girls to their academic environment. I wish, too, that we might hear whether this summer inflow of life from the working world is influencing the scholastic life of the regular students, and how. I was reading the other day how gloriously the sons of Oxford celebrated the centenary of their famous debating Union; how prime ministers, archbishops, lord chancellors, in a word, all kinds of distinguished men, filled the long tables in the big Oxford Town Hall to celebrate the Hundredth anniversary of 'the nursery of public men in the teething stage' (as Mr. Asquith described it). Just think what it has meant to the life of the British Empire that for one hundred years her most distinguished men have had the habit of leaving càres of Church and State behind for a few hours, in order to run down to Oxford and to take part with the undergrads in a hot debate concerning some vital and burning question of the hour! The older men bringing to the debate the maturity and wisdom which life has given, and drawing from the young men new life and enthusiasm. What noble training for all!

"I wish with all my heart that our Summer School may do something like that.

"President Park points out in her recent report that the undergraduate of today is interested in her studies only when they link themselves with her life. Perhaps the Summer School is destined to be the living link between our cloistered learning and hot, palpitating life."

In February and March the Class Editor went on a cruise to the West Indies, visiting Bermuda, the Bahamas, the Panama Canal Zone, the island of Curaçao, Cartagena, La Guayra and Caracas in South America, Trinidad, and a number of small islands in the groups whose names make such an appeal to the imagination—the Greater and the Lesser Antilles, the Windward and the Leeward Islands.

As many of the stopping places are in Spanish speaking countries, if one wishes to learn at the moment about the things seen and the places visited, it is needful to know something of that language. The study of that language being one of the hobbies of the C. E.'s old age, it added greatly to her pleasure not only to be able to gain information, but to find that years of toil over exercises and compositions so late in life had been profitable.

Unsigned Series. Letter Number 2.

"I can't pay a truer tribute to friendship than by saying that I am always glad to see your handwriting, even when I know it is the vehicle of the stern daughter of the Voice of God. My cheque for twenty-five dollars goes by this mail to the treasurer.

"If I were going to have any adventures this summer I would gladly confide them to you, but after two years of wandering my place is in the home, and we shall vegetate in our little house in the south shore of Long Island, christened The Lantern, with a reminiscence of Bryn Mawr. Today I am occupied in helping my young husband to pretend he is eighty years old."

1897

Class Editor, Mary Campbell, Walker Road, West Orange, N. J.

'97's MAY DAY REUNION

As you all know there was a sudden inspiration that our informal Reunion should be held on May Day, May 10th. We had luncheon at the College Inn at 12.45. In spite of the threatening weather and the consequent doubt as to whether or not the May Day Revels would be held, we had a goodly company. Those present were Bertha Rembaugh, Elizabeth Towle, Mary Fay, Gertrude Goff, Elizabeth Higginson Jackson, Mary Riddle, Mabel Searle, Eleanor Brownell, Claribel Stubbs, Mary Converse, Mary Peckham Tubby, Sue Blake, Elizabeth Caldwell Fountain, Grace Albert, Elizabeth Sedgwick Shaw, Margaret Nichols Smith, Mary Campbell, Frances Fincke Hand, Frieda Heyl, Alice Cilley Weist, Helen Biddle; and besides these there were six of '97's "Eight Daughters" now in college: Delia Smith, Dorothea Shipley, Anne Tierney, Mary L. Levering, Ruth Tubby, and Olivia Fountain. We were very sorry that Mary Hand and Peggy Brooks could not be with us.

We missed all of our absentees greatly—but where were you, oh faithless four, who gave us the hope of your presence and failed us; where were you, oh Clara Landsberg, Margaret Hamilton, Clara Vail Brooks, and Paradise Alley? And we were also more than sorry that we could not get word in time to our Class Baby, Helen Hutchins Weist, so that she might be with us at luncheon.

The most exciting moment of our luncheon was that in which our newest · '97 daughter appeared—Sylvia-Ann — Eleanor Brownell's newly adopted daughter. She is the greatest possible acquisition to the class, and is a lovely baby. She celebrated her first birthday on May 10th by coming to the Reunion.

Aimée Leffingwell McKenzie and her husband will sail on June 3rd to spend the summer in England and France. Aimée has been chairman of her County Branch of the League of Women Voters in Urbana, Illinois. She has to her credit three conventions: Chicago in November; Ann Arbor in December, and Buffalo in April.

Emily Brown has changed her address to 5 Bedford Avenue, Binghamton, N. Y.

Ida Gifford had a very serious operation last fall, and had to be idle a long time. Now she is back in the world of work again.

Julia Duke Henning is returning to her old home—her country place—this spring, and so cannot come on for reunion. But she promises on her "sacred oath" to be on hand for 1929.

Elizabeth Towle insists that she has no news of herself since she returned from her two years in Turkey. But she lives a very happy life with her delightful father at 10 Elliott Avenue, Bryn Mawr.

Emma Cadbury, Jr., spent six months abroad last summer and autumn. After delightful visits in England and Scotland she went over to Poland where she "spent two weeks visiting centers of relief work which are under the care of English and American Friends. It was an intensely interesting way to see something of this strangely fascinating country." Emma, after her return to this country, received a request from the American Friends Service Committee to go out to Vienna as their Representative in the International Center. Part of her letter is quoted below:

"Most of the relief work is closing this spring, but we have the administration of a fund raised in America for fighting tuberculosis in Austria. Financial help is given to hospitals, dispensaries, etc., and is given also for the education and support of teachers who go about the country schools teaching hygiene, child care, dietetics, etc.

"This is directed to the prevention of tuberculosis and is very enthusaistically received by the older people as well as the children.

"I am looking forward with much interest to my first visits to the various centers. One of our tours of inspection includes Gratz, and I have already written to Mabel Haynes Leick to ask if I could meet her for luncheon. She has replied most cordially and asked me to pay her a visit. She seems very keen to hear about Bryn Mawr and very sorry she can't go to the reunion.

"Many of you know how beautiful Vienna is and how delightful are the people. They are keeping up their music at the cost of other things and are getting bravely on their feet. But there is very bitter political rivalry, and still much sad poverty.

"Be sure to give a warm message of love to '97 and tell them I am very, very sorry not to be at the reunion."

Ella Eberman Cornwell writes good news from her four boys. It is a particularly wonderful record since she has been ill for seven years. The oldest boy will graduate from Yale in June. Jack and Ned (twins) are at Yale now. Dan comes next; he is sixteen and has not gone away from home.

Lydia Foneke Hughes and her husband sailed two weeks ago for Genoa to spend a luxurious six weeks' loaf in Florence, Venice, and Caroline's adorable house on Lake Lugano.

The four boys are thriving. Dudley, after four years in Oxford, was ordained to the Deaconate last October, and has been teaching in Salisbury School in Connecticut, where he will be for another year. Rowland is an ensign in the Navy and has been for three years (since graduation) on the U. S. S. "Pennsylvania", Division flagship of the Pacific Fleet. Arthur is a Sophomore in Princeton. Young Stanley is at a "Little Boy's" school out here in the country (Newport, R. I.).

Alice Cilley Weist's daughter is academic secretary of the Children's University School, 10 West 72nd Street. John Rollin Weist, aged twenty-one, is through Harvard and has a job with the Condé Nast Publishing Company, selling advertisements for their Shoppers and Buyers Guide. He has only been at it two months but seems to be doing well. He is a good athlete and made the Dean's list in his last semester, although he carried six courses where four are usual. Edward Cilley Weist, aged just fifteen, led the Lower Middle Class at Phillips Exeter Academy last term, being the only boy to "make" the first honor group. He has had A in first year Greek straight through the year. He plays the piano rather well for only two years' study.

Alice Jones MacMonnies has been staying in Dover, New Jersey, at Hotel Dover attending to selling some timber on a property which she and Mr. MacMonnies own.

Corinna Putnam Smith and her two elder daughters, Rebecca and Frances, sailed for England on May 6th, for two months.

Molly Peckham Tubby's daughter, Ruth, will graduate in June. Then Molly and Ruth and Mr. Tubby will sail on June 21st for Europe. They will leave Ruth in Paris for the winter to study at the Sorbonne.

Beth Fountain's daughter, Olivia, will go abroad in June after her graduation.

Anna B. Lawther has been elected delegate-at-large to the Democratic National Convention. She says in her letter: "I hope that '97 will be in New York at the time of the Convention and will look in at us as we attempt to nominate the man who is to be our next President." (N. B. by the Editor: Republicans please note Anne's prophecy.)

Anne is still Democratic National Committeewoman for Iowa. As you all know she is an Alumnae Director of Bryn Mawr.

At the end of her letter she writes (and she writes with feeling and understanding, for she is really our class treasurer when there is any money in the Treasury which comes from other sources than a reunion), "I am glad to know that you have $11.36 in the savings bank. You will probably have to use the interest and part of the principal for stamps and typing."

She is quite right, but more than that, there would be no balance at all were it not for the fact that Elizabeth Higginson Jackson was so profoundly moved by the news of that $11.36 in the treasury that she at once sent a cheque for $5.00.

Mary Riddle writes that she is having a great deal of fun selecting pictures to hang in Chicago's Public Schools, running a house and some business, and painting a bit, when the picture market is dull.

Elizabeth Seymour Angel came to America last summer with her husband and her two boys. We are certainly sorry that she did not give us all a chance to see her and the family. Besides that she has had a visit to Paris and the Chiltern Hills (walking and climbing and trying to sketch in October rains). Now they are at the sea, while the children get entirely well after the measles.

Last summer Mr. Angel had an important war-memorial—with five figures—unveiled by Lord Beatty in Exeter. Another one in Bridgewater is to be unveiled this September—a group with Civilization as the central figure; and he is now at work on one representing Peace.

Elizabeth's elder boy, nine, is now in a "preparatory school," which means in England preparatory for a public school (probably Winchester or Westminster) at thirteen. He is as keen on sports as on studies. He has had Latin for four terms and does fairly well, but distinguishes himself in arithmetic. The smaller boy, five, taught himself to read several months ago and is absorbed in that and in every branch of activity or information. He is a most enchanting companion.

Elizabeth writes that she hopes that if any of our class come to England they will telephone her or write and let her see them, and she sends her love to all of '97.

1905

Class Editor, Mrs. Clarence Hardenbergh, 3710 Warwick Boulevard, Kansas City, Mo.

The Class of 1905 extends its sincere sympathy to Elsie Henry Redfield, whose husband, John Mansfield Redfield, died recently. Mr. Redfield met with an accident and died the day after without recovering consciousness.

1907

Class Editor, Eunice Morgan Schenck, Low Buildings, Bryn Mawr, Pa.

Esther Williams Apthorp has a new son, James Sargent Apthorp, born in April. Those of us who remember Esther's scorn of petticoats will appreciate that the child chose his sex with tact and discretion. Esther recently bought the house at 8 Carpenter Street, Salem, in which she has been living for several years. Her elder son, Bill, is two and a half.

Tinky Meigs spent the early months of the year not far from Esther at Devereux, Massachusetts. She is now living at home in Keokuk and was a member of the May Day Committee for Iowa.

Adele Brandeis is living in New York at the Bryn Mawr Club and is studying at the Art League.

Anne Jones Haines graduates from her nurse's training course in May. She expects to take a brief vacation in Maine, do some public health work in this country for a few months and then go back to Russia for five years or longer to start a training school for Russian nurses and to superintend work there which will approximate our Visiting Nurse work. 1907 may well be proud of Jonesy.

May Ballin has been wandering the world again; this time travelling in the West Indies.

Letitia Windle is opening a bookshop in West Chester.

Alice Hawkins writes: "I have gone back to my old job from which I had leave of absence when I went abroad. Louise Watson and I gave up our Greenwich Village apartment, to the great relief of our respective families, and took one in the sacred precincts of Murray Hill. We live opposite J. P. Morgan, and it is a most respectable neighborhood. But, in spite of the phalanx of detectives guarding the Morgan property opposite, our apartment was recently robbed and we lost all our famous jewels, furs, etc. I see something of Tony Cannon, who has an office in the same building as mine. She is doing two part-time jobs and, true to type, is working at least three-quarter time on each. When last heard from she had taken on the chaperoning of some dances to be held in the Brooklyn high schools. One evening recently she and I and May Ballin and Margaret Morison and Elizabeth Pope Behr had dinner together at the Bryn Mawr Club. Grace Hutchins was expected but she telephoned that it was her turn to be cook at the Community House and she couldn't get away. We wanted to have Margaret Bailey, but she was buried in New Canaan, as it was a school vacation. Louise Watson, Bernice Mackenzie and I have taken a house for the summer at Sound Beach, Connecticut, and plan to commute for three or four months. If we don't manage to sublet our apartment in town our next move will be to the debtors' prison."

Lelia Woodruff Stokes is showing commendable spirit in planning to sail for Europe with her husband the end of June, leaving her five children in this country, Jo and Allen in a boys' camp and the three little ones in her country cottage.

Margaret Reeve Cary and her husband set forth on June 27th for the Canadian Rockies and Alaska, taking their three children with them. In its way, also, a spirited undertaking.

Margaret Ryan Noonan writes the Class Editor that for the past eight years she has been married and living in Seattle, Washington. She has two daughters, Constance and Doris Mae, aged seven and four years respectively. She has travelled up and down the coast since she has lived in the Northwest from Alaska to Southern California and down into Mexico.

Harriot Houghteling went to California in February. While there she met and lunched with Eleanor Ecob Sawyer and Alice Sussman Arnstein. In April she was touring the Atlantic seaboard for the Grenfell Association and she is now polishing off the Campaign for the Endowment of the Music Department in Winnetka, Illinois, before setting forth for Labrador in June.

Alice Gerstenberg is much interested in the founding and the financing of a Civic Theatre in Chicago.

Has all 1907 observed that Margaret Reeve Cary is President of the Alumnae Association and Peggy Ayer Barnes its Vice-President? You can't keep a good class down!

1909

Class Editor, Mrs. Rollin T. Chamberlin, 5492 South Shore Drive, Chicago, Ill.

To Edith Brown Abbot the class extends sympathy in the sudden illness and death of her sister. Edith is very busy bringing up two small daughters.

Fannie Barber Berry has been teaching in New York this winter, "with a little dancing and bridge on the side," and various pleasant week-end trips. Fannie sails on June 17th, to spend the summer in Italy and France.

Alta Stevens Cameron left Chicago the middle of May, with her two small sons, to spend the summer with her mother, Mrs. Charles A. Stevens, at Delavan, Wisconsin.

Dorothy Smith Chamberlin will spend part of June and July at Asquan Lake, Holderness, N. H.

To Grace Wooldridge Dewes the class extends sympathy in the death of her father, in Baltimore in January. Grace spent six weeks of the winter at Olympia, Florida, where the golf and bathing were very fine. For the summer Grace expects to take her three daughters east to the Atlantic Coast, to get some salt sea air. 1909's class daughter, Grace Heding Dewes, is now taller than her mother.

Antoinette Hearne Farrar is planning a visit, this summer, with her three children to her sister, Frances Hearne Brown, in Winnetka, Illinois. All Antoinette's Chicago classmates are rejoicing at the prospect of seeing her again.

Helen Brown Haggerty (Mrs. Lawrence Wilburt Haggerty) has a son, Walter Eliot Haggerty, born in March. Helen has abandoned the library at the Naval Station, Hampton Roads, Va., and is now living at Stratford, Conn.

Helen T. Gilroy sails in July for China, where she will be an Assistant Professor of Physics at the Canton Christian College, Canton.

1911

Class Editor, Louise S. Russell, 140 East 52d Street, New York City.

Norvelle Browne and Mary Taylor sail for England June 24th. They plan to walk along the coast of Cornwall and in the Scotch Highlands, and to take trips down the rivers Wye and Thames in a double sculling gig.

Anna Stearns landed in New York the last part of April after several months spent in Italy and on the French Riviera.

Elizabeth Taylor Russell is turning her legal mind to real estate and is prepared to supply you with everything from a remodeled garage studio in New York to a large estate on Long Island. She is with the firm of Lee and Carter, 665 Fifth Avenue.

Marion Scott Soames has returned to Wales after spending a few months with her family in Chicago.

Leila Houghteling spent a month in California this winter. She is now back at the University of Chicago, where she will work part of the summer.

Louise Russell spent Easter week with Helen Henderson Green in Petersburg, Va., incidentally helping her to celebrate her wedding anniversary.

The following members of the class were at Bryn Mawr for the May Day Pageant: Dorothy Coffin Greeley, May Egan Stokes, Anna Stearns, Norvelle Browne, Helen Emerson Chase, Charlotte Claflin and Louise Russell.

Dorothy Coffin Greeley spent a few days with Norvelle Browne in New York in May. She is planning to spend her summer at their new summer camp in Northern Michigan.

1915

Class Editor, Mrs. James Austin Stone, 2831 28th Street, N. W., Washington, D. C.

1915 will have had its ninth reunion by the time these notes are published, and those of us that are fortunate enough to be there will have gleaned quite a bit of news about one another. It had been the class editor's intentions to write every member of the class urging those who could not come to reunion to send some news of themselves for the June BULLETIN, but owing to attending the A. A. U. W.

Convention and the 1001 others that also took place in Washington in April, these letters were not written. Doc, the old dear, wrote me a letter of her own accord from the other end of the earth, and this news, with other bits gleaned from the highways and byways, and from helpful friends in other classes, is hereby given.

Doc writes from French Indo-China (wherever that is) as follows: "The best piece of news I have, is that I now have a daughter four months old, Helene Elisabeth, born October 15 (This is Doc's second child, the first being a boy). We are now settled in Hanoi, small unheard-of capital that thinks itself the center of the earth. It is a good town and we are glad to return to civilization after the wilds. My baby girl was born in Haiduong, where there are about thirty Europeans. This is a regular town. There are several thousand. Best wishes and thanks for the interest of the class in this old vagabond. As ever, Doc."

Candace Hewitt Stevenson has a son, Peter Cooper, born in April, weight nine pounds, and reported to be "gaining steadily."

Dorothea May Moore is on a trip around the world, and will therefore not be at reunion. Likewise, Louise Hollingsworth is sailing for Europe in June, accompanied by Virginia Baker, '16.

A clipping from the St. Louis Globe-Democrat for April 12 gave the following news of Hadley Richardson Hemenway and her husband: "St. Louis readers of O'Brien's Best Stories for 1923 will be interested in the fact that the name of Ernest Hemenway appears upon the dedicatory page. . . . Mr. and Mrs. Hemenway and their small child are now living in Paris. Mr. Hemenway's short stories . . . have won him distinction in Europe. He was in the service during the war, and when wounded was sent to an Italian hospital, where he met the King of Italy, who, with other visitors, was enthusiastic about him, for Mr. Hemenway is as distinguished in appearance as he is in his profession."

Anne Hardon Pearce, from her farm in Florida, wrote in March that about April 1st "we shall begin digging the new potatoes for which they (urban 1915) will pay fabulous prices. . . . Of course the labor is all negro and at that time the bandana handkerchiefs and songs are resurrected, but instead of 'Old Black Joe' it's 'Down at the Cross' and other strange incantations." Anne ends with a plea that is strongly endorsed by the class editor. "I wish 1915 would give a thought to its isolated members and contribute generously of its news. I always feel as though I'd been robbed when I see only about three items in the space allotted to 1915 in the BULLETIN."

Please, everyone who was not at reunion send in some news of yourself for the next issue of the BULLETIN without further notice.

1917

Class Editor, Isabella Stevenson Diamond, 1111 M Street, N. W., Washington.

Martha Willett writes that she is busy and still enthusiastically enjoying English Folk Dancing and "Girl Scouts"— of the latter she is secretary of the Massachusetts State Camp Committee. Martha says she is studying and dancing Morris and Country Dances and occasionally teaches the latter. Norwood is still her headquarters.

Ginger Litchfield is studying art at the School of Fine Arts and Crafts in Boston. She expects to spend her coming summer in Florence and Venice for the purpose of studying the Italian Masters.

Anne Davis Swift writes from 1207 E. 60th Street, Chicago, about her new daughter, Lilias Howland, born March 13th.

Bertha Greenough writes me that she saw Nats McFaden Blanton in Richmond, Virginia, and was introduced to Nats' new daughter. Nats will have to furnish further details at Reunion. I know no more.

Marion Halle Strauss wrote Con she is most anxious to attend reunion, but with two small kiddies to consider she can't be sure until she's on her way. Marion's address is 1533 East Boulevard, Cleveland, Ohio.

Gladys McMillan Gunn writes that her two months' old son and moving her family to Jacksonville, Florida, will prevent her attending reunion. Gladys' new address is care of The Florida Motor Company, 430 West Adams Street, Jacksonville.

Lucy Harris Clark writes from 737 North Topeka Avenue, Wichita, Kansas, that she, too, cannot attend reunion. Lucy adds that although Bryn Mawr graduates swarmed the earth, she has the distinction of being the only one in Wichita.

Elizabeth Cheney is now in Columbus, Ohio (484 Jefferson Avenue) and expects to be present at reunion.

1919

Class Editor, Frederica Howell, 211 Ballantine Parkway, Newark, N. J.

Cyril Adolphus Outerbridge Mumford and Martha Ann Eis were born March 24th, their respective mothers being K. Outerbridge and Dot Peters. Pete writes: "I am fast becoming a hardened mother." Cyril is K's second, her one-year-older being "a whacking big girl with thick reddish golden locks and a captivating smile."

Frank Allison Porter has a daughter, Jane Allison, born December 12th. She returned to St. Louis with her husband in the fall after an exciting year in Serbia.

Enid MacDonald (Mrs. Elmer Winters) has a son, David Gordon, born November 26th. She is living in Lancaster, and begs '19 to come see her; address care of W. T. Grant Company, Lancaster, Pa.

Dot Chambers has returned to her job with the Y. W. C. A. in Constantinople, where her address is 19 Rue Sera Selvi, Taxim Square. She appears to have made great progress with the captain and ship's carpenter of the Fabre liner Madonna on which she sailed.

Ruth Woodruff and Nanine Iddings are planning a trip abroad together this summer. Until then Ruth, in addition to her old job, is teaching a "night school class of so-called coming citizens," in Camden, and Nanine is "teaching ABC's in a mill school" of Gastonia, N. C.

Faff Branson Keller returned in September from a trip to France and England with her father.

Mabel Lafferty reports an A.M. from Penn last year, and teaching English at the Kensington High School now.

Another great brain! B. Hurlock is rounding out her years in the Psych Department of Columbia with a Doctor's Dissertation for her Ph.D., called "The Value of Praise and Reproof as Incentives for Children, as Shown by Their Performance in Mental Tests."

Nan Thorndike has left her saleslady job at Jay's and is now with a specialty shop known as Miss Moore's in Boston. She is frightfully intrigued with merchandising.

Libby Carus returned last June from eight months in Europe. For three years she has been running her own farm, New Cranford, at Benton Harbor, Mich.

Marj Martin Johnson writes of doing Junior League work in Montreal and being busy with her house and our Class Baby,

a beauty, judging by her photograph. She promises a welcome to any of '19 visiting the city for any reason and recommends the winter sports.

Helen Huntting is taking history courses at Minnesota University for an A.M., and studying music of the more serious kind.

Mudge Butler spent the fall in Los Angeles and is now back in Washington, where her father is a Justice of the Supreme Court.

Pi Driver Rock writes that she is busy as "housewife" of a 70-acre ranch near Santa Barbara, and sends a photo of her two girls, Mary and Dodo, very cunning, ages 6 and 4.

Jinkie Holmes is sailing, June 7th, to take in "Italy, the coast of Dalmatia and England."

Betty Biddle Yarnall has a colored Sunday School class and is tutoring in English two aspirants to the B. M. Summer School. She says she is "having a glorious time being married" and adores cooking.

Helene Johnson is selling life insurance for the Equitable Life.

Another life insurance lady is Edith Macrum, who has a job in the Sales Research Division of the Phoenix Mutual Life in Hartford. Her address there is 73 Greenfield Street.

Edith Howes is doing nutrition work with the Philadelphia Interstate Dairy Council. She was in Labrador last summer with the Grenfells, and loved it.

The following hot one from Ernestine Mercer: "There isn't any news about me, now that the hockey season is over, but I can tell you that Jean Wright is spending the winter in Paris, and is living at 1, Place des Vosges. 'Nuff said."

Catherine Taussig is teaching history at Miss Thomas's School, South Norwalk, Conn.

Helen Spalding is a Senior Visitor for the Provident Association in St. Louis. She sails, June 14th, for Spain, Italy, France and England.

Adelaide Landon is studying at Union Seminary as well as carrying on her fine Church work in New York.

Jane Hall Hunter's address is 416 Boulevard, Westfield, N. J.

Dot Hall writes that aside from her job as teacher in the Roland Park Country School her "real occupation is schooling a young hunter."

Fritz Beatty wrote Buster that she was

teaching in Nashville and was crazy about it. Her pupils "are the large, husky football 'men'" of the Peabody Demonstration School.

Tip writes of seeing Bocky Chadbourne and Lib Fauvre in Boston in February, where Lib was taking a Domestic Science course (no less!), before departing for New York and Florida. Bocky was working in her father's office and studying typing.

Corinne Mendinhall has just announced her engagement to Gordon Catty.

1921

Class Editor, Kathleen Johnston, 1754 Massachusetts Avenue, Washington, D. C.

Elinor West will be married on June 7th to Mr. Frank Wing Carey, of Dresher, Pa. F. Howard '21, E. Harris '21 and E. Pharo '22, will be attendants.

1923

Class Editor, Dorothy Meserve, 148 East 78th Street, New York City.

The Class Baby has arrived. Ann Fraser Brewer is the proud possessor of a daughter who upon her arrival became the most important member of the class. We lack details as to appearance, name, and disposition, but we are certain that she will do us proud in every particular. Ann is getting along splendidly.

A great many people returned to college for May Day, among them Eric, Ros Raley, Allie Smith, Marian Bradley, Helen Rice, Mary Adams, Jinks Brokaw, Mary Chesnut, Frannie Childs and Aggie Clement. Wang Holt arrived a week too late, through a slight oversight on her part.

Dorothy Burr was awarded one of the two scholarships in Archaeology given by the American School of Classical Studies in Athens, and so will spend another year in Greece.

Mary Adams has returned from her trip through England with the All-American Hockey Team.

Katharine Raht and Grace Carson are taking their A. M. examinations this spring.

CONTENTS

SCHOOL DIRECTORY

FERRY HALL
A Resident and Day School for Girls
LAKE FOREST, ILLINOIS
On Lake Michigan, near Chicago

. College Preparatory, General and Advanced Courses. Departments of Music, Home Economics, Expression, and Art. *Supervised Athletics and Swimming Pool.*

Eloise R. Tremain, A.B., Bryn Mawr, Principal

THE
Mary C. Wheeler Town and Country School
PROVIDENCE, RHODE ISLAND

Preparation for Bryn Mawr and College oard Examinations

Out door sports   Junior Country Residence

HILLSIDE
A School for Girls
NORWALK   CONNECTICUT

In a beautiful New England town, one hour from New York. Girls from all parts of the country. Four residences, schoolhouse, gymnasium. Extensive grounds. Preparation for all colleges. Special courses. Outdoor life. Horseback riding. Catalog.
    Margaret R. Brendlinger, A.B., Vassar
Vida Hunt Francis, A.B., Smith, *Principals*

The Harcum School
BRYN MAWR, PA.

Prepares for Bryn Mawr and all leading colleges
Musical Course prepares for the Department of Music of Bryn Mawr College
EDITH H. HARCUM, Head of School
L. MAY WILLIS, Principal

MISS RANSOM *and*
MISS BRIDGES' SCHOOL
HAZEL LANE, PIEDMONT (Suburb of San Francisco)

College Preparatory

MARION RANSOM } Headmistresses
EDITH BRIDGES

MISS MADEIRA'S SCHOOL
1330 19th St., N. W.   Washington, D. C.

A Resident and Day School
for Girls

LUCY MADEIRA WING, A.B

MRS. DAVID LAFOREST WING
Head Mistress

The Shipley School
Bryn Mawr, Pennsylvania
Preparatory to Bryn Mawr College
Alice G. Howland, Eleanor O. Brownell,
Principals

The Ethel Walker School
SIMSBURY, CONNECTICUT
Head of School
ETHEL WALKER SMITH, A.M. Bryn Mawr College
Head Mistress
JESSIE GERMAIN HEWITT, A.B. Bryn Mawr College

THE MISSES KIRK'S
College Preparatory School
PREPARATORY TO BRYN MAWR COLLEGE
Individual instruction. Athletics.
Clovercroft, Montgomery Avenue, Rosemont, Pa
Mail, telephone and telegraph address: Bryn Mawr, Pa.

MISS WRIGHT'S SCHOOL
Bryn Mawr, Pa.
Prepares for Bryn Mawr and
College Board Examinations

Miss Beard's School for Girls
ORANGE, NEW JERSEY
A country school near New York. College preparatory, special courses. Art, Domestic Arts and Science. Supervised physical work. Agnes Miles Music School affiliated with Miss Beard's School.
MISS LUCIE C. BEARD, Head Mistress

ROSEMARY HALL
No elective courses
Prepares for college
Preferably Bryn Mawr
Caroline Ruutz-Rees, Ph.D. } Head Mistresses
Mary E. Lowndes, Litt.D.
GREENWICH   CONNECTICUT

The Katharine Branson School
ROSS, CALIFORNIA   Across the Bay from San Francisco
A Country School   College Preparatory
Heads:
Katharine Fleming Branson, A. B., Bryn Mawr
Laura Elizabeth Branson, A. B., Bryn Mawr

THE AGNES IRWIN SCHOOL
2009-2011 Delancey Place, Philadelphia
A College Preparatory
SCHOOL FOR GIRLS
JOSEPHINE A. NATT, A.B., Headmistress
BERTHA M. LAWS, A.B., Secretary-Treasurer

SCHOOL DIRECTORY

In the circle at the left is one of the electric locomotives that will replace the steam engines.

10 locomotives will take the place of 25

Electric locomotives draw long trains 650 miles over the Rocky Mountains on the Chicago, Milwaukee and St. Paul. Eventually most of the railroads in America will be electrified — engineers estimate that this will save more than a hundred million tons of coal a year.

The General Electric Company is electrifying the Mexican Railway between Orizaba and Esperanza. On the first section—with many curves and heavy grades— 10 *electric* locomotives will take the place of 25 *steam* locomotives.

Economies resulting from electrification will repay the cost of the improvement within five or six years.

GENERAL ELECTRIC

The BRYN MAWR ALUMNAE BULLETIN

REUNION

COMMENCEMENT

JULY

1924

Vol. IV   No. 7

BRYN MAWR ALUMNAE BULLETIN

OFFICIAL PUBLICATION OF
THE BRYN MAWR ALUMNAE ASSOCIATION

EVELYN PAGE, '23, *Editor*

GERTRUDE J HEARNE, '19, *Business Manager*

EDITORIAL BOARD

LUCY M. DONNELLY, '93
ELEANOR FLEISHER REISMAN, '03
CAROLINE MORROW CHADWICK-COLLINS, '05

ADELAIDE W. NEALL. '06
MAY EGAN STOKES, '11
MARGARET REEVE CARY, 1907, *ex-officio*

Subscription Price, $1.50 a Year   *Single Copies, 25 Cents*
Checks should be drawn to the order of Bryn Mawr Alumnae Bulletin
Published monthly, except August and September, at 1006 Arch St., Philadelphia, Pa.

VOL. IV	JULY, 1924	No. 7

UNDERGRADUATE–ALUMNA

Commencement week followed its usual course, and has by now passed into peaceful obscurity. Nine classes, ranging from 1892 to 1923, held their reunions and renewed for a short time their undergraduate days. The Baccalaureate Sermon, Senior Luncheon, Senior Banquet, Alumnae Supper, and Senior Singing followed each other in their appointed times. Garden Party, on Wednesday, led up to the serious business of Commencement.

On Thursday, June 5th, the college brought to a close its thirty-ninth academic year. During that time, some two thousand five hundred women, differing in character and ability, have received their degrees and left the college to occupy the rest of their lives in many and various ways, but no matter how different the preceding and the succeeding years of their lives may be, all of these women have in common four years of kindred experience.

Class succeeds class, and the general life of the college continues almost as if the students had not changed. For the students themselves the progress from Freshman to Senior is nearly imperceptible, and the transformation of a Senior to an Alumna is little more abrupt. For most people, Commencement does mark a physical break; that is to say, the majority leaves the campus and its studious occupation. But there is no reshaping in the mental life of a student at the time of graduation. If each one were to leave behind her what she has gained, and were to forget the habits and observances of college life, then the time spent would lose its greatest value.

The undergraduate on becoming an

Alumna does not change her personality or begin a new existence. She carries with her for all time the teaching and the imprint of the college. In this sense, no one really graduates; no one forgets or abandons her more deep seated student life.

The Alumnae Association is delighted to welcome to its membership the Class of 1924. We hope that the class will come to recognize, as we do, that its members have not lost their place in the college, but have joined a large group of women who have perhaps been able to contribute more to the welfare of the college as Alumnae than as undergraduates; that the college has not ceased to belong to them, but has become still more their responsibility, since its name will always be linked with theirs.

President Park received the degree of Doctor of Laws from Oberlin University, Oberlin, Ohio. It is interesting to know that this honor has been bestowed upon President Park by an institution with which her family has been connected for a long time. Her uncle and one of her cousins were Professors at Oberlin, and her father and mother lived there for some time. We hope to be able to publish in the October BULLETIN what Oberlin thinks of President Park and Bryn Mawr.

ANNOUNCEMENTS

Beginning with the October issue of the BULLETIN, the class notes of every class, whether odd or even, will appear in every number. Each class will be allotted its share of space. We hope that by this arrangement we shall be able to print news more promptly and so make the BULLETIN more interesting to all its readers.

Material for the October issue should be sent to Evelyn Page, Taylor Hall, Bryn Mawr College, before September 10th.

The Editor is extremely sorry that she was unable to print all of the notes of 1892, 1904, and 1908. The material omitted will be published in the October BULLETIN.

The moving pictures of May Day are now being rearranged and captioned, and will be ready for distribution at the request of Alumnae or other people interested after October 1st.

Bryn Mawr has joined with Wellesley, Harvard, Princeton, Yale, and Dartmouth in a combination moving picture in which each college has a certain amount of film. This will be shown all over the country and in Europe under the auspices of the Associated Educational Bureau. The cost to each college is $750. In order to pay for this a Bryn Mawr Calendar is being issued by the publicity office. If any Alumnae care to contribute to this fund, they should send in their Alumnae Fund contribution so designated.

Reunion

The reunions held this year were smaller than usual on account of May Day, but not less enthusiastic. Merion was occupied by 1892, 1893, 1894 and 1918; Denbigh by 1923; Pembroke-East by 1916 and 1917; Pembroke-West by 1899, and Rockefeller by 1915. Each class held its supper, and carried on its business, joining with the other classes in the regular festivities. We are sorry, and yet proud to relate that 'Varsity gloriously

defeated the Alumnae at both waterpolo and basketball. If it had not done so we should have been convinced that the standard of athletics had fallen since our time. The parade on Alumnae Day was a great success, the class of 1899 carrying off the prize for the best costume. The members of the class dressed themselves in the costumes which they had worn

(Pacific and Atlantic Photograph)
May Blakey Ross and Margaret Stirling Thom as bridesmaids, Dorothy Fronheiser Meredith as a Freshman, and Katherine Houghton Hepburn as a suffragist in the Alumnae Day Parade.

at various times during their lives, beginning with the garb of the entering Freshman of 1895, and showing their college attire, their wedding garments and their professional clothing, such as the barrister's gown and the Y. W. C. A. uniform. Three of the "results"—their children—brought up the end of their parade, which was led by Emma Guffey Miller, 1899, who, as their candidate for the presidency, was dressed in senatorial purple.

The Alumnae Supper took place on Tuesday night in the Gymnasium. Elizabeth Winson Pearson, 1892, acted very ably as

toastmistress. She was introduced by Margaret Reeve Cary, 1907, President of the Alumnae Association, and she herself introduced the rest of the speakers. They were: Pamela Coyne, 1924; Helen Butterfield Williams, 1918; Agnes Clement, 1923; Florence Hitchcock, 1916; Mary Mitchell Moore, 1915; Thalia Smith Dole, 1917; Emma Guffey Miller, 1899; Caroline Morrow Chadwick-Collins, 1905, and President Park. President Park's speech was not written out beforehand, and so we were not able to secure it as a whole for the BULLETIN. We congratulate ourselves, however, on being able to print the greater part of it from stenographic notes taken down on the occasion. Of the other speeches we have been able to secure one in full —Mrs. Miller's delightful account of " '99 and Politics."

We are glad to say that we have the promise of Mrs. Chadwick-Collins' speech together with the final financial statement of May Day for publication in the October BULLETIN. The report could not be printed in this issue, as bills are still coming in, and the account has not yet been closed.

The moving pictures of May Day which were shown at the Alumnae Supper following Mrs. Chadwick-Collins' speech belong to the college, and are to be shown all over the country. They are very clear, and give an extremely good idea of the whole of May Day.

· PRESIDENT PARK'S SPEECH

Last June I spoke of the admission examinations as the academic problem of the year, and we have now finished the first of the five years which we asked for the testing out of our plan. The problem of this year, and it is not yet solved, is the curriculum, and I should like if I may to talk about this immediate question primarily as it interlocks with the continuous question of the Freshman's delayed adjustment to college.

The complicated and puzzling problem of a decided change in the curriculum has been sporadically discussed in the Faculty during five or six years, but this year the Faculty Curriculum Committee has worked over a definite proposal and made a preliminary presentation of its report. No final action will be taken on it until next winter. It is a question on which each member of the Faculty rightly needs to express his mind and individual opinions need careful discussion before general or final action is taken. I should like, however, to speak to you from my own point of view about the report in relation to the difficulties of the Freshmen.

The Freshmen present, it seems to me, the greatest difficulty that the colleges meet. They must obviously have a particular and a thoughtful treatment, but the fact that this particular and thoughtful treatment is being given should not be too plain to them or to the other classes because part of the value of their new experience lies in the fact that in their minds it is a lesson common to all the group which they have joined. The Freshman needs on the one hand the strange, new, instructive spur of independence. She needs on the other hand information, advice and explanation to reach the decisions which she is to color with her independent judgment. She oscillates between these two needs. If she is over-protected by her academic guardians she and the college run the risk of a prolongation of Freshman attitude and accomplishment for more than one year and the further risk that the spontaneous interest with which she comes to college will be lost because she does not feel that the change from school to college gives her a fresh point of view and a fresh motive for

work. On the other hand if she is left too much alone on the ground that any individual adjustment, however slow, is better than an adjustment imposed from above there results for her and the college an intolerable waste of her time and her energy.

In the first week of her Freshman year she chooses and sets to work at courses which will form a fourth part of all that she will take in college. How does she choose in this important matter? She comes from her school with a choice based on her own experience, often the experience of her own like or dislike of a teacher, or of the success or failure of her own record. Or she has already been seized by other students who have told her that certain courses are easy or can be crossed off her list and forgotten at the end of the year.

No Freshman understands what the college is trying to do or realizes that its curriculum is built on a careful educational plan. Nor do I think she can understand. She probably has not enough actual information to be able as she enters college to judge properly the form in which the college is presenting to her its idea of preparation for life. Nor if she had that information could she, I fear, be made to attend at that particular moment. She is busy with other things. She has very little time and very little hearing for any kind of theory as to how she may choose her work, charm the officials never so wisely. By the exigencies of time, hers and everyone's else, she is forced into making her choice in a hurry and she ends by seizing on certain blocks of work and doing her best with them through the year. At the close perhaps of her third or fourth year she realizes that with these blocks she has made a rough kind of pattern, that out of it all she has a roughly unified whole. But she does not go into the maze with any sort of clue as to the way in which she as an individual is going to work it out.

So I myself have come to the point of wishing to try an experiment. If neither a warden, a dean, nor a president can make quite plain to a Freshman why "required subjects" are required, why "elective subjects" are elective, that all courses are parts of a whole, that they are loosely related and how—if all this cannot be made clear to a young student in a few hours and yet she needs to know it as soon as possible in order to make her regard her college education intelligently, then should we not try what can be done by a slower method more scientifically applied? Many of us in our college work have found a certain unification in a philosophy course, a correlation of ideas, of values, an understanding of the relation of various subjects which before had seemed isolated units. I think that a course in reflective thinking must be presented to a student of more maturity than a Freshman as she comes into college. But I should like to try to get earlier and perhaps more generally something of the same result.

The Curriculum Committee has presented to the Faculty a plan for an experimental course which attempts to provide a string on which other college courses can be strung, so that if we cannot make a Freshman understand in her first days at college what she is coming here for, slowly by a daily classroom instruction she may herself find that unifying agent. The Committee had in mind a course which should present in succession the development of the great ideas of civilization, not in the form of history but as one problem following another problem, with an indication of how those problems were solved, of how one problem led to another, of what one age after another met as its great central difficulty, as its great central experience. We hope very much that in that way the questions of history proper, of economics, of sociology, of philosophy, of the development of the human mind, psychology and social psychology, would suggest themselves naturally to the student's mind as points of approach to something she could see ahead of her, lines on which she would want to work, and that as she went on through college such a course as this would again give her something to turn back to so that she could see how her knowledges connected with one another and formed parts of a great whole.

The course which the Committee had in mind has not approved itself to the Faculty in the form in which it was presented and we have asked to work on it for another year. I hope very much that we may present another report of such a kind that

the Faculty may be willing to experiment with it for a short term of years and see whether it solves any of the Freshman's difficulties, whether it gives a core for the other work of the college and possibly an interest which the girl finds less ready to hand in what seem to her more strictly continuation subjects, language, mathematics and history.

The Faculty has decided, though the method of carrying out its decision has not been worked out in detail, that there shall be a single major subject and that in favor of it the old group of two majors more or less closely connected be given up, that in that major subject the good student shall do at least three years of work and that with it, and building it up, shall be one or two other subjects closely allied to that phase of her major subjects which interests her most, so that we may say that a girl goes out of Bryn Mawr to an infinitesimal degree an historian, a French scholar or a chemist.

We do not know what this change will lead to in the end; I think to the comprehensive examination as that certainly follows logically where the student's interest is a field not separate courses. I think it will lead to some form of tutorial system because such work in a field and not in separate courses means that chinks have to be filled up, and that seems to be most adequately met, where the system has been tried, by discussion and outside reading, often put in charge of younger instructors or older graduate students.

The Faculty has also agreed on another matter—on a general policy of reduction of the required hours. If by the change and intensification of the major work we increase the specialized work of the college then, we felt, there must be more place in the college curriculum for elective work. We have at present only ten hours of elective work, the minimum offered by any woman's college. And if the elective hours are increased then the required hours must be decreased. In what form that decrease will be decided I do not know. The general policy has, I think, been agreed upon, though the questions of reduction remain to be discussed.

From the Freshman point of view there is one other thing I should like to say. The girl who comes away from her home and into as completely new an environment as Bryn Mawr or as any college, I think, finds herself very much at a loss spiritually. I don't mean in religious matters so labeled alone, I mean in many matters of the spirit. She finds many people thinking very differently from herself, with different ways of thinking and different content of thinking. She finds that stress is laid on new things, and that things which have seemed to her in her home and in her school extraordinarily important are ignored. At Bryn Mawr we have always been glad that the emphasis has always been laid constantly and consistently on the value of the use of the reason. We have been taught to apply the cold light of truth and accuracy to the subjects, material and immaterial, that were presented to us for our thought. We none of us, I think, would question the value of that for a moment or give up any smallest fraction of our lesson, but I have been wondering as I have come back to Bryn Mawr what could be done for the Freshmen which would make that college attitude a little more understandable and a little less hard to them, make the break between the more colored, warmer life that they are accustomed to seem a little less abrupt. For that I have no solution to offer at all. I cannot help believing, however, that in some way or other we must find a way of presenting spiritual forces without sentimentality but with warmth of feeling, making their presentation true and accurate as we have been taught to desire it to be without drawing it so harshly that the girl finds it unreal and out of place in her scheme of life.

'99 AND POLITICS

By EMMA GUFFEY MILLER, 1899

Madame Toastmaster and Fellow Citizens:

We have been told that one swallow does not make a summer, nor does one politician necessarily represent a whole class, but lest some of you think that the subject of politics is pertinent to myself alone, I intend to show you that the word politics is synonymous with the history of '99 since we left this quiet Quaker college for the turmoil of a noisy world.

The quarter of a century which has elapsed since Bryn Mawr sent us forth as her then best finished product, has been the most unusual and in many respects the greatest political period of our country's history.

When we stood here twenty-five years ago receiving our diplomas, the United States had but lately fought its first war beyond its confines in order to rescue a neighboring island from the oppression of an antiquated European monarchy, and we were beginning to talk of "carrying the white man's burden" by assuming control of the Philippines, 10,000 miles from our own seat of government.

While our nation was going outside its old boundaries in influence and government, the women of the United States were rapidly going outside the home into business and industry.

Soon an American President was pleading for reciprocal trade relations among nations, and before long another chief executive was demanding that two great world powers, one European, the other Oriental, should bring peace to the world by making peace themselves.

Thus while the nation was gradually but irrevocably being drawn into world events, the women keeping pace with their country's foreign movement were asking for political equality and demanding economic security, and therefore it should have been no surprise to those following the trend of events that our country definitely took its place in world affairs in 1917, and our women gained their political freedom just two years later.

In those broadening and exhilarating years from 1899 to 1919, the members of my class, whether they wanted to or not, were like our Presidents and statesmen, being forced into outside affairs.

Whether we all fully realized the onrush of events which were to sweep us into the political sea, none of us dared resist the tide after we saw Miss Thomas swimming far in advance of her more timid sisters who still stood on the shifting sands of an outworn political and economic era.

And '99 having been well trained under Miss Thomas, plunged breast high into the suffrage sea, there to struggle until finally the high ground of the Nineteenth Amendment was reached.

With political equality a fact, the next step was perfectly natural and now you will find us filling all sorts of political positions from school director to Assistant U. S. District Attorney.

Statistically, we do not all seem to be identified with active political life and organizations, for we boast one physician, two lawyers, one dramatist, one advertising manager, four Ph. D.'s, three college professors, two college deans and eight teachers, but to prove that the majority of us are successful politicians we point with pride to thirty-seven happy husbands surrounded by ninety-nine clever children and one grandchild.

We used to hear that woman's place was in the home, but now I am convinced that woman's place is in politics, for she will never have the right place in the home until she takes her proper place in politics.

Next week some of us are going as onlookers to the Republican convention at Cleveland, where that party's candidate for President will be nominated, and two weeks later one of us is going to the Democratic convention in New York to cast her vote nominating the next President of the United States.

And now perhaps you would like to hear from a practical politician how she got there!

It was not due to family influence, nor to political pull. The honor was given to me by voters of the Thirty-fifth Pennsylvania Congressional District in recognition of the nights I had talked on the corner soapbox because we could not get a hall to speak in; it was granted as a reward for the many times I had boarded a train at midnight and landed at dawn; it was offered to me in payment of the weary hours I had spent on foot and in motor trying to spread our gospel over the county and State.

After all, there is a deep feeling of loyalty and compensation in political organizations which is almost akin to devotion to an ideal, and the poorer the voter, the deeper the feeling.

You will often hear parties criticised for not sending certain so-called high type persons to Harrisburg, or Washington, or to their national conventions to represent them there.

Now political organizations are made up of average human beings who are in politics because they enjoy the excitement, or who feel they have something to give to their party, or who want something for themselves or for someone else, and most of them are willing to work and sacrifice for their party's advancement.

And yet it is astonishing to hear political complaints made by the so-called intelligent voters who never do anything but cast their ballot on election day, and many of them do not even do that. If you will compare the registration of the "kid glove" wards in our Pennsylvania cities to that of the "hob nail," you will find the latter has a registration per cent. almost double the former.

Now I have had experience with both types of voters—the educated and the uneducated—and nine times out of ten I have found the man on the street far better informed politically and usually far more willing to make concessions for the common good than the college graduate.

Not long ago I heard of a brilliant university professor who refused to vote for delegates to a national convention unless they first declared their stand on birth control, and agreed to work for its endorsement by the party platform. Now the platform of a political party is written to get votes, and the platform makers are not going out of their way to offend a large body of voters who are opposed to or entirely ignorant of birth control, however much you and I may approve of it.

The professor in his study may not realize the futility of such a request, but the man on the street does.

That is why we get so little real reform in this country. Cloistered people decide things ought to be changed without going into the history or psychology of the matter and the result is we have a lot of laws which are not enforced. Do not look horrified, I am not a second Dr. Nicholas Murray Butler yet, for there are other laws beside those covering the Eighteenth Amendment which are not enforced, but the so-called wet and dry issue proves the point. That one issue is so constantly kept in the foreground by misunderstanding enthusiasts or cunning politicians to the detriment of far more important legislation.

It seems to have settled down to a war between the bigots on the one side and the spigots on the other, while the uninterested citizen in between is either so parched by the one or so drenched by the other that he scarcely knows what to think, and the result is indifference, hypocrisy and corruption. Here is where I hope the women are going to do better than the men. Of course, the ballot is still too new to us to to be little more than a toy, but I trust we are beginning to realize that it has more sides than one and to use it properly we must think of candidates in other terms than their wives' clothes and of issues as being something greater than personal desires.

If the women of America are ever going to count for anything politically, they will have to begin their work and their reforms by going into the political parties as they find them, and then do their renovating and cleansing from the inside. Then and not until then will we even glimpse that Utopia of which we all dream.

It isn't easy to thread one's way through the maze of political entanglements and partisan prejudices which abound on every side, but at least we supposedly trained thinkers ought to try.

I wonder how many of us realize that the food we eat, the clothes we wear, the books we read, and the World Peace we all covet, are cheap, high priced, obtainable or possible according to the way a few men interpret the needs and wishes of the millions who elect them to office.

People vote for vast war expenditures and then complain of heavy taxes; they vote for an exorbitant tariff and then complain of high prices; they fill the United States Senate full of Pharisees and then complain of our foreign policy.

If Miss Thomas taught our generation to strive for their political emancipation, I hope President Park will teach this generation to strive for political intelligence.

That is the message I believe a class that has lived through stirring political times would like to leave with you.

We left Bryn Mawr in the heyday of our youth and we return tonight in the mellowness of middle age.

In the interim we have passed through all the great and fine experiences of life, and as we have developed from immature youth to seasoned age we have seen our country grow from a timid and awkward provincial to a moral and spiritual world leader, for despite petty politics and crafty politicians, the faith and peace of the world still rests with us.

A hundred years from now if we could choose twenty-five years in which to live from two thousand that had passed, I believe '99ers would choose these years we now celebrate as our silver jubilee.

We are thankful to have lived through them. Failures and disappointments have been ours, but whatsoever good we have attempted, whatsoever worthwhile we have accomplished, that belongs to Bryn Mawr.

Alumnae Activities

MARY RUTTER TOWLE, 1899

Assistant United States District Attorney for the Southern District of New York

Mary Rutter Towle, 1899, entered the New York University Law School in 1908. In 1910 she went into the law office of Bertha Rembaugh, 1897, taking her state bar examinations from there. She was admitted to the bar in 1912, and a year later went into partnership with Miss Rembaugh in the firm which is still known as Rembaugh and Towle. In June, 1921, she was appointed by Colonel William Hayward, the Federal District Attorney, an Assistant United States District Attorney for the Southern District of New York. In this capacity Miss Towle represents the United States in actions to which the Government is a party, either as plaintiff or defendant. Most of these actions are brought in the Federal Courts and involve some Federal statute. Miss Towle's work has to do principally with civil suits, her only criminal cases being those brought at the instance of the Collectors of Customs, such as smuggling cases. Her civil work includes civil customs cases, such as the collection of unpaid duties on imports and suits on various kinds of customs bonds; contract cases, many of which have to do with uncompleted war contracts, admiralty cases, cases brought for damages for injuries to Government property, and cases brought to recover penalties for violations of miscellaneous statutes. These cases are sent to the United States District Attorney's Office either through the Attorney-General or by the various Government departments, such as the Treasury, War, Navy, and Labor Departments.

A very interesting side of Miss Towle's work is the bringing of admiralty actions against ships which carry aliens into the port of New York and permit them to leave without inspection. Many of these aliens are listed as members of the crew and although forbidden to come ashore they evade the law in various ways. For every alien getting ashore the ship may be forced to pay $1000, which it is the duty of the District Attorney's office to collect. Technically, the ship may be sold at auction, but actually the company owning the ship puts up a bond for the amount. It has happened since the war that some of the law-breaking ships are owned by the United States Government. When an alien leaves such a ship, the District Attorney's office is in a quandary. Can the Government sue the Government? The unfortunate representative of the United States would have in that event to bring suit and to defend it as well. In fact, suit cannot be brought, although in extreme cases the captain of the ship, when he can be proved to be personally negligent, may be held responsible.

Miss Towle also represents the Government in cases concerning the New York Harbor Act. Ships coming into the harbor have dumped objectionable substances, among others oil, in such quantities that the practice has become a menace to health and safety. In a test case, the owners of the ship urged that oil was not an injurious substance. The chief of the New York Fire Department, however, testified that oil floating on the waters of the harbor drifted in around the piers in such a way that with a high tide a fire started in the inflammable wood would be almost impossible to control. Testimony was offered by an officer of the American Game Protective Association as to the effect of the oil upon fish, and by a representative of the New York City Health Department as to its injurious effects on human beings bathing in the polluted water. The case was decided in favor of the Government, and established a precedent for other cases of the sort.

There has been very few women engaged in this kind of work. Susan Brandeis, 1915, is a Special Assistant to the United States District Attorney for the Southern District of New York. Mrs. Willebrandt has held the position of Assistant Attorney General at Washington. We are proud to say that of these three, two are Bryn Mawr graduates, and that Miss Towle was the first woman in the United States to hold the position of Assistant United States District Attorney.

(*Pacific and Atlantic Photograph*)

PRESIDENT MARION EDWARDS PARK AND PROFESSOR WILLIAM ERNEST
HOCKING OF HARVARD UNIVERSITY

Commencement

On Thursday, June 5th, seventy-two members of the Class of 1924, fifteen Masters of Arts, and four Doctors of Philosophy received their degrees. The exercises opened with an Introductory Address by President Park, which the BULLETIN is extremely glad to have the opportunity of publishing.

PRESIDENT PARK'S ADDRESS

Another Bryn Mawr class reaches today the hour of its graduation from the college. For four years wisdom has cried aloud to you at the entrance of the gates, at the coming in of the doors. You have lived in classrooms, libraries and laboratories. Lecture, discussion, experiment, examination—examination, experiment, discussion, lecture has passed over your heads. True, you have emerged often into gymnasiums and playing fields; there have been longer holidays of play or travel and shorter holidays of reading, music, theatre and gaiety. But on the whole, it is the discipline of intellectual work that you have passed through and in the end you will find that the scholarly purpose, however vague it was, which brought you to college will, as you look back, unify the heterogeneous memories of your life in the college, memories that now rush in a turmoil through your minds. The graduate candidates for degrees come with perhaps soberer minds. They know something already of the vanity of human desires and the occasional tragedy which befalls human effort—intellectual as well as moral. On the other hand, they have already built up a confidence in themselves, in their powers of hard work, of perseverance, and in their ability to work alone and to take independent steps in the fields of knowledge.

To do you all honor, the college has assembled today its Directors, Faculty and Staff, your parents and your friends, the Alumnae who returning have awakened old memories, memories which were asleep to them, but still stirring and vivid realities to you, and lastly these old friends of the college whom we beg each year to return on this pleasant occasion as we might invite them each early June to contemplate a trim garden coming on into bloom.

As a preface to the actual events of the day I give a word of Bryn Mawr's own history.

I have found the year eventful day by day and uneventful in its entirety. The college has had an unusually large registration this year because it added to the number who can be put into the halls of residence the sixteen Freshmen who lived in East House below the Inn. The experiment of allowing students to live off the campus, mild to the last degree in the form in which Bryn Mawr has three times tried it, has never proved successful—perhaps, I am bound to say, because the college has felt so sure of its residence policy that it has put only half-hearted effort into any experiment which takes its students outside. At all events, we are all discouraged again over our lack of success in working out the difficulty, and next year we shall go back to the number of resident students who can actually sleep (or wake and talk) under our own roofs.

In avoiding a smaller local problem we hedge in settling a larger one. I suppose that every executive of a woman's college is this year dwelling on the increasing pressure of the numbers who wish to come to college and so on the requirements, whether examinations, intelligence tests, reports, certificates or interviews, that we are devising. By the use of some invention like the Cape Cod cranberry sieve we wish to make sure that after the June shaking up only the largest, plumpest and handsomest brains remain in our baskets. This pressure of numbers of applicants comes uncomfortably enough at the same moment with the increasing scarcity of good teachers in college and school and with the conviction that the insidiously convenient lecture system has had its day, its long day, and that recitation and discussion require smaller classes and hence more, not fewer teachers. We seem to need either new colleges, larger endowments for old colleges, or a system of thriftily broadcasted class discussions. Therefore we all rejoiced over the possibility which was recently held out of the foundation of a new endowed college for women in Bennington, Vermont. If its promise proves good we shall welcome it as European veterans welcomed fresh American troops in some hard-pressed corner of the fighting line of France. I hope that its sponsors will persist in wishing to attack the problem of women's education from a new angle so that from the girls who want and ought to have something other than the standard academic college curriculum a natural flow in its direction will be at once set up. Apparently, the type of college outlined will receive students who turn away and are turned away from our avowedly bookish courses and our tender hearts if not our tender consciences will be to a degree relieved. But I could wish that a plan could be carried out for a type of college which would stir the rest of us more roughly; which would demand exclusively honor work, for instance, or offer only the two last years of college and those for honor students only. It would reform a lagging president if she saw her darlings, intellectually speaking, packing up at the end of two years to go to a place where the work would be stiffer, their independence more encouraged and their interest more keenly quickened. Meanwhile and until that super college comes into being as our provocative rival we shall continue like Shelley's charioteer "to drink with eager lips the wind of our own speed," a mild breeze, or, vulgarly speaking, raise ourselves by our own bootstraps, a tedious and discouraging affair.

So among the rest Bryn Mawr has proceeded on her way this year like a flagellant, spurring herself on, and successfully to the standard of other Bryn Mawr years. Indeed, full undergraduate work was done with unusually good records until the interruption of May Day came. Just what devastation May Day wrought to courses and examinations and students' records I am not sure; for faculty estimates widely differ and returns are not all in. Before May Day came off I felt toward it as a pacifist does toward war. I wished to save the generations of faculty and students yet unborn from its menace. But when I saw it, its beauty was so great as to be convincing. Against the background which we have inherited from the older days of the college, the bold clear color, the vigor and precision of the dancing, the finished beauty of action and speech in the plays made a whole which I think cannot be repeated elsewhere and cannot lightly be forgotten here. It seems clear to me that we have some vague duty in regard to its continuance and we are all, enthusiasts and doubters alike, setting our brains to work on the problem of presenting the pageant with great simplification and no less vigor and beauty and interest.

The graduate work has not to the same degree as the undergraduate suffered from the May Day tidal wave and has moved more steadily through the year. You have before you in your programmes the list of appointment of scholars and fellows, still not quite complete, for 1924-25, and you can see before you, no longer quite complete, the roster of fellows and scholars of the current year. Bryn Mawr feels pride and assurance in its graduate work—assurance shown practically in the choice of thirteen former members of its graduate school on the instructing and administrative staff of the college. Side by side with her 2300 bachelors of arts the college sets her 150 doctors of philosophy and her 300 masters of arts.

The Graduate and Curriculum Committees of the Faculty have been busy throughout the year and the results of their work as finally acted upon by the Faculty will in due course be reported. The trend in both groups of recommendations has been toward greater elasticity of requirements with a maintained demand for the old level of scholarship. The Thorne School works and plays by our side, the Summer School for Women Workers in Industry takes our places next week when we leave them and carries on our love for intellectual things and our liking for discussion and still more discussion into the hot nights of an unscreened Bryn Mawr summer. And the Music School over whose future we have such ardent hopes moves on its delightful, pleasure-giving way as though it feared no discontinuance, indeed, as though no money were needed to support it, but that it would live ethereally through the years on the words of gratitude we gave it.

I cannot say even these few sentences about the college year without mentioning the great change which will come to the college at its close in the retirement of Professor Charlotte Angus Scott. Her absence from the college halls will be only less strange to us all than the absence of President Thomas. For thirty-nine years since the beginning of the college Professor Scott has taught successive generations of undergraduate and graduate students mathematics and under her eight graduate students have taken their doctor's degree. She belongs, of course, not to Bryn Mawr alone but to the world of learning. Yet we may speak of her on this platform out of our own experience. A scholar of great learning and imagination, a teacher with a perfected method of teaching, observant of and interested in her pupils, a wise, able and untiring counsellor in all faculty affairs, her name may well stand for all that the graduates of Bryn Mawr honor most. She takes with her in her retirement the gratitude and the admiration of us all and from her pupils of all generations their deep affection.

Professor Fonger De Haan, professor of Spanish since 1898, also retires this year. His wide learning and his skill in teaching have given to the Department of Spanish at Bryn Mawr a wide reputation throughout the country. The corresponding departments at both Smith and Vassar are headed by his pupils, and he has trained excellently well many Bryn Mawr undergraduates and graduates in Spanish in the twenty-six years of his terms.

There have been gifts to the college in addition to the regularly contributed scholarships and fellowships recorded in the programmes which you hold. Two delightful and increasing funds at the college's disposal are given by her two warmest groups of friends, her daughters and her daughters' parents—if I may say so: $5000 from the Alumnae of the various geographical districts for the undergraduate scholars of their districts, a growing number at the college, and $6000 from the parents of students now in college, given to the college to make up the actual cost of tuition and in turn given by the college to students in need of assistance. Twenty-one of these so-called grants in aid have been made for next year and we still have a sum which we are keeping in reserve for the crises which are bound to occur.

The Alumnae have added gifts from their famous yearly fund (a fund which in our old age is to be our greatest resource, I feel confident), $1000 for books and $4000 for various other exceedingly good causes. $1000 has been left to the college by Helen Adair to be known as the William R. and Martha S. Adair Fund, the income to be used for the purchase of books for graduate work in economics. $2000 has been

left to the college by Randall Durfee, the income to be used for a scholarship to be named in honor of his wife of the Class of 1892, the Abby Brayton Durfee Scholarship. Toward the Marjorie Walter Goodhart Memorial Fund $2500 has been given this year to be added to the $12,500 contributed to this fund in October, 1922. From John D. Rockefeller, Jr., the college has received a gift of $6400 for the Carola Woerishoffer Department, $5300 to be applied to the deficit of the Department, and $1100 toward current expenses; also a promise of $1100 for next year. There was a special gift for May Day from Charles D. Rogers of $1000. Miscellaneous gifts amounted to $2000.

Seven pictures have been received from Miss Ann Thompson in memory of her aunt, Miss Anne M. Clark, two by Manfra, two by William M. Chase, one Redfield, one Hopkinson-Smith, and one Lawson. They are hung temporarily in Denbigh so that anyone may enjoy them immediately without waiting for Miss King's formal authoritative word on their disposition in the fall.

I now come back to my starting point, the Senior Class, the candidates for graduate degrees. You have come to the actual moment when the college is ready to confer upon you those degrees for which you have presented yourselves—the traditional seals of standing for which centuries of young scholars have longed and sacrificed and which connect you with an ancient lineage and name.

The college regretted very much that on account of illness President Rowland Angell of Yale University was unable to give the Commencement Address. The Faculty and Directors were, however, very happy in inviting Professor William Ernest Hocking, Alford Professor of Natural Religion and Moral Philosophy at Harvard University to speak at Commencement. Professor Hocking's address was one of the most interesting, if not the most interesting, address that has ever been given at Bryn Mawr. We cannot, unfortunately, quote it in full, since it has not yet been written down for publication. We can, however, print a summary of it, and as we have heard that it is to be published in the *Atlantic Monthly*, we can advise the readers of the BULLETIN to watch for it there.

OUR IMITATIVE AGE

By Professor W. E. Hocking

We are often reminded of a paradox in our national life; we are an individualistic people, and yet we are an imitative people.

We are imitative in our thinking—and thought is the beginning of any independence worth having. I do not mean that we imitate Europe—as is often said—in science, architecture, letters, etc. We are getting bravely over that trait of national infancy. I am thinking rather of the beliefs we live by. We have no authoritarian caste; we do not take our beliefs by vertical imitation. We imitate horizontally— we imitate each other. Opinions travel through social sets; party can substitute for private judgment as in few places; even judgment of right and wrong are warped by our special allegiance. In the matter of behavior and taste, the abolishing of social distinctions opens the gate for emulation; and each of a hundred financial strata madly imitates the extravagance of the next higher level.

The coexistence of individualism and imitation is not an accident. One produces the other. Individualism shows itself in competition; and competition necessarily imitates. Two fighters, and two rivals in business, are driven to scrutinize every advantage of the other, and to adopt it. This is especially visible in the social field. Parents seek advantages for their sons and daughters, and incidentally train them in keen comparisons during their most plastic years, with the inevitable result of making them replicas of each other, empty of individuality.

No society can survive without something like imitation. A leader implies a group of followers. A great nation can only hold together if ideas spread rapidly. Our fault does not lie in too great loyalty to our principles nor to the men who are fit to lead. In the contrary, we are rather fickle in our allegiances,—we treat truth itself as if it were a matter of fashion, and could go out of season. Something like imitation is necessary: but it is not imitation,—it is appropriation. Imitation copies the external thing: appropriation finds its inner meaning. Imitation is necessarily fickle, because it only takes the husk; appropriation keeps alive what it takes, because, like the food we eat, it makes it part of ourselves.

The chief problem of education is to distinguish between imitation and appropriation. The copyist is everywhere, carrying off an apparent success, passing examinations, and learning to applaud in the right place, but failing to get an education. Men and women bring to college habits of imitation or appropriation already formed. It would be well if some test could weed out the imitators; they are the ones who with the mask of education add to the element of sham in public life and culture, to the detriment of the college, the impoverishment of the community, and the loss of their own souls. Cultivation is nothing unless it is original.

Imitation tends to cure itself. It is bound to bring about a revulsion, in the form, perhaps, of an outburst of frankness or a cult of self-expression such as we find in some members of the "younger generation." The revulsion is likely to take the form of attacking the model, because one hates one's earlier servility to it. The cult of self-expression tries to build something with the resources of internal vacuity. It necessarily fails. It is not rejection of culture that we want: it is the art of appropriation. There is such an art. Two of its elements may be mentioned.

First, getting rid of the comparative consciousness. We can overcome the too eager concern with our neighbor's opinion, or with the prevailing labels, such as "radical," "conservative," which undertake to ticket doctrine with social approval. The only important quality of an opinion is its truth or error, not its novelty, its age, its liberality.

Second, finding each one for himself a private way to some ultimate good. Each one has such a way, whether through science, beauty, philosophy, affection, or prayer. The quality of loneliness determines one's power to discriminate in social relations. Given the integrity of the private self, the wealth of the world can be owned; while to the imitator his own possessions remain alien.

A delightful luncheon on Dalton Green followed the Commencement Exercises. For the first time in history it was served by the college. The Director of Halls may be complimented upon so successful an innovation.

Minutes of the Council Meeting

Held June 4, 1924, in Taylor Hall

Margaret Reeve Cary, 1905, President of the Alumnae Association, presiding. The meeting was called to order at ten o'clock. The condensed minutes of the St. Louis Council Meeting, held November 8, 9, and 10, 1923, were read and approved.

REPORTS OF DISTRICT COUNCILLORS

District I. No Report.

District II. Report by Sarah Atherton Bridgman, 1913, Councillor for District II. Three scholarships are to be offered by New York City in 1924-25, to the following value: $500 to a Freshman, $300 to a Junior, and $200 to a Senior. In addition $300 was offered to a Sophomore, but was not accepted as there was no longer any need for it. Eight hundred and fifty announcements have been sent out to schools, offering a scholarship of $1400 (for the four years) to a girl entering Bryn Mawr in 1925. The money was raised as follows: $310 at a rummage sale, $1320 on hand or pledged. New Jersey has offered $500 to a Freshman for 1925, and $250 to its scholar now in college. Eastern Pennsylvania expects to have $1100 for next year.

District III. Report by Margaret Free Stone, 1915, Councillor for District III. A lecture recital by Mr. Alwyne cleared over $200. Plans are made for a series of such lecture recitals before Philadelphia Orchestra Concerts for 1924-25, both in Baltimore and Washington. A Joint Scholarship is to be given by these cities to a girl entering next fall, for which there are two candidates. $300 has been promised to a Sophomore. $500 has been raised by Baltimore for The Mallory Webster Memorial Scholarship. Richmond hopes to endow their yearly $100 scholarship for which they now have $500. The Southern District is to be organized if possible along state lines. Nathalie McFadden Blanton, 1917, is to be State Chairman for Virginia.

District IV. Report by Julia Haines MacDonald, 1912, Councillor for District IV. The report was read in the absence of the Councillor by Katharine Holliday Daniels, 1918. Following the November Meeting of the Alumnae Council in St. Louis, District IV held a conference in Indianapolis, at which forty-two Alumnae were present. The conference has had two splendid results: the added interest, locally, in Bryn Mawr affairs, and the organization of a Bryn Mawr Club in Kentucky. District IV has now only one state, West Virginia, in which there is no local Bryn Mawr organization. The District has two regional scholars, one of whom, a Junior, is being financed by the Bryn Mawr Club of Cincinnati. This student has just been awarded the Anna Hallowell Memorial Scholarship and a special scholarship for her Junior year in addition to her regional scholarship. The second student has just completed her Freshman course and is being financed by the Bryn Mawr Clubs of Cleveland and Indianapolis. Both students were prepared by public schools. District IV has offered a Freshman Regional Scholarship for 1925, but no suitable candidate has yet been found. A change in policy will probably be made next year, so that the regional scholarships may be offered to students in both, public and private schools.

District V. Report by Caroline Daniels Moore, 1901, Councillor for District V. The report was read in the absence of the Councillor by Margaret Ayer Barnes, 1907. District V has a scholarship fund but no candidate. It has decided, in order to keep the interest of the district and to encourage girls from there to come to Bryn Mawr, that the district should not give its money to another district, as it did last year, but hold it until suitable candidates shall have been found.

District VI. Report by Helen Tredway Graham, 1911, Councillor for District VI. The report was read in the absence of the Councillor by Emma Guffey Miller, 1899, former Councillor for District II. The first regional scholar from the district will enter college in the autumn. The aim of the district is to create a larger group directly interested in the college—that is to get more students to come to Bryn Mawr.

District VII. No report.

REPORT OF THE CHAIRMAN OF THE CAMPAIGN FOR THE MUSIC ENDOWMENT

Alice Carter Dickerman, 1899, Chairman of the Campaign for the Music Endowment and the Auditorium of the Students' Building, reported that most of the New York Committee's efforts had so far been bent to secure a proper office organization, and lists of prospective donors. A basis for an active campaign in the fall has been laid. The General Education Board, The Carnegie Corporation, and the Juillard Foundation have been unable to appropriate any funds for the Department.

To date the Committee has raised (not counting May Day proceeds nor Reunion gifts) thirty thousand, two hundred and ninety-one dollars ($30,291), about one-third of which has been paid in. For next year it has underwritten Mr. Alwyne's salary (which it was imperative to do in order to retain him); and it may continue to use for current expenses the $500 income from the Elizabeth Hopkins Johnson Scholarship Fund. The Committee, however, has not felt justified in arranging for the lease of Wyndham, Mr. Willoughby's salary being a prior lien on any endowment funds for next year.

Mrs. Miller announced for the class of 1899, that their reunion gift was to be $2500, to be given to the auditorium in appreciation of the work of Alice Carter Dickerman.

REPORT FROM DISTRICT V

Margaret Ayer Barnes, 1907, reported that it was difficult in District V to raise money for Bryn Mawr so soon after the Endowment Drive. The district is, however, unwilling to allow the Music Department to be lost to the college. Of the $7000 raised in the district only $500 was con-

tributed by outsiders. The committee feels that it is unwise to ask for money from the parents of girls enrolled to enter Bryn Mawr in the future, unless they are personally known to some member of the committee.

REPORT OF THE CHAIRMAN OF THE SCHOLARSHIP COMMITTEE

Helen R. Sturgis, 1905, Chairman of the Scholarship Committee reported that there are fourteen regional scholars in college now; this represents $5000 pledged and paid. The minimum cost to put a girl through one year of college if she is a resident, is $807, if she takes laboratory; $777, without laboratory fee; or $932 if the scholar comes from Philadelphia. Therefore the regional scholarships do not cover expenses.

Sixty-nine scholarships are available in college; this means one for every five and a half undergraduates. They vary in size from $50 to over $500. Besides these scholarships, $2410 was loaned to undergraduates needing assistance in 1923, and the Parents' Fund helped a great many. Fifty-one undergraduates held scholarships this year; the total sum of money given in scholarships was $20,100. The spreading of good publicity for college and specific information is impossible without personal visits and contact with schools.

REPORT ON REGISTER

By Ethel Cantlin Buckley, '01, *Treasurer*

The Alumnae Association, in April, published an abridged register, of which 2000 were printed; not 1000 have been sold. There will not be another register published during the year 1924-25. It is especially hoped that Alumnae will purchase this register, as it is valuable as an address book.

Mrs. Cary announced that Helen Taft Manning, '15, had been elected Alumnae Director.

The next meeting of the Council will be held on November 18th, 19th and 20th, in Washington, the first business meeting being held on Tuesday afternoon, the other business meetings to be Wednesday morning and afternoon, and the last business meeting to be Thursday morning.

Class Notes

1892, 1893, 1894

These three classes (the last meeting informally) held a reunion together in Commencement week. The celebration began with a tea given by Lucy M. Donnelly, '93, in her apartment in Low Buildings, on Monday, June 2. President Park was the guest of honor. Others specially invited were Miss Isabel Maddison, Mrs. J. Elmer Wright, and Mrs. Chadwick-Collins. In the evening there was a business meeting, at which Helen J. Robins, '92, presided. Addresses were made by Mrs. Cary, President of the Alumnae Association, and by Miss Kelly, who represented the Finance Committee. It was voted that the reunion gifts of the classes, with a few exceptions, be appropriated to the James E. Rhoads Scholarship Fund. Afterwards thirty sat down to supper in Denbigh Hall at tables decorated with flowers sent by Alice Belin Dupont, '92.

Present from '92: Alice Belin Dupont, Helen Clements Kirk, Frances Hunt, Abby Kirk, Mary T. Mason, Grace Pinney Stewart, Helen J. Robins, Edith Wetherill Ives, Elizabeth Winsor Pearson.

Present from '93: Jane Brownell, Louise Brownell, Lucy M. Donnelly, Margaret Dudley Walker, Margaret Hilles Johnson, Elizabeth F. Hopkins, Helen Hopkins Thom, Mary Hoyt, Annie Logan Emerson, Elizabeth Nichols Moores, Lillian V. Moser, Nellie Neilson (Henrietta R. Palmer could stay only for Lucy's tea), Bertha H. Putnam, Amy Rock Ransome, Harriet F. Seal, Helen Thomas Flexner, S. Frances Van Kirk.

Present from '94: Fay MacCracken Stockwell, Emilie N. Martin, Anna West West, Margaret H. Shearman.

Dr. Charlotte A. Scott had been invited to be the guest of honor at the dinner; she wrote:

"I am sorry that I cannot do what you ask. It has been necessary for me to recognize that it is not advisable for me to accept any invitations of the kind. I appreciate the invitation, the kind thought that has prompted it and the friendly recollections that lie behind it. I am sincerely sorry that I cannot show my appreciation by accepting. Please express my regrets to the other members; I certainly have not forgotten the old days in Merion Hall."

Elizabeth Pearson as toastmistress called first upon Helen Robins to speak of "Yesterday." Helen rallied to the defense of the aged and aging, cheered on those who are no longer flappers, insisting that experience and maturity of judgment have value, the fruits of which should be passed on to the next generation: in other words, the help of a mother and a teacher is still needed by the Freshman.

The next toast, "Today," was to have been responded to by Susan Walker Fitz-Gerald, who, however, was detained by important business in the Massachusetts Legislature of which she is a member. She telegraphed her wishes for a jolly time.

Emilie Martin, '94, Professor of Mathematics in Mount Holyoke College, the next speaker, said on the subject of "College and Alumna" that the last thing the Faculty wishes the Alumnae to do is to meddle with the curriculum. What they can do successfully is to give, and to give when more giving seems impossible. She touched upon the advantage to Bryn Mawr of buying the library of mathematical books owned by Dr. Scott, and she ended with a fine tribute to her as a teacher of the greatest ability and a woman of absolute sincerity of character, who thirty-one years ago had given to the speaker an ideal that was a living influence today.

The "Future" was discussed by Louise Brownell Saunders, who defended the youth of the present day as Helen Robins had defended "crabbed age." She challenged her listeners to realize that America of the future will be a totally different country from the America of the Atlantic Seaboard and of Puritan tradition, and one with far broader sympathies.

There were many flashes of wit and gaiety in the speeches and in chance remarks of the diners; these cannot be reproduced by the reporters who now find to their regret that the plain outline of events is more firmly fixed in mind.

At the end of the supper Edith Wetherill Ives and Louise Brownell Saunders presented their daughters, Elizabeth Ives, '24, and Olivia Saunders, '26. (Other members of the three classes who have or have had daughters in Bryn Mawr are: Evangeline Walker Andrews, Susan Walker FitzGerald, Mary Taylor Mackenzie, '92, Elizabeth Nichols Moores, Margaret Dudley Walker, all of '93, and Elizabeth Mifflin Boyd and Anna West West, '94.)

The next morning only '92 appeared in the procession. Six members marched, wearing costumes designed by Mary Mason, emblematic of the fact that '92, the fourth class to enter college, was called the fourth wheel of the college coach and used the wheel in all class affairs.

Messages came from these absent members:

'92

Helen Bartlett wrote from her present home, the Webster Hotel, Chicago, "For one who is not quite strong the trip is too long. I shall remember you all at the date of the celebration and I send warm and loyal greetings to the Class of '92."

Lucy Chase Putnam wrote: "You girls who had the time for your full course will never know what a beautiful and brilliant part in my life Bryn Mawr was. Such joy to study again! Such inspiration in the college! Such admiration of the girls years younger than I! How grateful I was that the young things took me in so kindly and made me one of themselves! The songs I sang there so gladly did not half pay for all I received."

Edith R. Hall, Bessie Stephens Montgomery, and Mathilde Weil had all hoped up to the last moment to come to the reunion.

'93

Eliza Adams Lewis wrote: "I cannot tell you how more than sorry I am that I cannot be with you all on the second."

Mary Janney Atkinson sent her best wishes for a happy reunion.

Grace Elder Saunders, who was in Boston as proctor of the Bryn Mawr examinations there, sent good wishes.

Louise Fulton Hucker, until the morning of the supper, expected to come, but was kept at home by a sudden illness.

Lucy Lewis, now travelling in Europe, wrote in a letter that came June 2: "I would that I could drop down on Bryn Mawr College on that day, but flying is still too dear and too insecure to tempt me. Remember me to each one of the reunionists and remember all that happens so that you can some day tell me just how each one looks and acts."

Mary Belle McMullin, who married the Rev. Michele Frasca this spring and is now in Italy on her wedding journey, sent good wishes.

Rachel Oliver rarely leaves Tryon, N. C., she writes, the climate of which is necessary to her health. She sent greetings.

Evangeline Walker was going to a hospital on June 3 for a slight operation. She wrote to '93: "My love to all of you. I shall be with you in spirit and I hope everything will go off beautifully."

SOME STATISTICS

'92 has twenty-five children and three grandchildren.

'93 has forty-eight children and three grandchildren.

EDITH WETHERILL IVES, '92.
S. FRANCES VAN KIRK, '93.

1894

Class Editor, Mrs. Randall N. Durfee, 19 Highland Avenue, Fall River, Mass.

The class was very happy to celebrate its Thirtieth Reunion with '92 and '93. The Class Editor was sorry not to be present, but Anna West, Margaret Shearman, Emilie Martin, and Fay MacCracken Stockwell report a splendid time.

Elizabeth Hench writes of her last summer's visit to Newnham College, where she had formerly spent a year.

Fay MacCracken Stockwell is the Executive Secretary of the Institute for a Christian Basis of World Relations, which is held at Vassar College this July.

Marie Minor and Martha La Porte both were prevented from attending the reunion on account of school duties. Marie writes—"Sorry I cannot see '94 again, hope for better luck at the Fortieth, after I retire."

Elizabeth Mifflin Boyd's daughter Lysbeth, ex-1925, was married in May to Henry P. Borie of Philadelphia.

Emilie Martin is very busy at Mt. Holyoke College. Besides her teaching, she is secretary and member of many important faculty committees.

Emma Bailey Speer plans to spend the summer in Scotland with her three children.

1899

Class Editor, Mrs. Percival M. Sax, 6429 Drexel Road, Overbrook, Philadelphia, Pa.

'99 celebrated its Silver Jubilee in gala fashion. On Sunday, June 1st, Emma Guffey Miller arrived to take possession of headquarters in Pembroke West, and by Monday afternoon had welcomed the following members of the class: Molly Thurber Dennison, Carolyn Brown Lewis, May Blakey Ross, Margaret Hall, Mary Hoyl, Sybil Hubbard Darlington, Ellen Kilpatrick, Elsie Andrews, Marion Ream Vonsiatsky, Dorothy Fronheiser Meredith, Jean Clarke Fouilhoux, Margaret Derling Thorne, Madeleine Palmer Bakewell, Anne Boyer, Aurie Thayer Yoakam, Cora Hardy Jarrett, Dollie Sipe Bradley, Martha Irwin Sheddan, Sara H. Stites, Charlotte Hubbard Goodell, Sara Thaws Hess, Kate Houghton Hepburn, Mary Towle, Edith Chapin Craven, Alice Carter Dickerman, Mary Browne, Evetta Jeffers Schock, Evelyn Morris Cope, Katherine Middendorf Blackwell, Ethel Hooper Edwards, Etta Davis, Ethel Levering Motley, and May Schoneman Sax.

A Philadelphia newspaper printed the following account of '99's part in the parade:

"The 1924 graduating class at Bryn Mawr College had an opportunity yesterday to see what the graduates of twenty-five years ago looked like when the Class of '99 in late Victorian period costumes of high-necked shirtwaists, trailing skirts and 'sailor' hats on high pompadours marched proudly and grandly down the campus in the annual Alumnae Day procession.

"There were thirty-five representatives of the class in line and they carried placards telling their history from the time they entered the college to the present. They were easily the best-costumed alumnae class and won the prize, a basket of flowers.

"One sign, 'Our First Basketball Team,' showed a sextette in long skirts and thick blouses, a striking contrast to the knickered, lightly clad members of the '24 championship team.

"Following the sign, 'When We Married,' came Mrs. William Carter Dickerman, of New York, who was Alice Carter, of Philadelphia, in her wedding gown of twenty years ago, accompanied by four bridesmaids also in 'period' costume. The bridesmaids were Mrs. Pembroke Thom, of Baltimore; Mrs. Thomas Ross, of Doylestown; Miss Elsie Andrews, of Merion, and Mrs. Charles M. Bakewell, of Cambridge, Mass.

"The next sign, 'Some Results,' was followed by five of the ninety-nine children born to members of the Class of '99. They were Frances and Charlotte Goodell, daughters of Mrs. Horatio S. Goodell, of Houghton, Mich.; Miss Joy Dickerman, daughter of Mrs. Dickerman; William Sheddan, son of Mrs. Ralph Sheddan, of Germantown, and James Sax, son of Mrs. Percival M. Sax, of Overbrook. Mrs. Sax also carried a large doll in a golf-bag as proxy for Mary Florence Sax, six months old, the youngest class baby.

"The first class grandmother, Mrs. John R. Fordyce, of Hot Springs, Ark., was also represented by proxy. Mrs. Thomas Hepburn, of Hartford, Conn., a prominent social and civic worker, illustrated the class spirit of '99, which was keen for suffrage and the freedom of the sex, by appearing in a tight black satin costume of short jacket and breeches with 'Votes for Women' emblazoned on her chest.

"Mrs. Emma Guffey Miller, of Pittsburgh, sister of James F. Guffey, Democratic boss, appeared as the class candidate for President of the United States. She was dressed in a purple toga with a chaplet of gilded oak leaves—or possibly, fig leaves —on her head. She marched with a proud stride in time to the music. She is a delegate to the Democratic National Convention.

"Other members of this class in line, following a sign announcing 'Professions We Represent,' were Miss Mary R. Towle, of New York, Assistant United States District Attorney; Mrs. Carolyn Radnor Lewis, of New York, advertising manager for a big silk manufacturing company; Dr. Mary N. Brown, of Baltimore, and Sara H. Stites, Ph. D., Dean of Simmons College, Boston."

The following poem was written by Cora Hardy Jarrett, and read at the Class Supper:

GRACE AFTER MEAT

Our life is like a table spread,
  Where feasting we have sat;
And some have counted calories,

And some have prayed for fat.
Our meat, our poison—both are there
   To feed our veteran ranks;
'Tis for a varied bill of fare
   I rise to render thanks.

First for the joys of memory,
   That magic of the past;
How lasting on its tablets be
   The things we *want* to last.
Sweet sound the bells of memory yet,
   Like silver chimes they strike;
'Tis also sweet how we forget
   The things we did not like.

A quarter-century ago
   (Like yesterday it seems)
Our wishes swarmed like butterflies
   Through gardens of our dreams.
Thank Heaven that some of them came true
   To bless our earthly lot,
And oh, thank Heaven devoutly too
   That some of them did not!

The years have brought us sober joys
   And pleasures and renowns,
For some of us have girls and boys,
   And some have laurel crowns.
Some of us have our jewels here,
   These classic shades to roam,
And others of us thank our stars
   That ours have stayed at home.

Lo, some rejoice because their locks
   Have kept their youthful hue,
And some are just as pleased to find
   That gray's becoming too.
And when the jest has died away,
   While still our board is bright,
Have we not all one grace to say
   When we say grace tonight?

For dawn, for noon—and afternoon,
   For bud and flower and leaf,
For hope and faith and happiness
   And oh, not least, for grief;
For Bryn Mawr's light of courage high
   Down all that way to shine,
Full five-and-twenty milestones long
   We've come since '99·

The day mounts high, the day declines
   Towards the quiet west,
And who shall dare of any hour
   To say, "It is the best"?
Where five-and-twenty years ago
   Our untried feet have stood,
Let us thank God for all His years
   That we have found so good.

1900

Class Editor, Mary Helen MacCoy, State Rehabilitation Building, Albany, N. Y.

The following members of the class returned to college for the May Day Fete: Julia Streeter Gardner and her daughter Rosamond, Cornelia Halsey Kellogg, Johanna Kroeber Mosenthal and her daughter Barbara, Jessie Tatlock, Susan Dewees, Daisy Browne, Mary Kilpatrick, and Maud Lowrey Jenks. Small Cornelia Kellogg walked in the procession in a quaint costume.

1904

Class Editor, Emma O. Thompson, 320 S. Forty-second Street, Philadelphia.

"Those who knew Deaconess Katharine E. Scott, who was for seven years principal of St. Hilda's School, Wuchang, China, and who died in Peking on August 26, 1923, feel that they would like to express their love and admiration for her by a memorial in China. Almost simultaneously in China and America groups of Deaconess Scott's friends decided that a memorial which in some living way perpetuated her memory would be most in accord with the purposes of her own life. It seemed to both groups that the most fitting memorial would be a scholarship fund, the income of which would be sufficient to send some prominent Chinese girl from St. Hilda's School to college in China. It is estimated that $3000 or $4000 gold would be enough for this purpose. Until the fund is completed, the income on such money as we might receive could be used to help some Chinese young woman in college or it might be added to the principal. It is proposed to erect a small tablet in the chapel at St. Hilda's School, telling of this memorial fund."

The members of the Class of 1904 at the Twentieth Reunion Dinner voted to contribute as a class to the Memorial for Katharine Scott. Please forward your contribution to Isabel Peters, 6 East 69th Street, New York City.

The class contributed to the Alumnae Association Fund so generously that $404.50 was added to our Scholarship Fund.

Alice Schiedt Clark, 2136 Van Hise Street, Madison, Wis.

"Things here are running smothly, the babies are fine—the least will be eight next month and when I now get up last in the mornings and they all three bathe and dress themselves with only an occasional review of neck and ears by me, I realize that they are now far from being babies. I am auditing a physics course at the university to keep my mind from complete stagnation and also catalogue my husband's pamphlet collection.

"The first snowdrops and crocuses are out, but today covered with ice and a light fall of snow.

"Paul and I hope to begin to learn golf this spring, and hope we are not too middle-aged to get the rudiments."

A reunion letter from Katherine Curtis Pierce says:

"The story ought to begin with the last reunion, I suppose. I missed that, as we were in England. We had gone over for a little while in France and then England for the rest of the summer. It was a most successful and interesting trip. One of the things I enjoyed most was seeing a good deal of Harriet Southerland Wright while we were in London and again in the country when we arranged the trip so that we might be together and also that her daughter and my youngest son might become acquainted.

"The other summers we have spent on our farm in Maine. We usually go away for a holiday in the spring. Two years ago we went to Pass Christian, last year to England for two months. This year we went earlier and spent six weeks fishing in Florida.

"But really I like New York the best and have a very good time being very busy. As my big boys are at boarding school and my little boy at school most of the day I have time for various outside things, mostly church work, the Woman's Auxiliary and some of the organizations at St. George's.

"My political activities are limited to being almost the only Democrat in our little town in Maine. That means that I have a high-sounding title that requires no work to go with it."

Elizabeth Gerhard

"There isn't very much to tell you for the class news for our twentieth birthday,— just about the following:

"I have been teaching French at Rogers Hall for a number of years and feel quite at home in New England. I am planning to spend the summer in England and France, travelling with my mother and sister. My present hobbies are horseback riding and Mah Jong; when I cannot do the one, I can do the other."

The class enjoyed one of the jolliest reunions that they have ever had. Thirty were present at the informal dinner at the home of Patty Rockwell Moorhouse. Helen Howell Moorhead told us of her very interesting experiences in Geneva. Mary James told of the wonders of Wuchang, and invited us to visit her. Lucy Lombardi Barber refused to speak of the wonders of Poland, because she was so interested in the wonders of 1904. She declared we were all apparently just the same. Anne Buzby Palmer and Helen Arny Macan delighted us with a familiar antique song. The greatest surprise was the birthday cake aglow with many candles. We wish you could all have shared the cake and the good time with us.

Several of the class are planning to spend the summer in Europe—Jane Allen expects to travel in Norway and Sweden, Hilda Vauclain goes to Lausanne, Switzerland, Gertrude Klein spends the summer in France, Clara Wade will travel in England, Emma Thompson in Italy and Switzerland. Dr. Mary James will go to New England for part of the summer and sail for China in September.

Following is part of a letter written to a classmate by Clara Cary Edwards: "I reached India on October 1st. Cecil did not come until six weeks later. He has visited all the principal rug-making centers in the country (and, of course, I have travelled with him) and besides, we have stopped at all the interesting towns we could manage to squeak in. It has been a wonderful time for us, really. We have seen so much that is new and interesting. The weather has been delightful, too; we could scarcely have taken the trip we did at any other part of the year—and certainly could not have taken it with Arthur, because a child droops so quickly in the heat. Before Cecil came, Arthur and I visited Quetta, Lahore, Amritsar, and Simla. The last is one of the most beautiful places I have ever seen, perched high on a mountain with deep valleys full of pines and cedars all about and magnificent views of great snow-covered mountains in the distance. But I don't think I should like it in the summer, when it is full of fashionable crowds; we got there in late October, when most of the summer people had gone home.

"Another wonderful place we went to was Srinagar, in Kashmir. The whole family were together there, and we took a houseboat and had such a good time on it. Cecil and I amused ourselves in the evenings by jointly writing an article on our Kashmir experiences.

"And just before we sailed, Arthur and I had a few days' visit with Melanie Atherton Updegraff (1908) who lives in a little place called Nipani, eighteen hours by rail south of Bombay. Unfortunately, I did not meet her husband or her older little girl (eight years old), because they were off somewhere in the south where the little girl was to be put into a missionaries' boarding school. Eight years seems pretty young for a child to be sent away from home, but there were no school facilities near by; Melanie will go to the same place for two or three months in the hot season, when the little girl will live with her, and then there is a two months' holiday in the cold season. We did see little Ann, three years old, who is a picture, with a great bush of kinky pale gold curls all over her head. She is very fat and rosy-cheeked, too, and full of life and mischief—a darling. Melanie's house is charming, and she has it arranged so artistically. But the nearest white people are twenty-five miles away, and Mr. Updegraff travels a great deal, teaching and preaching in the villages, so that Melanie is much alone.

"Well we have finally decided, after much cogitation, to go to England instead of retiring to live in Italy. It is Arthur really who has decided us, although I am not at all sure that he will have as good an education in England as he would have if we were to live in Italy and send him to an English public school. Doing that he would have the advantage of two distinct points of view instead of one.

"Our first job on arriving in London will be to find a place to live in. I suppose we shall live in the suburbs—again because of Arthur—although I personally should much prefer to live in town for at least a few months. I feel that it will take me six months or a year to get my fill of theatres and shops and lectures and art galleries. I am going to try to get Arthur into a boarding school for little children

that we know of, for just a month or two or three, until we have a house. I could not very well drag him about with me, looking at houses and buying furniture. We have no furniture at all, of course, and I feel rather like a bride, now that we are going to buy everything new once more.

"I had a long letter from Kathrina Van Wagenen Bugge the other day. She has two little girls, four years old and one year old. She says that she means to put the older one into a Chinese kindergarten next year.. After two years, she will go to a Norwegian school (in China) and will prepare for Bryn Mawr in Norwegian. She will certainly be a thoroughly internationalized young lady by the time she graduates from college. She already speaks English (their home language), Norwegian (with her playmates), and Chinese (with the servants and her nurse).

"I must stop and give Arthur a little reading lesson just to help pass the day for him. He has finished his first book, but cannot read very much yet."

A French Art Magazine recently published a very interesting account of Edith McMurtrie's work.

1906

Class Editor, Mrs. Harold K. Beecher, 1511 Mahantongo Street, Pottsville, Pa.

Anna Bess writes, "I wish I had time to write you further, but the whole Grenfell family; or at least the branch of it from this side of the water, is going to England in a few days. The International Grenfell Association has an exhibit in the Newfoundland pavilion of the British Empire Exhibition which is being held at Wembley, just outside London, during this summer, and we are going to oversee that for a bit. Then the Doctor is trying to secure a new hospital steamer, either building one in some English or Scotch seaport, or trying to buy one second hand. Then he is to lecture about two months in England and Scotland.

"In September, the children return with my mother to the United States, and my husband and I are going on a semi-lecture and semi-pleasure tour around the world. This will be the first time in thirty-two years that the Doctor has not been in Labrador; but his Directors feel that the time has come when it is imperative that he should have a complete change of thought, as he has been very closely occupied with the details of his work, both in the professional work on the coast and the even more exacting strain of lecturing in England, Canada and the States.

"Everything is going so well on the Labrador and the North Newfoundland Coasts, and the Doctor has such a fine staff, that he and I are leaving with very easy minds."

Marjorie Rawson met Elsie Barber in Philadelphia and motored out to Bryn Mawr two days for the May Day Fête. They saw Mary with her handsome daughter (our Class Baby) annd Adelaide Neall and Mary Withington and Nan Pratt and Josephine Bright. Then Marjorie went to visit Elsie at her beautiful country place, and from there very fortunately writes us the news that Elsie is a distinguished member of the Maryland legislature.

Caroline Richards McKnight tells us the good news that she still has the same husband and same two boys she had when last she gave a report of herself, and, she adds, "the boys, aged eleven and twelve, seem very normal physically and mentally, which aside from age applies to husband also. We live on a lemon ranch, with about 4000 chickens as a side issue, so if any members of the Class are in our vicinity, come out and help gather the eggs."

Anna Mack says she is still alive in Scranton and even after these eighteen years able to navigate and take an interest in things. She has the honor—and trouble —of being President of the Visiting Nurse Association and then adds, "But who wants to know that?" (1906, in the distance, with one voice, "We all do.")

1908

Class Editor, Mrs. William H. Best, 1198 Bushwick Avenue, Brooklyn, N. Y.

Eleanor Rambo has an article in a recent number of *The Classical Weekly*, entitled "The Literary Inspiration of Botticelli, *Pallas, and a Centaur*."

Anna Welles Brown writes:

Care of American Consulate,
Constantinople, Turkey.

Dear 1908:

My private life is so happy that I haven't much to say about it. When one's husband is completely devoted, one's three children normally well and intelligent, one's household running so that three meals (and tea) appear on the table at the appointed hours, is there much to tell? Something about the particular color that my home life takes on from its surroundings, perhaps. Yes, my cook is Russian and speaks not a word of any other language. The children's governess comes from Dalmatia and speaks French with us. One maid is Greek, the other is a product of the French Sisters' orphanage, and does not know her nationality. We speak French and Turkish in the household.

The house we live in is owned by a Turk, and he and his family still occupy two-thirds of it. The part we occupy was the "Selamlik" and consequently has a seperate entrance. Our front windows look out on the Bosphorus and give us a perfectly enchanting view. At the back of the house is an old garden, completely walled in, a perfect playground for the children, with shady spots for summer and open spots for winter. Running water and electric light we have; beyond that, an absolute lack of modern conveniences.

To cover the five miles which separates us from the city we have an automobile and a Tartar (or Russian Moslem) chauffeur to drive it.

As for my public life, clubs and other organizations exist here as elsewhere, and I am not immune from connections with them. The American Club, the Junior Red Cross, the Y. W. C. A., even the Golf Club have their committee members, and like the rest I fell into line. In fact I am afraid I have acquired the committee habit—but it was at Bryn Mawr I started it, and I am not ashamed. This sort of work has its local color too; because apart from organized effort we all must do a share of direct relief. Unemployment and poverty in all its forms are unhappily as characteristic of Constantinople as are black veils and Turkish coffee.

My contacts with Roberts College, and with Constantinople Woman's College are many. I did see President Thomas when she was here in 1922, and she sent me some lovely roses when my baby was born. The same summer, a little earlier, I proctored entrance examinations for a candidate of the Class of 1927. The Alumnae that come this way are few and far between.

Grace Woodelton received her Doctor's Degree in Osteopathy in January, and when last heard from was in Orlando, Florida, "recuperating from the strain and excitement of State Board examinations."

Elsie Bryant Goodwillie reports, "I was in Columbus recently as a delegate from the Toledo branch of the A. A. U. W., when the state association was formed, and had tea with Ethel Beggs Hall. She has two lovely children."

Margaret Copeland Blatchford writes: "This winter, aside from housekeeping and looking out for my three children—jobs which you all know too well to listen to details about, I am trying to concentrate on two main jobs, work on the Winnetka School Board, and a puppet show.

"The puppet show is most dear to my heart and perhaps some of you would be interested. There are seven or eight married women working on it, and we do everything ourselves—make dolls, costume them, paint scenery, make furniture. It is like old college days and you can imagine the good time we have. A Bryn Mawr girl wrote the play for us, "Snow White and the Seven Little Dwarfs," in the most lovely verse. Another member wrote the music, and the stage was made for us by a husband. We had a very successful time last spring giving the play before a great many schools in Winnetka and Chicago, at a Chicago Literary Club, for fashionable charities and orphanages. Our idea eventually is to give it for orphanages and hospitals, where our small theatre can be carried to those who don't get out. Our dolls are smaller than those of Tony Sarg, but move in much the same way, though we think ours walk better.

"This fall we started on Dickens' Christmas Carol, which is delightful for puppets, but did not get it finished for Christmas, so have put it away for next year; and are now working on 'Old Pipes and the Dryad' and *Dr. Doolittle*. Today I am in despair trying to make a dog and three goats with poor success."

1910

Class Editor, Marion Kirk, 4504 Chester Avenue, Philadelphia.

Irma Bixler Poste writes that all her time is devoted to seeing to the food, clothing and cleanliness of her family, and she finds nothing else to report. Her three children are all in school now.

Ethel Chase Selinger, 24 Gramercy Park, New York, has a daughter, Beverly, born March 6, 1924.

Mary Agnes Irvine is planning to go to Europe this summer, and also—to bob her hair. There will be many in the class to sigh over the loss of that hair.

Clara Ware Goodrich has a second baby, a boy, born in April. The name will be announced later.

Alice Whittemore, 437 West 59th Street, visited Pat Murphy for a few days in May. Alice is now secretary of the Department of Surgery in the College of Physicians and Surgeons in New York. During this past winter she has been taking a course at Columbia in statistics.

1912

Class Editor, Mrs. J. A. MacDonald, 3227 N. Pennsylvania Street, Indianapolis, Ind.

In Memoriam

MARY SCRIBNER PALMER

April the Thirtieth

Nineteen Hundred and Twenty-four

It is with great sorrow we report the sudden death of Mary Scribner Palmer, in Chicago, on April 30, and realize how many will miss her charm of happiness and loyal friendship. She leaves four children, Mary Ellen, Scribner, Curtis Chapin, and an infant daughter, Lucy Margaret. Margaret Scribner Grant, ex '06, was her only sister. Our deepest sympathy is with her family. A fund to be used for books for the Library of the Music Department has been started in recognition of Mary's love for music. to be called the "Mary Scribner Palmer Memorial Fund."

1914

Class Editor, Dr. Ida W. Pritchett, The Rockefeller Institute, Sixty-sixth Street and Avenue A, New York City.

Helen Carey was married, on April 30, to John V. McMahon, in Stamford, Conn. Mr. and Mrs. McMahon will live in Tulsa, Oklahoma.

Josephine Niles McClellan (Mrs. William McClellan) has a son, born in April.

Christine Brown Penniman (Mrs. Dushane Penniman) visited in Florida during the winter.

Eleanor Gale and Harriet Sheldon stayed

with Julia Tappan for a while in Baltimore this winter.

Mary Schmidt Kurtz (Mrs. William H. Kurtz) has a fourth daughter.

Elizabeth Ayer Inches (Mrs. Henderson Inches) has a son, born June 1. She and her husband and her two children are going to Cohasset for the summer.

Helen Shaw Crosby sailed from New York on June 10 with her husband and two children. She is planning to live abroad for a year and a half. Her headquarters will be in Paris, but she hopes to do a lot of travelling.

Evelyn Shaw McCutcheon stopped in New York and Boston on her way home from Treasure Island.

Alice Miller Chester has been in Florida for a month with her husband and children. While there she distinguished herself as a fisherman, catching the largest fish that has ever been caught.

Marianne Camp Newberry has returned from India.

Jessie Boyd Smith is at Bay Head this summer.

Lillien Cox Harman was in Boston for three weeks in May. Cad, Edwina, Libby, and Helen Shaw gave her numerous parties.

Elizabeth Colt Shattuck has taken a house at New Canaan, Connecticut, for the summer.

Dr. Ethel Dunham and Dr. Martha Elliott are keeping house in New Haven, where they are working.

Dr. Katherine Dodd has gone to Russia.

1916

Class Editor, Mrs. Webb I. Vorys, 63 Parkwood Avenue, Columbus, Ohio.

Anne Jaggard Kopper (Mrs. Edward Kopper, Jr.) is the proud mother of four children, three boys and a girl.

Dorothy Deneen Blow (Mrs. Allmand Blow) is president of the Tulsa branch of the Association of American University Women and was sent by them to the National Conference in Washington this spring. Also she was sent as a delegate from the Tulsa Junior League to the Association of National Junior Leagues in Denver, from May 7 to 10.

Adeline Werner Vorys (Mrs. Webb Vorys) was sent as a delegate from the Columbus Junior League to Denver. Here Dodie and I had a great reunion, except, of course, we did not begin to see enough of each other. While in Denver I stayed with Merle Sampson Toll, 1915 (Mrs. Oliver W. Toll), and enjoyed her adorable family and home.

1918

Class Editor, Mrs. Julian B. Cohn, 5154 Westminster Place, St. Louis, Mo.

Whether through a printer's mistake or a plain optical delusion, the *College News* put us down as Reuning in LIGHT blue scarfs!

The first event of our Reunion was Ruth's picnic, on Saturday, May 31, a lovely affair, down in a handsome meadow—giving a merry chase to Stairy and the others who drove straight from York to the Old Mill! At the Class Meeting which followed, Helen Walker was made permanent Secretary, and Ruth Hart Williams Class Collector again. Then Helen's booklets of our chequered careers were given out, and a copy has been mailed to all those not present. If perchance you did not get yours, notify Annette Gest, who, by the way, has gone to Spain so that maybe your chances for an immediate reply are not what they should be!

The Class Supper was a lively one, with thirty-two present, as follows: Anna Booth, Ella Lindley Burton, Sidney Belville Coale, Louise Hodges Crenshaw, Katherine Holliday Daniels, Marion O'Connor Duble, Bessie Downs Evans, Lorraine Fraser, Mary Gardiner, Annette Gest, Harriet Hobbs Haines, Laura Heisler, Mary Safford Hoogewerff, Henrietta Huff, Teddy Howell Hurlburt, James Marion Israel, Katherine Sharpless Klein, Virginia Anderton Lee, Helen Hammer Link, Dorothy Kuhn Minster, Cora Neely, Alice Newlin, Bethed Pershing, Leslie Richardson, Ruth Rhoades, Helen Schwarz, Mary Scott, Ruth Cheney Streeter, Beulah Fegley Weir, Helen Butterfield Williams, and Ruth Hart Williams.

Of these about twenty-five stayed for the week-end, and we had an exhibition of pictures, beautiful to behold, featuring the perfect baby and the perfect husband as well. On Sunday we all migrated to Annette's house in Overbrook for tea, after which there was a general dispersion. Probably Pinkie got back to college without her license because the car looked so indigenous! She and about six of the rest stayed on for Alumnae Supper, while Buttie even went so far as to speak, and nobly, too, at Alumnae Supper.

Those who did not get back this time missed a lot—but let them take heart, they were missed still worse!

1920

Class Editor, Helen Zinsser, 6 West Ninth Street, New York City.

Peggy Dent was married in Paris on March 12th to René Jean Daudon, of Chatillon-sur-Seine, France. M. Daudon served as lieutenant in the late war, was twice wounded, and received the Croix de Guerre. They are living temporarily in Marseilles.

Teresa James was married to Edward Karrick Morris, on Thursday, May 1st, in Washington, D. C. Mr. Morris is a Williams man, ex-1919; was in the Naval Aviation, and is now in the insurance business.

May I, through this column, express on behalf of our class the deep sympathy we feel for Teresa James Morris in the death of her father and grandmother in the last few weeks.

Marion Gregg King (Mrs. Clarence H. King) has a daughter, Marion, born May 18th. Her address is, St. Louis Country Club Grounds and Cella Road, St. Louis County, Mo.

1922

Class Editor, Serena Hand, 48 West Ninth Street, New York City.

In spite of a great deal of rain, many of 1922 came back to the reunion at May Day. Everybody who could not be there will want to know more about May Day than about reunion, for after all that is what we were all there to see. Having taken part in the last one we could not help being critical and taking a comparative view of things. The costumes were more elaborate than ours and it was perhaps on the whole a more finished production than in 1920, but when we looked anxiously at the characters in the different plays, we felt that although the new generation set a high standard we had probably done as well in our day.

As we were having a formal reunion we were told to wear our costumes and to march in the procession. Attired in our dark blue smocks and swinging large straw hats on ribbons we rode in the wagon drawn by the famous May Day oxen and felt as though we had a good share in the pageant.

There was no place for us to stay in college, so were placed in various houses on Elliott Avenue in the village. We talked till late, drank muggle like undergraduates and smoked like Alumnae. Saturday night we had a dinner at the Cottage Tea Room. We elected K. Peek toastmistress and N. Jay manager of the 1925 reunion. The following people came back for all or part of the time: E. Anderson, C. Baird, E. Bennett, E. Brown, C. Cameron Ludington, B. Clarke, D. Cooke, M. Crosby, D. Dessau, E. Donohue, A. Dunn Carpenter, A. Fountain, K. Gardner, V. Grace, E. Hall, S. Hand, E. Hobdy Hobart, N. Jay, H. Jennings, M. Kennard, M. Krech Cowles, A. Nicoll, J. Palache, K. Peek, E. Pharo, G. Prokosch, M. Rawson, C. Rhett, E. Rogers, M. Tucker, M. Tyler, M. Voorhees and J. Gowing.

E. Anderson has a job for the summer in the J. Walter Thompson advertising company.

E. Brown is going abroad in June to join her family.

B. Clarke is planning to go to the Frost School of Architecture, in Cambridge, next winter.

M. D. Hay and S. Hand are going abroad this summer with their families, who are going to the meeting of the American Bar Association in London.

H. Jennings has been elected President of the Graduate Club at Bryn Mawr for next year.

Story Kirkbride has announced her engagement.

V. Liddell Pickens is living in Hickory, North Carolina.

A. Nicoll and M. Voorhees are going abroad this summer.

J. Palache is spending the summer in Paris with M. Palache, '24 and E. Glessner, '25.

P. Norcross Bentley has a son.

M. Tyler has gone abroad for two months with Mrs. Herbert Satterlee and her daughter.

M. Speer is planning to study in England next winter.

N. B.—Please note that of the twelve news items above six are statements that various of 1922 are going to Europe. The editor would please like the more interesting news about those staying at home.

SCHOOL DIRECTORY

SCHOOL DIRECTORY

The whole world in your hands

General Electric motors enable one great mill to produce paper enough in a day to cover a 13-foot road from New York to Chicago. Other G-E motors run the huge presses which can print as many as 300,000 newspapers an hour.

So, served by electricity, you breakfast like a king—an electric percolator and an electric toaster on your table, and the world's news in your hands!

Rivers that now furnish power for great mills once ran wastefully away. Not in the United States alone, but all over the world, equipment made by the General Electric Company is transforming idle rivers into hard-working servants.

GENERAL ELECTRIC

The
BRYN MAWR
ALUMNAE
BULLETIN

PRESIDENT PARK'S SPEECH

THE SUMMER SCHOOL OF 1924

OCTOBER

1924

VOL. IV   No. 8

Bryn Mawr Alumnae Bulletin

OFFICIAL PUBLICATION OF
THE BRYN MAWR ALUMNAE ASSOCIATION

Evelyn Page, '23, *Editor*
Esther L. Rhoads, '24, *Business Manager*

EDITORIAL BOARD

Lucy M. Donnelly, '93
Eleanor Fleisher Reisman, '03
Caroline Morrow Chadwick-Collins, '05

Adelaide W. Neall, '06
May Egan Stokes, '11
Margaret Reeve Cary, 1907, *ex-officio*

Subscription Price, $1.50 a Year   *Single Copies, 25 Cents*
Checks should be drawn to the order of Bryn Mawr Alumnae Bulletin
Published monthly, except August and September, at 1006 Arch St., Philadelphia, Pa.

Vol. IV	OCTOBER, 1924	No. 8

EDITORIAL

We realize as never before, on reading President Park's speech at the opening of College, how many students wish to come to Bryn Mawr, and to what straits the administration is put to fulfil what President Park has called its duty as a "public servant of Education." It also brings home to us a problem that the Alumnae Association must face in a few years. With the increasing numbers of those who wish to come to College, and with the steadily decreasing numbers of those who wish to come only for a year or two, Bryn Mawr will inevitably be faced even more seriously than now with the problem of providing its students with living accommodations. Whether it is true that the students of the highest standing have chosen Bryn Mawr, or whether the schools are teaching their scholars better the technique of taking examinations, it is certain that never before have the standards of the entering class been as high as they are today. To turn away such students would defeat the aims of the College.

This Spring Wellesley faces the prospect of a nine million dollar drive for endowment and equipment, to mark its fiftieth anniversary. Within the next ten years Bryn Mawr must also undertake a drive for buildings and equipment which will mount into the millions. Of this sum a part must be set aside for a new dormitory, to the necessity for which the fifteen Freshmen at East House bear silent testimony.

HILDA WORTHINGTON SMITH, 1910

At the time of year when we welcome the entering Freshmen we have to say farewell to the Summer School students. Greatly as we always regret this necessity, we regret it still more now because our farewell must for a year include its Director, Hilda Worthington Smith, 1910, who has been granted a well-earned leave of absence.

It would be very difficult for Alumnae to express their appreciation of Miss Smith's work in modest terms. Their pride in her is self-congratulatory because she is one of Bryn Mawr's own people, who has not only had the same four years of experience which all its graduates have had, but has shared with them to a great extent her later work. We are very proud to think that the Summer School has for four years been directed by an Alumna of Bryn Mawr; that during these crucial years it has been safely guided through the problems which inevitably confronted it during its infancy; and that a project at first considered a visionary experiment has under her leadership been unquestionably acknowledged a great step forward in the progress of workers' education—so universally accredited, indeed, that schools like it are being organized all over the world.

With four years of exhausting work behind her, Miss Smith has certainly more than earned a year's vacation. She goes on her travels with the admiration and good wishes of every Alumna. We shall look forward to welcoming back to Bryn Mawr the person who has made it possible, to quote President-Emeritus Thomas, for us "to see as in a vision how industrial peace may come into the world, how learning, art and literature and beauty may be reverenced by all alike, and how friendship and mutual understanding may be brought about before it is too late."

ANNOUNCEMENTS

The final May Day Report will be published in the BULLETIN as soon as the May Day account is closed.

All contributions to the November BULLETIN must be sent to Evelyn Page, Taylor Hall, before October 10th.

The Editor regrets very much that she has been forced to cut a part of the class notes of 1903, 1908, 1913, 1915, 1916, 1918, and 1923. The notes omitted will appear in the November BULLETIN.

In order to include in the October BULLETIN President Park's speech at the opening of college, the new faculty appointments, and information concerning the Freshman Class, the publication date of this issue was set at October 10th instead of October 1st.

The Association to Aid Scientific Research by Women announces the offer of the Ellen Richards Research Prize for the best thesis written by a woman on a scientific subject. This thesis must embody new observations and new conclusions based on independent laboratory research. Requests for circulars and application blanks should be addressed to Mrs. Samuel F. Clarke (Secretary), Williamstown, Mass.

Marion Edwards Park, LL.D.

The following presentation was made by Professor C. H. A. Wager at the Conferring of Degrees of Oberlin College last June:

"It is with especial pleasure, Mr. President, that I present to you, for the degree of Doctor of Laws, a woman whose relation to Oberlin makes it peculiarly appropriate that we should recognize the eminence which she has attained in the academic world. The daughter of a clergyman whom this community remembers with respect, she is also the grand-niece of that admirable lady, long resident among us, who was for ten years president of Mount Holyoke College, Elizabeth Storrs Meade. Miss Park's career as a scholar, teacher and administrator, as well as the charm and effectiveness of her personality, have gained for her a very high distinction. There are many colleges that are larger than Bryn Mawr, and many that are older. There are colleges that are better known to the man in the street. But there is no college in this country, I am not sure there is a college in any country, where the pursuit of learning for its own sake is more frankly and practically recognized as the sufficient reason why a college should exist. In an age when almost every reason but the chief one is offered for the pursuit of what is called higher education the success of such a college is a source of deep gratification to all who care sincerely for the things of the mind. I have the honor to present to you for the degree of Doctor of Laws, Marion Edwards Park, President of Bryn Mawr."

Daughters of Bryn Mawr Alumnae and Former Students in the Class of 1928

STUDENT	MOTHER
Amram, Elinor Beulah	Beulah Brylawski, 1898-99 (died 1924)
Gregson, Margaret	Edith Goodell, 1904
Gucker, Louise Fulton	Louise Oliphant Fulton, 1893
Hepburn, Katharine Houghton	Katherine Martha Houghton, 1900
Hess, Margaret Straus	Sara Straus, 1895-97
Huddleston, Jean Fuller	Mabel Parker Clark, 1889
Hulse, Margaret Hartley	Margaret Ann Reynolds, 1900-02
Morgan, Edith Sampson	Lilian Vaughan Sampson, 1891
Rose, Cornelia Bruère	Emmie Cornelia Bruère, 1898-99
Saunders, Margery Elder	Grace Elder, 1897
Thorpe, Theodora	Helen Prentiss Converse, 1901
Wilson, Nancy	Anne Maynard Kidder, 1903
Yandell, Hope Gay	Elizabeth Sanborn Hosford, 1892-95

President Park's Speech at the Opening of College

This assembly opens formally the fortieth year of the college. The turning of many wheels has made it possible. The college has washed and aired and ordered itself this summer, done its business, filed its records, made its appointments. The faculty and students of last year have gathered themselves from the lands, from the east and from the west, from the north and from the south. Of the newcomers, undergraduates here and in other colleges have moved down the slow road of the curriculum to the Bachelor's degree and appear here today as graduate students. Small girls have studied and recited, grown older, filled out cards and written examinations that they might today with shining morning faces take their places among the Bryn Mawr undergraduates. All this activity is consummated and crowned at nine this snapping October morning and will appear from the moment of the end of chapel transmuted into another form of activity. We have exerted ourselves singly to get here, now we shall exert ourselves unitedly to stay—a much more cheerful way of working.

.   .   .   .   .   .

The graduate school has the usual number of registrations. Sixteen resident fellows have accepted appointments one each in Latin, Romance Language, History, Economics and Politics, Education Psychology, Archæology, Mathematics, Chemistry, Biology; two in Social Economy and Social Research, three Grace H. Dodge Fellows and one Bryn Mawr Intercollegiate Community Service Association Fellow—young women who have either already entered on the work leading to the doctor's degree or whose plans are arranging themselves to that end, the shock troops of our small army. The foreign scholars this year come from Great Britain, France, Germany, Denmark and Hungary; two British Scholars from the University of Oxford and one from the University of Edinburgh; one Danish Scholar from the University of Copenhagen; one French Scholar from the Universities of Nancy and Strassburg; one

Hungarian Scholar from the University of Budapest; one German Scholar from the University of Munich and one from the Universities of Heidelberg, Freiburg and Rostock. For the first time the scholar selected by the Chinese Scholarship Committee is a graduate; not an undergraduate student, an A.B. of 1922 from Ginling College, China.

One hundred and eighteen Freshmen are entering the college, eleven fewer than last year. No one of them has a record lower than a good pass, and no one of them carries a condition; the college has never admitted a class with so fair a start, with so little impedimenta. Good speed to them!

The matriculation scholar for New England, that is, the student passing the best Bryn Mawr examinations from a New England school, Barbara Channing, from the Winsor School, Boston, is transferring her entrance to 1925. The matriculation scholar from New York, New Jersey and Delaware is Josephine Young from the Brearley School, New York; from the Middle and Western States, Carolyn Elizabeth Asplund, prepared by the Monticello Seminary, Godfrey, Illinois; and from Pennsylvania and the Southern States, Alice Josephine Bonnewitz, prepared by Miss Madeira's School, Washington. Candidates receiving honorable mention in the entrance examinations —i. e., the students with the second highest standing in each of the four districts—are Frances Putnam from the Girls Latin School in Boston, Margaret Harper McKee of New York City, prepared by the Brearley School, Georgia Wilson of Richmond, Virginia, prepared by St. Catherine's School, Richmond, and Helen Montgomery Hood of Chicago, prepared by the Chicago Latin School.

Nine regional scholarships, including two from New England, have been awarded by the alumnae of the district each to a favorite daughter. Carolyn Asplund of Santa Fe, New Mexico, prepared by the Monticello Seminary, Illinois, holds the St. Louis College Club Regional Scholarship. Elizabeth Bethel of Washington, prepared by

Miss Madeira's school holds the Washington and Baltimore Regional Scholarship; Frances Cookman of Englewood, New Jersey, prepared by the Shipley School, has received the New Jersey Regional Scholarship. Frances Louise Putnam of Boston, prepared by the Girls' Latin School, Boston, is the First Regional Scholar from New England. Catherine Field of Montpelier, Vermont, prepared by Bishop Hopkins Hall is the second Regional Scholar from New England. Margaret Gregson of La Grange, Illinois, prepared by the Lyons Township High School, La Grange, has received the Regional Scholarship from District 5; Yildiz Phillips of Pittsburgh, prepared by the Schenley High School, Pittsburgh, holds the Regional Scholarship from Western Pennsylvania. Katharine Shepard, of New York City, prepared by St. Agatha's School, New York, holds the New York Regional Scholarship, and Sara Beddoe Walker of Philadelphia, prepared by the William Penn High School, Philadelphia, is the Regional Scholar from Eastern Pennsylvania.

Of the 118 Freshmen, nine are non-resident. In order to make entrance to the college possible this year for fifteen more students than could be housed in the college halls East House has again been rented. To those of us who are responsible it has finally come to seem the more just choice in a dilemma which forced us to consider not only questions of our own administration but the responsibility which we share with other colleges and universities as public servants of education.

The intention of the President and Directors at the close of the last college year was to fill the vacant rooms in the halls with the most satisfactory applicants for the entering class. Last year's Senior class was smaller than usual and unexpectedly few students withdrew voluntarily from college during the summer. With fewer available rooms on the list than in any previous year, we found ourselves after receiving the results of the Bryn Mawr and Board examinations faced with a great number of candidates for entrance whose examination average ranged from a credit to a high pass, whose school records buttressed their examinations and who by dint of their successful attempt to meet the Bryn Mawr requirements had established some claim on the college. If we closed our lists when the halls were filled applicants with a high pass average whose school records and recommendations showed they could not be differentiated from the group directly above them except by the wisdom of Solomon or by his arbitrary methods must be rejected and left to make application in August at other colleges whose lists were as full as ours. The President of the Board of Directors and myself both decided that we could not refuse to accept as many more entering students as would fill the numbers of East House rooms. We were obliged to reject many more students who in the old years of less pressure would have been admitted, who have fulfilled all requirements and who we have every reason to think are ready and able to do college work.

Where should the fifteen extra Freshmen be put? The best solution would undoubtedly have been the assignment to East House of four students of each college class, so that the conditions of the resident halls could prevail there in little, but in late August a revision of the arrangements of the upper class students was impossible. Or the college could use East House as it uses Bettws-y-Coed—as a small graduate house—and assign to the Freshmen the graduate rooms in the halls which would thus be left empty. In this case the uniform and low charge for graduate students would have made East House a financial loss to the college. More important than that, the number of undergraduates we could have added would have been cut. Graduate students, older women, with the necessity upon them of far stiffer and more concentrated work than the undergraduates know must have separate rooms and therefore only eleven graduate rooms in college could have been released for undergraduate students. We have therefore assigned the rooms to fifteen Freshmen.

I hope I have made it possible for you who have heard me breathing out threatenings against a house outside the campus to understand the reasons why I have been driven into changing my opinion for this year. "He answered and said, 'I will not' and afterward he repented and went." Everyone connected with the administration of the college will try mightily to prove that hard though it may be, it is still possible to carry a few hundred feet away from Pembroke gates the gains and privileges of college residence, whatever that vague but real virtue is which added to the formal academic work goes to make up the training of the college graduate. And I shall hope for the assistance of every undergraduate of Bryn Mawr to the same end.

I have come back this winter with a "concern." That is a word which as a member of a Quaker-founded college I have a right to use and a state of mind in which as a college president I have a right to indulge.

The reason why we are gathered in this crowded room this morning is that we may *learn*. We are at Bryn Mawr for one, two, three or four years to collect various facts of geography, history, science, language, and so forth, to organize those facts so that they are more conveniently usable, to learn a method of drawing conclusions from given facts, and at last to venture on the basis of our conclusions the composition of a picture of life, observing the relation of each of us to herself, to other individuals like herself, and to the universe as a whole, that is, forming individual philosophies, threads on which to string our actions.

I fly high but I start humbly—"to gather various facts of geography, history, science and language." My concern in the Quaker sense is with this first step because my concern in the ordinary sense is with you as students. The particular advantage of the period of your education formed by the four college years is the opportunity these years give to accumulate facts and the opportunity to learn a safe method of deduction. On these two abilities depend the first steps in the building of one's philosophy. As I read newspapers and hear conversation I believe that these steps are constantly skipped. Conclusions like airplants flourish without roots. I spent six weeks of my holiday in Austria. When later I met Americans outside Austria, for there were few inside, I heard the most surprising dicta as to Austrian food, Austrian economic conditions, her attitude toward her loan, toward Germany or Italy. From the smallest bone of fact was created an astonishing animal of generalization. And I ought to confess that I joined the other amateurs and capped their generalizations with my own! At least my dinosaur was as good as theirs. The Austrians on their side were I suspect doing something quite comparable though perhaps it would be

harder to stick to humdrum deductions when one was paying 70,000 kronen for his dinner and could easily carry a million in his purse.

Now if many people always constitutionally jump the first step in the formation of a picture of life, namely, the gathering of facts, and if in an abnormal time everyone tends to do so; if conclusions are perennially drawn from non-facts or half-, third- or quarter- facts; and if on the other hand the most convenient fact-gathering period in your lives is that in which you now find yourselves—then let us recognize both the danger to be avoided and the opportunity to be seized and set to work with energy, with persistence and above all with accuracy to accumulate and to treasure. I believe that European forms of education teach the art of acquiring and retaining accurate information better than anything we have developed. We are hazier, less quick at producing the fact and less retentive of it. Our vocabularies are less exact, our memories less well trained. And I am not only urging you to acquire a neater and a sounder mental process. The actions that follow this irresponsibility in reasoning, that is, the drawing of conclusions from inaccurate and insufficient data taken with the later incorporation of such conclusions in one's philosophy brings about not merely unconvincing arguments but rigid beliefs and explosive emotions, all kinds of stupidity and irresponsibility.

Faculties can teach facts and ways of using them, but students should demand them and outside class-room and laboratory should make their private hoards. We are sure to have at Bryn Mawr this year much discussion of politics, social conditions, and religion. Let us make a resolution together that such discussion shall to the best of our ability have its feet on the ground, nothing unproved, vague, inaccurate, presented as proved, definite, true. It is playing with fire. For certainly as a result of the discussions, our points of view will crystallize, our philosophies will continue to take shape. Beyond this winter's discussion stretches before you what seems illimitable time. For that time as well as for the immediate hour there is safety only in a ground work of fact. Remember the wise words of the wise Leonardo—"Nothing can be loved or hated unless first you have knowledge of it."

The Summer School of 1924

By *HILDA WORTHINGTON SMITH, 1910, Director*

A responsive, intelligent and open-minded group of one hundred and two industrial workers, stimulating teachers eager to work together for the best interests of the School, and the experience of the past three years as a foundation for future work have made the past term intensely interesting in its daily development, and very satisfying in its results. Many of those who have been at the School before agree that this term has been more satisfactory than any other, in the standard of classroom work attained, the amount of studying done outside the classroom, and in the general development of individuals in the group. For the students, as in the past, it has meant the long-desired "opportunity to study in the day time," new ideas, new friends, a broader conception of life as a whole, and of their own responsibilities as industrial workers. For the faculty it has meant everything from "a stimulating experiment with a new method of teaching," to "an exciting spiritual venture, involving so much that is fundamental that it becomes part of one like a religious experience." For both groups it means a determination to make sure that an increasing number of eager-minded workers shall have similar opportunities, and a new inspiration to push forward the movement for workers' education.

Although one hundred and twenty students were admitted this spring, a number of applicants had to withdraw, until the School opened with one hundred and two students. Of these one hundred and two, fourteen were second-year students, so far the largest group that has been able to return. The nationalities included our first Macedonian student, from New York, and our first Mexican girl, a garment worker from Los Angeles. As the result of the decision of the Joint Administrative Committee last winter, the group of hotel and restaurant waitresses were eligible for the School, and were represented by two girls, one from Denver and one from Syracuse.

The efforts of the District Committees last winter in recruiting well-qualified applicants, and in enrolling them in preliminary classes in English or Economics bore fruit this summer in the standard of classroom work, and in the ease with which the students as a whole adjusted themselves to their new program. We have come to expect that the first two weeks of the School term will be a period of intense despair, on the part of students and faculty, and that many students during that time will feel hopeless about their ability to keep up to the standard of school work. For the first time this year, this atmosphere of depression was absent during the interviews held with individial students at the end of the first ten days. With a very full schedule, and stiff requirements of outside papers and reading, almost every student felt confident that she would in time be able to cope with her assignments, and that the work was interesting and not too difficult. A new plan of registration was tried this summer by which the first two days of the term were set aside for the psychological tests and for individual interviews with each department. A carefully planned series of tests was given early enough so that the results were available before the final grouping of students for tutoring sections, and were so successful as a guide in this classification that it is hoped they will be experimented with further another year. The faculty also have learned much during the past three years in regard to the amount of reading which may be required, and the kind of assignments which will be of the greatest help to the students. Short, definite assignments have taken the place of long general reading lists, and as a result, the students realize that they are capable of mastering the material if they give time to it, and do not become so discouraged. An indomitable spirit in overcoming difficulties, a capacity for concentrated hard work, and a cheerful determination to measure up to the required standard were characteristic of the students of 1924.

With equal enthusiasm they flung themselves into the program arranged for health and recreation. As someone remarked, it was unusual to find in the group such a combination of serious-minded purpose in work ,and such light-hearted enjoyment of play. Either one or the other quality might have been expected, but the combination created a new atmosphere in the School. Characteristic of a majority of the students was what might be called a provincial outlook, typical rather of the small town than of the large industrial center. The subjects discussed as a matter of course in previous Summer Schools were at first new and strange to many of these students. They were interested, but ignorant even of the meaning of words with which the majority of former students had long been familiar. The difference in the psychological atmosphere this year may be due to the fact that in many districts the chairmen made a special effort to recruit students from smaller industrial cities and towns, with the result that these applicants, while they were well qualified by education and in most cases showed a high degree of mental ability, were on the whole less experienced, because they had had less contact with the problems characteristic of the larger industrial centers. When finally gathered at the School, however, the student group represented a typical cross section of the rank and file of women workers in the United States, and the new problems met this summer may well be considered the problems which all those concerned with workers' movements in this country will have to face.

Many interesting features of the work of each Department were introduced into the life of the School. Readings of poetry and plays in the cloister; star-gazing through the big telescope on Denbigh Green; a special poetry number of the "Daisy," with a series of remarkable prose poems written in the English classes; a week-end Forum on the "Bargaining Unit of Labor,"—these and many other events made up the fabric of our community life. The series of concerts arranged in connection with the course in the Appreciation of Music began this year with what has been referred to as a "stupendous performance," —a concert of folk music, given by a group of ninety people of many nationalities who came out from Philadelphia to sing or play for the School. The program was unique both in the history of the School, or of the College, and was as much appreciated by the different groups of singers who for the first time saw each other in costume and heard the folk music of other nations,

as by the faculty and students of the School. Fifteen Scotch bag-pipers, in full regalia, with kilts swinging and pipes playing, led by a big drummer, marched up and down Senior row to call the School together. Forty Russian singers, in elaborate costume, a group of Welsh dames in their long red cloaks and high black hats, Czecks in their gay peasant dresses, a high-spirited Italian with a concertina, Swedish, and Negro soloists all combined to render a program of folk music which will be long remembered by all those who heard it that afternoon.

In the School organization for the summer, the same plan was used as in previous years, students and faculty electing representatives to the Council, which is the central executive committee, and appointing joint committees of students and faculty to manage minor matters of administration.

Joint committees of students and faculty, and the faculty themselves in separate meetings, studied various questions of curriculum and school policies. As the School goes on, each year there are more applications from small industrial communities and more possibilities of forming new committees to work with the applicants and to raise their scholarships. This extended geographical distribution does not seem altogether desirable, as it so often means isolation and discouragement for the student who returns to her own town. A suggested plan for next winter, which has been approved by the faculty provides in each district that a study shall be made of the cities and towns where there is the greatest concentration of women employed in industry, and that for the most part the applicants for the School shall be recruited from the localities in each district where there are the greatest number of women workers.

The outlook for continued financial support for the School is encouraging. The scholarship fund of $20,000 and the additional $10,000 needed for the winter work of organization has been secured as usual through the district committees. Each year there is a growing list of individuals and groups sincerely interested in making possible the work of the School. It is hoped that further effort may be made to secure endowment to add to the $10,000 given two years ago by Mrs. Willard Straight. The former students of the

School take more and more responsibility in raising the scholarship fund. Dances or concerts given by the Summer School Alumnae in New York, Chicago and Philadelphia brought substantial additions to the treasury. From the South came an unexpected $100, the gift of ten girls working in a cotton mill who had through the efforts of two former students been inspired to work and save for this contribution. The Bryn Mawr undergraduates outdid their former efforts with a gift of $1200—six scholarships, and this wider interest in the College promises to develop further in the future.

By a vote of the Executive Committee of the School last spring it was decided that a Director and an Assistant Director should carry on the work for this next year, in order that much-needed traveling may be done in the interests of the district organization. On this organization depends the whole question of selection of candidates, their preliminary training for the school, the effectiveness of the Alumnae organization, and securing the scholarship fund. For this coming year, during the leave of absence of the Director, Miss Clara Taylor, a graduate of the University of Wisconsin, has been appointd to carry on the work. Miss Taylor brings to the School a thorough equipment of academic training and practical experience, unusually well adapted to the needs of the organization. Her graduate work was done at Wisconsin with Professor Commons, and at Columbia. Later she was in charge of the industrial work of the Y. W. C. A. in several Western States, and was sent to Russia by this organization for two years during the war to make a survey of employed women in Moscow. She has been closely in touch with the development of Reed College, in Portland, Oregon, and at various times has been appointed by the United States Government to make studies of employed women in this country. As an executive of the National League of Girls' Clubs this past year she has helped to develop their organization and their educational program. Her familiarity with the field of adademic education and of the problems of workers' education in the United States will be of the greatest value in the work of the School for the coming year.

Miss Matilda Lindsey, for the past two years field representative of the National Women's Trade Union League, has been appointed as the Assistant Director of the School. Miss Lindsey, formerly a government printer in the Bureau of Engraving, was a first and second year student at the Summer School, for two years has been President of the Summer School Alumnae Association, and for the past summer and part of the preceding term was Assistant Director of the School, as the Labor representative. Her contribution in the past to the work of the School is proof of what she will be able to do for it in the future, through her wide contacts with women workers in the labor movement, and especially through her intimate knowledge of the former students. The School is extremely fortunate in being able to secure both Miss Taylor and Miss Lindsey for the coming year.

To sum up the actual progress of the School this year is a difficult thing, in view of the complexity of the problems presented both in the organization, and in the development of an educational method which shall prove effective in teaching this group of adult industrial workers. The fact that each year the students in going back to their own communities carry on a program of educational work, both in their own study classes and in helping to create opportunities for their fellow workers, means that the two months' term has a far-reaching effect, which cannot be measured by statistics or be adequately presented in reports. The Summer School after four years is an integrated and vital organization, friendly and informal in its atmosphere, sure of its educational purposes, and with an enthusiasm for the things of the spirit which cannot be duplicated in many institutions. Those who come within its borders, even for two months, cannot fail to catch something of the meaning of those large purposes, that determination to seek out fundamental issues, and to set free those creative forces which shall make real our vision for the future.

Final Report of the Elisabeth Blauvelt Memorial Fund Committee

Alumnae of Bryn Mawr have not forgotten the life and death of Elisabeth Hedges Blauvelt, Doctor of the Amoy Mission in China, who died at Saranac in 1912. To all who had the privilege of knowing her, as well as more especially to the group of classmates and friends who contributed to the memorial fund, this report is addressed by the Committee.

On the announcement ten years ago that

Tuberculosis Pavilion

a hospital to her memory was projected at Tong-an in the Province of Amoy, China, by the Reformed Church Board of Missions, the desire of Dr. Blauvelt's friends to share in some fitting memorial of her life and work took form in the decision to contribute to the hospital equipment by the gift of a small isolation or tuberculosis pavilion.

The Elisabeth H. Blauvelt Memorial Hospital was long delayed in building on account of war conditions. When the original fund given for the hospital by Elisabeth Blauvelt's family had proved insufficient, because of the abnormal increase in building costs, Dr. Mathew Vandeweg, the able

and devoted physician appointed in charge of the hospital, raised the sum necessary to complete it among the Chinese themselves. The main building was thus at last completed and opened in 1921. Other buildings were to follow, among them the Tuberculosis Pavilion, but these plans were interrupted by the sudden death of Dr. Vandeweg, who fell a victim to influenza in the fall of 1922. News comes now, however, that the Pavilion has been completed according to his design, and that the hospital is functioning in charge of Mrs. Vandeweg, a skilled trained nurse, and a Chinese doctor, pending the arrival of the "foreign doctor" who is to take Dr. Vandeweg's place.

It is a deep satisfaction to know that our little fund of $1000, placed in the hands of the Board of Missions in 1920, has sufficed to build the attractive and substantial brick pavilion of the picture, capable of housing from three to four patients, and of defying evidently both heat and time.

The Committee tenders its deep appreciation to the many friends who contributed to the Memorial for their forbearance with inevitable delay no less than for the generous good-will and warmth of sympathy which have made the task of collection an inspiring and grateful one. The "Classmates and Friends" who have shared in the building of the pavilion are as follows:

Dr. Helen Baldwin, Lydia Boring, Elsa Bowman, Harriet M. Brownell, Emma Cadbury, Jr., Mary M. Campbell, Lisa Converse, Katherine Innis Cook, Harriet Daniels, Rebecca Mattson Darlington, Clarrissa Smith Dey, Abigail Camp Dimon, Mary Crawford Dudley, Frank Eckerson, Mary Lawther Eddy, Grace Emery, Clara E. Farr, Margaret Horner Fearon, Elizabeth Caldwell Fountain, Josephine Goldmark, Pauline Goldmark, Marion Whitehead Grafton, Helen Haines Grenning, Margaret Hamilton, Laura Heermance, Friederika Heyl, Anna Scattergood, Hoag, Mary Delia Hopkins, Florence Hoyt, Elizabeth Higginson Jackson, Mary Warren Jewett, Elizabeth Hopkins Johnson, Leah Goff Johnson, Cornelia Greene King, Elizabeth Kirkbride, Dr. E. P. Kohler, Flora C. Langford, Anna Lawther, Frances Lowater, Mrs. L. M. Mitchell, Dr. Mary M. Morse,

Mary Neville, Tirzah Nichols, Ida Ogilvie, Marion Edwards Park, Ruth Furness Porter, Hannah Cadbury Pyle, Virginia Ragsdale, Harriet Randolph, May Levering Robinson, Herbert Scholfield, Margaret Shearman, Caroline McCormick Slade, Mary Northrop Spear, Charlotte Thompson, Emma Linburg Tobin, Dr. Catherine Travis, Caroline Foulke Urie, Dr. Joseph Warren, Fanny Sinclair Woods, Grace Clarke Wright, Edith Wyatt and Elizabeth Zimmerman.

(Signed) ABIGAIL CAMP DIMON,
PAULINE GOLDMARK,
ANNA SCATTERGOOD HOAG,
MARY DELIA HOPKINS.

Elisabeth H. Blauvelt Memorial Hospital, Tong-an, China

THE Publicity Office of Bryn Mawr College is making up a most attractive College Calendar for 1925. The Calendar will bear the seal of the college, and will be illustrated by four beautiful etchings of Pembroke Arch, Pembroke East, the Library, and the Cloister, by Mr. G. A. Bradshaw of the Trenton School of Industrial Art. The Calendar is to be printed on heavy hand-cut paper.

The Publicity Office also hopes to get out Christmas Cards. Information about these will be announced later.

The price of the Calendar is $1.00 if purchased at the Publicity Office, and $1.25 if ordered by mail. It will be ready for distribution early in November. The proceeds will go to the Drive for the Endowment of the Department of Music and the Auditorium of the Students' Building, through the May Day account, since the etchings were originally made for use in connection with May Day.

The Alumnae Fund

By MARY PEIRCE, 1912, Chairman

The Alumnae Fund has accomplished two great things this year. By means chiefly of the undesignated gifts it has made possible the publication of the *Alumnae Register*, which the College for financial reasons was unable to publish, and has bought Dr. Scott's library for the College. Eight hundred and four Alumnae, two hundred and thirty-four more than had given at this time last year, have sent contributions totaling $3,663.13 in excess of the amount received from Alumnae by September 1, 1923. Only one class has not been heard from, whereas five had sent in no reports at this time a year ago. In five classes the same number has given. Ten classes have fewer, and twenty-one more, contributors.

So far the report is good. But what of the more than four thousand Alumnae and former students who have not been heard from? Unless they respond there will be only a very small contribution for President Park's Fund, which has proved invaluable in the meeting of emergencies in the College, an inadequate appropriation for increasing the endowment of the James E. Rhoads Scholarships, small appropriations for a few of the other vital needs of Bryn Mawr College and none at all for some of the needs.

Bryn Mawr Alumnae, you are interested in sending to Bryn Mawr the type of student of whom your College can be proud. Are you as much interested in maintaining Bryn Mawr at a standard of which her future students can be proud? The Alumnae Fund is the authorized channel through which you can prove your interest. Are you making use of it?

REPORT BY CLASSES

Class	No. of Contrib- utors	Amount through Alumnae Fund	Amount through Music & Auditorium Drive
M.A.s	2	$12.00	$00.00
Ph.D.s	19	95.00	1.00
1889	13	387.00	
1890			
1891	2	25.00	1,025.00
1892	16	1,060.00	10.00
1893	19	281.50	
1894	13	172.00	
1895	11	197.32	1,000.00
1896	25	326.00	205.00
1897	Class Chest	750.00	5,015.00
1898	12	245.00	
1899	41	2,701.00	53.00
1900	28	378.00	2,050.00
1901	7	57.00	500.00
1902	3	55.00	100.00
1903	34	287.50	850.00
1904	22	343.00	5.00
1905	27	406.00	1,233.00
1906	17	302.00	500.00
1907	34	393.00	410.00
1908	36	473.50	540.00
1909	34	453.00	161.00
1910	18	146.50	60.00
1911	16	122.50	302.50
1912	30	459.00	250.00
1913	41	330.25	15.00
1914	28	308.00	165.00
1915	50	841.00	1.00
1916	27	373.00	
1917	11	172.00	1.00
1918	56	418.50	125.00
1919	26	380.50	50.00
1920	39	284.50	
1921	3	18.00	
1922	38	183.00	5,005.00
1923	22	291.00	
Outside		469.37	
Totals	820	$14,196.94	$19,632.50

THE COLLEGE BOOKSHOP

The Co-operative Society

The Bryn Mawr Co-operative Society has had a place among College Bookshops for three years. Previously the Bryn Mawr Bookshop was conducted by undergraduates, who were able, by working there, partially to pay their college expenses. They were, however, forced to spend a great deal of their time in routine work, such as accounts and orders, and also to be in the shop a part of each morning and afternoon, during the hours in which it was open. In 1920, President Emeritus Thomas decided that the undergraduates could not afford to spend the time which the Bookshop demanded, and that the Bookshop itself needed more attention than they had been able, or ever would be able, to give to it. In order to relieve them of too great a responsibility, and in order to give the other students more comprehensive service, she decided to form the Co-operative Society.

In 1921-1922, the society was established, under the direction of Mrs. George Wharton Barrington, the present manager, with a borrowed capital of $2,000, and stock, valued at $1,000, which had been taken over from the old Bookshop. The gross sales of the Bookshop, under the management of the undergraduates, averaged about $8,000 a year. In 1921-1922, the first year of the Co-operative Society, the gross sales were $13,000. in 1922-1923 over

$16,000, and in 1923-1924 over $18,000. In 1921-1922, dividends of 10 per cent. were paid to members of the Society on cash purchases, and 8 per cent. on accounts. About one-third of the original borrowed capital was returned. In 1922-1923, no dividend was paid to members of the Society, but the remaining two-thirds of the borrowed money was repaid. In 1923-1924, 35 per cent. of the net profits was retained by the Society to cover increased expenses and overhead. Of the balance, $620, or 32½ per cent., will be paid to the members of the Society as dividends, and the same amount to the Alumnae Fund for Undergraduate Scholarships.

Membership in the Co-operative Society has been opened to the Alumnae of the College. The membership fee ($2.00, payable in October) will be returned in September, 1925, with the addition of the dividend, which is determined by the amount of purchases during the year. The dividend is increased by 2 per cent. when the purchases are cash.

The BULLETIN has turned its book business over to the Bookshop, and its editors hope very much that the Alumnae will support and help to develop this new and active part of the College. The splendid record of the Co-operative Society in its three years of service is its best advocate before the Alumnae Association.

Faculty Appointments

Professor *Rhys Carpenter*, Professor of Archæology, returns after a year's leave of absence.

M. Claude Gilli, Associate Professor of Romance Philology, has been granted leave of absence for the year 1924-25.

New Appointments:

Joseph E. Gillet, Ph.D., University of Liego, Assistant Professor of Romance Languages at the University of Minnesota since 1921, appointed Associate Professor of Spanish.

Norreys Jephson O'Connor, A.B. and M.A. Harvard University, who has been Associate Professor of English Literature at Mount Holyoke College the past year, appointed Associate Professor of English Composition.

Hornell Hart, Ph.D. University of Iowa, Research Associate Professor in Sociology in the University of Iowa and Head of the Sociological Division of the Iowa Child Welfare Research Station since 1921, appointed Associate Professor of Social Economy.

David Vernon Widder, Ph.D. Harvard University, Instructor in Mathematics at Harvard since 1921, appointed Associate in Mathematics.

Dorothy Sells, Ph.D. London School of Economics, Special Agent United States Bureau of Labor Statistics, 1917-18; Employment Manager for Women, Waterville Arsenal, 1918-19; Director, Industrial Education for Women, Texas, 1919-20; Research worker under the Labor Section of the League of Nations at Geneva, 1922-23, appointed Associate in Social Economy.

Winifred Sturdevant, A.B. Bryn Mawr College 1909 and Ph.D. Johns Hopkins University, Instructor in French at Vassar College 1922-23, who has been studying in Italy this past year, appointed Lecturer in Romance Philology.

New Instructors in English Composition:

Katharine Louise Ward, A.B. Bryn Mawr College, 1921, and M.A. Yale University.

Grace Hawk, A.B. Brown University, 1917, Graduate Scholar in English and Fellow in English at Bryn Mawr College, Instructor in English Composition, Pennsylvania College for Women, Pittsburgh, 1921-23, and student at Oxford University last year.

Margaret Jager, A.B. Radcliffe College.

Other Instructors:

Marion Hendrickson, A.B. Smith College, Instructor in Italian.

Harriette Millar, A.B. Bryn Mawr College, 1923, Instructor in Spanish.

Frederick Pfeiffer, Ph.D. University of Zurich, Instructor in German.

Anna Marguerite Marie Lehr, - A.B. Goucher College, Reader and Graduate Student in Mathematics, Bryn Mawr College 1919-21; President's European Fellow and Fellow in Mathematics 1921-22, American Association of University Women Fellow and Student, University of Rome, 1923-24, appointed Instructor in Mathematics.

Dr. Marjorie Jefferies Wagoner A.B. Bryn Mawr College, 1918, and M.D. University of Pennsylvania; Interne at the Philadelphia General Hospital, 1922-24, appointed College Physician.

New Wardens:

Margaret Bailey Speer, A.B. Bryn Mawr College, 1922, Warden of Rockefeller Hall.

Mary Hardy, A.B. Bryn Mawr College, 1920, Warden of Denbigh Hall.

Marjorie Howland, A.B. Vassar College 1921, Warden of Merion Hall.

Julia Ward, A.B. Bryn Mawr 1923, Warden of East House.

Class Notes

1889

Class Editor, Harriet Randolph, 1300 Spruce Street, Philadelphia, Pa.

Susan Braley Franklin, Newport, Rhode Island.

"My outside interests and opportunities increase as I am longer at home, and my home duties grow greater as my father and mother need more of my care.

This year I enjoyed serving on the Committee for University Extension Lectures, and am serving for the next year as well. I have been Vice-President of our College Club and a member of its executive board. And I have tried to keep in touch with my ten little Sunday School girls, who have been in my class now for three years. For the third year, I have served as Examiner in Latin for the College Entrance Board, Old Plan Examinations, and have continued as Examiner for several girls' private schools, and as Reader in Latin for the College Board.

My school work has increased a little in interest and opportunity since I became Head of the Latin Department. When my predecessor was made Headmaster, he very generously handed over this position to me. It is delightful to work with a Headmaster who is himself a Classicist, and the Latin here is a more welcome subject in the curriculum than in many schools. I have three other teachers in the department, and the number of students taking at least two years of Latin is about 350. I love to teach, and think I learn how to do it better as some of my difficulties increase."

The following is from *Science* for May 16, 1924:

"Dr. Edmund Beecher Wilson, DaCosta professor of zoology in Columbia University, has been elected a foreign member of the Paris Academy of Sciences, in the Anatomical and Zoological section. Professor Wilson was elected on the first ballot, receiving 44 of the 47 votes cast.

In the same journal for June 27, 1924:

"At Harvard University the doctorate of science has been conferred on Edmund B. Wilson of Columbia University."

Professor Wilson was Head of the Department of Biology at Bryn Mawr from the opening of the College in 1885 until 1891.

His former degrees are: Yale, Ph.B., 1878, LL.D., 1901; Johns Hopkins, Ph.D., 1881, LL.D., 1902; Chicago, LL.D., 1901; Cambridge, Sc.D., 1909; Leipzig, M.D. (Hon.) 1909.

He is also a member of the National Academy of Sciences.

1892

Class Editor, Mrs. Edward Cameron Kirk, Villa Nova, Pa.

Abby Kirk.

Since 1899 I have been in Bryn Mawr and my sister and I are a little proud of the fact that in the twenty-five years of our small school over a hundred of our girls have entered the College. This year we are moving the school to new and delightful quarters at Clovercroft, Montgomery Avenue, Bryn Mawr.

I am fortunate in keeping in touch with the undergraduates also through the "Baby Greek" class, which I have had charge of since 1906. That interest in the study of Greek is not dead may be seen from the fact that the class this year has numbered twenty.

Helen Clements Kirk.

I married immediately after graduation, becoming thereby mother to two little girls, and the following year came a baby of my own. Twelve years later, having some measure of leisure, I began graduate work at the University of Pennsylvania, taking an M.A. in 1904. Another daughter, Marcella, was born in 1905, and Barbara in 1909. We lived in Lansdowne from 1895 to 1921, spending our summers at Lake Skaneateles, New York, or in Europe, and through these years I took the usual share in civic and neighborhood duties. In 1921 the three older daughters having married, we moved to Villanova.

Mary Taylor Mason.

1893-93, taught in Mrs. E. L. Head's School, Germantown; 1893-94, Graduate Student, Bryn Mawr; 1894-95, Europe, study and travel; 1896-97, taught in Mrs. Head's School; 1898, served on local school board, Thirty-eighth Ward; 1903, September 8th, resigned from Board of Education; 1908-09, spent winter in Italy; 1909-11, scientific pre-medical work at Bryn Mawr; 1915, M.D. Women's Medical College of Pennsylvania; 1915-16, Demonstrator in Obstetrics W. M. of Pa.; social service work, Barton Dispensary; 1917-18, Barton Dispensary and Home Service Red Cross. Worked for a number of years with Octavia Hill Association and worked as a volunteer for the Philadelphia Society for Organizing Charity during unemployment crisis, 1921-22:

Until I was married in May, 1897, I traveled much abroad and at home. Since my marriage my history has been chiefly that of my family. Before the war, my husband and I went to Europe several times with our children, but since 1914 we have spent most of our summers at our cottage at Buck Hill Falls, Pennsylvania. My son was married over two years ago and now I have a grandson seven months old. My daughter expects to be married this summer.

Lucy Chase Putnam.

The home and its problems, not highly valued nowadays, have been the field of labor of my mature years. I have learned to sympathize with the cook's wish for every evening out, with the desire of youth to have its own way, and the longing of old age to take still some part in life. I have no children to rise and call me blessed, and for my life-rating must rely upon the testimony of those who experienced the home I made. I am happy that '92 remembers me.

Helen Josephine Robins.

I could never afford to adopt children, as I think every childless woman of means should do, but I have spent many years of teaching in learning about other people's children. These I have at least protected from being made the victims of every new educational experiment in "English," and with them I have tried to share the splendid possessions that came to me at Bryn Mawr through work under Miss Gwinn and Dr. Shorey. I have also had the illuminating experience of living several years in Italy, where my school is now sending me to spend next winter.

Mathilde Weil.

I started with the Macmillan Company. When I returned to my home in Philadelphia they continued to send me manuscripts for reading and editing. There I drifted

into photography but eventually I was able to get back to New York and its book world as consulting specialist to a number of publishers.

Foreseeing the demand for a literary adviser who was equipped to tell writers whether their work was salable: if not, why not: if so, where, I founded the Writers' Workshop, which I am now most happily engaged in developing along co-operative lines.

1897

Class Editor, Mary M. Campell, Walker Road, West Orange, N. J.

Katrina Ely Tiffany has been made Chairman of the Finance Committee of the New York State Democratic Campaign Committee, which is to work for the election of Davis and Bryan. She is Vice-Chairman of the Nassau County Democratic Committee, and will attend the State Convention as an alternate from the Second Assembly District.

Frances Hand, with her husband and three daughters (Mary Hand is at Bryn Mawr) spent the month of August at a ranch in Wyoming, where they had wonderful riding and camping trips.

Mary Campell expects to visit Betty Bancroft, '98, for a few days at her camp in the pine woods, near Harrisville, Rhode Island.

Edith Edwards has taken an apartment at 97 Mt. Vernon Street, Boston, for this, and the following winter. Just at present, her heart and energies are much divided between her new play-house, and her ancestral estates, and also in a one-third ownership in two new motor-cars.

Marion Taber went with Elsa Bowman, '96, in August, on a wonderful motor-camping trip to Canada, in Elsa's Ford roadster.

Frieda Heyl visited Elizabeth Higginson Jackson, and her family, at her villa in West Chop, Martha's Vineyard.

Frances Arnold has started the great task of moving her cottage, "Overbrook," in Cornish, New Hampshire, to the new piece of land, which she recently bought.

At least one member of '97, was greatly mystified as to where *Delegate Anne Lawther* was at the Democratic Convention on the day that Davis was nominated. The ranks of the Iowans were searched in vain, with great regret at her absence. Had she, perchance, become discouraged and returned to her home in Dubuque?

1899

Class Editor, Mrs. Percival M. Sax, 6429 Drexel Road, Overbrook, Philadelphia, Pa.

Members of '99, in particular, and all Alumnae of Bryn Mawr, in general, were undoubtedly thrilled when they read that one of their very own, Emma Guffey Miller, had received 1½ votes for President of the United States. She is the first woman to be so honored since women have been eligible for the Presidency. Emma made an enviable position for herself at the Democratic Convention, her two speeches, the first seconding "Al" Smith's nomination, and the second against the Ku Klux Klan, being considered high lights in convention oratory. Having heard Emma hold forth for many years, we are not surprised that she did us proud, but the men who heard her were astonished that every word she said could be heard, that it was worth hearing, and that her speeches were both short and to the point.

Anne Boyer will spend the winter in Philadelphia doing laboratory work at the Hahnemann Hospital. Her address is, 918 Pine Street, Philadelphia.

Ellen Kilpatrick spent the summer at Ogunquit, Maine.

Jean Clarke Fouilhoux attended the Summer School of Politics at Williams College.

Cora Hardy Jarrett and her daughter, Olivia, spent August at the Bakewell Camp, at Hurricane, in the Adirondacks.

Herbert Seymour Darlington, husband of Sybil Hubbard Darlington, died in July.

Camille Erismann has been married to Mr. Ashbel W. Bryan. Her address is 216 East High Street, Bound Brook, N. J.

1903

Class Editor, Mrs. Herbert Knox Smith, Farmington, Conn.

Ethel Hulburd Johnston's children: Hulburd is at St. Mark's, and goes to Harvard in 1925. Betsey will be at Miss Walker's at Simsbury, where she expects to prepare for Bryn Mawr. Hugh, Jr., goes to St. Mark's in 1925. Ethel, the baby, remains at home.

Agnes Maitland Sinclair was married on June 5th to The Reverend Howell Smith Vincent, D.D. After December 1st, they will be at home in Peking, China.

Marjory Cheney is running for the General Assembly in Connecticut.

Margretta Stewart Dietrich is the champion motorist. She is now driving to Arizona for the third time since March.

Helen Calder Wallower has adopted a second child, a little girl.

1905

Class Editor, Mrs. Clarence Hardenbergh, 3710 Warwick Blvd., Kansas City, Mo.

Dilly Mallery, Jonesy Sturgis, Snippy Collins, Curly Swan, and the Class Baby, were together at Sugar Hill this summer. Take it from Snippy, the Class Baby is worthy even of 1905.

Mabry's eldest is preparing for Vassar, but her two younger daughters are staunch Bryn Mawrtyrs (aged 4 and 13).

Isabel and family are in their newly-built cottage in the Michigan wilds.

Patsy Gardner motored in Texas during May from one Boston to another, (3 Bostons in Texas!) searching "flora and fauna."

Katherine Southwick Vietor's daughter, Katrin, goes to the Brearley School.

Marian Cuthbert Walker and family spent a month in the Adirondacks. They moved into a new and larger house in Moorestown last fall.

Edith Longstreth Woods studied painting again for the summer at East Gloucester.

Alberta Warner Aiken has moved to Wayne, Pa.

Alice Heulings is spending last winter and next in Philadelphia, though not enjoying apartment life as much as her Moorestown home.

Edith Sharpless spent her vacation at a Japanese sea resort where about thirty European families go. She writes: "The Exclusion Bill should never have been, and I hope that people of goodwill in America will bestir themselves to get it repealed."

Coopy convalesced with Pity at East Gloucester until September, but will return home this fall. Mrs. Barker will spend the winter with her.

Griffy got her Ph.D. in absentia last June from the University of Michigan. Her subject was anent rhythm in prose.

1908

Class Editor, Mrs. William H. Best, 1198 Bushwick Avenue, Brooklyn, New York.

IN MEMORIAM

The sudden and tragic death, on September 2, of Sarah Goldsmith Aronson, at her home in Wayne, Pa., has brought grief to her family and many friends. With her died her little nine-months' daughter, Jean. Since this second baby's birth, Sally fought a gallant but losing fight to regain the health and buoyancy that had made her life so active, useful and happy. She is survived by a four year old son, Joseph, Jr., and her husband, Dr. Joseph Aronson, who is connected with the Phipps Institute in Philadelphia.

Mayone Lewis breaks the silence of several years to send greetings from California. The last we heard (editorially speaking) was when Mayone was planning a wonderful trip to Sicily, Tunisia and Algeria, camping, riding camels and donkeys, and seeing marvelous Roman ruins. "On our return," she now reports, "we sold the farm, at South Norwich, Conn., and toured New England that summer. In the fall we came out here via the Canal, and have made our home in Pasadena, which we love, with the ardor that California inspires in her devotees. We are busy making delightful new friends, planning to build a house, and enjoying the varied interests of this lovely little city. The Pasadena Community Players are a remarkable organization giving as fine presentations in every respect as the Theatre Guild (or any other group of players in the country, I am told). (Ed.—Terry, look to your laurels.) "Last summer we toured all over the Sierra Nevada Mountains, through the wilds of Oregon and back through the indescribable Redwood forests, closing our banner summer with a perfect autumnal month in San Francisco. Now we are planning to go east this summer to see our families and friends, and pack up our belongings for the final flight westward, for we expect to get our house built next fall and want to set up our Lares. If any Bryn Mawrtyrs come to Pasadena we should love to see them."

From Westerly, R. I., comes this from Lydia Sharpless Perry, "My private life is occupied by a white clapboard house on a river bank, a husband, a son, a daughter, a dog, a cat, a donkey, fourteen cows, a duck, and about a dozen chickens. My public life consists solely of the Commissionership of Girl Scouts, which, if you don't understand, means that it is my fault if any girl in Westerly rebels at washing dishes or quarrels with her brother or makes herself objectionable at a football game."

Anna Dunham Reilly has a fifth child, Robert Sears Reilly, born last January. His arrival did not prevent Anna from making a visit back to college for May Day, and to Boston for a week-end with Marjorie Young Gifford.

1909

Class Editor, Mrs. Rollin T. Chamberlin, 5492 South Shore Drive, Chicago, Illinois.

Dorothy I. S. Chamberlin has a daughter, Frances Dresser Chamberlin, born August 19th.

Barbara Spofford Morgan has returned to this country, with her husband and children, after a most interesting year spent in Europe.

Ellen Shippen, with her two sisters (Katharine, 1914), left New York in June, to spend a year in China. They drove from South Orange, N. J., to San Francisco, "camping out every single night, in tents attached to the car, and sleeping on the ground. We slept hard and soundly. I have never had such a good time, nor felt better," says Nellie. They sailed, August 4, on the "President Lincoln," and expect to spend the winter in Nanking.

Hilda Starzenski was in New York in June, helping her mother to break up her home and the Veltin School. The school was sold, and, "at the end of May, closed its prosperous career of thirty-seven years." Hilda is again at her home in Schenectady.

1910

Class Editor, Marion Kirk, 4504 Chester Avenue, Philadelphia, Pa.

Elsie Deems Neilson (Mrs. Carol K. Neilson) is expecting to be in California again this winter with her husband and little girl. She is going to teach in Los Angeles.

Frances Hearne Brown is planning to play on a hockey team in Winetka, Illinois, this fall. Last year, as captain, she made a stirring record, cheered on by her four children from the sidelines.

Agnes Irwin is returning to St. Agnes' School in Albany as teacher of Latin.

Louise Merrill Bennett (Mrs. Robert Russel Bennett) has been visiting in Philadelphia with her husband, who is assisting in the orchestration of the musical show, *Dear Sir.*

Edith Murphy climbed the majority of the mountains in the Presidential Range this summer, using the Ravine House at Randolph, N. H., as the base of her operations.

Mary Wesner is returning to the Ethel Walker School at Simsbury, Connecticut.

1911

Class Editor, Louise S. Russell, 140 East 52nd Street, New York City.

Anna Stearns visited Helen Emerson Chase at Sakonnet, R. I., this summer. While there, she and Helen spent an afternoon with Catherine Delano Grant and Ruth Wells.

Elizabeth Taylor Russell took a trip this summer to Canada, and up the Saguenay River. She moves, October 1st, to 328 East 51st Street.

May Egan Stokes spent the summer at Saunderstown, R. I.

I am sure that the class joins me in awed appreciation of the long and chatty appeals of the Class Collector. I hope that her efforts are meeting with an appropriate response!

1912

Class Editor, Mrs. John A. MacDonald, 3227 North Pennsylvania Street, Indianapolis, Ind.

Pauline Clarke has announced her marriage to Mr. Clinton Gilbert, of Washington, D. C. They will live at 122 Connecticut Avenue.

Mary Peirce left in June for Berkeley, Cal., to visit her sister.

Mary Alden Lane, of Redlands, Cal., was East in May, and attended May Day at Bryn Mawr.

Margaret Peck MacEwan has a daughter, Margaret Winthrop, born in May.

Polly Vennum Van Cleave has a daughter, Lucy Ann, born May 22nd.

Dorothy Wolf Douglas and her family are at Seal Harbor for the summer.

Maysie Morgan Lee (Mrs. William Lee) has a daughte, Roxa Lee, born July 22nd. She has also collaborated in an article, entitled, *Attempts to Demonstrate Functional Changes in the Nervous System During Experimental Insomnia.* The article appeared in the *American Journal of Physi-*ology for December, 1923.

Lorle Stecher's engagement has been announced to Mr. Charles Weeber, of Honolulu.

1913

Class Editor, Nathalie Swift, 178 East 70th Street, New York City.

Helen Lee Gilbert reports that she has a second child, a daughter, Helen Louise, born August 8, 1923. The Gilbert family is now living at 366 Washington Street, Norwich, Conn.

Clara Pond Richards has a second son, Gilbert Pond Richards, born April 3rd. "Puddle" lives on a farm in what she describes as "the wilds of rural New York." The address is P. R. 2, Perry, New York.

Dorothy Blake is spending the summer as usual in Castine, Maine. She plans to return early in the fall to the Grenfell Mission at St. Anthony, Newfoundland, to continue the school-teaching she did last winter.

Mr. and Mrs. Courtenay Crocker, with their three children, sailed from New York, August 9th, en route for Bangkok, Siam. Mr. Crocker has been appointed Adviser to the King of Siam. Maude Dessau has gone with the Crockers, and she, and Clara, and the children, stop for a month or more in Ceylon, in order to avoid the extreme heat in Bangkok.

Sarah Atherton Bridgman has gone abroad for a six weeks' trip.

Dorothéa Clinton Woodworth has solved the problem of combining home duties and a career. She has just received her Ph.D. in Latin at the University of Chicago with the honor of *magna cum laude.* She has done this in addition to her work in the Correspondence School, not to mention, managing the house and caring for little Howard Woodworth. So I think 1913 can congratulate her. Dorothea has taken the baby to Oregon for the summer for a visit with her family. She and her husband have decided to remain in Chicago next winter.

1915

Class Editor, Mrs. James Austin Stone, 3015 44th Street, N. W., Washington, D. C.

The ninth reunion of the Class of 1915 started with a class meeting on Saturday afternoon, May 31, at 4.30, in the sitting-room of Rockefeller Hall. About fifty members were present, and the spirit and atmosphere of our college days immediately manifested itself in the hectic arguments that arose on every question, and the plain-spoken opinions voiced on all sides. After that we all felt perfectly at home, and from then on, reunion was a grand success.

Room 34 in Rock was our headquarters, and almost always contained a group of 1915 discussing, among other things, our looks, "nine years after." We decided that, on the whole, we have improved in looks, and certainly our dispositions have softened with age. We also kept admiring our class costume, which was selected, and arranged for, by Edna Kraus Greenfield and Dora Levinson Kramer, who deserve much gratitude and praise. The dresses were both attractive and useful (I've worn mine steadily all summer). "Chickie" Heyl, our class baby, attended reunion in a small edition of the class costume, and looked adorable. We really had counted on getting first prize in the Alumnae Parade, but had forgotten that we were up against the beauty and brains of 1889. They deserved the prize all right, and even admitted that fact themselves!

There were fifty at the class supper Saturday evening in Rock. Peggy Free Stone was toastmistress, and interesting and amusing speeches were made by Mary Mitch, Mary Goodhue, Isabel Foster, Mary Gertrude, Golly and, Susan Brandeis. We missed Hat terribly, but she had sent us a wonderfully inspiring message, which was read by the toastmistress. Between speeches, of course, we sang all the old favorites, and were vastly entertained by Mary Goodhue's imitation of Huddy, and the "preacher and the bear" song by Mitch.

The supper ended by the singing of Auld Lang Syne in the traditional manner, after which we adjourned to finish our singing as we tripped lightly (?) about the flourishing crab-apple bush.

Sunday, Ruth Glenn Pennell had us all at her home on Old Lancaster Road to tea, and we enjoyed her hospitality very much indeed. Husbands were invited, and two brave ones came!

Monday, Anna Brown had a luncheon at her home in Overbrook for those staying over, of which there were thirty-six. It was a lovely occasion.

Then that evening, the Philadelphia 1915'ers entertained the rest of us at a picnic on the lower campus, and great was the formers' surprise to see the food disappear. We've decided we're still young or we wouldn't have such marvelous appetites! We had forgotten to make Carol Walton run around the table at the class supper on Saturday night, so we made her run around the circle, under much protest, at the picnic. The lucky man is a Mr. Hellyer. (More details later. Ye Ed. has lost her notes.)

Tuesday afternoon, there was a children's party on the lower campus, managed by Florence Abernethy Pinch. About fifteen handsome children came, and were much admired by those of us who looked on. All sorts of games were played, refreshments were served, and to cap the climax, Mr. Pinch brought over a pony and cart, and gladdened the heart of each child with a ride. As they were leaving, the children were given lovely, gaily-colored balloons, making their happiness complete. Florence and her husband certainly deserve a lot of credit for having such a successful party.

Mary Mitch was our representative among the speakers at Alumnae Supper Tuesday evening, and raised a number of important questions for us all to think about.

Some of us stayed over for College Breakfast and Garden Party, and a few for Commencement; and we all agreed that it was a wonderful reunion and that we owed a great debt of thanks to our Philadelphia members whose untiring efforts, under the able leadership of Adrienne Kenyon Franklin, reunion manager, made our reunion the unqualified success and satisfaction that it was.

The following were present for at least part of the time: Mary Albertson, Kitty McCollin Arnett, Rachel Ash, Mary Monroe Bagley, Zena Blanc, Frances Boyer, Susan Brandeis, Anna Brown, Mary Goodhue Cary, Mildred Jacobs Coward, Lucile Davidson, Atala Scudder Davison, Alice Humphrey Doermann, Gertrude Emery, Olga Erbsloh, Helen Everett, Angeline Spence Fitzgibbons, Marjorie Tyson Forman, Isabel Foster, Adrienne Kenyon Franklin, Betty Channing Fuller, Edna Kraus Greenfield, Marie Keller Heyl, Ruth Hopkinson, Ruth Hubbard, Ethel Robinson Hyde, Myra Richards Jessen, Marguerite Jones, Mildred Justice, Florence Hatton

Kelton, Gladys Pray Ketcham, Emily Noyes Knight, Dora Levinson Kramer, Vashti McCreery, Mary Mitchell Moore, Mary Gertrude Murphy, Ruth Tinker Morse, Ruth Newman, Susan Nichols, Florence Abernethy Pinch, Ruth Glenn Pennell, Esther Pugh, Cecilia Sargent, Katherine Sheafer, Miriam Rohrer Shelby, Elsie Steltzer, Peggy Free Stone, Cleora Sutch, Emily Van Horn, Carol Walton, Helen McFarland Woodbridge, and Isolde Zeckwer.

1916

Class Editor, Mrs. Webb Vorys, 63 Parkwood Avenue, Columbus, Ohio.

Juliet Branham was married to Mr. C. S. Williams, Jr., in the spring, and is living at 15 East 10th Street, New York City.

Dorothy Evans, ex-1916, was married on Saturday, June 21st, to Dr. Edward Sterling Nichol, of Chicago, and is now living at 141 S. Austin Boulevard.

1916's Reunion was a great success. It was very interesting to hear about the activities of each member of the class since graduation, for after eight years one has really something to say. At parting, I think everyone felt glad of the renewed contact with her classmates.

The first people to arrive Saturday afternoon were Helen Riegel Oliver (with her Buick), Lois Goodnow MacMurray, Bobby, Lucretia, Cedy Dowd, and Betty Washburn. Of course Dilly, as Warden of Rock, was on the spot. A song practice was immediately held, so that after dinner we were able to answer up at Senior Singing with not as many quavers as might be expected. We dined en masse with Dilly in Rock.

Sunday morning Con Kellen Branham arrived on the Federal from Boston. Eight years, and the cares of a family, sit very lightly upon her. Most of the day was spent in heated discussion of a class costume. In the morning, the costume started out as a long toga, but as the discussion went on, it dwindled and dwindled, until, at four P. M., nothing was left but half a breadth of the blue material, used as a scarf, and embellished with the numerals, 1916. The crowning touch was a White Lily paper drinking cup, worn at various angles on each of our heads, and tied beneath our chins with neat blue bows.

Annis arrived Sunday, and Cedy had to leave on the night train for her work in Cincinnati.

On Monday afternoon at five, a Class Meeting was held under the big, spreading, tree near Pembroke. Jeannette Greenewald Gordon, Doddie, and Clara Heydemann (who is teaching at Miss Wright's) swelled our numbers.

We boasted of a company of seventeen at the Class Dinner, Monday night, the following new arrivals coming for the occasion: Anne Lee, Helen Tyson, Emilie Wagner Baird, Florence Hitchcock, and Willie Savage Turner. The table was laid in Rock and arranged with flowers sent by Mrs. Branham and Cedy. Everyone appeared very dressy in real evening dresses. Punky was toastmistress, and everyone spoke more or less informally. During those few hours around the table we caught up amazingly on the history of each member of the class, for Con read letters from some of those not present, and everyone supplied data as she knew it. At intervals during dinner, we changed seats, so everyone had the benefit of the conversation at different parts of the table. The general theme of the married ladies was their occupation and contentment with husbands and children—a promising sign for anti-feminists.

Tuesday, we wore our above-described costumes in Alumnae Parade, and caused amusement but carried away no prize. Afterwards, the small group of members still remaining, lunched at Mrs. Miller's on chicken patties and Dutch bread.

Helen Riegel's care was a great asset, and should be rendered a vote of thanks. We filled in intervals by taking various drives in the country, to say nothing of innumerable trips to the Pike. And Helen, as manager, should be congratulated upon staging a most successful Reunion!

1918

Class Editor, Helen Edward Walker, 418 Oakwood Boulevard, Chicago, Ill.

"Peary" writes: "I have been waiting to have some real news to report, namely, the arrival of our fourth scion, a daughter, born on May 2nd, and unnamed as yet. She is, so far, of a very calm and placid disposition, and doesn't fully realize the strenuous life ahead of her, which is being prepared by her two older sisters, and one older brother."

Mary Allen was married on April 26th

to Mr. Samuel Sterling Sherman, of Bonita, California. They spent their honeymoon trout fishing and deer hunting in the Sierras.

Helen Whitcomb was married in June to John Sedgwick Barss, of Windsor, Conn.

1919

Class Editor, Frederica Howell, 211 Ballantine Parkway, Newark, N. J.

Fifine Peabody Cannon has a daughter, Jeannette Le Grand, born in May.

Betty Dabney Baker has a daughter, Barbara Carrington, born July 23rd.

Helen Huntting was married on August 12th to Edwin George Fulton, of Minneapolis. Faff Branson Keller and I went out for the wedding as matron of honor and bridesmaid, and had the most wonderful time possible. At the fitting of her bridal regalia, however, Helen ruined her drag with the dressmaker by shaking with mirth at what she saw in the mirror, and refusing to take her rôle seriously. Still, the wedding, which was in a garden at Lake Minnetonka, went off without a hitch. Mudge Butler and Marynia Foot, '21, were there, dispensing refreshments, and creating atmosphere as of old.

Louise Wood writes that she will continue at Miss Nixon's School in Florence this winter, teaching history, as well as continuing some of her secretarial work. Her letter came from St. Jean du Doigt in Brittany, where she was enjoying a rest, and awaiting the arrival of K. T. and Marian Moseley.

1922

Class Editor, Serena Hand, 48 West Ninth Street, New York City.

As Serena Hand has been in Europe, the notes of 1922 for this issue have been sent in by Nancy Jay.

Valeska Wurlitzer was married on August 28th to Mr. Henry A. Thoman.

Mary Douglas Hay and Serena Hand went to the Bar Association Convention in London with their respective parents. Among the festivities, they both attended the King's Garden Party. Serena has since been heard to boast that she left her glasses in Buckingham Palace!

Emily Anderson has been working since June in the J. Walter Thompson Advertising Company.

Josephine Fisher has returned from her winter at Cambridge, England. She and Frances Bliss were both counsellors at Camp Kenjocketee this summer.

Isabel Coleman is engaged to Mr. Norman Hughes. Mr. Hughes is an Englishman whom she met last winter when they were both studying at the Sorbonne.

Phoebe Norcross Bentley has a son, Cyrus, born last May.

Dorothea Cooke is engaged to Mr. E. Paris, also of Honolulu.

Margaret Tyler went abroad with Mrs. Herbert Satterlee and her daughter, Eleanor, this summer. Upon their return, they took a six weeks' cruise up the Saginaw on the Corsair.

Jane Bell Yeatman Savage has a son, born last June.

Katharine Peek has temporarily given up her job and gone home to Moline.

Nancy Jay has been working since April with Marlis Frocks, Inc., which is a wholesale dressmaking firm.

1923

Class Editor, Dorothy Meserve, 148 East 78th Street, New York City.

Star McDaniel was married on the 11th of September to Mr. Charles H. Heimsath. Her address for the coming winter will be 461 Whitney Avenue, New Haven, Conn.

Agnes Clement will be married to William F. Robinson, the end of November. He is an angel, an ex-Harvard football player, and Aggie's engagement rings are a band of diamonds and a band of emeralds.

Pick McAneny was married to Sherman Loud on the 27th of September. They are very much in love and will live in an apartment in Greenwich Village. The bedroom is too small for the bed, and there seems to be some doubt as to whether the bathroom will be big enough for the bathtub.

The thirty-first of May found nearly thirty members of 1923 reunited in Denbigh. Needless to say, we were delighted to be together after the strain of Freshman life in the world. The Reunion began with a class meeting. This, presided over by the class collector, and visited by a representative of the Alumnae Fund, was an excursion into the realm of high finance quite beyond our depth. However, we soon found relief at Senior Singing, where we vaunted a reunion song, and were warmly welcomed by **1925**.

Continued on page 26

Heaven Folk. By Waldemar Bonsels. Translation by Adele Seltzer. Poems done into English by Arthur Guiterman. Thomas Seltzer. New York, 1924. $2.50.

The author has woven a series of nature idylls about the central tale of a flower sprite, who has become mortal because he has looked at the sun. One is transported into another world; that of the meadow folk and the wild flowers. There is a delicate beauty about the book which makes one think of water colors, and a hidden depth of philosophical meaning, reminiscent of Maeterlinck.

David Balfour. By Robert Louis Stevenson. Illustrated by N. C. Wyeth. Scribner's. New York, 1924. $2.50.

The Boy Who Knew What the Birds Said. By Padraic Colum. Macmillan. New York, 1924. $1.75.

Isle of Thorns. By Sheila Kaye-Smith. E. P. Dutton & Co., New York, 1924. $2.00.

Sally Odiarne, M. M. (Mysterium Magnum) finds the call of her vagrant gipsy blood too strong for her. She takes to the road, but her restless desire to live is not satisfied. It is further complicated by her chance meeting and friendship with a young widower, whose whole being has been frozen into the mould demanded by strictest conventionality. This tale of conflicting personalities takes the reader along the highways and byways of Sussex and the Forest, in company with those wandering troupes, who own a life apart; a life that is at once sordid and fascinating.

In the *Isle of Thorns* the author is completely absorbed in her characters (and they are engrossing) with the result that one rather misses the call of the land, usually so characteristic of her work.

Footlights and Spotlights, Recollections of My Life on the Stage. By Otis Skinner. The Bobbs-Merrill Company. Indianapolis, 1924. $5.00.

Footlights and Spotlights is Mr. Skinner's delightful account of his early vicissitudes and later successes, from his debut at the Philadelphia Museum in 1877 as *Jim*, an old negro, to his triumph as *Hajj* in *Kismet;* to *Blood and Sand;* and to *Sancho Panza.* One may judge something of the varied fortunes and the crowded life which are the foundation of this autobiography when Mr. Skinner says:

"In taking an inventory of my professional experience, I find that I have played in all, three hundred and twenty-five parts; have appeared in sixteen plays of Shakespeare, acting therein, at various times, thirty-eight parts, and I have produced under my own direction thirty-three plays."

Mr. Skinner records the passing of the stock companies as the "slipping by of a group of old fellows who met life with a laugh—sterling lads of ready wit and admirable equipment. Often they may have taken themselves over-seriously; but the Lord keep their memories green! They possessed distinction and they respected the King's English!"

However, in summing up the many changes through which the art of the theatre has passed, Mr. Skinner claims that, "In all this mutability one vital, ineffaceable thing remains—The Spirit of the Drama."

Continued from page 24

Dinner in Denbigh was most jovial. We began with telegrams from some absent members, including one from Kay and D. M. from Havana. Then we drank the health of the class baby, Effie Leighton Brewer, and sent her a telegram, envying her youth and weight and inviting her to join us next year. Franny Matteson Rathbun and Pic McAneny enlightened us greatly on their respective situations and Ellie Mathews gave us some important points on the "Business Woman" from her own experience. Unfortunately Helen Wilson could not leave "Art." long enough to give us one of her traditional speeches.

Sunday, Miss Park invited us to tea at Penygroes. We all wanted particularly to see, "Our honorary and most honored member," and were delighted with the opportunity, and also by the pleasant time we had.

We carefully concealed our reunion costumes until Alumnae Day. Then we appeared as cowboys in green chaps, bandannas and slouch hats, carrying toy pistols, which proved quite attractive to some of '99's children. We sang *Wild and Wooly* and *Cheyenne*, which Rats had taught the band to play. Then we proceeded to captivate the movie men. They took a picture of us charging across the lower hockey field, brandishing the toy pistols and dropping on one knee to shoot. The grass was slippery, so some dropped further than intended, but it only made the picture more realistic. In fact, we may not recognize ourselves when we appear in the Pathé weekly. We have already appeared in one picture supplement as "the life of the party, all right, at the recent college frolics."

Our bliss was momentarily marred by discovering, just in time, that we had to have a speaker at the Alumnae Banquet. However, it was not too late to choose Aggie Clement who rose to the occasion for us beautifully, and made a fitting end to our first Reunion. Altogether, it was a great success. We only wished that more could have come back to enjoy everything with us.

1924

Class Editor, Mildred Buchanan, D-8 Powelton Apartments, Powelton Avenue and Thirty-fifth Street, Philadelphia, Pa.

It seems as if the Class graduated to Europe. Monkey Smith and Gwyn Anderson were at Grenoble and, from all accounts, they enjoyed it a lot. Gwyn is going to stay for the winter.

Felice Begg, Betty Hale, Bess Pearson, Sue Leewitz, Priscilla Fansler, Beth Tuttle, Sara Wood and Lesta Ford have all been travelling abroad. I believe Felice is planning to be at the University of London this winter. Lesta, Beth and Woodie will be in Paris.

Betty Howe, Helen Walker, Ginny Miller, Mary Minott, Plum Fountain, and Ruth Allen are sailing this fall.

Dog Conner, Lou Sanford, Becca Tatham and Charlotte Weiser were at Mr. Surette's Music School this summer.

Roz Pearce took a course in Applied Psychology at the Harvard Summer School.

Doris Hawkins tutored "somewhere in Maryland" and Elizabeth Henderson, in Maine.

Mitzi took Miss Lotz' place at Bates and was very successful.

Freda Rosenkoff took a course in practice teaching at the University of Pennsylvania.

Margaret Dunham travelled in the West, and that reminds me of the letter I had from Margaret Compton in which she said, "Manna from Heaven is the best way I can describe the Western conception of a Bryn Mawr graduate. They are crazy to get them."

Elizabeth Briggs was at a camp in Maine, where she learned farming. She has a job on Macy's training squad for the winter.

Louise Howitz is teaching English in the new Junior High School in Scranton.

K. Van Bibber and Mary Woodworth are teaching at the Bryn Mawr School in Baltimore. Chuck was at Summer School again this year.

Mary Rodney is advertising manager of her father's business. I understand she is going to do graduate work at B.M.C. in addition.

K. Nielson is back at college, too.

Martha Fischer and Molly Angell are studying at Yale.

Pamela Coyne has a position as Secretary in a music school in Chicago.

Married:

Roberta Murray to Mr. Thomas Fansler.

Betzie Crowell to Mr. H. J. Kaltenthaler.

Engaged:

Irene Wallace to Mr. David Vogels.

SCHOOL DIRECTORY

The Bryant Teachers Bureau, Inc.

711-12-13 Witherspoon Building   Philadelphia, Penna.

Friendly, personal interest; prompt intelligent service.

The Agency you will recommend to your friends.

WE PLACE MANY BRYN MAWR GRADUATES EACH YEAR

Cathedral School of St. Mary

GARDEN CITY, LONG ISLAND, N. Y.

A school for Girls 19 miles from New York. College preparatory and general courses. Music. Art and Domestic Science. Catalogue on request. Box B.

Miriam A. Bytel, A. B., Radcliffe, Principal

Bertha Gordon Wood, A. B., Bryn Mawr, Ass't Principal

St. Timothy's School for Girls

CATONSVILLE, MARYLAND

Founded 1882

COLLEGE

PREPARATORY

Miss J. R. HEATH } Heads of the School
Miss L. McE. FOWLER

MISS MADEIRA'S SCHOOL

1330 19th St., N. W.   Washington, D. C.

A Resident and Day School

for Girls

LUCY MADEIRA WING, A.B.

MRS. DAVID LAFOREST WING
Head Mistress

MISS WRIGHT'S SCHOOL

Bryn Mawr, Pa.

Prepares for Bryn Mawr and
College Board Examinations

ROGERS HALL

A SCHOOL FOR GIRLS

Thorough preparation for college entrance examinations. Graduate course of two years for high school graduates. Complete equipment. 40 minutes from Boston.

MISS OLIVE SEWALL PARSONS, B.A.
Principal
Lowell, Massachusetts

The Episcopal Academy

(Founded 1785)

CITY LINE, OVERBROOK, PA.

A country day school for boys from second grade to college. Separate lower school for boys from seven years up. Enjoys the patronage of Bryn Mawr Alumnae

WYKEHAM RISE

WASHINGTON, CONNECTICUT

A COUNTRY SCHOOL
FOR GIRLS

Prepares for Bryn Mawr and Other Colleges

MISS GILDNER'S PRINCETON SCHOOL

FOR GIRLS

Prepares for best eastern colleges and Board examinations. Also for Advanced College-entrance Two-year Graduate Course. Music, Art, Expression. Sports, Riding, Outdoor and Indoor Athletics. Estate of beauty. Mile from town.

Miss Laura M. Gildner, A.M., Director
Princeton, New Jersey

Smart Togs
for Sport
or Campus Wear

*A*T McCUTCHEON'S, the college girl can select Sport Frocks that are the perfection of simplicity and smartness. Hats that express the latest dictates of Paris in their clever shapes and Sweaters for every occasion in every color and style. The sweater illustrated is priced at $22.50 and the hat is $9.50.

Send for New Catalog No. 62

Our new thirty-two page Fall and Winter Catalog containing choice selections of linens, laces, hosiery, hats, sweaters and lingerie, is all ready to be mailed to you. Write for your copy to-day.

James McCutcheon & Co.
Department No. 62
Fifth Avenue, 34th and 33d Streets, N. Y.

SCHOOL DIRECTORY

COLLEGE WOMEN

Who know the meaning of thoroughness and who take pride in scholarly accuracy are in special demand for literary and editorial work of a high character.

We are prepared to give by correspondence

A Complete Professional Training

to a limited number of suitable candidates who are interested in fitting themselves for a second profession.

For further information address

The Mawson Editorial School

25 Huntington Avenue   Boston, Massachusetts

HILLSIDE

A School for Girls

NORWALK   CONNECTICUT

In a beautiful New England town, one hour from New York. Girls from all parts of the country. Four residences, schoolhouse, gymnasium. Extensive grounds. Preparation for all colleges. Special courses. Outdoor life. Horseback riding. Catalog.

Margaret R. Brendlinger, A.B., Vassar
Vida Hunt Francis, A.B., Smith, *Principals*

The Harcum School

BRYN MAWR, PA.

Prepares for Bryn Mawr and all leading colleges

Musical Course prepares for the Department of Music of Bryn Mawr College

EDITH H. HARCUM, Head of School
L. MAY WILLIS, Principal

THE Mary C. Wheeler Town and Country School

PROVIDENCE, RHODE ISLAND

Preparation for Bryn Mawr and College Board Examinations

Out door sports   Junior Country Residence

FERRY HALL

A Resident and Day School for Girls
LAKE FOREST, ILLINOIS
On Lake Michigan, near Chicago

College Preparatory, General and Advanced Courses. Departments of Music, Home Economics, Expression, and Art. *Supervised Athletics and Swimming Pool.*

Eloise R. Tremain, A.B., Bryn Mawr, Principal

MISS RANSOM and MISS BRIDGES' SCHOOL

HAZEL LANE, PIEDMONT (Suburb of San Francisco)

College Preparatory

MARION RANSOM } Headmistresses
EDITH BRIDGES }

The Katharine Branson School

ROSS, CALIFORNIA   Across the Bay from San Francisco

A Country School   College Preparatory

Heads:

Katharine Fleming Branson, A. B., Bryn Mawr
Laura Elizabeth Branson, A. B., Bryn Mawr

THE AGNES IRWIN SCHOOL

2009-2011 Delancey Place, Philadelphia

A College Preparatory
SCHOOL FOR GIRLS

JOSEPHINE A. NATT, A.B., Headmistress
BERTHA M. LAWS, A.B., Secretary-Treasurer

The Ethel Walker School

SIMSBURY, CONNECTICUT

Head of School
ETHEL WALKER SMITH, A.M. Bryn Mawr College

Head Mistress
JESSIE GERMAIN HEWITT, A.B. Bryn Mawr College

Miss Beard's School for Girls

ORANGE, NEW JERSEY

A country school near New York. College preparatory, special courses. Art, Domestic Arts and Science. Supervised physical work. Agnes Miles Music School affiliated with Miss Beard's School.

MISS LUCIE C. BEARD, Head Mistress

ROSEMARY HALL

No elective courses

Prepares for college
Preferably Bryn Mawr

Caroline Ruutz-Rees, Ph.D. } Head Mistresses
Mary E. Lowndes, Litt.D. }

GREENWICH   CONNECTICUT

The Shipley School

Bryn Mawr, Pennsylvania

Preparatory to Bryn Mawr College

Alice G. Howland, Eleanor O. Brownell,
Principals

THE MISSES KIRK'S

College Preparatory School

PREPARATORY TO BRYN MAWR COLLEGE
Individual instruction. Athletics.

Clovercroft, Montgomery Avenue, Rosemont, Pa.
Mail, telephone and telegraph address: Bryn Mawr, Pa.

The Baldwin School

A Country School for Girls
BRYN MAWR   PENNSYLVANIA

Preparation for Bryn Mawr, Mount Holyoke, Smith, Vassar and Wellesley colleges. Abundant outdoor life. Hockey, basketball, tennis.

ELIZABETH FORREST JOHNSON, A.B.
Head

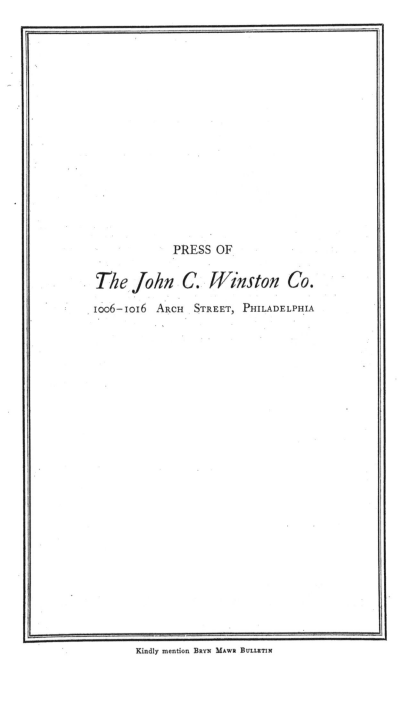

PRESS OF

The John C. Winston Co.

1006–1016 ARCH STREET, PHILADELPHIA

After the third light-less night, the business men took matters into their own hands. "If the city won't pay for the lights, we will," they told the city council.

Where was Lima when the lights went out?

MAZDA, the Mark of a Research Service. It is the mark which assures the user of the lamp that the manufacturer had advantage of the most recent findings of the Research Laboratories of the General Electric Company. Invention moves from the ideal to the real. So the researches of men trained to investigate and experiment make impressive contributions to human progress.

As part of an economy program, Lima, Ohio, tried turning out the street lights. The trial lasted three nights.

One newspaper summarized the result as "the probability of a crime wave, increase in the number of traffic accidents, and the loss to Lima business houses of a gigantic sum during the holiday season."

GENERAL ELECTRIC

тhє
зRУη mАШR
АLUmПАє
BULLєтIП

A YEAR IN GREECE

NOVEMBER
1924

. IV   No. 9

BRYN MAWR ALUMNAE BULLETIN

OFFICIAL PUBLICATION OF
THE BRYN MAWR ALUMNAE ASSOCIATION

EVELYN PAGE, '23, *Editor*
ESTHER L. RHOADS, '23, *Business Manager*

EDITORIAL BOARD

LUCY M. DONNELLY, '93
ELEANOR FLEISHER REISMAN, '03
CAROLINE MORROW CHADWICK-COLLINS, '05

ADELAIDE W. NEALL, '06
MAY EGAN STOKES, '11
MARGARET REEVE CARY, 1907, *ex-officio*

Subscription Price, $1.50 a Year   Single Copies, 25 Cents
Checks should be drawn to the order of Bryn Mawr Alumnae Bulletin
Published monthly, except August and September, at 1006 Arch St., Philadelphia, Pa.

VOL. IV   NOVEMBER, 1924   No. 9

FINANCE

In the course of a year one difficulty after another rises to confront its unsuspecting victims, and this year is no exception to the rule. With our American trust in the dollar we are dismayed to find that even large sums of money may have their awkward aspect. When we saw the report of the Alumnae Fund last month we were rightly elated. The increase in the number of contributors and the increase in the amount of money contributed are so encouraging that we look forward with confidence to a time when by the co-operation of every Alumna the Association and the college will be assured of a substantial and permanent income.

There is one aspect of the Alumnae Fund, however, which is to be regarded with some anxiety. The sums of designated and undesignated money are about equal. In turning to the list of objects voted upon by the Association last February, we notice that three of the objects are for so definite an amount that a set sum of money *must* be raised and paid over this year, namely, the James E. Rhoads Scholarships, Dr. Scott's Library and the expenses of the Alumnae Association. These total $7,697.07. $555.00 has actually been designated to these ends, leaving $7,142.07 to be paid from undesignated money.

When we turn, on the other hand, to the credit side of the account, we find that the Alumnae Fund has received $6,366.57 undesignated. Out of this money the bills of the 1924 Alumnae Register have had to be paid to the amount of $2,383.80, since the cost of the Register was $3,479.25 and the receipts so far have totalled only $1,095.45. The total of undesignated money available is, then, $3,-982.77 to cover bills amounting to $7,142.07.

The only conclusion to be drawn from these figures is that when the Alumnae Association votes to appropriate money it must give money to cover its appropriations. We appeal to the members of the Association not to leave its officers in possession only of a large sum of designated money which they cannot use to carry out the wishes of the Association. The Fund must have more and more a large income of undesignated money, so that there will no longer be a temporary surplus on one account and a deficit on another. The contributor of undesignated money gives not to one but to all of the objects of the Alumnae Fund.

We trust and believe that the end of the year will find that the Alumnae have responded to this plea. We ask them to reassure us soon, and to relieve their officers of echoing Shylock's complaint, "My shekels, oh my shekels!"

Radcliffe College has recently opened a new dormitory, Briggs Hall, in which a room has been named by the Class of 1925, in honor of President Marion Edwards Park.

ANNOUNCEMENTS

Any Alumna wishing to purchase 1925's Class Book should send her name at once to Elizabeth Smith, Denbigh Hall. The price of the Class Book will be $3.00.

The Council is to be held this year in Washington on November 18th, 19th and 20th. The principal topics to be discussed are the publication of the Alumnae Register, the Campaign for the Endowment of the Music Department and the Auditorium of the Students' Building, and the designation of money through the Alumnae Fund. The officers of the Association will welcome suggestions as to other topics for discussion, or expressions of opinion on these topics from individuals or groups of Alumnae.

All contributions to the December BULLETIN must be sent to Evelyn Page, Taylor Hall, Bryn Mawr College, before November 10th.

A Year in Greece

By DOROTHY BURR, 1923

*(Miss Burr was awarded the European Fellowship in 1923. She spent last year at
the American School of Classical Studies in Athens, and was awarded
by the School one of two scholarships for 1923-24
given to its most brilliant students.)*

A year in Greece was a bewildering year, a year of sensations geographical and geological, of travel and study and tramps and Museums, of Revolutions, peasants, teas, and excavations.

The most important experience, of course, was the country itself—for its unexpected beauty, continually charming and predominating. To have to climb picturesque gorges to a temple, to study on an acropolis set splendidly among mountains by the sea, to dig near the foothills of Arcadia, gave me a continual sense of pleasure. Archaeology suddenly moved from the dark bounds of Room E, Taylor Hall, to a boundless territory. Travel was one of the most important ways of study and travel made me more and more aware of the surprisingly high key of the whole country—its bare mountains catching an opalescent light at evening, its bitter blue bays, its ruddy plains, its hills crowned by a gray classic fort or by a crumbling Mediaeval castle. I grew to know the physical things of the country that had seemed literary—the white spike of the asphodel, the merry armies of anemones, the pink oleander in dry river-beds, the myrtle, the laurel, and the oaks of Arcadia.

Through this background, I passed from the places which I had known before—like Delphi, steep and hot and full of the glitter of the beaks taken at Arginusae and the great bowl of Croesus, or Thermopylae, where I dabbled my hand in the hot springs, or Olympia, where I saw Hermes knee-deep in plaster to be moved from danger of earthquakes, or Sparta, in a luxuriant valley, singularly inapt for Spartan severity, and so on—to the places which I had not known before, that made Greece fuller and deeper—Levadia, where one consulted the oracle by going down a hole in the earth feet first, honey-cakes in one's hand; Mistra, a dead Byzantine city of gay churches and pale silent streets; Gla, a mysteriously walled island in what was once a lake, a fortress deserted probably when the Dorians came. Personal contact created a curious point of view. I remember Sparta for its beer, Megalopolis for its fleas, Thebes for worse, far worse, Mycenae for the family named Agamemnon, Orestes, and Helen, Athens for its hot baths!

In the autumn, we traveled in a group through Central Greece and the Peloponnesus; in the winter, we studied in Museums—queer Daltons!—in the spring, we traveled severally wherever we chose. I chose Arcadia with Betty Barber, ex-'24, and Elizabeth Vincent, '23, and didn't regret it! For there I saw white kids in deep grass, snow-drifted Cyllene where Hermes was born, abundant flowers when "diffugere nives"—all in rather Horatian and Virgilian flavor. In this setting we talked of May Day and Reunion—things but half credible. I ruined a pair of shoes in the Styx—for its water has always destroyed everything except an ass's hoof—but I must admit that it did my foot no harm. We visited an ancient monastery built in a cave, where jewelled crosses and delicate missals touched one's dim ideas of the Byzantine Empire to life and color. And then I went to Crete, to lose my breath even more over the varnished dark original frescoes of bulls and maidens and Blue Boy and ladies in bustles. We had the good fortune to be shown Knossos by Sir Arthur Evans. I stumped, in hot Cretan boots, over the floors of glittering crystal slabs curled by the heat of the fire which destroyed the palace. How I rejoiced in a glass of cool water from a Minoan well in Evans' garden!

But these (with a good deal of minute and technical archaeological study) were not the only new and vivid sensations of the year. There were personal contacts with lecturers from the other schools, with Dörpfeld, the famous German Archaeologist, whom I heard on the Acropolis where he had found so much, and later on the boat, where he talked forever to my eager ears in delightful private chats on the Phoenicians and Ithaca. I met the Greeks, too, cosmopolitan Greeks who talk French and do not visit the Acropolis, and peasant Greeks who are lovable in naïveté.

Peasant Greece, indeed, was most interesting, chiefly because of its primitiveness of mind. Whatever revolutions or shootings go on in Athens to enliven one's Sundays—the Greeks wed, murder, and bury on Sunday—the peasants do as their ancestors did, ploughing with the same sort of plough, going to the spring in the evening with the same sort of jug (though less lovely), daily migrating to the fields from their huddled villages of sun-baked brick, red tiles, and uncertain balconies, with all the family—the donkeys, the goats, a sheep or two, a ferocious dog, the babies in the women's arms, the baby animals on long unsteady legs, the plough, the copper sulphate for the vines, and the lunch in a coarse bag of fetching color and design. All through the country one meets the man who has been to America, the "Hello-Boy," we call him because he invariably greets one with, "Hello boys, where you from, how you like this country?" To these men, America is ideal; one even carried in this pocket the time-table of the Buffalo and Erie Railroad on which he had worked. Yet, though they wear five-dollar gold pieces as watch charms and usually a collar—in memoriam—they make no effort to tidy up a land which would infinitely repay a little sanitation. To ride sideways, whining a folk-song, on a toddling donkey while their wives work, to sit in a café, drinking liqueurs and Turkish coffee while the sun burns their unirrigated land, is to them the sweetest way of life. Never have I seen people who cared so little about making money. They often refuse to accept money for all sorts of courtesies; they overlook chances of adding to their resources. Perhaps it is dullness; in Delphi they keep no postals of one of the most superb views in the world because, when they had had a set made, "the first party that arrived bought them all. What can we do?" Perhaps it is laziness; an Arcadian Hello-Boy said, "In America, you are rich, but then you are always working; if I have enough to eat and so on, why should I work hard all day?" And, ah, what a tempting and lovely leisure is the midday siesta in the light regular wind, when the lizards curve quickly over the hot stones in the burning land beyond one's magic dome of fig-tree shade!

One thing which I had not foreseen was this leisurely spirit, this Orientalism. On my arrival, I suddenly found myself in a city of uneven earth streets (in the outskirts), of houses white and pink and blue, addicted to lavender or green shutters and frilly rosy antefixes, of blazing days when all is quiet and of violet evenings when the people chat from window to balcony and the goats come home, tinkling various small bells. Byzantine churches suggested the East—with their bulging domes and quaint squat bodies secreting a glimmer of mosaic and silver lamps in their dark insides. What an Oriental pattern!—incense and nervous bells; ghastly beggars sprawled on the streets; vegetable vendors with solemn donkeys; shops hung with the rich tapestry of Greek embroideries and cluttered with brass and old silver, with Turkish china in tan and turquoise, with stiff terra-cottas and small bad vases; copper glowing in Hephaestus Street; rugs and eikons and priests' purple and gold robes; tiny scarlet shoes with blue pompons dangling in ranks before one's eyes. Of course, the Class Baby must kick in a pair of such scarlet shoes, and I shall involve myself with sealing-wax and Greek stamps as soon as I return.

Crete, however, was the most Oriental, for there the Turks stayed longest. There were lean minarets, fountains carved with scrawls, green cages at the upper windows for the harem, and many men in fezzes, soon to leave. Greece is not the East, but the East lies just beyond her seas.

To me, the most exciting experience of all, perhaps, was excavating—though I found but little. It is a tiring life, that rising daily at five-thirty to stand by blazing trenches which produce, oh, so slowly. But it is absorbing—so absorbing that it is hard to leave, even at evening, to stop sifting earth between one's fingers for Byzantine earrings and beads, or pulling bronze rings off green finger bones, or scraping with one's knife, seeking, ever seeking the quaint precious letters of an archaic inscription. Coins, blue and emerald of patina, little heads of Hera, say, or a smiling Aphrodite, strange recumbent old women, ugly with hoary age, the braceleted hand of Athena, or the shiny leg of an anonymous gentleman might turn up—one was always guessing. I was usually so much dissociated from the outer world that the realization would come over me as a shock, when I tramped in my trousers down to the second breakfast, that Commencement was going on in the unbelievably modern campus, and that Bryn Mawr, too, was hot.

The workmen were characters such as I had never known, wide-eyed as children and easily discouraged. I had many from Mycenae, who, when they could not find anything, would cry, "But in Mycenae it was all gold, all gold." I thought of Schliemann. We had refugees from Smyrna, who could understand no Greek, and who had a great fondness for hacking away at bed rock. We had an episode with one Bunting, a Russian of Miami, Florida, according to his version. He threatened to kill people with a large knife and ended in the village gaol, being fed by our cook because the handcuffs hurt his hands. At the excavations, we lived with a rich widow, who was about to marry off her niece. They began the trousseau by buying wool from sheepgrazing Argos and carding it on the front porch. The villagers were most interested in the discoveries in their fields. In the evenings, a procession would visit the trenches, men, who hoped for the gilded goat which had once stood in the marketplace, women who clasped their hands crying, "What ancient things, what ancient things!" and who begged to be allowed to see whether there were any water in the wells we found.

In all, then, Greece held many sights and sounds and suggestions. Among them, I found certain experiences infinitely illuminating. I caught the whiff of the East that the Greek must have caught. I knew the mountains and places which formed the accepted background of his literature. I had individual encounters where he had had individual encounters. I anxiously watched the growth of the new olive-tree by the Erechtheum as the Athenians had watched after the Persians had burned the original. I even tried to scale the cleft up which the Persians came to burn it. I climbed behind the pediment of the Parthenon like any workman (if less comfortably). I swam in the Aegean, seeing Salamis and Aegina over the tops of gay waves. Best of all, I saw things that had become immortal through literature. At evening, Hymettus purpled as it had purpled when Socrates drank the hemlock; frogs, in Lake Stymphalus, committed the thrumming uproar which must have suggested to Aristophanes their excellent qualifications as a chorus; at sunset, around the corner of the citadel of Mycenae, came a boy with his flock—a piper, that shepherd, though more quarrelsome than the pipers of Theocritus; attacking dogs turned in fear when we picked up a stone—as Homer said they turned; on the Areopagus sat an owl—Athena's owl, Bryn Mawr's owl. These experiences make up slowly but profoundly an understanding in what has passed—no small nor valueless possession.

THE Publicity Office of Bryn Mawr College is making up a most attractive College Calendar for 1925. The Calendar will bear the seal of the college, and will be illustrated by four beautiful etchings of Pembroke Arch, Pembroke East, the Library, and the Cloister, by Mr. G. A. Bradshaw of the Trenton School of Industrial Art. The Calendar is to be printed on heavy hand cut paper.

The Publicity Office also hopes to get out Christmas Cards. Information about these will be announced later.

The price of the Calendar is $1.00 if purchased at the Publicity Office, and $1.25 if ordered by mail. It will be ready for distribution early in November. The proceeds will go to the Drive for the Endowment of Department of Music and the Auditorium of the Students' Building, through the May Day account, since the etchings were originally made for use in connection with May Day.

Schedule of College Events

Approved by the Schedule Committee, Spring 1924

Wednesday, October 1st ....College opens. Parade night.

Saturday, October 4th ....Christian Association Reception.

Wednesday, October 8th ....Reserved for President's Reception to the Freshmen.

Friday, October 24th ....Lantern Night.

Saturday, October 25th ....Reserved in case of rain on Lantern Night.

Saturday, November 8th ....Junior Play.

Saturday, November 22nd ....Sophomore Play.

Wednesday, November 26th .....THANKSGIVING VACATION begins at 12.45 P. M.

Monday, December 1st .........THANKSGIVING VACATION ends at 9.00 A. M.

Friday, December 5th ....Swimming Meet.

Friday, December 12th ....Swimming Meet.

Thursday, December 18th ....Maids' Party.

Christmas Parties. Christmas Carols.

Saturday, December 20th ....CHRISTMAS VACATION begins at 12.45 P. M.

Tuesday, January 6th ....CHRISTMAS VACATION ends at 9.00 A. M.

Saturday, January 10th ....Sophomore Dance.

Friday, January 16th ....Lecture by Dhan Goupal Mukerji.

Monday, January 19th ...:.....VACATION.

Tuesday, January 20th ....Collegiate Examinations begin.

Saturday, January 31st ....Collegiate Examinations end.

Annual Meeting of the Alumnae Association.

Monday, February 2nd ....VACATION.

Tuesday, February 3rd ....VACATION.

Second Semester

Wednesday, February 4th ....Second Semester begins at 9.00 A. M.

Saturday, February 28th ....Freshman Play.

Friday, March 6th ....Gymnasium Contest.

Saturday, March 7th ....Christian Association Conference.

Friday, March 13th ....Gymnasium Contest.

Friday, March 20th ....Announcements of European Fellowships.

Fellowship Dinners.

Wednesday, March 25th ....SPRING VACATION begins at 12.45 P. M.

Wednesday, April 1st ....SPRING VACATION ends at 9.00 A. M.

Friday, April 10th ....GOOD FRIDAY VACATION.

Saturday, April 18th ....Track Meet.

Senior Play.

Saturday, April 25th ....Track Meet.

Friday, May 1st ....May Day Announcements.

Glee Club.

Saturday, May 2nd ....Glee Club.

Friday, May 15th ....Freshman, Sophomore, and Junior-Senior Suppers.

Monday, May 18th ....VACATION.

Tuesday, May 19th ....Collegiate Examinations begin.

Saturday, May 30th ....Collegiate Examinations end.

Friday, May 29th ....Sophomore Reception to the Seniors.

Saturday, May 30th ....Senior Reception to the Faculty.

Sunday, May 31st ....Baccalaureate Sermon.

Monday, June 1st ....Senior Supper.

Tuesday, June 2nd ....College Bonfire. Alumnae Supper.

Wednesday, June 3rd ....College Breakfast. Garden Party.

Thursday, June 4th ....Conferring of Degrees.

Close of fortieth academic year.

Graduate Fellowships for Belgian Universities

The C. R. B. (COMMISSION FOR RELIEF IN BELGIUM) Educational Foundation announces that a limited number of American graduate fellowships for study in Belgium during the academic year 1925-1926 will be awarded by April 1, 1925.

These fellowships were established to commemorate the work of the COMMISSION FOR RELIEF IN BELGIUM during the Great War and to promote closer relations and the exchange of intellectual ideas between Belgium and America.

A candidate for a fellowship, to be eligible,

(1) must be an American citizen;

(2) must have a thorough speaking and reading knowledge of French;

(3) must be a graduate, at time of application, of a college or professional school of recognized standing in the United States. (If a member of the faculty of a college or university, the candidate must hold a grade below that of associate professor);

(4) must be capable of independent study or research;

(5) must have definite plans for his proposed work in Belgium;

(6) must be in good health. (A satisfactory medical certificate must be submitted before confirmation of an award.)

Preference in selection is given to applicants between the ages of 25 and 33 who are unmarried and who intend to take up teaching or research as a profession. Applications must reach the Committee by Feruary 15, 1925.

Each fellowship for the year 1925-1926 carries a stipend of 15,000 francs plus tuition fees, payable in Belgium, and first-class traveling expenses from the residence or university of the holder in the United States to and from the university in Belgium. The fellowships are open to men and women. The fellowships are tenable for one year.

For the year 1925-1926 not more than six fellowships will be awarded. Fellowships may be held in any one of the following subjects:

Bacteriology	International Law
Botany	Mathematics
Chemistry	Medicine
Civil Engineering	Mining Engineering
Classical Philology	Paleography
Egyptology	Philosophy
Electricity	Physiology
French Literature	Psychology
Geology	Surgery
History	Zoology

American fellows will be required to report in Brussels by October 1, 1925, and to reside in Belgium for at least eight months. The Fondation Universitaire of Belgium assists the fellows in arrangements for their academic work. Fellows may choose the Belgian university or technical school which they wish to attend, but, in general, such choice will be indicated by their subject of study so that they may obtain the maximum benefit from the available opportunities. In special cases fellows may enroll at more than one university.

The Foundation reserves the right to withdraw a fellowship and terminate payments in case of conduct that is, in the opinion of the Foundation or its representatives, prejudicial to the interests of the Foundation.

Application blanks and further information may be obtained by addressing the Fellowship Committee, C. R. B. Educational Foundation, Inc., 42 Broadway, New York, N. Y.

CORRESPONDENCE

(The BULLETIN was delighted to receive the following letter from Margaret Bates Porterfield, 1905. We hope that others will follow her example and write us about their experiences, either for the Class Notes, or for this section.)

St. John's University,
Shanghai, China,
September 25, 1924.

We—including husband, and the two children—are still at St. John's University, where my husband has built up, and is now holding down the Biology Department, and carrying on sundry activities. One of these is his membership in the American Company, Shanghai Volunteers. These with the other Volunteer Units and the Marines from British and American Ships are at present guarding the Shanghai settlement against the Chinese armies in the Civil War now going on.

Last week the armies attacked each other and there was heavy bombarding about ten miles from here. The University is just outside the settlement, but there are two hundred British Marines barracked in the park across from this compound and a little patrol boat on the Soochow Creek that bounds two-thirds of our property. The Settlement is International, and no belligerents are allowed in it. The thing to be feared is retreating, leaderless soldiers bent on looting. Crowds of Chinese refugees have flocked to Shanghai. I can see them in little boats passing the house, crowded in, with their possessions and sacks of food. Last week, Lu's—the Chekiang general's—soldiers tried to conscript in the big Chinese village at our gates, but the police stopped it, so that all the compound servants have passes with stamps to show in case anyone wants to snatch them. The Hangchow-Shanghai Railroad runs very near, and we can watch load after load of Chekiang soldiers being carried to Shanghai and beyond. You see, Shanghai is in Kiangsu Province, but is ruled by a Chekiang man (the military governor), and the Chinese sentiment is with him (Southern) rather than with the north. Now that the forces 'round Peking have taken up the cudgels, the thing may be "a regular war." Most people say that the state of affairs is much worse than under the Empire.

We had a fine month's vacation in the mountains, a day's journey from Shanghai. Going up was comparatively easy, though just as we got on the train that was (after four hours going) to connect us with a launch and four more hours, we heard that owing to the drought and lack of water in the canals there would probably be no launch. However we did find a boat of sorts and finally arrived. Coming home, after war had been declared was full of uncertainty. We waited till most of the rush was over, and one misty morning at five-thirty we piled into sedan chairs, and with plenty of water bottles, and food enough in the tiffin basket for siege and all, including a train of luggage coolies, set out down the mountain through the bamboo groves and later along the brilliant green rice paddies of the plain. We reached the waterway, to find no launch, but a mass of little Chinese houseboats. We squeezed in, feeling as if we were entering an enormous turtle, the tops are so rounded and the boats so clumsy looking. After five hours, part of the time being towed, we were glad to untangle our stiff selves from the piles of baggage and humanity, cooks, amahs, and Chinese and foreign travellers. At Hangchow we had two hours to wait and everyone paraded the platform, or spread out tea. We were more than relieved to find the train service was still as per schedule. A troop train came in, and we watched the men and were told they had walked (I don't think Chinese soldiers *march*) from Hankow to Foochow, quite a little trot, and then to Hangchow. I never saw so many kinds and varieties of footwear, from cloth shoes to pseudo-foreign leather ones. Their equipment seemed to be tied on with string or any old thing, and they had no guns (too precious to trust them with, I suppose). Soldiers in this country are about the lowest order and never to be trusted. They turn brigand and mutiny if not paid or if it suits their plans. . . .

This winter I am teaching Peggy, running the school magazine for St. Mary's Hall (a Chinese girls' school) and helping two blind Chinese students of the University with French, as well as tending my vegetable garden and doing my share in a lot of compound affairs, the Church, etc. I'd give a lot to see Bryn Mawr and some '05ers.

Bryn Mawr Books

Friends With Life. By Anne C. E. Allinson. Harcourt, Brace and Company, New York, 1924.

As one who has been in very close touch with the so-called "younger generation," Mrs. Allinson is in an advantageous position to discuss some of the problems which confront young men and women today. She has had the opportunity and the ability to share and solve many of their difficulties. The magic which has allowed her to enter thus intimately into the lives of others seems to be an unusual combination of sympathy and common-sense. As her title suggests, Mrs. Allinson's goal is to seek out the means of living on terms of friendship with life. Her solution is not based on emotionalism, nor on the prevailing synicism. She demands that one should face the facts; that one should meet life and its perplexities with an inner honesty—far above the common code—in order that one may find, "some general terms, widely applicable, upon which this life may become a friend."

Her purpose thus set forth, Mrs. Allinson proceeds to treat in a sane and cheerful manner, which does not conceal a deep earnestness, various aspects of our modern ethical life. She deals with power, happiness, and religion, as they concern the individual, without hide-bound dogmas, but in a spirit of suggestion. Power, she says, increases as we look beyond ourselves to the ultimate aim; as we universalize every personal experience; and as we conceive a passion for great ends. Happiness, she analyses as, "the color laid by some inward light upon all that we do and are."

Abreast of her time, Mrs. Allinson does not hesitate to attack the more intricate problems of human relationships. She writes on the freedom of the individual within the family. Everyone, she asserts, has the right and desire to develop himself, but the freedom necessary for such development need not conflict with the claims of family life; rather, it should raise their value. She considers with understanding the relations that exist between mothers and their unmarried daughters, between husbands and wives, and between men and women in the business world. On every question she takes a definite but thoroughly human stand.

Mrs. Allinson appropriately closes her book with an essay on Friendship, and at the end of the essay, she cleverly binds the whole of her work together in the following paragraph:

"Thus, wherever person touches person, the word "friend" best describes the most perfect relationship. And so it is between the individual and his existence in this world. To be friends with Life means to transform a fatally necessary connection into an intimacy which is free and beautiful and noble."

High Lights and Twilights of Morningshore. By Sarah Satterthwaite Leslie. Ralph Fletcher Seymour, *Publisher.* Chicago, 1924. $2.00.

High Lights and Twilights of Morningshore is a volume of poetry combined with rhythmical prose. Prose and verse together form a sequence descriptive of a garden and a place. The garden is particularly enchanting.

"Larkspur wreaths are being woven, pointed spur in spur encased.
Forming crowns, pink, white, and purple, from the blossoms interlaced.
Honeysuckles twining over lift their mimic bugles red .
To the giant trumpet-creeper, towering lordly overhead;"

Flowers, gardens, islands, meadows give Mrs. Leslie the subjects of her poems, often by suggestion, often by their own intrinsic beauty. Sometimes she is contented with their homeliness and simplicity, and then again she expresses their magnificence, as, for instance, in her poem on the evening primrose:

"Let the red rose flaunt to the flaming sun.
Wan treasure of moonlight the night's chosen one !"

Mrs. Leslie concludes her poetical diary with a Ballade reminiscent of Wordsworth:

"Oh, earth, adorned in beauty bright,
    Could I but fathom, wandering free,
The visions of my inward sight
    And test thy utmost mystery. . . .

Oh, life, scant taste of what may be,
    To us, who long for range more wide,
Thy promise is eternity,
    And in my heart doth hope abide."

Campus Notes

The newest thing at the opening of every college year is the Freshman Class, and the BULLETIN would be unreasonable if it did not devote a great part of this section to its members, as a supplement to President Park's speech which appeared in the October issue. Thirteen Alumnae have daughters in 1928. The geographical distribution is wide. Out of a class of 118, New York City claims twenty-seven, while ten come from New York State. Twelve students are residents of Philadelphia and fifteen are natives of Pennsylvania. There are nine from New Jersey, seven from Illinois, seven from Massachusetts, four from Connecticut, four from Missouri, four from Ohio, one from California, four from Maryland, two from Minnesota, one from Colorado, one from Arkansas, three from Washington, D. C., one from Vermont, one from Arizona, one from Virginia, and one from Louisiana, New Mexico, Oregon and Rhode Island.

Seventeen Freshmen hold Scholarships.

Two members of the Freshman Committee are now chosen by the Juniors, and the other three are elected by the class. The Committee members elected by the Juniors this year are Mary Hopkinson, formerly Mayor of the Winsor School in Boston, Josephine Stetson, formerly head of Self-Government at Rosemary Hall.

For the third consecutive year the Sophomores defeated the Freshmen on Parade Night. The Freshman song this year was written to the tune of "Row, row, row your boat." At present the Freshmen have forgotten this reverse in the intricacies of registration and medical examinations, and in the introduction to new studies both athletic and academic.

The Christian Association welcomed the Class of 1928 in the Gymnasium on Saturday night, October 4th.

Margaret Stewardson, '25, President of the Christian Association, stressed the value of the Association as a help towards the co-ordination of facts in the individual and in college. The spiritual influence links the separate activities into a constructive whole which is encouraged by the comprehensive and tolerant nature of the Christian Association itself.

The presidents of the Self-Government Association, the Undergraduate Association, the Graduate Club, the Athletic Association and the Managing Editor of the *College News*, followed with self-explanatory speeches, poetically, humorously or seriously expressed.

The students have all shown great interest in the Summer School and its problems, and are eager to hear about the workers in industry. The Summer School has stimulated them to keen attention to economic and political questions. The Liberal Club has arranged a program for speakers, and has made an arrangement whereby a number of students will have an opportunity to discuss current events with groups of factory girls. The aim of the club "is to develop a fair and open-minded attitude toward all industrial, social and international questions and to develop an interest in questions of modern art, drama, music and literature." Delegates were sent to an Intercollegiate political conference which was held at Vassar over the week-end of October 18th.

The sixteen colleges who joined with Vassar were Barnard College, Mount Holyoke, Wellesley, Bryn Mawr, Skidmore School of Arts, Goucher, Marymount, Wilson, Yale, Harvard, Amherst, Dartmouth, Williams, Haverford, Colgate and Smith. Many of the colleges were represented by three delegates each.

Bates House was run this summer entirely by Bryn Mawr students. The Head Worker was M. Faries, 1924, who was assisted by thirty-two volunteers. In all there were 117 children, no girls over twelve, and no boys over ten, including fourteen nursery babies. The committee refuses to be satisfied with last year's achievements, however, and expects next summer to have a uniform for the children, and to make Bates House "a model establishment."

The Sophomore Class is to perform Sir James Battle's *Quality Street* on Saturday evening, November 22nd. The Juniors have just announced their choice of *The Amazons*, by Sir Arthur Pinero. *The Amazons* was first produced at Bryn Mawr in 1896, when President Park took the part of Oorts. The play is to be coached by Katherine Ward, 1921.

Varsity was defeated in its first game on Saturday, October 11th, by the Germantown Hockey Club.

In the game of October 22, however, 'Varsity defeated the Merion-Main Line Team by a score of 3-1. Dorothy Lee, 1925, is 'Varsity Hockey Captain for this year.

On Monday, October 20, the Department of Music gave the first of a series of four concerts to be held this year. The program was given by Mr. Harold Samuel, probably the greatest interpreter of Bach. Mr. Samuel, an Englishman, came to this country at the invitation of Mrs. F. S. Coolidge, and through her generosity was enabled to play at Bryn Mawr. He found a large and enthusiastic audience. The chapel proved so inadequate for his hearers that it was necessary to throw open the doors at the back and place chairs in the hall for those who would otherwise have been turned away. Mr. Horace Alwyne, Head of the Music Department wrote of him in the *College News*, "It is a rare thing nowadays to find an artist who is willing to put aside all opportunity for personal display and aggrandizement in order to dedicate himself entirely to the furthering of the appreciation of some noble and beautiful work of a non-popular order. This Mr. Samuel is doing by devoting himself to the music of Bach and giving programs entirely devoted to his music. . . . His evident personal delight in the playing of such music quickly became reflected in his hearers."

The program consisted of:

I. Chromatic Fantasie and Fugue.

II. From the "Well-Tempered Clavichord."
   Prelude and Fugue in A, Bk. II.
   Prelude and Fugue in C sharp minor Bk. I.
   Prelude and Fugue in B flat, Bk. I.
   Prelude and Fugue in F, Bk. II.

III. Short Preludes in C major and E major.
   Invention in A major.
   Bouree in E minor.
   Minuet in M major.
   Fantasia in C minor.

IV. Partita in B flat major.
   Prelude.
   Allemande.
   Courante.
   Sarabande.
   Minuets 1 and 2.
   Gigue.

The Music Department is to be highly congratulated not only upon the success of its class room work with a special group of students, but also upon its influence upon the whole undergraduate body. The keen interest in and appreciation of music manifested by the students is one of the best developments of the college in the past few years. Mr. Alwyne's achievement is recognized by the world as well as by Bryn Mawr. We were very much interested to read that he had recently had conferred upon him the degree of honorary fellow of the Royal Manchester College of Music, of which he was already an associate with distinction and gold medalist. Mr. Alwyne will play with the Philadelphia Orchestra on December 5th and 6th.

Lantern Night was held on Friday, October 25. The Freshmen and Sophomores were fortunate in having a beautiful, clear evening for the ceremony.

"Pallas Athena Thea," the Greek hymn sung by the Sophomores, was written by Bertha Haven Putnam and Madeline Vaughan Abbott as 1893's class song. It was first sung at Lantern Night by 1901. The Freshman hymn, "Sofias," was transposed by K. Ward, '21, and H. Hill, '21, from Pericles' funeral oration by Thuycides and was rewritten by Dr. Saunders, professor of Greek, two years ago. L. Reinhardt, '21, and H. Hill, '21, selected the music, part of the Russian services by A. F. Lvoff starting "Of Thy Mystical Supper."

Steeplejack. By James Gibbont Huneker. Two volumes in one. Charles Scribner's Sons, New York. 1923. $3.50.

Mr. Huneker chooses his devise from the *Steeplejack* of the *Seven Arts:* "I who write these words . . . have been a steeplejack. I have climbed to the very top of many steeples the world over, and dreamed like the rest of my fellows." It is a device that seems to characterize the quickly-turning tale that Mr. Huneker has to tell, filled with color, and brimming with the exuberant joy of existence. In his Apology, he describes with humorous charm his own position with regard to this autobiography, "Pray accept me as a steeplejack of dreams, a mediocrity, and these avowals merely as the chemistry of saturation and precipitation."

Mother Goose's Nursery Rhymes. Edited by L. Edna Walter. Illustrated by Charles Folkard. A. & C. Black, Lt., London. $3.50.

An unusually complete collection of nursery rhymes, old and new, with a wealth of charming illustrations. All the familiar rhymes are included, and one finds, in addition, many that are less well known, but equally delightful, such as:

"I won't be my father's Jack.
I won't be my mother's Jill.
I will be the fiddler's wife,
And have music when I will.

T'other little tune,
T'other little tune,
Prithee, love, play me
T'other little tune."

Pipers and a Dancer. By Stella Benson. The Macmillan Company, New York. 1924. $2.00.

The story of Ipsie, who must forever dance when the pipers play, and the pipers are her imagined public before whom she must enact various rôles. She is a victim to her own self-consciousness, her sensitivity to what she feels is her expected part. She is always thwarted by her own blindness to reality. Only once or twice does she escape herself. Ipsie is drawn with an insight that is penetrating, but rather cold. The analysis is colored more by irony than by sympathy. In the background move the pipers, her fiancé, and her future sister-in-law, and Rodd, who alone grasps something of Ipsie's tragedy:

"Why she's not alive. . . . She's lost life and God knows what she's found instead. Reality's the only thing she can't imagine."

The Boy Jesus and His Companions. By Rufus M. Jones. The Macmillan Company, New York, 1922. $1.25.

Doctor Jones tells in a simple but vivid manner of the early life of Jesus. The story is presented in the terms of every child's experience, and with an understanding that makes the figures of the Gospel narrative living people. Behind the story itself are the facts of history and geography, supplying a background that is at once accurate and colorful.

The Actor's Heritage. By Walter Pritchard Eaton. The *Atlantic Monthly* Press. Boston, 1924. $4.00.

"The finished art of the theatre is not a separate and splendidly isolated thing. It is part and parcel of the travelling-caravan show, the cheapest vaudeville, the meanest stock-company. The boy who rises to the peak of the human pyramid in the sawdust ring and then leaps off with a double somersault may be a Molière; the girl who blunders through some melodrama in the remotest provinces may be a Siddons." Such is Mr. Eaton's theme, and in the course of a number of delightful essays he embroiders upon it. David Garrick, Mrs. Siddons, Edmund Kean, Sol Smith, Macready, Mademoiselle Rachel, John Barrymore, Mrs. Bracegirdle, and many other personages, some shrouded in the midst of legend, some familiar figures of today come and go in his pages. The charming illustrations are most of them taken from old drawings and engravings, but even here, unlike most historians, Mr. Eaton recognizes the claims of the present. Indeed, he is daring enough to say that the present is in some degree better than the past, and that "truly, it seems hardly the time for us old fellows to prate of the Palmy Days."

Ariel. The Life of Shelley. By André Maurois. Appleton. New York, 1924. $2.50.

Sea and Sardinia. By D. H. Lawrence. Thomas Seltzer. New York, 1921. $5.00.

The Gallants. By E. Barrington. *Atlantic Monthly* Press. Boston, 1924. $3.50.

The Divine Lady. By E. Barrington. Dodd, Mead and Company. New York. 1924. $2.50.

Alumnae Activities

ANNA KING, 1908

Chief Clinic Executive at Cornell University

The Clinic of Cornell University Medical College has been operating now for nearly three years as a pay clinic for persons of moderate means. It aims to give sound medical service at cost to those who cannot afford the same treatments at private rates. After various financial vicissitudes it is now running nearly without a deficit and, although this is the so-called slack season, having approximately 10,000 visits a month. Each day about 425 persons enter its doors "to see the doctor."

A newspaper reporter recently spoke of these Cornell patients as the "white collared class" and elicited a letter from a woman asking if the clinic was for men only! Socially they are of all kinds,—clerks, mechanics, singers, salespeople, social workers, laborer, housewives, policemen,—those who are living on from about $1000 to $1800 a year, or if they have dependents perhaps considerably more.

I am asked to tell about the clinic executive staff, and its relation to the Clinic work. Modern medicine has such wide fields of knowledge and activity that it requires the co-operation of the patient to elicit information for an early and complete diagnosis and to bring about the modifications in the life of the patient necessary to carry out successfully many forms of treatment. It is the purpose of the clinic executive staff, which is composed of medical social workers, to assist in securing this co-operation and making it effectual.

Assistance to Patients in Various Clinic Procedures

The first of our duties is to admit the patients, assigning them to whatever department for treatment their complaint indicates, securing the broad skeleton facts of the patient's life which may affect treatment, explaining the operation of the Clinic, its fees, etc., learning whether the patient can afford these fees and if not, persuading him to go elsewhere; if, on the other hand, he can afford private rates, giving

him a list of specialists prepared by the Faculty. After the patient has seen the doctor we "route" him through whatever procedures the doctor has recommended, explaining preparations for tests and their costs and arranging for subsequent appointment at convenient hours. At Cornell patients are seen by appointment, the capacity of each department being estimated by the medical chief and only the authorized number of patients being admitted that day, all others receiving future appointments. Thus any patient having an appointment can feel secure in coming to the Clinic at that hour instead of having to crowd in early.

In connection with this "routing" of patients there is a certain amount of clerical work. To assist in this work clerks are detailed to us by the Director.

Special Services to Patients

Many patients need also those services which are the more generally accepted duties of the medical social service department. These one of the doctors in a manual for his medical staff has characterized in part as follows:

"Reviewing with the patient his mode of life and resources in order that a practicable plan for carrying out the instructions of the physician may be formulated. . . . In some instances she may discover obstacles to treatment which will necessitate a modification of plans and she will then consult the physician.

"Assisting in the diagnosis by bringing to light relevant facts pertaining to the patient's personal, environmental and industrial condition. . . .

"She may arrange suitable and agreeable hospital or sanatorium accommodations, recreation, employment, etc.

"In some cases she helps the patient's family to understand the medical treatment plan, and enlists their interest and co-operation. . . .

"She assists in prevention of the spread of infectious disease by specific instructions to the patient and by encouraging contacts to visit the clinic.

"She also assists in other forms of preventive medicine, such as in those illnesses which are caused by economic or industrial factors.

"By reason of her familiarity with the patient's home, work, interests, etc., she can further assist by maintaining continuity of treatment and following patients who have lapsed in attendance. . . . "

Assistance in Teaching and Research

Another duty of the clinic executive staff is to assist in teaching and research. The original purpose in establishing the Clinic was to furnish teaching material for the medical students of the College, of which the Clinic is one department, operating in the same building with the College. The clinic executives in some departments arrange for the return of patients to be used for study, explaining the purposes of teaching and winning their consent.

Another form of teaching in which the staff takes part is the training of medical social workers. During this past year ten students from the New York School of Social Work were assigned to us for periods of field work.

The clinic executive staff has been called on to assist in certain aspects of research studies which are being carried on. One of the most interesting studies undertaken is an attempt to analyze what constitutes clinic service. A group of doctors assisted by a special social worker have been analyzing what they have done for the regular clinic patients that they have seen during a certain period, "putting the microscope" on their own procedures.

During the brief years while this pay clinic has been running, the eighteen clinic executives have had to meet many vicissitudes. Herbert Spencer defined life as "the continuous adjustment of internal relations to external conditions." Cornell Clinic according to this definition is full of a fine vitality. It is a challenge to bring as much as possible to this new experiment of the medical profession in its ageless study and practice of the art of healing.

Class Notes

1889

Class Editor, Harriet Randolph, 1300 Spruce Street, Philadelphia.

Science, Sept. 5, 1924.

"At the conclusion of the meetings of the French Association for the Advancement of Science, the University of Liège conferred honorary degrees on M. Raymond Poincaré, Dr Rigaud, Director of the Paris Radium Institute . . . Dr. Paul Shorey, professor of Greek at the University of Chicago."

Doctor Shorey was professor of Greek and Latin at Bryn Mawr College from the founding of the College to 1892.

His other degrees are: A.B., Harvard, 1878; Ph.D., University of Munich, 1884; LL.D., Iowa College, 1905; University of Missouri, 1913; Johns Hopkins University, 1915; University of Michigan, 1915; University of Colorado, 1917; Princeton, 1920; University of Pennsylvania, 1921; Litt.D., University of Wisconsin, 1911; Brown, 1914.

Unsigned series. Letter No. 3.

"Maybe I could send a snap-shot or two of the interesting group in the Y. W. International Institute, in which I am much interested. We work chiefly with Chinese, Japanese, Korean and Filipinos, and all of them mixed up together. I am going to a Korean dinner next week, given by our Korean Committees ladies.

"Honolulu is lovely, getting ready for a big flower show."

1892

Mrs. F. M. Ives, 136 East 36th Street, New York City.

Edith Rockwell Hall.

My first few years after graduation were spent in teaching, partly in schools, and partly as private tutor, migrating with my charges between Washington and California. This was followed by two years of graduate work in History at Cornell and then by eight years as Associate Head (with Louise Brownell Saunders) and Head of the Balliol School, from which we had the pleasure of sending several students to Bryn Mawr.

After gathering from this adventure a rich harvest of enjoyment and spiritual profit, unfortunately not backed by profit of a grosser sort, I turned from academic work to social and industrial investigation. In the course of this I had several particularly interesting years, first as Inspector in the Enforcement of the Federal Child Labor Law (chiefly in the Georgia Cotton Mills) and, throughout the period of government control of the railroads, as Field Agent of the Women's Service Section of the Railroad Administration.

During the two years just past I have enjoyed a return to academic life as instructor in the History Department of Vassar College."

This year Edith Hall has opened a lunch room in New York at 32 W. 49th St.

Eliza Stephens Montgomery.

Until I was married in May, 1897, I traveled much abroad and at home. Since my marriage my history has been chiefly that of my family. Before the war, my husband and I went to Europe several times with our children, but since 1914 we have spent most of our summers at our cottage at Buck Hill Falls, Pennsylvania. My son was married over two years ago and now I have a grandson seven months' old. My daughter expects to be married this summer.

Anne Emery Allinson has just published a new book entitled *Friends with Life*.

1896

Class Editor, Mary W. Jewett, Pleasantville, New York.

Mary Northrop Spear has a granddaughter, born August 24th.

Katherine Cook spent the summer at her cottage at Lakeville, Conn., where E. Kirkbride, A. Dimon, M. Hill Swope, E. Bowman, O. M. Taber met for a picnic.

Marian Whitehead Grafton and her three children, 12, 14 and 16, were at Sea Girt, N. J., all summer. She is president of The League of Women Voters of Trenton.

Hilda Justice spent a month at Buck Hill Falls, a month with a friend on Long Island, a month at Southwest Harbor, Me., and took a week-end canoe trip in September in the Maine woods.

Laura Heermance centers her interest in housekeeping and five lively nephews and nieces.

Clara Farr gardened the summer away at her cottage in the White Mountains and took many trips in her car.

Anna Scattergood Hoag spent the summer at their farmhouse at Tamworth, N. H., coming home early in September for the wedding of her son, Garrett, to Margaret Ewing. The day of the marriage the house at Tamworth, 125 years old, burned to the ground.

Faith Mathewson Huizinga was in London three months in the spring, making trips to Wembly and other nearby points; returned to Thompson, Conn., in June, and expects to go to France in November to put her daughter in school for six months.

Hannah Cadbury Pyle motored to Amherst, Mass., by way of the Delaware Water Gap, and spent a week riding, driving, swimming, and digging on the farm of her sister.

Harriet Brownell was in Paris several months last winter and travelled in southern France, northern Africa, Sicily and Italy. This summer she has been studying at Grenoble, attending the League of Nations Conference, and driving through the Chateau country from Tours. Her sister, Jane, sails the middle of October to join her for the Winter.

May Crawford Dudley has been gardening—with great success—walking and climbing mountains at her summer home at Les Eboulements Centre, P. Q., Canada.

Gertrude Heritage Green has motored through Pennsylvania and New Jersey, and along the historic James River in Virginia. Most of her time, however, has been spent in the development of a new formal garden. About seventy-five plants, gathered from places with literary or historic associations, make this of unusual interest. All Bryn Mawtyrs are invited to stop in passing and see her treasures.

Euphemia Whittredge raises apples at Woodstock, N. Y.,—look for "Euphemia's Apples,"—Wealthys and Baldwins. She prefers this outdoor life to interior decorating, doing the easier part of the work herself—pruning, thinning out the smaller fruit, and some of the picking and packing.

Ruth Furness Porter, husband and three boys spent the Summer in Norway, England and Scotland. They went to Iceland for a "week-end" on the way to the North Cape, and cruised down the coast, seeing most of the fiords, and having the excite-

ment of running onto a rock near Trond-
hjem, which laid the ship up for repairs
for four days. Landing in Southampton,
they motored for seven weeks from St. Ives
to Inverness, from the Trossachs to Wembly.

Clara Colton Worthington, after a Summer spent in Salt Lake City, with her
younger son, Bill, is leaving now for San
Francisco, Los Angeles, El Tovar, and
Kentucky, reaching New York about
Thanksgiving, where she will be till after
the holidays; part of the time at the Bryn
Mawr Club. Hood, her older son, graduated from Massachusetts Institute of Technology in June, and Bill is at Tome, Port
Deposit, Md.

Charlotte McLean passed her Summer vacation with a month at Longport, N. J.,
and another at Devon, Pa., reading Latin
for the coming year's work.

Elizabeth Palmer McMynn had an ideal
motoring and tramping trip through England, Scotland and North Wales with her
husband and some friends, staying a week
in London, where they were royally entertained by the English and Canadian Bar.
At home she is interested in Girl Scout activities with Alice Miller Chester, 1914.

Lydia Boring spent several weeks this
summer autoing through the Finger Lakes
Region of Western New York, west to Chi-
cago via the Erie Boulevard, Toledo and
South Bend, and home by way of the Old
National Roads Trail.

Leonie Gilmour took a business trip to
the summer places along the coast of Cape
Cod and Cape Ann for several weeks. Her
son, Isamu Noguchi, has suddenly come
into notice as a sculptor, one of the Sunday papers having recently shown a picture of him in his studio.

Abba Dimon spent a week in June with
Bertha Ehlers at her camp at Bolton Landing, Lake George; the middle of July, with
her niece and another eleven-year-old,
she packed in to Morehouse Lake two and
a half miles over a trail, put up a tent and
enjoyed four days of continuous rain;
visited K. Cook at her hilltop bungalow at
Lakeville, Conn.; went to Annisquam for
two weeks; spent a few days with the
Goldmarks at St. Hubert's; made a three-
day trip with The Tramp and Trail Club
of Utica over Labor Day, climbing Mt. Mc-
Intyre; and ended her summer with a two-

day jaunt to Pleasant Point Club on Lake
Ontario.

Mary Jewett opened The Flower Shop
last April in Pleasantville, N. Y., which
combines cut flowers, plants and nursery
stock with a variety shop—pottery, baskets,
bridge prizes, party favors, etc. It is on
one of the through highways north from
New York through Westchester County—
she hopes '96 will stop when passing.

Grace Baldwin White with her family,
boys eleven and sixteen, daughter thirteen,
were all summer at their cottage on Pe-
conic Bay. She would always be glad to be
looked up by '96 in Summit.

Tirzah Nichols enjoyed the sea at Provincetown, Mass., during the month of August.

Mary Boude Woolman went this Summer
to Alaska, and the Canadian Rockies, seeing gold-mining at Cripple Creek, and the
Klondyke and being properly thrilled by
Pike's Peak, Mt. Rainier, the Selkirks and
the Alaskan Inland Passage.

Sophie Reynolds Wakeman spent week-
ends at Lake Club House near Hornell, N.
Y., and motored to Saratoga with her husband to attend the Conference of the State
Health Dept. In September they took their
two sons, who are midshipmen in the United
States Naval Academy, back to Annapolis
by auto.

Clarissa Smith Dey was in Maine four
months this summer at Tenant's Harbor,
where she has a summer home.

Pauline Goldmark spent the Summer in
the Adirondacks, as usual, where she was
a near neighbor of our class president, who
seems to have astonished her by her "youthful vigor and enthusiasm for mountain
climbing." Her city address is 195 Broadway, as the Goldmarks have given up the
house in Ninety-fourth Street and will
eventually go to Hartsdale to live.

1900

Class Editor, Helen MacCoy, 4 Chestnut
Street, Albany, N. Y.

Owing to the splendid co-operation of
the Class, in replying to inquiries for Class
Notes, we have the following items of pecul-
iar interest:

Susan Dewees was arrested for speeding
in her new red Stutz. Her license was removed for driving while intoxicated.

Dorothea Farquhar has been divorced for
the fourth time.

Edith Wright won a pearl necklace from H. R. H. while playing baccarat at Monte Carlo.

Cornelia Halsey won second prize at the Dancing Marathon contest at Coney Island.

Hodgie has the extreme distinction of being a member for next winter of Mme. Pavlowa's ballet. She will appear under the stage name of Mme. Petrova Serchmikoff, and will star in the tone poem of the Scarlet Peacock.

Lotta Emery has opened a wet wash laundry in her home town and is baking raisin bread on the side. Patronize your home merchant.

Don't forget when you're touring through Baltimore to stop at Mary Kil's roadside stand on St. Paul Street, where she dispenses tonics, chewing gum, hot dogs, and Oh, Henrys.

Watch for other issues of the BULLETIN where news of similar interest will appear.

1904

Class Editor, Emma O. Thompson, 320 S. 42nd Street, Philadelphia, Pa.

Evelyn Holliday Patterson, 1622 Ridge Avenue, Evanston, Ill.

There is nothing special to say about my children except that they are both very interesting and satisfactory. Emie should enter college in the fall of 1929 and as she takes school examinations calmly, I hope she will not have to put in an extra year on preparation, that is if anyone at all gets into college. She is not a C. K. T. and neither is Wallace.

Katharine Curtis Pierce, 9 East Ninety-fourth Street, New York City.

There is nothing I would rather do than talk about my children, but it is difficult to do it with proper restraint.

I have three sons whose ages are eighteen, fifteen and seven. My two oldest boys are at Groton. Curtis is in his last year there and expects to go to college in the fall. He is a fine big boy, interested in all the various activities of school life, is a member of the school crew (rowing is his favorite sport), played on the second football team, is Press Editor of the school paper, etc. He is rather reserved and makes friends slowly but surely and is very loyal. He is always dependable and has good, sound judgment for a boy of his age. During his vacations he goes to parties all the time and enjoys them thoroughly. He spends a little while each summer at the Groton Camp acting as "Faculty." He gets on splendidly with little children, especially his little brother. Their devotion to each other is very remarkable.

Henry is not reserved or shy at all and knows and likes everybody. As he is only in the third form he has not had a chance to make any school team, but he plays football and baseball on the lower club teams and is a very good sport. Drawing takes most of his time and he thinks now he is going to be an artist; he has a gift I am sure. He enjoys parties as much as his brother does. He is a very amusing and lively boy, gets a good many black marks at school and is in everything that is going on. His warm-hearted and affectionate nature keep him from doing anything that would really trouble us though.

Ben is still at home with us, of course, and goes to St. Bernard's School. He is ambitious and works hard. He has already skipped one class and may skip another this year. He is sociable, too, and assumes that everyone is his friend, and is usually right. He tries very hard to imitate his big brothers and is rather old for his age, as he is so much with them. He is very much on his job and practical.

Clara Woodruff Hull, Waverly, Pa.

Our youngest, John Laurence Hull, was born March 29, 1924. Esther Sinn and I are keeping pace with each other—you have heard no doubt of the arrival of her little Richard. We now have each three sons and one daughter.

Many of the class children are not accounted for in this news. Will those of you who have not responded to our appeal write a few lines now for the next issue?

1905

Class Editor, Mrs. Clarence Hardenbergh, 3710 Warwick Boulevard, Kansas City, Missouri.

Kathryn Grotevent "decided that the only thing to do in these troubled times of inadequate housing conditions was to buy a house"; which she has done at 304 Winona Street, Germantown, Philadelphia.

Theo Bates has just returned from China, where she spent a delightful year. Her only regret in coming home is that she missed the latest civil war.

Margaret Thurston Holt has a second son (third child) September 21, at Portland, Maine.

1906

Class Editor, Mrs. Harold K. Beecher, 1511 Mahantongo St., Pottsville, Pa.

Helen Lowengrund Jacoby writes of an uneventful Summer at White Plains, but says her husband has usurped enough excitement for all the family, "for he spent last Winter in Japan engaged in reconstruction work for the Mitsui Company, where he met many interesting people and formed a very high estimate of Japanese manners and morals." Helen was asked to accompany him but would not leave the children.

Louise Fleischmann Maclay has a son born in June whose name is Alfred Barmore Maclay, Junior, but he is called Hal for short.

Maria Smith is doing graduate work in Latin at the University of Pennsylvania, and teaching Latin at the Shipley School.

Alice Lauterbach Flint motored to Nova Scotia with her husband for their vacation period, but found the roads so poor that they returned by boat, and had an unpleasant experience in one of the hurricanes that came to our shores this Summer.

Helen Sandison with her sister Lois (B.M. '16) stayed in their Poughkeepsie house until the middle of Summer getting Vassar's 325 Freshmen safely entered. Then at Ogunquit for a month of pure recreation.

(There might be more 1906 notes if the Editor could get more replies to her postals.)

1907

Class Editor, Eunice Morgan Schenck, Low Buildings, Bryn Mawr, Pa.

Lidie Babb Weadley, ex-1907, died on August 31, 1922, after an illness that lasted since February. In fact, she had never fully recovered her strength after her heroic fight with a forest fire in 1913. Her friends in 1907 wish to extend their sympathy to her aunt, Miss Mary M. Babb, of Strafford, Pennsylvania.

The Class also extends its deepest sympathy to Mabel Foster Spinney, whose husband, William Spinney, died early in September.

Mary Isabelle O'Sullivan has been abroad on a special travelling scholarship doing research at the British Museum for her Ph.D. dissertation.

Peggy Ayer Barnes reports a series of lyric postal cards from Mabel from the Lake Country.

Margaret Augur spent all summer at Greenwich, overseeing the building of Rosemary's new hall.

Harriot Houghteling returned to her work with the Grenfell Mission in Labrador, the end of June. This Winter she and her sister, Leila Houghteling (1911) have taken an apartment at 1210 Astor Street, Chicago, "where they hope any members of the Class, passing through the city, will, etc., etc."

1908

Class Editor, Mrs. William H. Best, 1198 Bushwick Ave., Brooklyn, N. Y.

Louise Hyman Pollak has been appointed a Trustee of the Cincinnati Public Library, and anticipates an interesting and very strenuous term of three years. She writes: "We are trying to get the voters to pass a bond issue for the building of a new library, which we need very badly; and if the bonds carry at the election, the seven trustees will have a big job."

Another reason why this fall will be strenuous for Louise, is that she has been elected First Vice-President of the League of Women Voters, and is swamped with demands for speakers for election. We feel sure she will need all the extra vitality she stored up during her summer in Colorado Springs.

Anna King's "much beloved job" is in the Cornell Clinic, a department of Cornell University Medical College. She is Chief Clinic Executive, with a staff of some seventeen medical social workers and thirteen clerks. (Incidentally, Anna's correspondence came to us via her own private secretary.)

Comments by Mrs. Laurence Todd (Constance Leupps Todd) on her year in Europe:

"I remember years ago when Betty Martin said it was possible to take young children to pre-war Europe comfortably, it staggered my imagination. We found it true, even for post-war Europe, from which we returned in October. We spent the winter in Italy, at a perfect little hotel on the Fiesole hillside above Florence, and in May we parked the children (boys, five and seven then) in Paris with an American governess, and Mr. Todd and I went up to Berlin, and thence to Moscow.

And there we saw what we believe to be the only orderly, sane, peace-promising country in Europe. It is of course very much in the making still. Eight years of civil war, famine, typhus, and blockade are enough to reduce any country to its lowest terms. For two years they have been building; and building in a way the world has never before seen. I tell everyone to read Anna Louise Strong's new book, *The First Time in History* for an informed and graphic and very interesting picture of it. Anna Louise was at Bryn Mawr as a student for a year, proving the authenticity of her account."

1909

Class Editor, Mrs. Rollin T. Chamberlin, 5492 South Shore Drive, Chicago, Illinois.

Mary Allen is living at 7 Hilliard Place, Cambridge, Mass., with Pleasaunce Parsons and Mary Nearing. They want it known, so that any "1909ers or B.M.'s in general" who may be in the neighborhood, will not overlook them. Mary Allen did volunteer work through the Spring on the General Allen Committee for German Child Feeding. Later she spent a month on a Wyoming ranch.

Frances Browne is reported as having spent the Summer in England.

Dorothy Child was seen recently in Philadelphia, "addressing a class of ninety-one Board of Education Nurses." The same reporter says, "Dorothy is doing wonderful work with Child Nutrition in the Public Schools." Can't you tell us more about it, D. Child?

Bertha Ehlers says, "I still have the best job in the world, selling life-insurance, and I expect to keep on having it. With Life Insurance in the Winter, and Lake George in the Summer, life is very full." The Lake George camp is off by itself, with nothing about it but woods, and water,— "It's the sweetest place in the world."

Frances Ferris was attending the Harvard Summer School last Summer.

Mary Nearing is continuing the study and practice of architecture and landscape architecture.

Shirley Putnam O'Hare has returned from Europe, and is now living in Waltham,

Pleasaunce Parsons has just delighted the Editor with a long and newsy letter. She says, "Mary Nearing and I were talking about the BRYN MAWR ALUMNAE BULLETIN, and complained about the paucity of news of 1909. Later we agreed in justice that we had not contributed anything ourselves for a long time. So, just to give us the whip hand over non-co-operative members, I'm sending you a line or two." The Editor hopes that other members of the Class will read, mark, learn, and act accordingly! The Class will sympathize with Pleasaunce in her loss of her father last January. Since then, the Florida home has been sold, and Pleasaunce is now living with May Allen and Mary Nearing. "We are only four minutes walk from Harvard Square, so there is no good reason why any 1909ers, passing through Boston should not make us a visit." Pleasaunce has been occupied temporarily in the editorial office of the *Open Road*, a young men's magazine.

Lucy Van Wagenen spent June at Bar Barbor, Maine, "my usual Summer practice." Then she went abroad. She says, "my first trip, and I am much thrilled. I visit a week in London, fly to the Hague, visit in Frankfurt, take a walking trip in the Bavarian Alps, go to Paris and then to Southern France and Italy. Home in October, to begin my New York season.

Mary Goodwin Storrs writes from China, Shaown Fukien, of floods and famines and revolutionary bandits. But still they smile and sing, "What's the use of worrying if it does rain all the while, if you've a tin of milk to feed your child, just pack up your troubles in your river box, and smile, smile, smile!" They spent the Summer at Kuliang."

1910

Class Editor, Marion Kirk, 1013 Farragut Terrace, Philadelphia, Penna.

Mabel Ashley is back again at the Lenox School, as secretary, after giving up her work for a while on account of a rundown condition. Apie describes her Summer as spent in a hammock, so perhaps she will find a Winter spent at the typewriter somewhat more interesting.

Helen Bley Pope is teaching Greek and Latin at Hunter College, New York. She has recovered her American citizenship by virtue of the Cable Law, and has shortened her name to Pope, to avoid further difficulties. She has begun studying at Columbia University and expects sometime to get a Ph.D. there. Her address is 7 Grammercy West.

Grace Branham is continuing her teaching at the Dominican College at San Rafael, California, and will soon take the veil there.

A letter addressed to Annina De Angelis at 38 N. Burnet Street, East Orange, New Jersey, has been returned. The Class Editor will be glad if Annina will send her the correct address and give an account of herself for the past year or more.

Elsa Denison Voorhees returned from a trip to Europe in May and spent the Summer with her family on their farm in New Hampshire. They had a small music and rhythm school there, and learned a lot about rhythmic dancing. The three children are now attending school, and Elsa is enjoying her leisure in studying music again.

Beth Hibben Scoon reports the acquisition of a new car, which she is slowly learning to run,—or rather learning to run slowly, she says, for her average speed is ten miles an hour. Beth and her family spent the Summer in Greensboro, Vermont. Mr. Scoon is now teaching philosophy instead of classics. Their little boy is now in the third grade.

Janet Howell Clark is still at Johns Hopkins, but has now attained the dignity of associate professor of Physiological Hygiene. She reports that she has just written a book called "Lighting in Relation to Public Health. It's a very dull book." Little Anne Janet is splendid and is in the second Primary grade. (It is good to know that Janet does not find all her offspring dull.)

Elizabeth Tappan is teaching Latin at Vassar College.

1914

Class Editor, Ida Pritchett, 155 E. 73rd St., New York City.

Laura Delano Houghteling (Mrs. James L. Houghteling), went to Fairhaven with her family this Summer.

Helen Shaw Crosby (Mrs. William A. Crosby) has gone abroad with her entire family.

Edwina Warren is reported to be making money in the insurance business, and sailing the rest of the time.

Leah Cadbury is still being Secretary to the Manager of the Old Corner Bookshop, each of them having a large desk in a 2x4 room in the new store, and Cad admits that she adores her job. She went to Miss

Applebee's hockey camp this Summer. She is giving up her "Country House" this Winter because she thinks she is getting too old to stand the leaks in the roof! She hopes to stay in Concord, however.

Eugenia Jackson Comey (Mrs. Arthur Comey) spent the Summer partly in Cohasset, and partly in climbing with her husband and her two children.

Dorothy Godfrey Wayman (Mrs. Charles S. Wayman) ex-1914, has returned from Japan, and is living in Dedham.

Anne White Harper (Mrs. Paul Harper) has a son, born in May.

Nancy Cabot Osborne (Mrs. Maurice Osborne), ex-1914, has a new baby, born last Spring.

Eleanor Allen Mitchum (Mrs. Colis Mitchum) has a daughter, born in June.

Betty Lord went abroad this Summer with her family.

Isabel Benedict is running the library at the Western Electric in New York.

Ida Pritchett has an apartment this Winter at 155 East Seventy-third Street, New York, and will be charmed to supply tea to members of the Class almost any time. She would be charmed likewise to receive news items for the BULLETIN from members of the Class unable to call her bluff about tea, and she would like to announce that the old threat to manufacture news items if the present dearth of authentic ones continues, still holds good and may go into effect almost any minute. She would like to add that her abilities in this line have lost nothing with age, and to earnestly advise the Class to be warned in time!

1915

Class Editor, Mrs. James Austin Stone, 3015 Forty-fourth Street, Washington, D. C.

Susan Nichols has announced her engagement to Mr. Harold Trowbridge Pulsifer, Harvard 1911, owner and publisher of the *Outlook*. After November 1, her address will be 9 East Tenth Street, New York City.

1916

Class Editor, Mrs. Webb I. Vorys, 63 Parkwood Avenue, Columbus, Ohio.

Anna Sears Davis (Mrs. Warren G.) has a second child, a son, born July 21, 1924. She has named him Gilbert Sears Davis.

Margaret Mabon Henderson (Mrs. David

K.) has a third little girl, Agnes Davidson Henderson, born on July 12th.

Margaret Russell Kellen (Mrs. Roger S.) has a third child, a second daughter, Mercy Kellen, born on June 27th.

Dorothy Packard Holt (Mrs. Farrington) has a second daughter, Frances Jane, born on June 21st.

Louise Dillingham has been traveling in Europe this summer with her three sisters, and this fall she will study at the Sorbonne, doing work for her Ph.D.

Clara Heydemann will teach in a girls' school in California this winter.

Helen Chase Rand (Mrs. Rufus) has another little girl, born in the spring.

Buckner Kirk sailed for Europe on May 27th.

Fredrika Kellogg Jouett (Mrs. John H.) is now living in San Antonio.

Dorothy Deneen Blow (Mrs. Allmand) has been in Estes Park, Colorado, with her family for the summer.

Lilla Worthington Kirkpatrick (Mrs. James H.), in spite of two young sons, has a half-time job in New York City.

1918

Class Editor, Helen Edward Walker, 418 Oakwood Boulevard, Chicago, Illinois.

Ruth Cheney Streeter spent the Summer with her growing family at Nantucket, and writes: "In my present condition of servitude it is just as well that there is no romance to report!—unless you would call a glimpse of the Prince of Wales at the Polo Match romance. Considering that there were several thousand other Americans present, however, the edge of my enthusiasm was dulled."

Margaret C. Timpson says that she is occupied in looking for a job; that she returned last June from a trip around the world, and does not know when she will start off again; and that she has bobbed her hair, an item which was not intended for publication, but which is too good to keep.

Molly Cordingley Stevens has moved to "North Andover forever!" where she is busy planning to build a new house in the Spring. She writes: "Two wonderful months of travel in France, Italy, Switzerland, England and Scotland. We crossed with twenty-five Bryn Mawrters, and Dr. and Mrs. Grenfell. Just missed connections with Buffy in Northern England.

Second honeymoons are a close second, as we found out while travelling. A nice visit from Helen Walker during the wedding festivities of a mutual friend brought back vividly our College days. Another bobette is Helen."

Marian O'Connor Duble has a son, Peter Wright Duble, aged eight months.

Helen Whitcomb was married in June to Mr. John S. Barss, and is living in Andover, Massachusetts.

Adelaide Shaffer Kuntz is lost for the time being, three communications to her at three different addresses having been returned. The Class Editor will appreciate any information as to her correct address.

Laura Pearson Pratt spent the Summer in Squirrel Island, Maine, "with a small retinue, consisting of four children, two nurses, seven dogs, and three trunks." Her third daughter, born in May is "now named Lalla Joan Pratt, is fat, placid, and still fairly interesting to Hildreth, Betty, and Amasa Pratt, 2nd."

Martha Bailey is at present travelling in England, and on the continent.

Frances Buffum was married on May 22nd to Mr. Arthur Snyder, and is now in England.

Katharine Dufourque Kelley is keeping house and motoring week-ends, mostly in New England. She writes that Tude Huff has been abroad all Summer, and is now in Egypt.

Marjorie Jefferies was married on August 9th to Dr. George W. Wagoner, of Johnstown, Pennsylvania. Doctor Wagoner holds the Hunterian Fellowship in Surgery at the University of Pennsylvania Hospital for 1924. Mrs. Wagoner was Physician to the Summer School, Bryn Mawr College, 1924, and is Associate Physician to the College 1924-25 term.

Two letters arrived too late to be included in the reunion booklet, so we quote from them here.

Helen Alexander writes, from Cloudcroft, New Mexico: "I was highly insulted to read in the booklet that I was among those whose addresses were unknown. I, who have always at least had an address! El Paso was a bit warm, to put it mildly. After a few days of 100 and over, I tossed up my job, and am going to have a perfectly grand loaf in New Mexico. Cloudcroft is a lovely summer resort in the mountains, 9000 feet elevation, if you please!

Have been here two weeks and shall stay over the Fourth of July for a three-day rodeo to be .held then. Have my eye on a cattle ranch where I hope to spend several months. It should be interesting to Eastern eyes. I am hoping to come to New York next summer and see you all."

Martha Bailey writes: "My *modus vivendi* has been a compromise—of course. One year I stay at home, keep house, play golf, work on half a dozen charities, even teach a Sunday School class, in short, am thoroughly dull and domesticated. Then I depart for Brazil or Sicily and a series of the most ridiculous adventures. That trip to South America seemed more like a fairy tale than real life, one of the kind where you have a magic ring and all your wishes are fulfilled. Of course, sometimes, like Midas and other wishers, I wished I hadn't.

One of the absurd things I did on my last trip to Europe was to register for a summer course at Cambridge. I went there, lived in the college halls, and went to the college lectures, long enough (three days) to make me appreciate Bryn Mawr, and then I bolted to London to see Lucy Chew.

Now it's time for me to be off again. I had arranged to sail on April 16th, but went to the hospital instead, which completely annihilated my plans. So now, tonsilless and planless, I am awaiting developments, with a passport made out for India and Italy, England and Africa. But I hope that wherever I go, I shall have the good luck to run into some of 1918."

1919

Class Editor, Frederica Howell, 211 Ballantine Parkway, Newark, N. J.

Great days for matrimony—

Nan Thorndike has announced her engagement to Dr. John Rock of Boston, Harvard 1915. She is to be married in January.

Annett Stiles is engaged to Mr. Sidney F. Greeley, Harvard 1915, of Winnetka, Illinois. Mr. Greeley is now working in Framingham, Mass., where Anne expects they will live after the wedding.

Mary Ewen was married to Mr. Stephen Milton Simpson on August 30th. Her new address is 449 West 123rd Street, New York City.

Corinne Mendenhall is to be married to Mr. Gordon Catty on November 22nd.

Faff Keller is Assistant Mathematics Instructor at the Shipley School, and Bi Lab Demonstrator at College. In her spare time, she runs her house and daughter, and does her father's office work—mere trifles!

Tip's address this Winter is 99 Pinkney Street, Boston. She is sharing a flat with several other girls, among them Elizabeth Cope '21.

Helen Huntting Fulton's address is 516 University Avenue, Southeast, Minneapolis.

The Class wishes to express its deep sympathy to Eleanor Marquand, whose father, Professor Allan Marquand, died late in September after a long and trying illness.

1920

Class Editor, Helene Zinsser, 6 West Ninth Street, New York City,

It is with great sorrow that we record the death, in September, of Anna Eberbach Augsburg. The Class extends its sincere sympathy to her husband and her mother.

1921

Class Editor, Betty Kellogg, 144 Buckingham Street, Waterbury, Conn.

Nancy Porter was married on May 24th to Michael W. Straus. Her address is 1018 North State Street, Chicago, Ill.

Betsey Kales' engagement was announced this Summer to Dr. Francis Straus, Nancy's brother-in-law, and when last heard from expected to be married in August, and live this Winter on the West Side in Chicago, completing the third year of her medical course. That was in July, when Betsey was starting for Montana again in the Ford. Her trip was interrupted by an attack of sciatica, which caused her fiancé to order her return.

Grace Hendricks was married on July 4th to George W. Patterson, Jr. Her four dogs did not sit in the front pew as reported.

Stoney was married September 20th to Archibald Iovine McColl.

J. P. and Eleanore Boswell are still decorating the staff at Rosemary, J. P. in the Latin department, and Eleanore as head of the English department.

Marg Archbald has a job in Philadelphia as private secretary to a lawyer. She is living at the College Club, 1300 Spruce St.

Among those who sailed for Europe this Summer were Biffy, Copey, Becky Marshall, Silvine, and Bettina Warburg The full passenger list will be published later.

Mary Baldwin returned this Summer from a year's trip in Europe.

Kindly send us some more news items!

1922

Class Editor, Serena Hand, 40 West Ninth Street, New York City.

Ethel Brown is at the School of Social Work in New York.

Anna Dom is teaching in New Mexico.

Edith Finch will be at Bryn Mawr this Winter as Miss Donnelly's reader.

Dorothy Ferguson, Eleanor Gabell, and Mabel Meng were in France this Summer.

K. Gardner and Jeannette Palache are teaching in the Buckingham School in Cambridge.

Serena Hand is studying at Columbia.

Elizabeth Hall is teaching at Wykeham Rise.

Mary Douglas Hay is spending the Winter in Europe.

Octavia Howard is finishing her training this year at the Union Memorial Hospital in Baltimore.

Ray Neel is teaching at Miss Walker's School.

Alice Nicoll is teaching at the Holton Arms School in Washington

Cornelia Skinner is acting in a play called *In His Arms*.

Margaret Speer is Warden of Rockefeller Hall.

Katherine Stiles was married to Mr. Caroll Harrington on October 4th, at Fitchburg, Massachusetts. They are going to live in Providence.

Sylva Thurlow wrote from Cambridge:

"There are wonderful opportunities here for hearing good music, a concert almost every week. And two of the research people at the labs play beautifully and have me in quite often and play for me.

"I love the work here and the people and the lovely walks among old buildings and through quaint villages. I have just come back from a two weeks' holiday, part of it spent in Birmingham, where there was a constant round of dances, theatres, teas, etc., and the rest in Wales, where we spent a whole week climbing mountains and watching the sea. It was glorious and did me worlds of good. I took Carlyle's *French Revolution* along with me to read, but somehow it would not go well with Wales, so I ended up with Jeffery Farnol.

"I have not seen any really good plays since I've been here. Cambridge is too small a place to get the good campanies and I have not yet seen London. That has been saved for Easter vacation.

"I do wish you were here for some walks. There is the dear little river Cam with its willows and stone bridges, and everywhere are little villages with thatched-roofed houses and old gardens. Here and there one finds a great house with imposing gates and lawns, and not far away is an old cathedral begun in 900. So one never is at a loss for something to see. The trouble is to find time to see it all. Research keeps one tied down quite a bit, but then the work is so fascinating that I hardly mind being tied down.

"While I was away I was taken to see Stratford-on-Avon. Harvard was born there, also, in a lovely old house with heavy oak beams. The Shakespeare house is very fine, but it is rather spoiled by a lot of horrible old men and women acting as guides, who drag you from something you want to look at to something you don't and who all have to be tipped. One does nothing but tip in England. And I do hate old places all fixed up for you to look at, but I suppose they must do it."

Margie Tyler has announced her engagement to Mr. Samuel Paul, of Chestnut Hill, Philadelphia.

Mildred Voorhees has a new job in the Charity Organization Society in New York.

1923

Class Editor, no one, *pro tem.*

Celestine Goddard is continuing her job as secretary to Mr. E. C. Carter, former head of the Y. M. C. A. (during the war).

Haroldine Humphreys is playing the part of the Nun in the *Miracle*, alternating with Rosamond Pinchot, and appearing about three times a week.

Ann Fraser Brewer returns to New Haven with her husband, who is just taking his Ph.D. exams in English, and her daughter, Effie Leighton, who is a perfect darling, and has big blue eyes like her mother. I have just been visiting Ann, and from all I can see, I think Effie will make a splendid geologist.

Helen Hoyt will study "Religious Education" at Teachers College in New York, and will take her M.A. in that subject.

Hi Price and K. Strauss symbolize the charm and culture and social development of the Class, as they have not yet taken to gradding or to stenography. K. knows a great deal of geography, due to her recent trip around the globe; speaks pidgin English and can ride in a rickshaw with the utmost grace.

Gussie Howell has been visiting Florence in California, and they both expect to come East late in September.

D. M. sailed on the 4th of October to spend the winter in Paris, studying at the Sorbonne.

1924

Class Editor, Mildred Buchanan, Powelton Apartments, Philadelphia, Pa.

Mary Rodney, Elizabeth Henderson, Alice Bingeman, K. Nielson, and R. Murray Fansler, are doing graduate work at College. Mary Cheston, B. Ling, M. L. White, and Anne Shiras, are back finishing their courses.

Sully, Bess Pearson, and Buck were at Hockey Camp together. Sully has organized a team in New York, which she calls the "Pagans," because they play on Sunday.

Buck is at College, doing part-time coaching in place of Trev, who was kept out by immigration laws.

The Class was well represented at Parade Night. Becca and Rus were there in addition to the ones already mentioned as being at College.

Pam has a new job in Chicago with Marshall Field.

Elsa Molitor is taking a business course.

Freda Rosenkoff and Elizabeth Robbins are substituting in the schools around Philadelphia.

Ellie Requa, and Lou Sanford spent a few days at College. Lou is studying music.

ENGAGED

Eliza Bailey to Mr. Frederick Wright.

MARRIED

Katherine Blackwell to Mr. Frederic A. Cammann.

Marie Louise Kirk to Dr. Julius Lane Wilson.

Irene Wallace to Mr. David Vogels.

CONTENTS

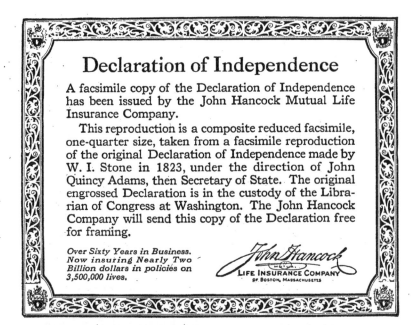

Declaration of Independence

A facsimile copy of the Declaration of Independence has been issued by the John Hancock Mutual Life Insurance Company.

This reproduction is a composite reduced facsimile, one-quarter size, taken from a facsimile reproduction of the original Declaration of Independence made by W. I. Stone in 1823, under the direction of John Quincy Adams, then Secretary of State. The original engrossed Declaration is in the custody of the Librarian of Congress at Washington. The John Hancock Company will send this copy of the Declaration free for framing.

Over Sixty Years in Business.
Now insuring Nearly Two
Billion dollars in policies on
3,500,000 lives.

John Hancock
LIFE INSURANCE COMPANY
OF BOSTON, MASSACHUSETTS

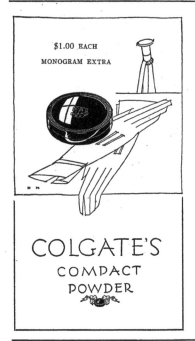

$1.00 EACH

MONOGRAM EXTRA

COLGATE'S
COMPACT
POWDER

A Worthwhile
Baby Gift

Means' BASKETWEAVE BABY BLANKETS

Your friends will be delighted to receive one of these downy blankets for the new arrival. A Basketweave Baby Blanket, warm and fleecy, will be a most fitting gift and one that the mother will always appreciate.

The Basketweave Baby Blankets are soft, warm and light in weight with the texture and durability that only a masterpiece of the hand loom can have. They will not shrink or lose shape in washing.

These wooly coverings give adequate warmth without being burdensome in weight. And the lifetime wear of the Basketweave Blankets wins unvarying popularity.

Colors: White blankets banded with blue, pink or buff. Solid blue, pink or buff blankets banded with white.

Bassinet size 30x40 in., $5 postpaid
Crib size 36x50 in., $7 postpaid

ORDER BY MAIL or send for
folder and sample of material.

Means Weave Shop
38 Howe Street : Lowell, Mass.

SCHOOL DIRECTORY

The Bryant Teachers Bureau, Inc.

711-12-13 Witherspoon Building   Philadelphia, Penna.

Friendly, personal interest; prompt intelligent service.

The Agency you will recommend to your friends.

WE PLACE MANY BRYN MAWR GRADUATES EACH YEAR

Cathedral School of St. Mary

GARDEN CITY, LONG ISLAND, N. Y.

A school for Girls 19 miles from New York. College preparatory and general courses. Music. Art and Domestic Science. Catalogue on request. Box B.

Miriam A. Bytel, A. B., Radcliffe, Principal
Bertha Gordon Wood, A. B., Bryn Mawr, Ass't Principal

St. Timothy's School for Girls

CATONSVILLE, MARYLAND

Founded 1882

COLLEGE PREPARATORY

Miss J. R. HEATH } Heads of the School
Miss L. McE. FOWLER }

MISS MADEIRA'S SCHOOL

1330 19th St., N. W.   Washington, D. C.

A Resident and Day School

for Girls

LUCY MADEIRA WING, A.B.

MRS. DAVID LAFOREST WING
Head Mistress

MISS WRIGHT'S SCHOOL

Bryn Mawr, Pa.

Prepares for Bryn Mawr and
College Board Examinations

ROGERS HALL

A SCHOOL FOR GIRLS

Thorough preparation for college entrance examinations. Graduate course of two years for high school graduates. Complete equipment. 40 minutes from Boston.

MISS OLIVE SEWALL PARSONS, B.A.

Principal

Lowell, Massachusetts

The Episcopal Academy

(Founded 1785)

CITY LINE, OVERBROOK, PA.

A country day school for boys from second grade to college. Separate lower school for boys from seven years up. Enjoys the patronage of Bryn Mawr Alumnae

WYKEHAM RISE

WASHINGTON, CONNECTICUT

A COUNTRY SCHOOL FOR GIRLS

Prepares for Bryn Mawr and Other Colleges

MISS GILDNER'S PRINCETON SCHOOL

FOR GIRLS

Prepares for best eastern colleges and Board examinations. Also for Advanced College-entrance Two-year Graduate Course. Music. Art. Expression. Sports. Riding. Outdoor and Indoor Athletics. Estate of beauty. Mile from town.

Miss Laura M. Gildner, A.M., Director
Princeton, New Jersey

The Bryn Mawr College Calendar, 1925

A Beautiful Calendar printed on hand cut paper and illustrated by delightful etchings of Pembroke Arch, Pembroke East, the Library, and the Cloister, by Mr. G. A. Bradshaw.

A limited number of copies will be printed

The Calendars may be obtained from the Publicity Office, Bryn Mawr College, and from local Bryn Mawr Clubs after November 15th.

Price each, at office *$1.00*
Price each, on mailing orders . . . *$1.25*

SCHOOL DIRECTORY

COLLEGE WOMEN

Who know the meaning of thoroughness and who take pride in scholarly accuracy are in special demand for literary and editorial work of a high character.

We are prepared to give by correspondence

A Complete Professional Training

to a limited number of suitable candidates who are interested in fitting themselves for a second profession.

For further information address

The Mawson Editorial School

25 Huntington Avenue   Boston, Massachusetts

HILLSIDE
A School for Girls
NORWALK   CONNECTICUT

In a beautiful New England town, one hour from New York. Girls from all parts of the country. Four residences, schoolhouse, gymnasium. Extensive grounds. Preparation for all colleges. Special courses. Outdoor life. Horseback riding. Catalog.

Margaret R. Brendlinger, A.B., Vassar
Vida Hunt Francis, A.B., Smith, *Principals*

The Harcum School
BRYN MAWR, PA.

Prepares for Bryn Mawr and all leading colleges

Musical Course prepares for the Department of Music of Bryn Mawr College
EDITH H. HARCUM, Head of School
L. MAY WILLIS, Principal

THE
Mary C. Wheeler Town and Country School
PROVIDENCE, RHODE ISLAND

Preparation for Bryn Mawr and College Board Examinations

Out door sports   Junior Country Residence

FERRY HALL
A Resident and Day School for Girls
LAKE FOREST, ILLINOIS
On Lake Michigan, near Chicago

College Preparatory, General and Advanced Courses. Departments of Music, Home Economics, Expression, and Art. *Supervised Athletics and Swimming Pool.*

Eloise R. Tremain, A.B., Bryn Mawr, Principal

MISS RANSOM and MISS BRIDGES' SCHOOL
HAZEL LANE, PIEDMONT (Suburb of San Francisco)

College Preparatory

MARION RANSOM } Headmistresses
EDITH BRIDGES

The Katharine Branson School
ROSS, CALIFORNIA   Across the Bay from San Francisco

A Country School   College Preparatory
Heads
Katharine Fleming Branson, A. B., Bryn Mawr
Laura Elizabeth Branson, A. B., Bryn Mawr

THE AGNES IRWIN SCHOOL
2009-2011 Delancey Place, Philadelphia

A College Preparatory
SCHOOL FOR GIRLS

JOSEPHINE A. NATT, A.B., Headmistress
BERTHA M. LAWS, A.B., Secretary-Treasurer

The Ethel Walker School
SIMSBURY, CONNECTICUT

Head of School
ETHEL WALKER SMITH, A.M. Bryn Mawr College
Head Mistress
JESSIE GERMAIN HEWITT, A.B. Bryn Mawr College

Miss Beard's School for Girls
ORANGE, NEW JERSEY

A country school near New York. College preparatory, special courses. Art, Domestic Arts and Science. Supervised physical work. Agnes Miles Music School affiliated with Miss Beard's School.

MISS LUCIE C. BEARD, Head Mistress

ROSEMARY HALL
No elective courses
Prepares for college
Preferably Bryn Mawr

Caroline Ruutz-Rees, Ph.D. } Head Mistresses
Mary E. Lowndes, Litt.D.

GREENWICH   CONNECTICUT

The Shipley School
Bryn Mawr, Pennsylvania

Preparatory to Bryn Mawr College

Alice G. Howland, Eleanor O. Brownell, Principals

THE MISSES KIRK'S
College Preparatory School

PREPARATORY TO BRYN MAWR COLLEGE
Individual instruction. Athletics.

Clovercroft, Montgomery Avenue, Rosemont, Pa.
Mail, telephone and telegraph address: Bryn Mawr, Pa.

The Baldwin School
A Country School for Girls
BRYN MAWR   PENNSYLVANIA

Preparation for Bryn Mawr, Mount Holyoke, Smith, Vassar and Wellesley colleges. Abundant outdoor life. Hockey, basketball, tennis.

ELIZABETH FORREST JOHNSON, A.B.
Head

In spite of its size and the enormous power developed by this reversing blooming mill motor it reverses many times a minute. Its maximum rating is 22,000 h.p., equivalent to the muscle power of 176,000 men.

"The 100,000 Man'

Look closely at the picture of this great motor installed in the plant of a large steel company, and you will see the monogram of the General Electric Company, an organization of men and women who produce equipment by which electricity does *more* and *better* work.

Of Napoleon it was said that his presence on the battlefield was equivalent to 100,000 additional men. "The 100,000 man," his enemies called him.

Napoleon dealt in death. Big General Electric motors, like the one in the picture, lift heavy loads off human shoulders, and contribute to the enrichment of life.

GENERAL ELECTRIC

The
BRYN MAWR
ALUMNAE
BULLETIN

"NO GREATER GIFT"

THE WASHINGTON COUNCIL

ANATOLE FRANCE

DECEMBER
1924

Vol. IV   No. 10

Bryn Mawr College Calendar, 1925

A Beautiful Calendar printed on hand cut paper and illustrated by delightful etchings by Mr. G. A. Bradshaw.

A limited number of copies will be printed

The Calendars may be obtained from the Publicity Office, Bryn Mawr College, and from local Bryn Mawr Clubs; the proceeds will be devoted to the Music Drive.

Price each, at office $1.00
Price each, on mailing orders $1.25

(Cheques payable to Bryn Mawr College)

BRYN MAWR ALUMNAE BULLETIN

OFFICIAL PUBLICATION OF
THE BRYN MAWR ALUMNAE ASSOCIATION

EVELYN PAGE, '23, *Editor*
ESTHER L. RHOADS, '23, *Business Manager*

EDITORIAL BOARD

LUCY M. DONNELLY, '93
ELEANOR FLEISHER REISMAN, '03
CAROLINE MORROW CHADWICK-COLLINS, '05

ADELAIDE W. NEALL, '06
MAY EGAN STOKES, '11
MARGARET REEVE CARY, 1907, *ex-officio*

Subscription Price, $1.50 a Year   *Single Copies, 25 Cents*
Checks should be drawn to the order of Bryn Mawr Alumnae Bulletin
Published monthly, except August and September, at 1006 Arch St., Philadelphia, Pa.

VOL. IV   DECEMBER, 1924   No. 10

THE ALUMNAE COUNCIL

The Alumnae Council is fast making for itself a history that is both interesting and distinguished. In glancing back over its old minutes, and over the plan for its organization, we are keenly interested to see how it has grown in membership and in scope, how many famous Alumnae have attended its meetings, and how many problems have been solved in its sessions.

The Council has, besides the transaction of the business that comes before it, a twofold function. It gives the Councillors who come together once a year from great distances a feeling of the unity of the Alumnae of Bryn Mawr. They hear of the achievements of the College, of the difficulties it has surmounted, of its needs and of its beauties. They see women of early and recent classes, brought together with a common interest and a common purpose. They not only receive information, but on returning to their homes they carry to their constituents the facts and impressions which they have gathered. Aside from this geographically widespread influence, the Council arouses both interest and activity in the place in which its meeting is held. The local Alumnae and even those who have only a slight or no connection with the College are given a concrete example of the lively part played on its behalf by its graduates. The name and reputation of the College are thus made more real and the aims of the College and its Alumnae are better understood.

The Council is made possible through the efforts of a few devoted Alumnae. It is not a small thing to ask twenty-five busy women to drop their other occupations and spend three or four days away from home, working exhaustively over a body of material, in order to carry home with them for the benefit of their constituents clearly formed opinions and information based on fact. Nor is it a small thing for the few Alumnae, living in one city, to entertain the Council during its meetings. When we look back on the succession of hospitable and delightful hostesses who have opened their houses to the Councillors, we realize what a great deal of effort they expended, not only without complaint, but with enthusiasm.

The full account of the meetings in Washington has been printed on a later page. Here we can only publish our appreciation of the hospitality of the Washington Alumnae. As one of the Councillors said, "The Washington Council was distinguished by its serenity, by the way in which both business and pleasure were made easy." We congratulate Margaret Free Stone, 1915, Councillor for the District, and the members of the Washington Bryn Mawr Club on their intelligent and delightful management of the Council meetings.

MUSIC AT BRYN MAWR

(The following editorial is reprinted from the "College News" of November 19th, by the kind permission of the Editor of the "News.")

The services of the Alumnae to the College are many and important; but perhaps they have made no greater gift than the Music Department. Their work in founding it has been more fruitful than donations of books to the Library, or even of scholarships; for they have made possible the study, elementary and advanced, of an art. No one can deny the value of music as an art, or even as a large part of true culture. Nor can anyone who has had really intelligent instruction in the playing of an instrument or in the history and theory of music, fail to realize the severe mental discipline of music study. Contrast, for a definite and local example, the effort of concentration needed in an ordinary lecture course with that required in the History and Appreciation classes. You can take down the words of the professor almost automatically; but you cannot discuss the form, material and characteristics of a piece of music unless you have listened to it intently.

There is another aspect of the Music Department for which we must express our gratitude to the Alumnae, the evenings of informal music. By giving us the Department they have made possible delightful hours of singing, playing and listening, under wise and stimulating leadership. Thus music loses the artificiality of the "concert habit" and becomes a natural form of expression. We can never repay the Alumnae for their service in forwarding the growing intimacy with music at Bryn Mawr.

ANNOUNCEMENTS

The publication date of the December BULLETIN has been put at December 5th in order to include the account of the Washington Council.

All contributions to the January BULLETIN should be sent to Evelyn Page, Taylor Hall, Bryn Mawr College, before December 10th.

"No Greater Gift"

Two Impressions

By *MARGARET AYER BARNES*, 1907

Radnor students' sitting room on a chill November afternoon—the great curved bow of the window—the blue upholstered furniture — the "good" engravings—the glowing coals of the Radnor fire, rose and black with an occasional flicker of blue and gold flame. Outside the narrow casements a pale blue sky, dim sunlight, high white clouds and bare maple branches tossing in the Bryn Mawr wind. The occasional tramp of student feet in the carpeted corridor — a banging door in a distant wing—a laugh and scuffle of steps on the bare stairway —an inquiring undergraduate glancing in at the open door, curiosity fading from the casual young countenance, indifference taking its place— "O, the Alumnae!"

It is the Alumnae, right enough, some thirty of us, gathered together on the blue furniture this chill November day, intent, as is so often the case with Alumnae, middle-aged and dreary as we needs must be, not on the memories of youth and springtime that our surroundings might well awaken, but on a sordid discussion of ways and means. It is the Music Department that we are discussing and the hope of its permanent endowment, and the discussion would seem to a disinterested witness to be rather a fruitless one as all within that room are already convinced of the value of the Department and the crying need for its support and continuance at Bryn Mawr. President Park speaks to us and voices her profound belief in its educational worth, not only for the forty odd students actually enrolled in the music courses, not only for those who can take part in the informal recitals and sing in the choir, but for the rank and file of the undergraduates whose experience is enriched by the introduction of music into the cultural background of the College. Professor de Laguna tells of Mr. Samuel's recital in Taylor Hall at which the undergraduate audience listened to an entire program of Bach and called for encores which were gladly given by an artist known to be critical in such matters, an artist whose enthusiastic response to applause was evidence that in his opinion (and in the immortal phrase of Mr. George Bernard Shaw), "the audience was a success." Lucy Donnelley adds her word of commendation for the distinction and color that the inclusion of music in the curriculum brings to the life of the College. Eunice Schenck says that no one who has watched the work of the Department for the past three years can question the rigor and integrity of its intellectual standards. She refers to the attitude of the undergraduates and says that the three new classes that have come to the College finding music established there have registered surprise and consternation at the incredible rumor that the Department was endangered by lack of funds and that Bryn Mawr might be without music in the future. She tells us this question is under continual discussion by the students at the moment and that there is but one opinion on the campus, that the Music Department is of vital significance to the life of the College. Frances

Fincke Hand speaks for the interest of the Board of Directors of the College in this problem and Margaret Reeve Cary for that of the Executive Board of the Alumnae Association. Julia Langdon Loomis tells a little of the work of the indomitable New York Committee which has for four years borne the burden of the Department's support. Then Alice Carter Dickerman, their chairman, who has given in unstinted measure for those four years her constructive enthusiasm, moral support and financial aid to their collossal task, rises to introduce a figure as gallant as her own, Mr. Horace Alwyne, the Professor of Music, to whom we owe the success of its courses, the enthusiasm of its students, the success and enthusiasm on which we stand as on a rock in our quest for permanent endowment. He tells us what he thinks of his Department, of its aims and achievements, of the value that he feels it has as a part of that elusive type of training, changing yet unchanged, for which his little Alumnae audience has so much loyalty—Bryn Mawr education.

The meeting is over. The thirty Alumnae in Radnor sitting room are convinced of the worth of our cause. We were convinced before the meeting began. There are thirty Alumnae in that Radnor room. There are twenty-five hundred in the world beyond it. How make them see and feel and understand the critical emergency that has arisen at Bryn Mawr. We wonder a little wearily in spite of the high wave of enthusiasm that has just broken over us. As we are wondering we hear again Mr. Alwyne's voice, "There's a Monday night musical at Miss Ely's tonight. Just the regular thing. If any of you would care to come."

Miss Ely's long, low music room, chairs ranged around the wall, two grand pianos at the window end, a student orchestra tuning its instruments—a scene not particularly evocative of memories in the mind of the average Alumna. But we who have crossed the arch and the orchard in answer to Mr. Alwyn's invitation know that just across Merion Avenue stretches the long yellow line of Pembroke's lighted windows and that over the tops of the apple trees the towers of Pembroke are outlined against the winter sky. The room itself is the temporary possession of the College for the use of its Department of Music. It is so lovely in its simple, informal dignity that we wonder if the very practical auditorium for which we are all so conscientiously striving will ever quite take its place in the heart of the student body. It is filled to overflowing with residents of the campus. Along the walls are casual members of the Faculty and staff, Faculty wives, Alumnae, visiting mothers of students, an occasional Bryn Mawr neighbor, interested as never before in an informal gathering. Hovering over the two pianos are Mr. Alwyne and his assistant, Mr. Willoughby. Professor Brunel is tuning his violin in the midst of the student orchestra. Some fifty students are perched along the great round window seat at the end of the room, their bright heads and eager faces outlined together with the vivid flowers of Miss Ely's branching geraniums against the small black window panes. Two hundred more are sitting on the floor, a confusion of color and sound, yellow heads and brown, an occasional carrot top, laughing faces, bright evening frocks and dark day dresses, a chattering child in a brilliant sweater, a bright red head rising above the tawny fur of a leopard-skin coat. Movement, color, shrill young voices, and always laughter. If anywhere the middle-aged Alumnae can be diverted from that dreary preoccupation with ways and means to those memories of youth and springtime, it will be here. The room is crowded, the doorway is filled, students are standing in the hall and sitting on the steps of the stair beyond. Mr. Alwyne steps forward and strikes a chord on the piano. Instantly silence falls. The last undergraduate stumbles over the feet of a classmate and sinks with a stifled giggle to her seat on the floor. Every face is turned to the piano in eager anticipation. The program begins.

We have first two Bach chorales sung at sight by the audience from mimeographed copies of the music, copies painstakingly prepared by Mr. Willoughby for a penniless department that can afford no sheet music. Then comes a Fantaisie by Schumann played by two students on piano and cello and by Mr. Brunel on the violin. Two folk songs follow, "Po li'l' Lolo, she gwine die" from the Creole, rendered with spirited humor by the student audience, and the more delicate "Moon" from the Japanese. Two students are called from their seats on the floor to play Scenes from Ravel's Mother Goose on two pianos. Then the whole room sings "Bonnie Laddie, Highland Laddie" from a Scotch series written to order by Beethoven, Mr. Alwyn explains, for a Scottish patron. The evening is unbelievably, and all too soon, almost ended. A gesture from Mr. Willoughby and the choir rises. The concert ends, as it began, with Bach and Palestrina chorales. The last note dies and the spell is broken. The musical evening

is over. Pandemonium breaks out in the student audience in an instantaneous burst of talk and laughter and a simultaneous movement toward the door. Breaks out and is quieted again, instantly, by the chord struck on the piano. Mr. Alwyn has an announcement to make. "The choir is singing some church music at the Rosemont church next Thursday afternoon in illustration of the course in appreciation of music. Mr. Willoughby will play some organ music later." Again the diffident invitation: "If any of you would care to come."

In a moment we are standing in Miss Ely's orchard, wondering again, preoccupied Alumnae that we are, just what we can do about it. For the spirit that we saw illuminating the faces of those intent undergraduates must be kept alive in Bryn Mawr. Evenings of this kind must not vanish from the life on the campus. The discipline and training that has made them possible must be continued in the curriculum. In the *College News* of November 19th the students themselves have said, "The Alumnae have made no greater gift to the College than the Music Department. Their work in founding it has been more fruitful than donations of books to the library or even of scholarships, for they have made possible the study, elementary and advanced, of an art. By giving us the Department they have made possible delightful hours of singing, playing and listening under wise and stimulating leadership. Thus music loses the artificiality of the "concert habit" and becomes a natural form of expression. We can never repay the Alumnae for their service in forwarding the growing intimacy with music at Bryn Mawr."

"A growing intimacy with music at Bryn Mawr under wise and stimulating leadership" — we could not improve upon the students' phrase. The work of the Department cannot continue without funds. The budget of the College is already overcrowded. If that music room full of eager students could be transported throughout the country on a magic carpet no further publicity nor propaganda would be needed for the campaign. Can the 2,500 Alumnae in outlying districts be led to visualize for themselves this emergency on the Bryn Mawr campus? If so, permanent endowment for the Department of Music will be assured Bryn Mawr.

Alumnae Activities

ISABEL COOPER, ex-1913
Artist at the Tropical Research Station of the New York Zoological Society

Everyone has his private dream of the ideal job, but few are as fortunate in the realization of this aspiration as is Isabel Cooper, ex-'13. In the June issue of the *Atlantic Monthly*, Miss Cooper describes how her dream has been more than fulfilled:

"A long while ago, I formed a vague magnificent idea of the perfect job for a young woman with artistic tendencies. It was to be so interesting that it would seem more like play than work; it was to require extensive travel in rare and foreign lands: and it was to make some use of the artistic tendencies. I used to dream of such a job as I went bleakly about my various occupations, such as assisting at the legerdemain of interior decorators, or degrading oriental perfections to terms of modern rug-factory . . . And lo, the dream came true. The perfect job is mine. The vague magnificent idea had given me no hint of the fantastic delight in store for me. Several years ago I began to try my hand at sketching animals from life, at the Tropical Research Station of the New York Zoölogical Society, in British Guiana. Lately this nebulous project has become a real and fascinating job—Staff Artist of the Station."

Miss Cooper is more than Staff Artist of the Station at Kartabo Point on the Essequibo River; she is also Staff Artist for Mr. Beebe, the Director of Tropical Research, which means that she was a member of the party which sailed from New York on the steam yacht Noma, in the Spring of 1923 on the Harrison Williams Expedition to Galapagos. Miss Cooper's scientific preparation for this position was almost nil, but scientific ability is not the only, nor always the most important consideration in the selection of the personnel of such expeditions. Miss Cooper tells of one member of the party whose interest in the technical goal was only spasmodic, whose specimens would burst their containers at odd moments of the day and night with startling retorts and suffocating odors, and yet who added more to the ultimate success of the group than an expert who failed to see either the beauty or the humor of the undertaking.

On these expeditions, Miss Cooper's particular field is the sketching from life of the various specimens, especially those whose colors fade or change at death, or which are distorted by preservatives. Brilliantly-colored snakes, for example, lose their gorgeous pigments when they die, and become the brittle lack-lustre creatures that grace the defunct foliage of museum exhibits. These living models are sometimes partially anæsthetized, but more often not. Miss Cooper holds her bright-hued subjects in one hand and reproduces their fantastic coloring with the other. Frequently the wriggling, scaly tails of her models wreak havoc among her paints and inks, and often her wily prisoners effect an escape. Once after she had been working with a large boa constrictor for several days, and the snake was almost dead from chloroform, she allowed an inexperienced photographer of the party to borrow it. The unsuspecting photographer arranged the coils of the somnolent reptile to suit his purpose and then went in search of his cameras. When he returned the boa constrictor had vanished. The yells of the thwarted and terrified photog-rapher soon brought the rest of the party to the scene of action. After a short search, the unhappy boa was recaptured and another dose of chloroform was administered, but the enthusiasm of the photographer had waned.

Of course the greatest interest and thrill for Miss Cooper comes from the fact that she has opened a new field and must invent her own technique as she goes along. Art schools do not offer courses in snake-painting, and only experience can train one to hold venomous serpents without repulsion. Dozens of unexpected and perplexing questions arise with every model, and there is no comforting precedent to which one may turn.

Some examples, although not nearly enough, of Miss Cooper's unique work are to be found in Mr. Beebe's account of the expedition to Galapagos (*Galapagos, World's End*, Putnams.) From these one can gain some idea of the intricate patterning and colors of her subjects, and of the accuracy and delicacy of her sketches.

The Alumnae Register for 1924 contains not only information on addresses, marriages, children, and occupations, but also the geographical distribution of Alumnae, class lists, and statistics. It is on sale at the Alumnae Office, Taylor Hall, at a price of $1.35.

Anatole France

By *EUNICE MORGAN SCHENCK*, 1907

(The following appreciation was given in a speech in Chapel, which Miss Schenck made shortly after the death of Anatole France. The BULLETIN is very grateful for the opportunity of publishing it.)

A fortnight ago, ten miles of French people followed through the streets of Paris to a bookstore on the banks of the Seine, the body of Anatole France. In front of this bookstore the funeral services were held: there were tributes by the President of the French Republic, and by a representative of the French Academy, the Elegy from Gluck's *Alceste* was sung by the chorus from the Opera House—a pagan ceremony, our newspapers were careful to point out. In the apartment over the bookstore Jacques Anatole Thibaut, who later called himself Anatole France, had been born eighty years before, and to the bookstore, which was his father's—and the booksellers of Paris have a great tradition of scholarship and culture,—there came during his boyhood the men of letters of that day, and the talk was good. The father was one of that race of urbane skeptics that the eighteenth century established in France and he passed a point of view on to his son. But the mother was a devout Catholic, poetic and sensitive and she told her boy the mediæval legends and introduced him to the thought of the church. In the finished Anatole there is no question that the skeptical, urbane father left the deeper mark; there is no question that with the years the church lore he had from his mother was turned to purposes that all good Catholics deplore, but the man who believed *pity* to be one of the two greatest human attributes learned this pity from his mother and the tenderness of his *Jongleur de Notre Dame* is a testimony to her influence.

Other influences at work on him— his quarter of old Paris; the statue of Voltaire, the greater skeptic, at his door and radiating back from the Seine those particular streets that hold the most precious of the antiquities and works of art Paris has to sell in her shops, and through these streets the little Anatole walked to school, learning to love the beauty of the past. In his school he found not a teacher for whom he has anything good to say, a lot of pedants dry as dust, but the great traditions of the literature of Greece and Rome which even his teachers would not spoil for him, and in that incomparable autobiography of his, the first volume of which, *Le Livre de Mon Ami*, is given over to his earliest years, he pictures the little boy that he was, digging away with his dictionary in his room at night, weeping passionately first over his Homer and finally over Euripides, who taught him to understand, he writes, what grief really is.

A spirit acutely sensitive to beauty and a mind both intensely curious about all human experience and able to penetrate and comprehend strange phases of human experience—this is the record of the inner life of the young Anatole France at the time he began to formulate his philosophy. What was it destined to become? A philosophy claiming all beauty and experience as its right, and in passing in review the development of human thought, arrested by the interest of everything, but incapable of arriving at any judgment; refusing, therefore, any faith, any rule of life, any system of morals, because it believed that in all these things was to be seen the passing judgment of a few generations of men and nothing more.

And yet this man, so apparently detached, so completely absorbed in his work and his personal life, came out finally into the life of his day and became one of the most violent partisans in an incident that developed more violent partisan feeling than any other in modern history, the Dreyfus case. You remember how Captain Dreyfus, a Jewish officer in the French army, was unjustly accused of high treason and was for years the victim of an inflamed anti-Semitic prejudice. Anatole France, with Zola, Clemenceau and others, became an ardent believer in the innocence of Dreyfus and a defender of his cause. Anatole France came out of the mêlée persuaded that the Catholic Church had fostered and encouraged the anti-Semitic movement against Dreyfus. This made of him an avowed enemy of the Church, whereas, before, he would not have admitted himself an enemy of anything. His experience with the Dreyfus case seems also to have been the determining force in making him an avowed enemy of the existing order of things, for he became convinced that both sides in the struggle were vicious and ignoble and that modern civilization could breed nothing good. What has been called his arraignment of Modern France in *Penguin Island* is really an arraignment of the modern world. The last step in this development made of him a Communist, our modern brand of revolutionary, but he was a communist *and* a pacifist. *His* revolution should not come by blood, and so he was read out of the International Communist party, controlled from Moscow, he and other Communists of distinction.

He was not only a Communist, he was convinced that we are on the verge of the complete breakdown of our civilization. This conviction he linked with his literary after-fame with a gentle melancholy. Among the last pages he published, in the third volume of his Autobiography, *La Vie en Fleur*, he wrote to this effect: "Those of us who are writing now will be caught up by the coming whirlwind and will exist for posterity no more than the writers of the last years of the Roman Empire exist for us. The world in the near future will be so different from our world that it will have no interest in what we thought or in what we were."

Until our world is swept away, however, we may enjoy Anatole France. One hesitates to approach him with the critic's jargon, for he was scornful of the function of criticism. French writers agree in calling him the master of them all for the chiselled beauty of his style. It is difficult to find other voices as unanimous. He is a storm center where his matter is concerned. To the skeptics he will always be an unalloyed delight. He is *their man*. To the rest of the world, except to that group to which he is anathema, he stands as one of the great intellectuals of his generation, and I like to use the term intellectual in connection with a man in whom there was no pose. Here was a mind marvelously endowed with curiosity and penetration that took as its field for research the strangely changing and still more strangely unchanging opinions of men through the ages and touched them with these two qualities that so rarely mingle and yet were so perfectly blended in Anatole France— irony and pity.

The Washington Council

By FRANCES FINCKE HAND, 1897

The Council opened its fourth meeting at Washington, on Tuesday, November 18th, at the house of Mrs. Robert Johnston, 1754 Massachusetts Avenue. The day was beautiful and Washington charmed us all, but at 2.30 P. M. promptly Mrs. Cary called the meeting to order and the work began. The Executive Board had arranged that the bare bones—the finances of the Association—should be considered first, and there was interest, intelligence and dispatch in the discussion. The Council showed itself a very adequate and satisfactory size for general discussion and group decision.

After dinner Mrs. Barnes sketched the history of the Music Endowment Drive from the appointment of the committee by Miss Thomas in 1921 to the present time. Many of the Council members had been at the college on Monday and had heard the concert given by the students and Mr. Alwyne in the Music Room at Gertrude Ely's house. The sight of that room filled with students listening with intentness to the choir singing Gregorian chants, the delightful playing of two pianos and a cello by the students themselves, and the spontaneous and spirited singing of them all was an experience that made vivid to us the beauty and importance of this department. We realized the debt we owed to Mrs. William Carter Dickerman, the Chairman of the Music Committee, who had made the opening of this department and its continuance for three years possible. With conviction the Council voted to recommend to the Alumnae Association that it undertake the completion of the Fund for the Endowment of the Music Department.

The following day we listened to the reports of the Councillors. As we passed from one section of the country to another we became aware of our resources and felt again that intangible bond which binds us together. The number of scholarships raised in the various districts, in many and diverse resourceful ways was satisfactory and encouraging.

The Academic interest was greatly added to by the very able speech of President Park. She spoke at the A. A. U. W. Club House, to a room full of university women, many of them our own Alumnae, but many the Alumnae of other colleges. Her subject was, "The College and the Experimental School," and a more frank, closely-reasoned and adequate presentation I have never heard. Mr. Stanwood Cobb, of the Progressive Education Association, presided at the meeting.

Our hostesses, Mrs. Stone, Miss Johnson, Mrs. Jessup, Mrs. Jordan, Mrs. Wright, Miss Eastman, and the other Washington Alumnae had arranged our time in so pleasant and varied a manner that our social diversions refreshed us and gave us a sense of leisure. There was an agreeable tea at the house of Mrs. Wright, where the guest of honor was Mrs. Charles Evans Hughes, a delightful

The members of the Council and a few Washington Alumnae received by Mrs. Coolidge at the White House, at the time of the Council Meeting in Washington, D. C.

morning reception at the White House, where we were presented to Mrs. Coolidge and photographed with her in our midst on the East Porch of the White House, and our own friendly informal dinner, where we sat forty-two strong, about a long table hospitably presided over by Miss Eastman.

Miss Park talked to us again about the college, the students, the activities, the problems, the life there, which is different and yet strangely the same, so that we felt ourselves back again on the campus with the gray buildings framing it. This council meeting gave us a sense of quiet, a flavor of the past which helped us to finish our business easily, brought us to one mind, and quickened our appreciation of the beauty and opportunity of Bryn Mawr.

Meetings of the Council

Held November 18, 19 and 20, at 1754 Massachusetts Avenue, Washington, D. C.

MINUTES

The meeting was called to order at 2.30 o'clock, on Tuesday afternoon, November 18th, Margaret Reeve Cary, 1907, President of the Alumnae Association, presiding.

Roll Call

Executive Board

Margaret Reeve Cary, 1907—present

Margaret Ayer Barnes, 1907—present

Katharine Sergeant Angell, 1914—present

Eleanor Marquand, 1919—present

Ethel Cantlin Buckley, 1901—present

Alumnae Secretary, Evelyn Page, 1923—present

Chairmen of Committees

Frances Fincke Hand, 1897, Academic Committee—present

Elizabeth Cauldwell Fountain, 1897, Finance Committee—absent

Caroline Morrow Chadwick-Collins, 1905, Publicity Committee—present

Helen Sturgis, 1905, Scholarships Committee—present

Ethel Dunham, 1914, Health and Physical Education—absent

Alumnae Directors

Frances Fincke Hand, 1897—present

Pauline D. Goldmark, 1896—present

Martha G. Thomas, 1896—absent

Louise Congdon Francis, 1900—absent

Anna B. Lawther, 1897—present

Chairman of Class Collectors, Mary Peirce, 1912—present

District Councillors

I. Mary Richardson Walcott, 1906—present

II. Sarah Atherton Bridgman, 1913—present

III. Margaret Free Stone, 1915—present

IV. Julia Haines MacDonald, 1912—present

V. Caroline Daniels Moore, 1901—present

VI. Helen Tredway Graham, 1911—present

VII. Florence Martin, 1923 (representing Eleanor Allen Mitchum, 1914)—present

Members from 1924

Jean Palmer—present

Marion Angell—present

Councillor-at-Large

Helen Taft Manning, 1915—present

The condensed minutes of the meeting of the Council held June 4, 1924, in Taylor Hall, were read and approved.

FINANCE

Presentation of the proposed Budget for 1925 by Ethel Cantlin Buckley, 1901. Mrs. Buckley indicated three new items on the Budget: A full-time salary for the Assistant Alumnae Secretary; appropriations for office equipment; and traveling expenses for the Regional Scholarships Chairmen. She then presented the problem of designated money. On account of the designation of money for certain objects and the failure to send in undesignated funds, the Alumnae Association faces a deficit of $3,475.21. We must, therefore, ask (1) for more undesignated money; (2) that when the Association directs a definite purchase, it must be contingent on the possession of the money.

M. S. C. That the Council recommend a revision of the wording of the Alumnae Fund Card.

In the absence of Elizabeth Cauldwell Fountain, 1897, Mrs. Cary reported that the Finance Committee has been meeting continually and giving great aid to the Association.

Mary Peirce, 1912, announced that the total of the Alumnae Fund was now $15,410.44, of which $8,069.37 was designated, and $7,341.07 undesignated. The total number of contributors is 899. In addition, $15,138.10 has been received by Mr. Wing from Alumnae for the Music Endowment and the Auditorium. The Alumnae Fund cannot control appeals to Alumnae which the Association authorizes or which individuals institute for purposes outside the college. Dues are not appeals. The increasing amount of designation has brought about a serious difficulty.

M. S. C. That all money given by Alumnae to the College be listed in a supplementary list to the Alumnae Fund, this plan to be put into effect as soon as possible.

REPORTS OF DISTRICT COUNCILLORS

District I. Report by Mary Richardson Walcott, 1906, Councillor for District I. Two Freshman Regional Scholars have been sent to College this year. Money was raised by subscription and by a lecture. New England is in need of a Chairman and a definite plan for raising money for the Music Drive. A small musicale held in the Spring, at which Mr. Alwyne played, met with an enthusiastic reception. At a meeting of the New England Alumnae Association and the Boston Bryn Mawr Club, a letter from Leah Cadbury, 1914, was read, which suggested that money might be raised for Bryn Mawr both in Boston and elsewhere by selling books on a commission basis, and by opening book stores to sell books on this basis for the Doubleday Page Bookstore Co.

(Reports of District Councillors were continued on Wednesday morning.)

TUESDAY EVENING, 8 P. M.

Discussion of the Drive for the Endowment of the Music Department and the Auditorium of the Students' Building.

Margaret Ayer Barnes, 1907, presented the history of the Drive from the time of the appointment of the Committee by President-Emeritus Thomas in 1921, to the resignation tendered by the Committee to President Park in November, 1924. The Committee had added in March, 1924, at the request of the Association, to its proposed aim of $300,000 an additional $100,000 for the erection of the Student's Building. It has raised about $40,000. The Committee has worked under the greatest difficulties, and is to be congratulated upon its achievement.

M. S. C. That the Executive Board invite the choir and the little orchestra to stay after mid-years and give a concert for the Alumnae before the Annual Meeting.

M. S. C. That after general discussion, it is a sense of the meeting that the raising of the funds for the Music Department will be less interrupted if the present Music Committee remain in office until the Annual Meeting, and that this sense of the meeting be communicated to President Park.

M. S. C. That Mrs. Barnes, Mrs. Dickerman, Mrs. Collins and Miss Page prepare a statement of the history of the Music School Drive to send to the Alumnae through their Councillors, and that an article about the Music Department Concert of yesterday and its atmosphere be printed in the next BULLETIN.

M. S. C. That it is a sense of this meeting of the Council to recommend to the Alumnae Association that the Alumnae Association undertake the completion of the Fund for the Endowment of the Music Department.

WEDNESDAY MORNING, 9 A. M.

REPORTS OF DISTRICT COUNCILLORS *(continued)*.

Report of *District I*. Report given Tuesday afternoon.

District II. Report by Sarah Atherton Bridgman, 1913, Councillor for District II.

Three Regional Scholars have been sent this year from New York City. The necessary $1,000 was raised by a special Theatre Guild children's play, by a bridge party, and a rummage sale. The Committee offers a $500 scholarship for next year, but has had no applications. The By-Laws of the New York Association are being amended so that the responsibility for raising the money is given over to a Ways and Means Committee.

New Jersey is sending two Regional Scholars. The $750 was raised by card parties and the sale of certain articles. New Jersey hopes in ten years to have a $5,000 endowment for the scholarships.

Western Pennsylvania has one scholar in College and has two applicants for next year. The Pittsburgh Bryn Mawr Club held a meeting in October.

Eastern Pennsylvania has two Regional Scholars in College. $600 of the necessary $800 was raised by a moving picture given at the Merion Cricket Club and the Germantown Y. M. C. A.

The Carola Woerishoffer Scholarship, $300 of which was contributed by the I. C. S. A. and $300 by individual Alumnae, can no longer be raised by contribution.

M. S. C. That it is a sense of this meeting that the Finance Committee arrange to have half of this Scholarship met under the Alumnae Fund.

A resolution proposed by Mrs. Bridgman was adopted.

M. S. C. That a vote of thanks be sent to each member of the present Music Committee in recognition of their service in creating at Bryn Mawr a department which singularly enriches the entire College, and is a valuable contribution to the history of culture in this country.

District III. Report by Margaret Free Stone, 1915, Councillor for District III.

Washington and Baltimore are each having a series of four lectures by Mr. Horace Alwyne before the Philadelphia Orchestra Concerts in those cities. Mr. Alwyne is also giving a recital in Washington. It is hoped that enough money will be raised for two years. $300 has been promised to a Sophomore, and $500 to a Freshman Regional Scholar this year.

District IV. Report by Julia Haines MacDonald, 1912, Councillor for District IV.

The District has two Regional Scholars now in College. There was no candidate for this year. The scholarships have so far been offered only to Public Schools. The Scholarship for 1926 will probably be offered also in private schools. All money is raised by entertainments.

The Bryn Mawr Club of Kentucky was organized in November, 1923. Alumnae have spoken about Bryn Mawr in as many schools as possible. Advertisements of the scholarships have also been inserted in the school papers.

District V. Report by Caroline Daniels Moore, 1901, Councillor for District V.

District V has four states in which there are practically no Alumnae. In the other states, the Alumnae are widely scattered. It is difficult to arouse interest in the scholarships, and difficult to get school preparation for Bryn Mawr. There is a Regional Scholar from the District now in College.

The District Music Committee consists of fifteen members. Chicago has raised $8,751 for the Music Drive, almost entirely from Alumnae. Mr. Alwyne gave a recital in Chicago last year. At the last meeting resolutions were passed whole-heartedly advising Alumnae support of the Music Drive.

District VI. Report by Helen Tredway Graham, 1911, Councillor for District VI.

The District covers 850,000 square miles and has 1/5000th of an Alumnae per square mile—in Texas 1/10,000th. Organization must be done by letter. It is hoped that the different states will organize themselves. A Regional Scholar from New Mexico was sent to Bryn Mawr this year. The Councillor is Chairman for the Music Drive in the District. In the future, it is planned to find scholars through the local Alumnae. The Council meeting in St. Louis last year

has greatly increased the general interest in the College.

District VII. Report by Florence Martin, 1923, representing Eleanor Allen Mitchum, 1914, Councillor for District VII.

San Francisco has raised the money for a scholarship, but has no acceptable candidate. The Alumni of Yale, Harvard, Princeton, Vassar, and Bryn Mawr have banded together to improve High School education in the District. There is little interest in the High Schools in the Eastern Colleges. There is also little in the Music Department.

Frances Fincke Hand, 1897, spoke on behalf of the Alumnae Directors reading interesting extracts from the minutes of the meetings of the Alumnae Directors during the past year. The five Alumnae Directors, she feels, since they see presented the problem of the College as a whole should be able to be of service to the Alumnae Association, but the Alumnae Directors should have more direct contact with the Alumnae, and a more direct contact with the Executive Board of the Association. Mrs. Hand spoke of the problem of the College being crowded in by new houses and the advisability of the purchase of new land.

M. S. C. That resolutions be prepared for the Annual Meeting directing the Alumnae Directors to ask the Board of Directors of the College to appoint a committee of Alumnae to study the whole problem of land and purchases.

M. S. C. That the Council, acting on Mrs. Hand's report, request the Executive Board to arrange a meeting once a year with the Alumnae Directors.

Discussion of the Scholarships Committee by Helen Sturgis, 1905, Chairman of the Committee. The Committee considers very carefully the total amount of scholarship money that should be given to any student. There is a great need for money for the traveling expenses of the Regional Scholarships Chairmen. There are nine Regional Scholars in College in the Freshman Class, nineteen in the College, which represents $6,800 raised by Alumnae. Students in Economics have been requested to make a study of average Undergraduate expenses in order to assist the Scholarships Committee in making awards.

M. S. C. That it is a sense of this meeting that the item of $250 for the traveling expenses of Regional Scholarships Chairmen be supported when it comes up at the Annual Meeting.

M. S C. That it is a sense of this meeting of the Council that the Publicity Committee prepare a Scholarship poster.

THURSDAY MORNING, 9 A. M.

Presentation of the Academic Committee by Frances Fincke Hand, 1897, Chairman of the Committee. The Committee membership last year was reorganized according to mittee. The Committee is going to make a report on Bryn Mawr women holding higher positions in colleges, and is studying the problem of graduate work and a graduate school in a small college like Bryn Mawr, with the plan also of studying the achievements of Bryn Mawr graduate students.

M. S. C. That in view of the brief time that has elapsed since the re-organization of the Academic Committee, it seems advisable that any discussion of the organization of this Committee shall be postponed for another year.

M. S. C. That if the Academic Committee sees fit to undertake a study of the administration of scholarships in other colleges, it is a sense of this meeting that it would be of great assistance in awarding Regional Scholarships.

The Register. Margaret Reeve Cary, 1907, announced that the cost of the Alumnae Register for 1924 was, so far, $3,479.25. The Executive Board decided not to publish a Register this year, but to send out tracers. The question now is the publication of a *Register* in 1926.

Caroline Morrow Chadwick-Collins, 1905, suggested the publication in 1926 of a supplement to the present Register, giving recent marriages, deaths, changes of address, and possibly children, and change of occupation. This will make possible the sale of the 1924 *Register*.

M. S. C. That the Council recommend to the Alumnae Association that the supplement to the Register, incorporating Mrs. Collins' suggestions, be published in 1926.

M. S. C. That it be the policy of the Alumnae Office that the Secretary supply to Alumnae only such information as is not given in the Register, or such as is a correction of mistakes in the Register.

NEW BUSINESS

M. S. C. That the Council accept with pleasure the invitation of the Pittsburgh Bryn Mawr Club to meet there next year.

M. S. C. That a vote of thanks be offered Mrs. Stone and all the members of the Washington Bryn Mawr Club for the careful arrangement and delightful entertainment of the present Council Meeting.

CONTENTS

BOOKS FOR CHILDREN

The Macmillan Company has issued a most attractive catalogue of Books for Boys and Girls, which will be sent to anyone desiring it upon request. The catalogue is fully illustrated, and each book in it is described both as to contents and as to the age of the child likely to be most interested in it. The Bookshop will be very happy to send out these catalogues immediately.

Dr. Dolittle's Circus. By Hugh Lofting. Frederick Stokes Company, New York, 1924. $2.50.

"This is the story of that part of Doctor Dolittle's adventures which came about through his joining and travelling with a circus." The Doctor had, in his travels in Africa, become possessed of a strange new animal—a pushmi-pullyu. He wished to exhibit it, and what could be better than a circus? After many trials the Doctor became manager of the 'Dolittle Circus.' The animals in the circus were all his friends, and he allowed them to wander free for half an hour a day. In fact, there were no rules, or hardly any. And if little boys wanted to see 'behind the scenes,' or to go into the elephant's stall and pet him, they were personally conducted wherever they wished to go . . . . For children everywhere were beginning to regard the Dolittle Circus as something peculiarly their own."

When We Were Very Young. By A. A. Milne. E. P. Dutton & Co., New York, 1924. $2.00.

Exceptional verses, delightfully illustrated.

The Court of King Arthur. By William Henry Frost. Scribner's, New York, 1924. $1.00.

Scribner's "Dollar" series is not only a delight to young bookworms, but a great relief to their parents. "The Court of King Arthur," one volume of this group, is an amusing and realistic account of King Arthur's court and his country. We are taken from London to Caerleon, from Tintagel to Camelot, and at each place are told of the adventures that happened there, and everywhere of "the sweet air and the great, glorious rocks, the cries of the sea-birds, the roar and the dash of the water, and all the sights and the sounds of the Cornish shore and the Cornish sea."

The Common Sense of Music. By Sigmund Spaeth. Boni and Liveright, New York, 1924. $2.00.

"This book," in the words of the author," is written on the assumption that musically all men are created free, though not necessarily equal. It is addressed to potential listeners rather than potential performers.

"It presupposes no knowledge on your part, and it admits no fundamental ignorance. It does not worry about the hair-splittings of the technical scholars, nor is it concerned with the maudlin exaggerations of the sentimentalists."

With this foreword, Mr. Spaeth launches out into a breezy treatment of the basic principles of music and its appreciation. One feels that at least in so far as music is concerned, the golden road to learning has been discovered. In spite of the somewhat flippant tone, the book contains much information that is valuable, and lasting.

Mr. Spaeth stresses the fact that, "the language of music is universal, for it is delivered through tones that everyone can hear, and in symbols that anyone can understand. And it has the vast advantage over any and every spoken language that even when it is imperfectly comprehended, it rewards the listener with a direct thrill of pleasure that no one can take away from him, and for which there is no substitute."

My Brother's Face. By Dhan Gopal Mukerji. E. P. Dutton & Company, New York, 1924. $3.00.

"It is the unwritten law of every Hindu that he shall visit the place of his birth at least once in twelve years." Mukerji, after twelve years in the western world, returns to seek again the peace and idealism of India. The language of the book is that of the Orient, full of imagery and aglow with color. When the author first glimpses India on his return, he describes it thus:

"India at last! The hills of the western Ghauts gleamed so intensely emerald that it hurt one's eyes to look at them. This afternoon of late May throbbed with colors clean and brilliant —russet and gold, purple and green, cerise and blue, alternated and mixed with one another as we drew near the wharf. Suddenly, all these warm colors—warm and vivid like the day—took supple and fully defined form. The ebbing and flowing currents of iridescence burning the strand, shaped themselves into Indian women walking slowly back and forth, drawing about them the long flowing ends of their saris."

From this book one gains an understanding of the moral and spiritual beauty that is the heritage of India, and likewise of the grave and immediate problems that face the leaders of her people.

Class Notes

1889

Class Editor, Harriet Randolph, 1300 Spruce Street, Philadelphia, Pa.

'89 was well and appropriately represented on the "Get Out the Vote Caravan," which toured Pennsylvania before the election in November.

Comments on '89's Class Notes in the BULLETIN by members of the Class:

April 30, 1924. "Indeed I have and do enjoy all the 'Notes' of all the Bryn Mawr people I know."

May 10, 1924. "I wish I had some thrilling news for your 'Notes.' They *are* good 'Notes' and I read every syllable eagerly."

1896

Class Editor, Mary W. Jewett, Pleasantville, N. Y.

Elizabeth Kirkbride spent some time in the Summer with K. Cook at Lakeville, Conn.; a little later she motored with the Goldmarks to Keene Valley. She will spend the winter in Albany with her sister, Mary.

Josephine Holman Boross and her two daughters spent a month at the Ausable Club in August.

Mary Gleim made a three months' pilgrimage this Summer to friends and relatives from the Pacific Ocean to the Atlantic and back. She writes: "While in Philadelphia, I had the joy of going to Bryn Mawr. The students had not arrived. on that lovely September day, but the College was there—stately, beautiful, fair Bryn Mawr. I spent two months on Frontenac Island, St. Lawrence River. Perhaps because of the contrast to the brown hills of Southern California, never before had the islands seemed so green."

Gertrude Heritage Green is president of the Woman's Club of Pennington, N. J.

1899

Class Editor, Mrs. Percival M. Sax, 6429 Drexel Road, Overbrook, Philadelphia.

Caroline Radnor-Lewis spoke at the Woman's City Club in Philadelphia in October on silk. She has been asked to make a speech on the feminine point of view before the Association of National Advertisers at their convention at Atlantic City in November. This is a great honor, as it has been some time since a woman has been the speaker there.

REUNION OF THE LAST OF THE VICTORIANS—1900, 1901, 1902, and 1903

A suggestion is now being entertained that the four classes beginning with 1900—who of course will hold their twenty-fifth reunion in June—should have a joint supper in Pembroke, with speeches, separate features, and other diversions.

The Committee is very eager to hear expressions of opinion from everyone concerned. What do you personally feel about it? Can you bear the idea of sharing your salt? Write to the member of the Committee who represents your class giving your reasons for and against. Your privacy wi l probably not be respected, but your opinion will be.

> LOUISE CONGDON FRANCIS, 1900;
> MARION REILLY, 1901;
> ANNE TODD, 1902;
> DORIS EARLE, 1903.

1902

Class Editor, Mrs. George Dudley Gregory, 1921 Nineteenth Street, Washington, D. C.

1902 has two daughters in the Freshman Class: Elinor Beulah Amram and Cornelia Bruère Rose, who is rooming with Nancy Wilson, daughter of Nannie Kidder Wilson, 1903.

Grace Douglas Johnston has bought a new house, and is now settled in it. Her address is 1520 North Dearborn Avenue, Chicago.

Elizabeth Lyon Belknap moved to Boston last winter, and is living at 81 Myrtle Street.

Cornelia Bruère Rose writes: "My family and I spent the Summer in the Adirondacks, where we helped stage the splendid memorial pageant for Inez Milholland at Meadowmount. I am deeply interested in the formation of student councils throughout the colleges of the country for the study and promotion of absolute equality of men and women."

Anne Rotan Howe is Director of Publicity for the Women's Republican Club of Massachusetts, which has recently opened a handsome new club house at 46 Beacon Street. Her elder son is a Freshman at Harvard.

Elinor Dodge spent the Summer at Straitsmouth Inn, Rockport, Mass.

Harriet Spencer Pierce (215 Hixon Avenue, Syracuse, N. Y.) ran a Summer branch of the Richmond, Va., Children's Shop at East Gloucester. She stayed with Anne Rotan Howe, who had a house at Gloucester for the season. Harriet's daughter, Cornelia, is at Rosemary Hall.

Marion Balch spent two months at Tryon, N. C., last Winter.

Marion Haines Emlen is now Chairman of the Bryn Mawr Alumnae Association of Eastern Pennsylvania and Delaware, and has been very busy getting up an entertainment for the Bryn Mawr Regional Scholarship Fund of that district. She has built a cottage at Mantoloking, N. J., where she and her husband and six children spent the Summer, except for a month of motoring along Cape Cod.

1904

Class Editor, Emma O. Thompson, 320 South Forty-second Street, Philadelphia.

Gertrude Buffum Barrows and "Patty" Rockwell Moorhouse were very much interested in the Regional Scholarships benefit performance, given by the Main Line Section of the District, at the Merion Cricket Club in October. At this benefit, Mr. McClintock showed his bird and animal pictures.

Dr. Alice Boring is President of the College Club at Peking, China. She is very busy and writes that in Peking everything, thus far, is quiet.

Leslie Clark bought a Dodge sedan in August, and very shortly afterward drove alone all the way from Cleveland to Middlebury, Conn. She stopped at Bedford, Bethlehem and Ardmore to visit other members of the Class.

Marjorie Canan Fry has taken a house at Ardmore, and plans to live there during the school year. Her two daughters have just returned from England, where they spent over a year, visiting an aunt. Marjorie's daughter, Betty, 1904's Class Baby, is at the Irwin School this year, preparing to enter Bryn Mawr. She has already passed her preliminary examinations.

Hilda Canan Vauclain's two daughters are at the Irwin School. Amelia has already made a number of points in her preliminary examinations, and plans to enter Bryn Mawr next Fall.

Margaret Reynolds Hulse's daughter, Margaret, is a Freshman at Bryn Mawr.

She is living in Pembroke East. She brought her college possessions in the identical trunk her mother used in 1900! We congratulate our first daughter who has chosen to follow in our footsteps.

Dr. Mary James has returned to her hospital in Wuchang, China.

Marguerite Gribi Kreutzberg and her daughter, Robin, have gone to Paris to remain a year. Robin will go to a French school and continue her preparation for Bryn Mawr, which she expects to enter in three years. Marguerite plans to study painting. Her address is Morgan, Harjes & Co.

Anne Buzby Palmer's daughter, Marion, has gone to the George School.

Isabel Peters visited Cary Case Edwards in her London home last August.

1905

Class Editor, Mrs. Clarence Hardenbergh, 3710 Warwick Boulevard, Kansas City, Mo.

Bailey Aldrich is a Freshman at Harvard. Doesn't this make "Lit" the only mother of a collegian?

Freddy is to sing the soprano part in a Cadman opera for the Denver Municipal Opera Co.

1906

Class Editor, Mrs. Harold K. Beecher, Pottsville, Pa.

The Class is not renowned for sending in news, but it does write in to ask when is our next reunion, so attention all. Our next reunion is in 1926, and headquarters are to be in Pembroke. No date yet set for the Class dinner.

Adeline Curry writes the tragic news that she spent the Summer at home nursing her two eldest sons, each with a broken leg. The eldest son is a Freshman at Williams, and the second son is in the Choate School. Adeline lunched with Elizabeth Torbet while in Boston and "had a wonderful time hearing 1906 news." (I wish the Editor could get some of that same news.)

Margaret Grant also has sad news to impart. Her sister (B. M. C., 1912) died last April. Margaret spent the Summer on her father's farm in Vermont with her small son, Charles, and the two oldest children of her sister. She has now returned to Cleveland, and has taken a house for the Winter at 2865 Fairfax Road.

Mary, our President, writes of a Summer spent as usual at Peach's Point with ten-

nis, bathing and sailing their principal occupation. The small knockabout which the
children raced (most unsuccessfully *à la
Mary*) was driven on shore during the
August gale and most unfortunately
smashed.

1907

Class Editor, Eunice Morgan Schenck,
Low Buildings, Bryn Mawr, Pa.

Margaret Ryan Noonan, ex-'07, has a
third daughter, Lorraine Elizabeth, born
September 8, 1924.

1908

Class Editor, Mrs. William H. Best, 1198
Bushwick Avenue, Brooklyn, N. Y.

From the *Evening Sun*, October 31, 1924:
"A tablet in memory of Miss Helen Sherbert, former teacher at the Teachers' Training School, will be unveiled at the Chapel
of the Nativity, Cedarcroft Avenue and
York Road, at 4 o'clock Sunday afternoon.

"The tablet is the gift of the Class of
1924 of the school. The presentation will
be made by Dr. Norman Cameron, former
principal of the school. Miss Sherbert died
December 6, 1923."

1910

Class Editor, Marion Kirk, 1013 Farragut Terrace, Philadelphia, Pa.

Sidney Garrigues Edwards announces as
the principal item of interest about herself
that she has moved into a house on Walnut
Lane, Haverford, and invites the Class to
visit her whenever it or they are in the
neighborhood.

Peggy James Porter has returned to her
home in San Francisco with her two children, Robert Bruce, aged eight, and Catherine, aged three, from a Summer on a farm.
The whole family is now engaged in taking
music lessons. (If the Class is to have an
infant prodigy in little Catherine, I think
Peggy should let us know immediately.)

Rosalind Romeyn Everdell says that her
Irish wit is ingrowing,—she is still able to
laugh at her own jokes, but can't make
others laugh at them. But she reports herself and family well and happy in spite of
such a handicap.

Margaret Shearer Smith writes to say
that they have two new babies in her home,
—one white and the other black; also a
very nice young calf, and five Gordon setter
puppies. Margaret's new baby's name is
Barbara Hathaway Kellogg Smith, and she

is now nearly five months old. Apparently
the Smiths do not think they have enough
young life about, for they are planning to
adopt a little boy of the same age as Barbara to keep her company.

Jane's Auntie writes that Jane sailed on
September 23rd on the New Pittsburgh for
Cherbourgh, together with Miss Friedman,
with the intention of spending a year in
traveling. They are to have a vacation in
Southern France or possibly Spain, and
then to visit labor schools in Germany and
England. Their address will be care of the
American Express Company, Paris.

1911

Class Editor, Louise S. Russell, 140 East
Fifty-second Street, New York City.

> The Class will be shocked and grieved
> to learn of the death of Mary Williams
> Sherman on October 10th after a week's
> illness. She leaves three sons, and a
> little girl, born August 29th. 1911 loses
> one of its most loyal and responsive
> members, and feeling our loss as we do,
> our sympathy goes out to her husband
> and her young children.

Frances Porter Adler with her family
spent August in the Keene Valley in the
Adirondacks.

Kate Chambers Seelye writes that Margaret Doolittle is back in this country. Has
anyone seen her?

If Kate had not said that they expected
to get home in 1926, it would be a little discouraging to learn that they are at present
engaged in building a house in Beirut.
They are enjoying the prospect of living in
one built just as they want it. Doctor and
Mrs. Chambers will also have an apartment
in it.

Margery Smith Goodnow has a third
child, a boy, born in June.

Ruth Vickery Holmes took a motor trip
to New Hampshire in August and climbed
Mt. Monadnock.

Phyllis Rice McKnight writes that after
being ill all Summer, she had an operation
in September and is slowly recovering. Her
little boy is "in fine health, sturdy and rosy
and very bright, talking a lot at twenty-one
months." (I quote her exact words, as the
last time that I reported on him I brought
down on myself a letter of reproach for
having described him as having red hair.

It seems he had none at all.) The other members of her family are a husband and two hives of bees. Her address is 45 Lowell Road, Schenectady, N. Y.

Mary Case Pevear writes that she has forsaken New England for the great Middle West and is now living in Oak Park, Ill., where her husband is employed. Her address is 542 Woodbine Avenue.

Mary Miner and Norvelle Browne discovered the British Isles on foot this Summer. It would be hard to mention a cliff in Cornwall that they haven't stood upon, a glen in Scotland that they haven't walked through, or a river that they haven't punted on, to say nothing of stone circles, Pict houses, cathedrals and abbeys all discovered by them. If you don't believe this account, ask them—they love to talk about their travels. (The Class Editor takes no responsibility for the statements contained in this paragraph.)

1912

Class Editor, Mrs. J. A. MacDonald, 3227 N. Pennsylvania Street, Indianapolis, Ind.

Mr. Daniel A. Tomlinson, Leonora Lucas Tomlinson's husband, died very suddenly during the Summer. The Class extends its deepest sympathy to Leonora. She will spend the Winter with her mother in Riverside, Calif.

Sadie Beliekowsky is studying at the University of Pennsylvania this Winter.

The 1912 Philadelphia Lunch Club held a special meeting on November 1st in honor of Lorle Stecher, who is sailing the end of November for Honolulu, where she will be married on December 5th to Mr. Charles Weeber.

Pauline Clarke Gilbert has a daughter, born October 12th in Chicago. Pauline's husband was doing special reporting of the Presidential election campaign for the *Philadelphia Ledger.* They returned to Washington about November 1st, where their address is 1224 Connecticut Avenue.

Carmelita Chase Hinton has returned from England, where she spent the Summer with her children. They lived in a caravan in Devonshire. Carmelita spent part of the time cruising in the Hebrides.

Dorothy Wolff Douglas' new address is 3 Orchard Street, Amherst, Mass.

Florence Glenn Zipf has a son, born on November 14th.

1915

Class Editor, Mrs. James Austin Stone, 3015 Forty-fourth Street, N. W., Washington, D. C.

Frances Boyer took an automobile trip through the Pyrenees and into the Alps last Summer. She is now studying at the Sorbonne.

Dagmar Perkins (Mrs. Edmund Summers Hawley) has a son, born in June. The Hawleys are living at 215 West Ninety-second Street, New York City.

Florence Abernethy Pinch and her husband have moved to Lake Villa, Ill.

Susan Nichols (Mrs. Harold Trowbridge Pulsifer) was already married when the announcement of her marriage was reported in the November BULLETIN. The wedding took place at her home in Oyster Bay on October 11th.

Helen Everett is again in Washington this Winter, and Florence Hatton Kelton has also joined the Washingtonians. Florence and her husband and two children have a house on Goddard Road, Battery Park, Md.

Mary Goodhue Cary has moved to Woodbrook, Baltimore, Md.

Helen Taft Manning, as one of the Alumnae Directors, attended the meeting of the Alumnae Council held in Washington, D. C., on November 18th, 19th and 20th.

Adey writes to remind us that we voted in June to raise at least $1000 as our reunion gift, each member of the Class having the privilege of designating the branch of the Alumnae Fund to which she wished her share contributed. (This includes, of course, the Music Department and the Students' Building.) We are still $300 short of the $1000 pledged, and have only until January 1st to raise this money. *Please, everyone,* whether you have already contributed or not, take stock of your finances and see what you can do. And DO IT NOW!

By the way, Adey (Mrs. Benjamin Franklin, Jr.) has a new address. It is 6814 Lincoln Drive, Germantown, Pa. All contributions welcomed with open arms.

The Class Editor is worn out, what with a new house, the responsibility before and during the Alumnae Council meeting in Washington in November, and being on the Board of Managers of the National Club, A. A. U. W. Kindly revive her spirits by sending in some *unsolicited* bits for the next BULLETIN, either about yourself or any other member of 1915. To appear in any particular BULLETIN, news notes must reach her by the 9th of the preceding month.

1916

Class Editor, Mrs. Webb Vorys, 63 Parkwood Avenue, Columbus, Ohio.

Georgette Moses has announced her engagement to Mr. Harry Gell. She expects to live in Palestine for the first two years after her marriage.

1917

Class Editor, Isabella Stevenson Diamond, 1111 M Street, N. W., Washington, D. C.

Lovey Brown Lamarche is in this country for a while, and is staying with her family at Sandwich, Mass.

Caroline Stevens Rogers has a son, Samuel Stevens, born last July.

Eleanor Jencks spent the past Summer in Venice. Con Wilcox is also abroad with her father.

Dor Shipley is deeply engrossed in politics with her husband, Thomas Raeburn White.

Con Hall writes that she spent the Summer with her sister, tenting in the wilds of Vermont. She says Mart Willett is as industriously engaged in Girl Scout work as ever.

Amie Dixon Bushman has a daughter, Barbara, born in September.

Mildred Willard writes that her chief interests are still the same:

1. Psychology: Still subjecting ex-soldiers "to the test" at the Veterans' Bureau in the mornings, and doing a little free hospital work, and a few "private patients" in the afternoons.

2. Tennis: Now Philadelphia champion, and also won the Jersey coast championship, and the Maryland mixed doubles.

3. Hockey: Playing badly, but enthusiastically.

Monica O'Shea writes that she still moves the merchandise and draws down the shekels in New York, which she says is interesting to her, but probably not to others!

Will Jane Kinsey be good enough to send me her present address? I am unable to get in touch with her.

1918

Class Editor, Helen Edward Walker, 418 Oakwood Boulevard, Chicago, Ill.

Mary Gardiner's address is Cacketts, Brasted, Kent. She is studying at the University of London.

Lucy Evans Chew has just returned from a Summer in Spain, Italy, France and England. Under the heading of the questionnaire of "Romance" she writes: "What a strange heading! I do not know what to answer. I find my Romance in traveling, I think."

Virginia Pomeroy McIntyre has a son, born in July, 1924.

Dorothy Harris was married to John H. Thompson in June, 1924.

Mary Allen Sherman writes: "A wonderful wedding trip with horses, mules and guide up onto Sierra San Pedro Martir, Baja California, Mexico. California is as nice as ever, and I recommend you all come to visit me. Where are "Teddy" Howell Hulburt and Adelaide Shaffer Kuntz?"

Sarah Morton Frantz was in Paris from October, 1923, to September, 1924, where her daughter, Margaret Wistar Frantz, was born on December 19, 1923.

Helen Hammer Link spens the Summer as co-director of Camp Kuwiyan, a Summer camp for girls from eight to fourteen, and the Winter taking care of her three children and her home.

Helen Butterfield Williams had a "glorious trip to Maine, marked by frenzied efforts to pick up a few nautical terms. The Class baby—no longer that—is hoping to go to kindergarten in October."

Helen Alexander, though indignant at not having been reached for news for the reunion booklet, has again had her postal returned to the Editor marked, "Return to writer, unclaimed." We wish she and Adelaide Shaffer Kuntz would each send in her correct address.

Ella Lindley Burton will spend the Winter in California again at 226 East Padre Street, Santa Barbara, from November 15th to April 1st.

1919

Class Editor, Frederica Howell, 211 Ballantine Parkway, Newark, N. J.

Oyez:

Sixth reunion is coming. Our President requests that one and all save the first of June for the great event, which will be staged in Pembroke. To quote Tip's letter to Editor of Notes (rather grim it is in the early stages, too) :

"You might add that we don't have another one until five years later, and as we will then all be thirty, and what's worse, on our way to forty, we'd better have a last look at each other while we've got the chance.

"Also tell them that elaborate plans are being laid for it, concocted by the fertile imaginations of you, Eleanor, Liz Fuller and Tige. (So far, of course, none of you have concocted anything, but I always have hopes.) At any rate, it's going to be a grand and glorious affair. How grand and glorious, none of them will ever know unless they attend it in person."

1920

Class Editor, Helene Zinsser, 6 West Ninth Street, New York City.

DEAR CLASS: I have neglected you shamefully! No notes for two issues! But the item below may explain everything to you and may grant me grace. Love is a wonderful but terrible thing. It seems to affect one's head as well as one's heart, and all outside correspondence seems superfluous. Now I know why parted lovers sigh and strong men need beef and iron. Forgive me, and please, all of you, send me juicy bits, so I can make this year's issue the very best we've had, and so my notes may be so enthralling that they will leave their mark long after I've gone to foreign shores to dive through foaming beer or sling a nasty noodle.

With love,
THE ED.

Helene Zinsser has announced her engagement to Hans Loening, of Bremen. Mr. Loening studied at the Universities of Freiburg, Goettigen and Marburg, where he made his Doctor. in Law in the Spring of '23. He is now working in Frankfurt, Main. (He's my third cousin once removed, but it's quite all right.)

The following letter has just been received from Isabel Arnold Blodgett, who is now living at 2 Prescott Street, Cambridge, Mass.:

Dear Zin: Are you the Secretary of the Class of 1920? Or, anyway, are you the kind fairy that sent me, as a present from the Class, the *Complete Works of Shelley?* I'm going to thank you for it, at any rate, and tell you it's the best present the Class could have chosen for me. And, incidentally, it quite adds to the tone of the living room!

Until next Spring, when I hope to see you at Bryn Mawr,

Affectionately yours,
ISABEL ARNOLD BLODGETT.

Marion Frost was married on Saturday, October 18th, to Mr. Russell Murray Willard, in Plainfield, N. J. The wedding was a double on with her sister, Frances. Dorothy Allen was one of the bridesmaids.

Mary Hardy is Warden of Denbigh Hall.

Alice Harrison is in the Advertising Department of Alfred Knopf & Co., the publishers, in New York City.

Monica Healea is teaching at the Buckingham School in Cambridge, Mass.

Helen Humphreys traveled and studied in Spain last Summer and is now teaching Spanish in the Senior High in Cleveland.

Elizabeth Luetkemeyer Howard (Mrs. Paul B. Howard) announces the arrival of Julia Howard on September 26, 1924. Weight, 8 pounds.

Kitty Robinson is living at the Bryn Mawr Club, 279 Lexington Avenue, New York City, and is working with Marsh & McLemon, marine insurance, learning insurance and translating.

Birdie Boleyn Zilker has left the wilds of Texas, and suddenly appeared at 1000 Park Avenue, New York City, Apartment 10D. She will be there until January, and is most anxious to "meet up with the old gang, as she has been out of touch with them for a million years. Any call from a Bryn Mawrtyr to Butterfield 1683 will be most welcome."

1921

Class Editor, Betty Kellogg, 144 Buckingham Street, Waterbury, Conn.

Kath Ward's engagement was announced last Spring to Robert Wilcox Seitz. Kath is back at Bryn Mawr this year as Instructor in English Composition, and when last heard from was coaching Junior Play.

Betsey Kales was married September 28th to Dr. Francis Howe Straus, of Hinsdale, Ill. We hear that they drove to the minister's in Windy Egg, the Montana to Chicago Ford, with only three interruptions, once when they ran out of gas, once when they dropped the ring out, and once when they were arrested for not having headlights on.

Darn says the '21 ranch representatives last Summer were Teddy, Luz Taylor and Jimmy James Rogers. Jimmy's address is 98 Glen Rose Avenue, Toronto. Darn herself is entering upon a career as pianist. She says she can now play "The Happy Farmer" very nicely.

At Johns Hopkins this Winter are Becky Marshall (studying for a Ph.D. in Economics!), Blissides in the School of Hygiene, and Lube in the Medical School. Both the latter are due to graduate this year, writes Blissides, putting it cautiously.

Flossie Billstein replies: "I am still secretary to an excellent architect who specializes in ecclesiastical work, and live in New York at 84 Grove Street."

Helen Bennet is "teaching the children at Miss Simonson's School a little English, gym, and singing, with plays and dancing thrown in. No self-respecting union would approve of my hours," she says, "But I love the work."

Biffy, like the angel she is, took time from her editing of the *Junior League Bulletin* to submit the following items:

"Copey, Goggin, Blissides, Silvine, Becky and I went abroad in June, disgracing the Royal Mail with the hilarity of our dining-room table. We took a walking trip around the edges of Devon and Cornwall, which was a huge success, although—or perhaps because—we did everything but walk. We took buses, trains, charabancs, pony-carts and trolleys, and occasionally strolled a few miles just to prove we knew how. Becky hopped, skipped and jumped all the way, with accelerated speed when she saw a bull —which genus to her includes indiscriminately all cows! Goggin sauntered placidly in our rear, with a pack twice her size. She's writing a book called *Travels as a Donkey*. After scattering ourselves around England we joined up again and went to Guernsey and then on to Brittany, which beside being the most entrancing country in the world, was well worth going to just to hear Becky burble French. *C'est trop plus* covered every occasion.

1922

Class Editor, Serena Hand, 48 East Ninth Street, New York City.

S. Aldrich has announced her engagement to Mr. Philip Drinker.

M. Crosby is corresponding secretary of the Junior League of Minneapolis.

A. Dom is teaching in New Mexico.

D. Ferguson is teaching in Lynchburg, Virginia.

E. Gabell and M. Meng are teaching at the Germantown High School. M. Meng is completing work for a M.A. in Sociology at the University of Pennsylvania.

A. Gabel is teaching in Moorestown, New Jersey.

J. Gowing is in her Junior year at the Woman's Medical College of Pennsylvania. She says that "It is pretty busy and awfully interesting."

V. Grace is teaching English at the Wadleigh High School in New York, and giving lessons in Greek to Mrs. Arthur Brisbane, wife of the editor of the *New York American*.

M. Kennard is doing chemical work in the laboratories of the Massachusetts General Hospital, in Boston.

L. Mearns is completing her work for a M.A. in the Columbia Business School.

O. Pell is teaching at the University of South Carolina.

M. Tucker is doing graduate work at Bryn Mawr.

1924

Class Editor, Mildred Buchanan, the Powelton Apartments, Philadelphia, Pa.

1924's cheering on Lantern Night was rather weak, there being three members present. Monkey, Buck, and Martha Hammond did their best, however, and fortunately were not called on for the Class Song.

Hootch is taking a business course in Seattle.

Martha Hammond was back for Junior Play, too. She is doing graduate work in Chemistry at Columbia.

Litch, Freda Rosenkoff, Margaret Dunham, Van Bib, Elizabeth Robinson, Martha Fischer, and Doris Hawkins also came back for Junior Play.

K. Brauns, Chubby, and Molly have been back for week-ends.

Molly and Jean are attending the Alumnae Council in Washington, as our class delegates.

Roberte is studying at L'Institute Pasteur, in Paris.

Monkey is taking a business course in Philadelphia.

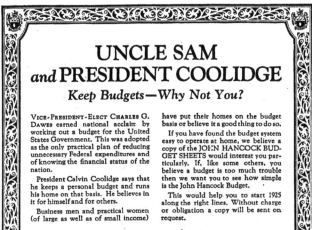

Kindly mention BRYN MAWR BULLETIN

SCHOOL DIRECTORY

The Bryant Teachers Bureau, Inc.

711-12-13 Witherspoon Building　　　　　　Philadelphia, Penna.

Friendly, personal interest; prompt intelligent service.

The Agency you will recommend to your friends.

WE PLACE MANY BRYN MAWR GRADUATES EACH YEAR

Cathedral School of St. Mary

GARDEN CITY, LONG ISLAND, N. Y.

A school for Girls 19 miles from New York. College preparatory and general courses. Music. Art and Domestic Science. Catalogue on request. Box B.

Miriam A. Bytel, A. B., Radcliffe, Principal
Bertha Gordon Wood, A. B., Bryn Mawr, Ass't Principal

St. Timothy's School for Girls

CATONSVILLE, MARYLAND

Founded 1882

COLLEGE
PREPARATORY

Miss J. R. HEATH ⎫
Miss L. McE. FOWLER ⎬ Heads of the School

MISS MADEIRA'S SCHOOL

1330 19th St., N. W.　　　　Washington, D. C.

A Resident and Day School

for Girls

LUCY MADEIRA WING, A.B.

MRS. DAVID LAFOREST WING
Head Mistress

MISS WRIGHT'S SCHOOL

Bryn Mawr, Pa.

Prepares for Bryn Mawr and
College Board Examinations

ROGERS HALL

A SCHOOL FOR GIRLS

Thorough preparation for college entrance examinations. Graduate course of two years for high school graduates. Complete equipment. 40 minutes from Boston.

MISS OLIVE SEWALL PARSONS, B.A.
Principal
Lowell, Massachusetts

The Episcopal Academy

(Founded 1785)

CITY LINE, OVERBROOK, PA.

A country day school for boys from second grade to college. Separate lower school for boys from seven years up. Enjoys the patronage of Bryn Mawr Alumnae

---

WYKEHAM RISE

WASHINGTON, CONNECTICUT

A COUNTRY SCHOOL
FOR GIRLS

Prepares for Bryn Mawr and Other Colleges

MISS GILDNER'S PRINCETON SCHOOL

FOR GIRLS

Prepares for best eastern colleges and Board examinations. Also for Advanced College-entrance Two-year Graduate Course. Music, Art, Expression. Sports, Riding. Outdoor and Indoor Athletics. Estate of beauty. Mile from town.

Miss Laura M. Gildner, A.M., Director
Princeton, New Jersey

SCHOOL DIRECTORY

If father did the washing just once!

If every father did the family washing next Monday there would be an electric washing machine in every home before next Saturday night.

For fathers are used to figuring costs. They'd say: "The electricity for a week's washing costs less than a cake of soap. Human time and strength are too precious for work which a machine can do so cheaply and well."

GENERAL ELECTRIC

Lightning Source UK Ltd.
Milton Keynes UK
UKHW020327221118
332685UK00006B/862/P